Wish you
were here

Wish you were here

THE OFFICIAL BIOGRAPHY OF

DOUGLAS ADAMS

Nick Webb

headline

First published in 2003 by HEADLINE BOOK PUBLISHING

10 9 8 7 6 5 4 3 2 1

Cataloguing in Publication Data is available from the British Library

Hardback ISBN 0 7553 1155 8
Trade paperback ISBN 0 7553 1166 3

Typeset in Palatino by Ben Cracknell Studios | Jon Schotten

Text design by Ben Cracknell Studios | Janice Mather

Printed and bound in Great Britain by
Mackays of Chatham plc, Chatham, Kent

HEADLINE BOOK PUBLISHING

A division of Hodder Headline
338 Euston Road
London NW1 3BH

www.headline.co.uk
www.hodderheadline.com

For Susan

Contents

Acknowledgements

I would particularly like to thank Jane Belson for her help and big-hearted agreement to let me have access to Douglas's papers. Jane and the other members of the family were patient with my clumsy questions when they were still shocked with grief. Janet Thrift, Douglas's mother, was brave to face a biographer so soon after her son's death and also deserves special thanks. In the diaspora of the Adams and Thrift families, Sue, Heather, Jane, James, Rosemary and Karena were generous with their time and invaluable insights in what must have been trying circumstances. Shirley Adams, from another branch of the family, gave me the benefit of her scholarly researches into the family tree. The Thrifts and Adamses are a remarkable lot.

Ed Victor, Maggie Phillips and Sophie Hicks at the Ed Victor Agency were unfailingly helpful. Pan Books were kind enough to let me look through their archives – my special thanks to Jacqui Graham for arranging it. Many others contributed interviews, or help with research, including Will Adams, Mary Allen, Sophie Astin, Nick Austin, Peter Bennett-Jones, Nick Booth, Trevor Bounford, Simon Brett, Jonathan

Brock, Dr Mark Bryant, Michael Bywater, Margo Buchanan, Jon Canter, Mark Carwardine, Maggie Crystal, Richard Curtis, Brian Davies, Professor Richard Dawkins, Sally Emerson, Don Epstein, Ken Follett, Susan Freestone, Jacqui Graham, Yoz Grahame, Peter Guzzardi, Bruce Harris, Richard Harris, Terry Jones, Michael Leapman, Jim Lynn, John Lloyd, Andrew Marshall, Simon Master, Debbie McInnes, Reverend Ian Mackenzie, Sonny Mehta, Isabel Molina, Chris Ogle, Michael Nesmith, Rick and Heidi Paxton, Geoffrey Perkins, David Renwick, Christophe Reisner, G.R. Roche, Kanwal Sharma, Martin Smith, Robbie Stamp and Caroline Upcher.

Published sources that were very useful were Neil Gaiman's *Don't Panic* and M.J. Simpson's *Hitchhiker's Guide*. They are essential reading for the serious buff; I have acknowledged them wherever they were the principle source of information. *The Best of Days?*, a collection of memories from Brentwood School and expertly published by the school itself, gave an insiders' flavour of life there. *The Greatest Sci-Fi Movies Never Made* by David Hughes is grimly fascinating. Neil Richards's *Starship Titanic Guide* is invaluable for navigating through the game and understanding the thought processes behind it. *From Fringe to Flying Circus* by Roger Wilmut is a lot of fun and helped to put the Cambridge Footlights phenomenon into perspective. My thanks to Punch Cartoon Library for permission to reproduce the Crum cartoon about hippos.

Douglas himself gave innumerable interviews, and a large proportion of them can still be found on the Internet. There are many websites, including the official one, on which information is posted by fans and then maintained and updated out of sheer enthusiasm. The World Wide Web is a very rich source for a researcher, but it is so diverse that it is only possible to acknowledge it in the broadest terms.

Finally I am grateful to Susan Webb for her help in transcribing the interviews and for her expert editing. The errors that remain are entirely mine.

A commendably brief introduction, but you may skip it if you like

Contemporary biography is the Area 51 of the literary world. There's a lot of circumstantial evidence that it exists, but very few get to visit. The rest of us wonder what the hell is going on behind the perimeter fence.

Biography set in the past is less mysterious. Disappearing from sight, the writer tunnels through a mountain of research – emerging, dazzled by the light, years later with a book. If this contains some entertaining history, sixteen pages of attractive pictures, an argument about the subject that can be supported – perhaps with a little casuistry – from the documentation, and it doesn't cost more than twenty quid (twenty-five if it's a whopper), the book is acceptable.

Boswell said that writing his biography of Dr Johnson was a presumptuous exercise. It is indeed an odd idea that you can squeeze someone's life between the covers of a book. Writing about somebody of the moment who died suddenly, and far too young, is trickier still. There are many people over whose feelings the author can clodhop, and they will all have a different view of the person from the one offered. Some of those views will appear not to refer to the same person at all. The biographer will have to rely less on historical records and more on people's fallible memories. ('Hmm,' they say, 'it was 1982 – no, I tell a lie, '84 – oh, the eighties anyway . . .') The whole truth that the courtroom witness so recklessly undertakes to deliver is a notion that should be melted down for scrap and deleted from legal procedure forthwith. The whole truth is unknowable – it can only be lived and not described.

In the case of Douglas Adams the difficulty is compounded. First of all he was immensely clever and gave such good interviews that he was in constant demand. Every time you think you've had an insight into the man, it turns out that he had it first – and expressed it with more wit than any biographer could muster, though in the process he turned such revelations into suspiciously polished artefacts.

To complicate matters further, he was wildly exuberant about his interests. Despite being the finest comic author since Wodehouse, this enthusiasm did not embrace writing (which he did reluctantly, and with enormous anguish). Any biography also has to deal with the fact that he was an enormously prescient and creative thinker, and much of what he thought was never located on paper.

Douglas's passions were lifelong; they resist any attempt to tidy them into phases. Why would he stop loving music because he discovered Apple Macs, for instance? Besides, as Kierkegaard said, life is lived forwards but understood backwards – thereby, in my view, imposing a subtle but misleading formalism upon a messy business. We human beings are rarely as consistent as characters in fiction from whom we expect a purposeful direction seldom achieved in real life.

With a straight chronology the word 'meanwhile' would soon become tiresome. Douglas was not conventional. This book abandons a strictly chronological structure in favour of illuminating aspects of a brilliant, engaging and complex man. You will judge whether this works. My hope is that at least the book will be good company – like the man himself.

Prologue

'A towel is about the most massively useful thing any interstellar hitchhiker can carry. For one thing it has great practical value – you can wrap it around you for warmth on the cold moons of Jaglan Beta, sunbathe on it on the marble beaches of Santraginus Five, huddle beneath it for protection from the Arcturan Megagnats as you sleep beneath the stars of Kakrafoon, use it to sail a miniraft down the slow heavy river Moth, wet it for use in hand to hand combat, wrap it around your head to avoid the gaze of the ravenous Bugblatter Beast of Traal (which is such a mind-bogglingly stupid animal it assumes that if you can't see it, it can't see you), and even dry yourself off with it if it still seems clean enough.'

The Narrator, Fit the Seventh, *The Hitchhiker's Guide to the Galaxy*

In the time of the Revolution, so the story goes, when the Terror was at its height, a French count, suitably disguised by scruffiness, made a run for the coast in order to escape to England. He was a cultured man, a flower of the Enlightenment, rational, charming and educated.

Just a few kilometres short of Boulogne and safety, he stopped to rest his horses and have a meal at a handy *auberge.* Even 200 years ago the roadside snack was treated with Gallic seriousness.

After a certain amount of large French small talk, the waiter got down to business. The dialogue went something like this:

'*Dis donc,* citizen. What would you like to eat? We can offer bread, some amusing cheese *paysanne,* and fresh eggs.'

'Thank you, citizen. The eggs sound good. Perhaps an omelette?'

'Of course, citizen. And how many eggs would you like in your omelette?'

Now, since birth the aristocrat's family had employed a team of people to look after his every need. Anticipating a hint of nasal drip, a servant would appear with a fine linen handkerchief before the well-bred nose needed blowing. The number of eggs that normally went into an omelette was not a fact with which the aristocratic mind had ever had to burden itself.

'Um. Douze, thank you,' he said.

'Douze? *Douze?*' said the waiter, aquiver with revolutionary suspicion. 'And what is it you do, citizen, may I ask?'

Doubtless the count did the French equivalent of dropping his aitches as he laboured to sound like a rough-hewn son of toil: 'I'm a carpenter, innit, citizen, me old mate.'

But it was too late. The waiter had clocked the refined accent, and one look at the count's soft hands, never sullied by manual work, gave the lie to the carpentry story. Nipping back into the kitchen, the waiter reappeared shortly with the chef, an enormous man equipped with a cleaver – a small preview of things to come.

Transported back to Paris, the count was swiftly guillotined.

Perhaps death is always absurd.

Douglas Adams was a comic genius and creative thinker, a highly complex man. His death, at the age of forty-nine, on 11 May 2001 in Platinum Fitness, a private gymnasium in Santa Barbara, was almost as daft, and really much sadder, than that of the *comte*.

He and his family had moved from London to Southern California two years before and had settled in Santa Barbara, or, more precisely, Montecito, a verdant village of Heinleinesque gated enclaves and huge houses looking like escapees from the set of Dallas. Douglas needed to be 'on the Coast' – not so much a location as a state of mind having nothing to do with the seaside but everything to do with Hollywood. Finally, after several decades of false starts and uncertain flirtations, it looked as if the film of *The Hitchhiker's Guide to the Galaxy** was going to happen.

Douglas loved it there. His wife, Jane Belson, enjoyed it too though she did suffer intermittent bouts of what long-term prisoners call gate

---

* 'Hitchhiker's' is written in a variety of ways even by Douglas's publishers. Scholars in millennia to come may read significance into the occasional sighting of a hyphen and the pitiable singularity of the hitchhiker. To appease my publishers, I shall endeavour to remain consistent.

fever. The affluent, cosmetically adjusted locals with those teeth that only Americans and people in television seem to manage, the Potemkin supermarkets with their rows of shiny technicolor fruit (tasting of nothing), and the endless days of dappled sunshine all contrived to give the place a certain unreality in her mind. 'Sometimes it could be a bit *Stepford Wives*,' she observed. But Jane was happy that Douglas was happy, and she had put her own career as a barrister on hold because she could see how much her husband wanted the movie to happen. They were both delighted that their adored young daughter, Polly Rocket Adams, took to California with joyful exuberance.

In appearance, Douglas Adams was like some large, friendly marine mammal. In his opinion, Elaine Morgan's* idea that evolution had taken the hominids through an aquatic phase had more virtue than conventional wisdom was prepared to grant it. Douglas never claimed that his liking for water stemmed from mankind's deep evolutionary past, though he certainly had an affinity for it. Exactly like the captain of the B-Ark on Golgafrincham, he took to his bath when stressed, and he regarded scuba diving as so pleasurable that it was bound to be illegal somewhere. He was huge, a smidgen over 6'5", left-handed, rather ill-coordinated, a little clumsy. He sometimes gave the impression of fitting awkwardly into the world. Eyes: brown; eyelashes: enviable – as long as a giraffe's; face: often lit with a half-suppressed smile, for he had a prodigious sense of humour and found the world funny when it wasn't tragic. He had a habit of looking into the middle distance and saying 'um' when thinking. 'Heroic' best describes his endowment in the nose department; his schnozzle was a mountain range of a thing.[†] He once observed that if he swam on his back in the sea, parallel to a beach, everyone would run screaming out of the water.

Obviously, food and drink were put upon the Earth for his pleasure. He was extravagant with champagne. He had a particular weakness for Japanese restaurants, but his lifelong affair with all restaurants was

---

* Elaine Morgan, *The Aquatic Ape Hypothesis* (Souvenir Press, 1997).

† In an article for *Esquire* magazine, reprinted in *The Salmon of Doubt* (Macmillan, 2002), Douglas notes of his nose that several speleologists had been up it, but those who had not returned became part of the problem.

disgracefully promiscuous. He was not put off even by the pretentious ones where every mouthful is a week's wages. Not surprisingly, he was prone to putting on weight and he had been hit by late-onset diabetes, known as 'Type Two' in the USA which boasts some of the most enormous bipeds on the planet (and where this form of diabetes has become almost epidemic). Douglas himself had been as heavy as 19 stone (266 lbs) but he had always succeeded in losing any excess. The diabetes was not acute and soon disappeared, but in 1999 he went on a round of medical checks – for he loved hospitals and doctors – and discovered that he had developed high blood pressure. He had reached that age when men used to rude health all their lives become uncomfortably aware that their bodies cannot do what they did at twenty.

An infamous writing block had persisted all decade, though he had found myriad interesting alternatives; to say he failed to write is like saying that Columbus failed to find India. Nevertheless, the missed deadlines – not quite an industry record, but impressive – were a source of anxiety, and occasionally despair, that had weighed upon him without remission.

Douglas's Internet and computer game business venture had also run into the sand. All over the landscape there had sounded the thunder of giant wallets being slammed shut by men in suits. Historians of the future will look back on the last two decades of the twentieth century with fascination and bewilderment. Was it something we'd eaten? Enormously canny and prudent investors used their elbows as they ran to the front of the queue clutching thick wads of their own and, more usually, other people's money in a headlong rush to finance telecoms and dotcom companies. Many of these boasted business propositions that depended on markets and technologies that were yet to be called into existence. The *Financial Times* estimates that this global financial bubble wasted $1,000 billion of real cash in ridiculous investments.*

---

* 'Glorious Hopes on a Trillion Dollar Scrapheap' by Dan Roberts, *Financial Times*, 5 September 2001, cited in Will Hutton's brilliant book *The World We're In* (Little Brown, 2002).

You may think: well, tough. All those acquisitive young men in the City with stripy shirts and spotty ties (to say nothing of those techies who could have been speaking Inuit for all the sense they made) – who cares if they lost a packet? After all, the Internet revolution threw up business ventures without number – some brilliant, some fathered by hope and greed. Presumably the ones with real merit survived while the crowds of dodgy ones melted away. But the truth is that many of those failed businesses were not nonsense; some were genuinely visionary and inventive. Douglas's venture, originally called The Digital Village, was years ahead of its time.

But building a business is hard to do within the time limits demanded by your free-range western venture capitalist. Such creatures have an icy spreadsheet where their hearts should be, and their expectations for the return of some whole number multiple of the initial investment rarely extend beyond three years. As long as the share prices were rising, this short-term myopia did not matter, but as technology stocks ramped up from optimistic valuations to down-right silly ones, eventually the overvaluation of tech stocks became unsustainable. When the high tide of money retreated and left thousands of enterprises flapping about on the beach like dying fish, the good suffocated along with the bad. Douglas's enterprise was not spared.

During these years too, the film of *The Hitchhiker's Guide to the Galaxy* was something that Douglas passionately wanted to be made. For nearly a quarter of a century the project had inched its way fitfully through a contractual maze and a development hell so capricious that even jaded Hollywood insiders smote their foreheads and sighed. Many times it had come to within an angstrom or two of greenlighting before, triumphantly, it found the right director and a workable budget. All seemed well at last, but then, in 2000, it foundered again.

Douglas had made lots of money. A rich author is paid in cash; his wealth is not tied up in the equity of some business, the value of which, as financial advisors sometimes forget to point out, can fall as well as plummet. A writer's assets are built in and enviably portable: talent and fingers. But Douglas was never as rich as people imagined. He was self-indulgent and hedonistic – and extravagantly generous both to individuals and his favourite good causes. The concept of Treat was seldom far from his thoughts, and he applied it to others as well as self. Money was for pleasure. His talent for making it was more than matched by his genius for spending it.

For all his warmth and humour, Douglas was sometimes hard to live with, a trait often shared with very creative people. In many ways he was an emotionally fragile yet precociously brilliant child. Children can oscillate between joy and gloom with mercurial rapidity, and anyone who has spent time looking after them knows that nature, for sound Darwinian reasons, has programmed the little so-and-sos with a certain egotism. Douglas was romantic, warm, funny, exuberantly enthusiastic and possessed of a quite exceptional brain; he also had his demons, and could be depressed, self-absorbed, sulky and difficult.

But, despite all the problems, by 2001 things were looking up. Admittedly, the film was still in the Horse Latitudes and drifting, but it was at least afloat. Douglas, who now had a personal trainer, was being conscientious about getting himself fit. Physically he appeared to be in better shape than he had been for years. The weight was melting away. The diabetes had gone. The marriage, that had had its turbulent moments, was happy. He and Jane (who in their household was invariably the standard bearer for practical intelligence) had recently bought a beautiful house, redolent of rural England in its charm, which won a local prize for the excellence of its presentation. They found it much more sympathetic than their rented mansion where at any moment one expected a soap opera star with big hair and an improbable suit to appear. Also they had made some good friends in Chris and Veronica Ogle, a local Australian couple.

Polly was happy there too. She was tall for her age, earnest, pretty and bespectacled. The outdoors life suited her, she loved riding and had also made friends with the Ogle boys, particularly the seven-year-old Joshua. Tom, Chris's youngest boy who was then five, was very fond of Douglas and missed him a lot when he died. 'He had great farts,' he said, and indeed Douglas was capable of the odd duvet-billowing eructation. It always amused him; one of the most memorable definitions in *The Meaning of Liff* was the Affcot – the sort of fart you hope people will still talk after.

The families were close. Chris is in the clothing business and successful in a field far removed from Douglas's own, something that was probably good for Douglas as the media world operates in an orgy of self-regard that can become oppressive. Douglas and Chris otherwise had much in common: their love for their children, an enthusiasm bordering on the reckless for Apple Macs, Mercedes cars, and good food and wine. They even sported the same make of fine but obscure wrist watch (an Ulysse Nardin).

In 2000, the families had enjoyed a blissful holiday together in Fiji. Douglas, a keen diver, had been so overjoyed with the experience that he had to call someone to share it. (Throughout his life if he found something pleasurable he would encourage others to try it.) He was thrilled to learn that his state-of-the-art cell phone would work there, so he stood clutching his high-tech gizmo in thigh-deep water in a cove on a tiny island, and rang Sophie Astin, his assistant in The Digital Village. With a certain edge to her voice, she reminded a contrite Douglas that the world was round even for him. In London it was darkest night; she had been fast asleep. Later Douglas discovered that the coverage was so good because they were only twenty minutes away from Castaway Island where Tom Hanks had starred in the movie of the same name. Apparently, he had arranged for a local satellite relay to be installed so he could ring his agent. 'What a pity,' Douglas said afterwards, with his writer's magpie instinct for an anecdote, 'that Tom Hanks had never made a road movie on the Pacific Coast Highway.' Mobile coverage is notoriously patchy along that route.

Above all, by 2001 the long pause between books had topped up Douglas's creative batteries. Writing had always been difficult, but now he had a treasure store of new ideas and was buckling down to the long-awaited book with extraordinary application.

Douglas liked cars, and, following a disastrous young-man's flirtation with Porsches, he developed a fondness for solidly engin-eered, luxury saloons like the Lexus or Mercedes. It amused him that they could look so respectable, but deliver an unnecessary quantity of horsepower if the driver were feeling daft enough. That final Friday, 11 May, he glided down to the gym in his Mercedes 500 as usual, in order to take some exercise and return home in good time for the arrival from England of his mother, Janet. She was already in the air, on a British Airways 747.

In the gym, Peter, his personal trainer, put him through a routine that had been especially devised for him – twenty minutes on an aerobic stair machine to be followed by stomach crunches. If you have tried a stair machine, you will know that pretty soon rivulets of sweat run like molten lead down your back; the thighs seem on the point of spontaneous combustion. But although the regimen was hard work, it was not dangerously excessive for a chap of Douglas's age and general state of health. He wore a heart monitor and Peter was there to keep an eye on him.

It was Douglas's habit to stop by after his exercise sessions at the Ogles' house, handily just opposite Platinum Fitness. They'd have a coffee, boast about their children and shoot the breeze.

Chris Ogle relished Douglas's appearances, looking righteously exercised, at his home. With the anguished clarity of retrospect he suspects that Douglas may have suffered a minor heart attack shortly before 11 May. After his session in the gym the week before he died, Douglas had as usual called by, but in an uncharacteristically distressed state. He was pale and very tired. He had to lie down, and he slept for hours while Chris busied himself preparing for a business trip to South Africa. Waking much revived, Douglas was still concerned about a slight tingling in his arm. However, his local hospital did some tests and could not detect anything serious. So it goes, as Kurt Vonnegut, an author much admired by Douglas, so aptly observed. So it goes . . .

But the health scare the previous week hadn't put Douglas off his regime. So on this day, as usual, he had finished with the torture of the step machine, and was ready for the stomach crunches. The very term sounds mediaeval.

Hitchhiker's Guide to the Galaxy fans will recall that Douglas attributed to the humble towel a miraculous potential for reassurance and utility. 'There's a frood who really knows where his towel is,'* the Narrator observes with admiration. The role of the towel traces its lineage back to the summer of 1978 when Douglas and various pals

---

* The Narrator, Fit the Eighth, *The Hitchhiker's Guide to the Galaxy* (Pan, 1979).

were on holiday in Corfu. Douglas was supposed to be writing, but a certain amount of hedonism and frolicking on the beach also featured. Douglas's towel – he needed one the size of a marquee's groundsheet – was forever going missing. Perhaps it had some homing instinct for the sea, like a baby turtle. Finding it became synonymous with being a really together, cool kind of guy.

You may be touched to learn that, feeling faint from the rigours of the machine, Douglas picked up his towel from Peter and clutched it to him before lying down on a bench. In these circumstances specialists advise that becoming horizontal may not be expedient, but the piercing clarity of retrospect takes no account of the reality of an enormous, sweaty man, probably feeling a little woozy, poised to topple like an uprooted tree.

He lay down. Peter glanced away for a second. When he looked back he thought that Douglas was messing about. Still holding on to his towel, he had rolled quietly off the bench. He had fainted. Peter called an ambulance, which efficiently speeded Douglas off to hospital. He never regained consciousness.

He had suffered a catastrophic cardiac arrest. Astonishingly – nearly instantaneously as it turned out, and mercifully without pain – his huge heart had failed him. Jane said he just stopped, like one of his beloved computers crashing and failing to reboot.

He was dead.

*   *   *

'I refuse to prove that I exist,' says God, 'for proof denies faith, and without faith I am nothing.' 'But,' says Man, 'the Babel Fish is a dead giveaway isn't it? It proves you exist, and so therefore you don't. QED.' 'Oh dear,' says God, 'I hadn't thought of that,' and promptly vanishes in a puff of logic. 'Oh, that was easy,' says Man, and for an encore he proves that black is white and gets killed on the next zebra crossing.

Most leading theologians claim this argument is a load of dingo's kidneys, but that didn't stop Oolon Colluphid making a small fortune when he used it as the central theme of his bestselling book *Well, That About Wraps It Up For God*.

Fit the First, *The Hitchhiker's Guide to the Galaxy*

It may seem odd to start with an account of Douglas Adams's world view, but it underpinned much of what he did. It is a key – not The Key, as such things do not exist outside self-help paperbacks – to how he thought.

Douglas published his first piece of commercial writing when he was twelve. It was a fan letter to the *Eagle*,* the smashing – and quite high-minded – boys' comic. It was 1965, the year Churchill died and the Beatles released *Rubber Soul*. Wily Harold Wilson was Labour Prime Minister. The Vietnamese War had started in earnest with a massive build-up of American troops and the heavy bombing of North Vietnam. It would be six years before Intel developed the first silicon chip. Marijuana was still a gesture of defiance, not just a recreational option, and long hair on men was considered by some to be a dangerous threat to the fabric of society. It was the sixties: in the West a whole range of flukishly favourable circumstances conspired to produce massive social change and the most spoilt generation in the history of the world.

Little of this upheaval reached Essex, however, where Douglas attended a school that was proud of having cherished the same values since 1558. His contribution to the boys' comic earned him ten shillings. In those days, before the decimal digits had fingered the eccentric British currency, ten bob (as shillings were known) was 50p in today's money. It was an amount large enough to have its own pretty brown note; with it you could buy twenty 6d (old pennies) chocolate bars. Douglas's letter, characteristically playful, described a state of high anxiety, the source of which – after some sneaky authorial misdirection – turned out to be the arrival of the *Eagle* itself.

---

* The *Eagle* (incorporating *Boy's World*), 23 January 1965. Buffs might like to know that the *Eagle* also published Douglas's first short story, a comic tale about a man losing his memory, on 27 February 1965.

Dan Dare was the *Eagle*'s most famous creation. An intrepid space pilot with a fine line in unflappability and cocked eyebrows, his origins lay in the fighter aces of the Second World War. Week by week Dan Dare, and his well-upholstered sidekick, Digby (what is it about heroes that they so often need a plump git as a foil?), would fight to save the universe from the evil attentions of the Treens and their mastermind, the Mekon, a small, green hominid whose vast cranium was swollen with malevolent intelligence. The Mekon travelled by anti-gravity saucer – which was just as well as it was by no means clear whether his spindly limbs would support the weight of that enormous head. The artwork, by Frank Hampson, was superb and mint copies of the comic are prized on the collectors' market. Years later the Mekon reappeared oddly in Douglas's life, played by Rick Wakeman, the legendary rock keyboard player, who performed as the malign alien in a production of *The Hitchhiker's Guide to the Galaxy* at the Roundhouse, one of London's largest venues for alternative theatre.

The *Eagle* fired the imaginations of a generation of British youngsters. It wasn't just Dan Dare whose adventures took the readers off-planet. Nearly every week in the centre of the comic was a double-page spread, in full colour, of a machine cut away in three dimensions to reveal its inner workings. These were artefacts with glamour: ocean liners, locomotives, record-breaking cars, jet fighters and so on. Also, executed with the same matter-of-fact verisimilitude – *as if such things existed already* – there were interplanetary shuttles, space stations and starships. The *Eagle* just took it for granted that such marvels were coming, and so did its readers. The world did not stop at the corner shop, or even at the edge of the atmosphere.

Douglas loved that comic. He was a boy who lived very intensely in his own head. At twelve he was already six feet tall. As an adolescent, and later as a man, he did not fit comfortably into the world.

Schools in those days – and it lingers on still – were firmly in the grip of the idea that a profound dichotomy exists between Art and Science. The British educational system pivots around that great divide. Very few children understand that a decision at thirteen to drop, say, Physics is an existential moment destined to affect their whole lives.

Their thinking is more along the lines of, 'What subjects do I like the most or tyrannize me the least?' From such factors as the scariness of the chemistry teacher are our futures determined.

C.P. Snow famously labelled this great divide the Two Cultures, and it has a long and ignoble history. Some commentators attribute Britain's decline as a world power to the tradition that its best brains learned Latin and Greek with a view to doing something mandarin in the Civil Service, rather than studying trade, technology or engineering.

A cultured gent, the sentiment ran, was a bundle of sensibility, sustained in town by a distant estate, who could talk fluently on any subject without doing it much damage or, God forbid, giving offence. Even today you can meet Brits at dinner parties who can – amusingly – say nothing all evening, but who nevertheless are quite sure that you're a better person if you appreciate *quattrocento* painting and have no clue how a television functions. John Brockman in the introduction to his book, *The Third Culture*, argues that such scientific illiterates are pitiably disabled when it comes to understanding how the world works.

Douglas was well-educated, but caught in the traditional system. The fork in the road labelled Art in one direction and Science in the other later struck him as absurd. Why not go straight on? But at the time the system obliged him to choose and, with his love of language and his finely attuned ear for the rhythm of a sentence, it is not surprising that he took the arts route.

But in another time, or under a less rigid educational tradition, the river that carried him off to Cambridge could have swept him into the great sea of science. Douglas stood on the bridge between art and science, waving madly in both directions. Cultured and well-read scientists abound, but arts people who can define Planck's Constant are rare beasts.

In his lectures, he was wont to observe that, in order to understand the human condition and how the world worked, in the nineteenth century you had to read the great novels of the time, but in the twentieth century the path to that kind of enlightenment came from reading science.

Douglas himself expressed it well in his response to a question about how his reading habits had changed:*

I read much more science than novels. I think the role of the novel has changed a little bit. In the nineteenth century, the novel was where you went to get your serious reflections and questionings about life. You'd go to Tolstoy and Dostoyevsky. Nowadays, of course, you know the scientists actually tell us much more about such issues than you would ever get from novelists. So I think that for the real solid red meat of what I read I go to science books, and read some novels as light relief.

Human beings are born with a sense of wonder. Occasionally one encounters kids who seem destined to be tomorrow's actuaries right from the off, but by and large it's true. Babies burble with glee as they discover a new sensation. How they laugh when they discover that banging a saucepan correlates with a bloody awful noise. But somewhere on the path to adulthood the world becomes familiar and fades to grey. Is it routine that does us the mischief, or the cynical knowingness we call sophistication? We diminish; as we age the level of our world goes down as if we were goldfish in a slowly leaking bowl. Douglas, with his wild enthusiasms, resisted this shrinkage passionately.

He continued:

The world is a thing of utter inordinate complexity and richness and strangeness that is absolutely awesome. I mean the idea that such complexity can arise not only out of such simplicity, but probably absolutely out of nothing, is the most fabulous, extraordinary idea. And once you get some kind of inkling of how that might have happened – it's just wonderful. And I feel, you know, that the opportunity to spend seventy or eighty years of your life in such a universe is time well spent as far as I am concerned.

---

* From the 1997 Channel Four documentary called *Break the Science Barrier with Richard Dawkins*.

Douglas never ceased to perceive the world in all its strangeness – and the more he read science (and he inhaled it wholesale in volume) the more mind-buggeringly* improbable it all appeared. The Krikkitmen in *Life, the Universe and Everything* had never seen the stars because their planet moved through an impenetrable cloud of dust. They were convinced that they were alone – if only because they could not see any universe to observe outside themselves. In this respect they had a lot more justification than we who are Earth-bound and refuse to look up. The night sky is heartbreakingly wonderful, and there's more beauty and complexity if we look the other way, down the size scale.†
Unfortunately, the Krikkitmen suffer a spasm of xenophobia when they discover that there is life elsewhere – indeed that the universe is teeming with the filthy stuff. Their mission, with a sardonic backwards glance at the much-parodied opening words of *Star Trek*, is to seek it out and destroy it.∞ Douglas's view of the Krikkitmen would be similar to his view of people who resolutely decline to learn what science can tell us about the universe we inhabit.

Of life, the universe and everything, it's life that's such an extraordinary predicament of matter. As far as we can tell, it's hugely outnumbered by inanimate material. Einstein said that the greatest mystery of the universe is that we can comprehend it. We struggle to describe how unlikely it is that some minute configuration of stuff on a speck of rock revolving around an undistinguished G-type star (in what Douglas called the unfashionable western spiral arm of the galaxy) should have stirred into life. For that stuff to evolve further to the extent that it became sentient is amazing. The fact that we human beings have compelling theoretical reasons to believe that we can make observations, and draw conclusions, that are relevant to the whole cosmos is

---

* Buffs might be interested to know that Douglas replaced this witty expression of amazement with the more conventional 'mind-bogglingly' in the Narrator's account of the Babel Fish in Fit the First. History does not record if this was pressure from the BBC, an expedient eye on the American market, or just the thought that such a graphic expression might distract.

† A star is much simpler than a leaf.

∞ This notion that alien life forms are not benign is, of course, common in a lot of SF and goes back to H.G. Wells's *War of the Worlds*.

improbable to such an extent that language can scarcely accommodate it. Douglas went through life shaking his head at the sheer implausibility that some organic molecule could self-organize into a stable form of slightly higher order, and eventually – via a process of great beauty but entirely without external purpose – turn into creatures as disparate as you, the reader, the possessor of the most complex thing we yet know of in the universe (the three-pound lump of human brain), and, say, a sulphur-metabolizing worm at a submarine volcanic vent. What is more, the journey took less than four billion* years.

The process by which this happened is called evolutionary biology. It was one of Douglas's intense enthusiasms and integral to his view of the world. Jokes about evolution abound in all Douglas's books. The Vogons are the only creatures who decide to do without it ('Evolution,' they thought. 'Who needs it?'), because they rectify their grosser anatomical inconveniences surgically.† Remember the Haggunenons of Vicissitus Three, whose chromosomes were so impatient that they quite frequently evolved several times over lunch so that if they were unable to reach a coffee spoon they would mutate into something with longer arms?∞ Or the cavemen from the early Earth who were out-evolved by a bunch of telephone sanitizers? Think of his contention that coming down from the trees was a big mistake, or that our troubles began in earnest when we emerged from the sea.

Evolution had fascinated him from his schooldays. Intellectually the pump had long been primed for his friendship with Professor Richard Dawkins. It was a true meeting of minds when they got together in 1990. At one point, Douglas had even contemplated taking a mature student's degree in zoology (it would have been one of his worthier displacement activities). Richard dissuaded him: Douglas was an inspired scientific generalist with an imagination far too effervescent for the sometimes grindingly repetitive nature of scientific procedure. His broad perspective

---

* There is now some controversy about whether ancient microfossils are really indicative of life. Life may be much younger than the usual c. 3.8 billion year estimate. See 'Proof of Life', *New Scientist*, 22 February 2003.

† *The Hitchhiker's Guide to the Galaxy*, p. 43.

∞ The Narrator, Fit the Sixth, *The Hitchhiker's Guide to the Galaxy*.

would not be well served by the tight focus of a single discipline.

The notion of God had appealed to Douglas when he was a schoolboy. God is, after all, the solution – transmitted to us by culture and tradition – to those big questions that trouble an enquiring mind. Douglas had worked in the school chapel and sung his heart out in the choir. But his religious impulse was really a search for meaning – and that is by no means the sole prerogative of those immersed in the organized religions. Indeed, by the time he was a student, the institutional answers to the question of meaning had become irrelevant. Once you have the dimmest inkling of the scale of the universe, the idea that a huge one of us (we humans being made in His image) created it all in order to place us in it becomes preposterous. Douglas lost his faith, he said, at the age of eighteen, when he heard a street evangelist and realized that what was being said made absolutely no sense at all. The great French mathematician, Laplace, dedicated his *Treatise on Celestial Mechanics* to Napoleon. '*Merci*,' said Bonaparte, but then added that he was surprised that Laplace had made no mention of God. 'Sire,' Laplace is supposed to have replied (only in French), 'I found I had no need to avail myself of that hypothesis.'

Douglas had no need for the hypothesis either. Indeed, he agreed with his friend, Richard Dawkins, whose book, *The Selfish Gene*, had such an influence on Douglas when he read it years later, that there is something sentimental and self-deceiving about any notion that puts man centre stage. 'Space', after all, 'is big. Really big. You just won't believe how vastly, hugely, mindbogglingly big it is. I mean, you may think it is a long way down to the chemist, but that's just peanuts to space.'[*]

Douglas was a radical atheist,[†] and quite unequivocal about using the term. If someone had suggested that he take Pascal's bet and recant on his deathbed to be on the safe side, he would have rejected such an indignity.[∞] He really did mean 'atheist' and not agnostic. The more he

---

[*]   The Narrator, Fit the Second, *The Hitchhiker's Guide to the Galaxy*.

[†] Interview with the American Atheists collected in *The Salmon of Doubt*.

[∞] Pascal's bet, the reader will recall, was the pusillanimous notion that being wrong about the non-existence of God carried such a potential downside that one might as well play safe on the deathbed and recant one's atheism. In the circumstances, it would be a minor concession when set against a possible eternity of extreme discomfort.

learned, the stronger his atheism became – but this was nothing as crude as replacing one paradigm with another.

One of the slanders frequently addressed to atheists is that their view of the world is mechanistic and reductive – a long, cold chain of materially determined consequences with each iron link of cause and effect stretching back to the Big Bang. Where in this account, argue the believers, is there room for spirit or free will? But Douglas thought that imputing such a position to atheists was absurd.* The more you know about how the world works, the more astonishingly wonderful it becomes.

His way of looking at things is infectious.

For instance, you are reading a book, a rectangular block of laminated wood pulp. Some huge vegetable, probably grown in a Scandinavian monoculture where no birds sing, has been harvested so that its fibre can be chemically and mechanically treated to make paper. Oil-based pigment has been squeezed onto the paper by machines. The resulting black marks are intended to convey information using an invention, language, so creative that it can generate sentences like this one which has probably never been written before in the history of the species. With luck you will still find it intelligible. If the wood-pulp tree were still standing, you'd want to lean against it.

In terms of quantum physics, you and the book are mostly empty space consisting of infinitesimally tiny nuclei surrounded by clouds of electrons whizzing round in (relative to the nucleus) hugely distant and ultimately unknowable orbital clouds that nevertheless can only possess discrete values. The nuclei contain still smaller components, and their numbers determine what you're made of. All but the very lightest elements in your body were synthesized in the thermonuclear hearts of stars and blasted into the universe by explosion. You're at the bottom of the gravity well of a planet that is moving at nineteen miles a second around its solar central heating unit that is one star of about a hundred billion in the local system. Gravity is – by millions of orders of magnitude – the weakest of all the binding forces of the cosmos, but it weighs heavily on you because you're so tiny compared to the mass

---

* Inebriated conversation in Frederick's restaurant in Islington.

of our planet. What's more, you're living in a thin envelope of dangerously reactive gases. You don't give this a moment's thought because, of course, you know all this is normal. Douglas didn't.*

But Douglas was not wide-eyed about science. He would not believe any old tosh because it made for a frisson-inducing yarn. As a good positivist he thought that you had to be entitled to believe a proposition on the basis of proper evidence. In many interviews he was asked what he would have done if he hadn't been a writer, a job at which he excelled but for which he was temperamentally one of the least well-suited people on Earth. His usual answer was software engineer/designer, a blend of science and technology that marries up extreme care with wild creativity. Douglas had no time for soggy science of the 'Was God a chair-leg?/Aliens made the pyramids' variety. Rather like his beloved Bach, whose music conveys emotion while adhering to strict musical forms, Douglas believed that the appeal of science was all the greater if it were methodologically rigorous, careful and difficult. In his opinion:

> Revolutionary changes to accepted models quite often come from outside the orthodoxy of any given discipline, but if a new idea is to prevail it has to be better supported in argument, logic and evidence than the old view, not worse. 'Feel-good' science is not science at all. Science Fiction is a great territory in which to play with the kind of perspective shifts that lead to new discoveries and new realizations. But imagination tempered with logic and reason is much more powerful than imagination alone.†

Douglas Adams had a gift for making us look again at the world and see how strange it really is. You remember those quizzes in comics and magazines when something is drawn from an odd angle or photographed from an unusual perspective? The circle with a thin bar projecting diametrically from either side that turns out to be a bicycling

---

* Douglas's riff on these lines was quoted movingly by Professor Dawkins at the memorial service at St Martin-in-the-Fields, 17 September 2001.

† Preface to *Digging Holes in Popular Culture – Archaeology and Science Fiction*, edited by Mike Russell (Oxbow Books, 2002).

Mexican wearing a big hat seen from above? Douglas's writing pulls a similar trick.

There ought to be a unit of pleasure to describe that moment when a joke or a sudden insight makes you see something clearly in a way you had never thought of before. In Douglas's honour such moments should be calibrated in Adamses, using the S.I. system. Femto-adamses for tiny but amusing surprises, right up to Tera-adamses for sickening lurches in world view. His ability to stand sideways on to the world, and think 'that's bloody peculiar' informs all his writing. He urged us to think differently, to take our eyes out for a walk.

Of course, very few live up there in the stratosphere of human thought all the time. Astronomers, their minds on the transcendent, live in torment in case a rival team publishes in the right scholarly journal first. It's comfortingly human. Our minds may encompass infinite space, but we still worry about status, sex and the milk bill.

Douglas Adams did enjoy an intense inner life of the mind – while he wasn't throwing parties and going to restaurants, that is. But his sense of wonder never left him.

chapter one

Not from Guildford
after all

'The main problem which the medical profession in the most advanced sectors of the galaxy had to tackle after cures had been found for all the major diseases, and instant repair systems had been invented for all physical injuries and disablements except some of the more advanced forms of death, was that of employment.

'Planets full of bronzed healthy clean-limbed individuals merrily prancing through their lives meant that the only doctors still in business were the psychiatrists, simply because no one had discovered a cure for the universe as a whole – or rather the one that did exist had been abolished by the medical doctors.'

The Narrator, Fit the Eleventh, *The Hitchhiker's Guide to the Galaxy*

It was half a century and a world away. In Britain, the 1950s were not famously colourful. If the nineties were a decade when everything had inverted commas around it, the fifties were like sitting through *The Mousetrap* over and over again in some church hall with rock-hard seats. You would say 'as joyous as the fifties' about as often as you'd remark that something was as droll as a Bergman season.

Internationally, Eva Peron, 'the mother of Argentina', died in 1952. Great swathes of Africa were still under European colonial rule. The Korean War ended in 1953 having cost almost three million lives. President Eisenhower was in the White House (twice), while Americans got richer and their cars, already the size of cathedrals, became larger and finnier with every passing year.

British society was one of those bottles of fizz that feel as hard as teak until the top is unscrewed and the pressure released. Dr Jonathan Miller, the director, writer and polymath, thinks that in many ways the fifties were a social extension of the thirties with habits of deference that did not change until a decade later.* A certain strangulated gentility ruled, especially in the suburbs whose sprawl had been contained by 'green belt' legislation just in time to prevent the whole of southern Britain below a line from the Wash to Cardigan Bay from becoming a housing estate.

Car ownership was only for the well-off. Television was grainy and black and white (405 lines to the screen and not today's 625), and it was by no means universal. The sets themselves were huge brown boxes containing valves that took a minute to warm up and stored energy long enough for a strange white dot to fade slowly from the screen when the power was turned off.

Despite their room-crushing dimensions, TVs had hanky-sized screens in front of which free-standing magnifiers could be placed. There were two channels, and on the BBC continuity gaps were filled with footage of a potter's hands shaping a clay vase. Spiffing chaps in dinner jackets or county women in evening dress would announce the next programme with voices of crystal-etching upper-class Oxbridge English.

The fifties were a time of damp gabardine macintoshes, ugly haircuts, hideously uncomfortable clothes, stodgy food, buildings of fashionable brutality inspired by scaled-up packets of cornflakes, and suffocating disapproval.† Beneath the surface all was churning. Kingsley Amis's *Lucky Jim* pierced the phoney moralizing with randy glee in 1954,∞ and John Osborne excoriated the stultifying hypocrisy of it all in *Look Back in Anger* (1956). But on the surface an oppressive and paralysing respectability prevailed.

In Cambridge in early 1951, Janet Donovan met Christopher Douglas Adams, who was twenty-four at the time. Janet was a nurse at Addenbrookes, the famous Cambridge hospital. She was rather pretty, then as now a pragmatic woman with a sympathetic, no-

---

* Interview with Sue Lawley on *Fifty Years On* (BBC Radio Four, 24 July 2002).

† The author remembers his mum getting into trouble with the neighbours in their block of council flats because she put out the washing on a Sunday.

∞ An unreliable informant reports that the condoms of the time were like the Russian *galoshki* (gumboots) of the Soviet era. He says it was 'like wearing a hot-water bottle on one's willy'.

nonsense manner. Despite being a staple of Mills and Boon romances, nurses tend not to be soppy. After all, if your daily routine consists of dealing with the ill and cantankerous public and its leaky orifices, soppiness could not survive for long. It was an unlikely liaison, but Janet was swept off her feet by the fascinating Christopher Adams. They quickly married (in Wisbech), and on 11 March 1952 Janet gave birth to Douglas Noël Adams, an infant hominid whose unusual intelligence would not be manifest for quite a while. Indeed, he was a markedly late developer in all but size, being a whopper even as a baby. Douglas's first name has a certain dynastic inevitability. Later one of his stock jokes was that he (initials DNA) arrived in Cambridge nine months before J.D. Watson and Francis Crick worked out the double helix structure of deoxyribonucleic acid.*

When somebody as extraordinary as Douglas Adams appears, there's a temptation to regard him as some kind of happy fluke, rather in the same way that townies imagine that meat never runs about a field but pops into being in sterile packs in huge supermarket refrigerators. But in both cases there is a long line of antecedents.

Doctoring was the family business, and it stretched back to the late eighteenth century. In four generations there were eleven male Dr Adamses and one woman surgeon. It was a Scottish dynasty of tall, clever men, and one that combined considerable talent with a strong sense of obligation to the public good. Interestingly, quite a few of those Adamses also wrote books, some were inspired teachers and lecturers and nearly all of them – perhaps all, but the records are incomplete – seem to have had an appetite and a gift for public speaking.†

---

* Quoted in *The Salmon of Doubt*. There is a joke that, despite the efforts of the editorial staff, will not die in the *New Scientist* magazine. It's so-called 'Nominal Determinism' whereby someone called Henrietta Bunn, for instance, is condemned to become a cake mix chemist. Douglas, given his passion for evolutionary biology, thought his initials funny, though entirely lacking any other significance.

† I am indebted to Shirley Adams, the granddaughter of Douglas's great-grandfather's sister, for her research into the family tree. This has many roots and branches, some huge and others tragically truncated, and it's something I will not attempt to describe. What with infant mortality, marriage between distant cousins, and age disparities it looks as if someone quite disturbed had tried to draw the Tube map from memory. Its compilation is a truly impressive and scholarly undertaking.

The great, great grand-daddy of them all was Alexander Maxwell Adams (1792–1860), who graduated from Edinburgh University and then practised in that city in Argyle Square, now the site of the Museum of Science and Arts. He left three sons who also became doctors. His great-grandson, also Alexander Maxwell Adams, author of a family history published in four parts by the *Hamilton Advertiser* in 1922, described him – somewhat obscurely quoting Thales* – as a man who 'took time by the forelock'. He was a popular man, who did a lot of unpaid work for the poorer folk of Edinburgh.

This was what saved him one day in 1828 after a mob mistook him for Dr Knox, the famous anatomist of Surgeons' Hall, who had been innocently implicated in the Burke and Hare murders. You will remember that Burke and Hare were the notorious body-snatchers who robbed the graves of the recently dead in order to supply, cash on delivery and no questions, corpses to the local medical school. (You may wonder how much important medical knowledge was hard won in such iffy circumstances.)

Body-snatching was a lucrative business – and one in which unsur-prisingly the anatomists favoured good, fresh material – so much so that Burke and Hare were tempted to regulate what the economists call the supply side, by not actually waiting for nature to take its course. They anticipated death, to the extent of murdering some of the rootless people in their own lodging house. Dr Robert Knox had his suspicions aroused when he saw the body of 'Daft Jamie' in the dissecting room, and raised the alarm.

Despite this, the doctor became something of a bogeyman. The mob, returning from despoiling his house, spotted Dr Adams, mistook him for Knox, and decided to string him up from one of the large brackets used to suspend oil lamps, then the only means of street lighting. Dr Adams's expostulations were in vain, the rope was around his neck; it looked very bleak. A century later, Dr Alexander Maxwell Adams (the fourth) was to describe matters, with that caution that marks a man of science, as 'an unpromising position'. Suddenly one of the crowd

---

* Thales of Miletus, pre-Socratic philosopher and cosmologist highly rated by Aristotle. They must have been a cultured lot, those doctors . . .

shouted out: 'What! Would ye hang the lang [tall] doctor o' the south?'
Dr Adams's practice was south of the Nor'loch.

Dr Adams survived this flirtation with the grim reaper to live on as
a well-respected Edinburgh doctor. He was the author of several
textbooks, including *A Treatise on Female Complaints*, some pretty bad
poetry, and a novel, *Gamoshka, or Memoirs of the Goodwin Family*.
However, he was best known for *Sketches from the Life of a Physician*
based on his experiences as a General Practitioner. It's engagingly
written, full of historically interesting detail and suffused with dry
humour. For medical men and women it is rightly viewed as a minor
classic.

His sons, Dr Adams, Dr Adams and Dr Adams, were all highly
regarded. William David had a distinguished career in Edinburgh.
Alexander Maxwell (the second of that name) became Professor at
Portland Street School of Medicine at the Andersonian University,
Glasgow, and then practised in Lanark where he went on to become
the Provost of Lanark, a job peculiar to Scotland that, as head of a
municipal authority or burgh, carries a lot of responsibility.

James Maxwell Adams (1817–1899), the middle son, also took the
road to Glasgow where he built up a large practice in medicine, with
added toxicology and engineering.* He invented the Adams Inhaler
for Respiratory Diseases, not only more efficient than the previous
model but much cheaper to manufacture. He composed many
innovative scientific papers on such subjects as heating by gas. (British
cities were black with soot from coal fires at the time.) In 1865 his subtle
forensic work, which involved devising from scratch a lethality
experiment with rabbits and a control group, contributed to the
conviction of Dr Edward Pritchard, who was accused of poisoning not
only his mother-in-law but also his wife. The creepy Dr Pritchard has
the unusual distinction of being the last man to be hanged in Glasgow
in public.

James was also a writer whose lively mind was manifest in the
eclectic range of his publications. *Sanitary Aspects of the Sewage Question*

---

* This information derives from a talk given by John Lenihan to a meeting of the
  Scottish Society of the History of Medicine.

was not one of his most commercial titles, but he also wrote about cruelty in lion taming, arsine poisoning, and the nutritional and chemical properties of wine. What is it, he wondered – *inter alia* – that makes the nose go a mottled cerise that betrays the imbiber no matter how excruciatingly tiptoeing his diction?

James was loved by his patients. In 1879, he was a shareholder in the Bank of Glasgow when it failed. Rather like a Lloyd's Name he had unlimited liability, but in contrast to many Lloyd's Names he paid up without cavilling even though he had to sell his house in the process. Astonishingly, a group of his friends and patients clubbed together and bought his house back for him, presenting him with the deeds in a fine silver casket.*

To tell the tales of all the medical Adamses would take too long. Suffice it to say that when Douglas Kinchin Adams (1891–1967), Douglas's grandfather and possibly the most brilliant doctor of them all, came along in 1891, the tradition of medicine and public duty was already firmly established.

Douglas Kinchin Adams, MB, ChB, MA, BSc, MD, FRCP, was another tall man of ferocious intelligence. 'Kinchin' is unusual even in Scotland; it was his mother's maiden name. Douglas K. Adams plunged into medicine with intellectual passion. He took his Bachelor of Medicine and Surgery degrees with honours, winning First Class Certificates in Midwifery, Surgery, Pathology and Medical Jurisprudence. Then he swiftly got his doctorate. While studying for his medical and surgical qualifications, he thought he'd also study for an MA and a BSc, both of which he acquired with distinction. He also proved his ability in research and practical medicine. In particular he refused to accept that neurological illness was unassailable, and as a result of his painstaking investigations he threw a great deal of light upon a group of nervous diseases called Generically Disseminated Scleroses (which include multiple sclerosis). His MD thesis on the subject won him the rarely awarded Bellahouston gold medal.

The Adamses always felt that they should give something back to

---

* Once again I am grateful to Shirley Adams for this information and the sight of the actual silver box containing the deeds to James's house in Glasgow.

the world, and Douglas Kinchin was no exception. Despite being a doctor and thus a member of a reserve profession able – indeed encouraged – not to go to war, he joined the Navy, in which he held a commission as a Medical Officer from 1914 to 1918, serving in the 'X' Cruiser squadron, then on the flotilla blockading the Belgian coast, and finally on a battle cruiser. Twice he was torpedoed, but escaped with little harm. By the time Douglas Kinchin was twenty-eight, he'd packed in more living and more learning than most of us manage in a lifetime.

After the war he returned to Glasgow, where his medical career was touched once more by grace. Medical lectures are notoriously dull, being largely of the hip-bone-is-connected-to-the-thigh-bone variety, but with more Latin. Kinchin's lectures at the University of Glasgow, however, were so coruscatingly brilliant that they attracted students and academics from other disciplines, prefiguring his grandson's immense talent for public speaking in general and the gift of making complex ideas accessible in particular. For years, Douglas Kinchin was Consulting Physician to the Western Infirmary in Glasgow where he established a reputation and a consultancy practice that stretched extensively over western Scotland. Family legend has it that he lost his life savings in the crash of 1929 and the subsequent Depression, but wealth was not that important to him. Finding out how things worked was what motivated him.

The same could not be said of his son, Christopher. The need for money – not that he ever had any of his own – and the things it could buy ran through his life like molten lava.

The Philip Larkin School of Developmental Psychology ('They fuck you up, your mum and dad/They may not mean to, but they do') embodies a certain melancholy truth. That's why everybody knows those lines. Larkin goes on to say that the parents had been fucked up in their turn. You may think that this is a sad, almost biblical account of damage, like a rugby ball being passed down the scrum of generations. The sins of the fathers visited upon the children, and so on forever. One can only take comfort from the fact that in many families the chain of grief is broken.

We cannot know now what made Christopher turn out as he did. Partly from loyalty, and perhaps because it's still too painful, Janet will not speak of him at all. 'Controlling, difficult, overwhelming, sulky, clever, charming, and complex' are the adjectives most commonly applied to Christopher by those who knew him. Douglas's own relationship with his dad was one of his inner demons that haunted him all his life.

It cannot have been easy for Christopher to have had a superman for a father, especially with the suffocating weight of tradition mapping out the path for the men in the family. If you cannot bear the burden of such a mythic mantle, you might take an ego-bashing which transmutes over the years into selfishness and sourness. Sons of famous fathers are known to have a tough time of it. Often they grow into perfectly pleasant and well-balanced adults, but some are never able to come out from their dad's shadow. Think of William Burroughs' son striving to be even more depraved than Pa (a tall order and a fatal aspiration), or of Evelyn Waugh's remark about Winston Churchill's son, Randolph. When told that he had undergone an operation for the removal of a small growth that turned out to be harmless, Waugh remarked: 'How typical of medical science to find the only part of Randolph that is not malignant, and remove it.'

Possibly Douglas Kinchin was so busy that he did not have enough time left over for his children, but there is no evidence of this in the folklore of the family. Besides, Christopher, impressed, perhaps oppressed, by the family's long line of brilliant and altruistic doctors, was strong-willed and determined to go his own way. Possibly Douglas Kinchin made his paternal disappointment with his son apparent, something that could have a wretched effect on a child, but details of Christopher's childhood are obscure. But it is known that he had an intense falling out with his elder sister, Pauline, for reasons now lost in the fog of time. It has been suggested that Douglas Kinchin's marriage had its problems, and that the children had been forced to take sides between mother and father. Whatever the source of the schism, it went very deep. Even when Christopher was in his forties and living close to Pauline in Eardiston, near Birmingham, they had scarcely any contact.

Christopher was highly intelligent, but he found it difficult to settle to anything for long. At the time he met Janet he had just finished a degree course at St John's, Cambridge (where he had been from 1949 to 1951), and for reasons that remain obscurely complex he had embarked upon a course of divinity at Ridley College, the school of theology in Cambridge. He had no vocation for the church, and became very dissatisfied with it as an institution, yet he did have – something his son was destined to share – an extreme curiosity about whether there was any purpose to the world. St John's records suggest that he was ordained, but the Johnian Office there admits that their documentation covering that period is incomplete. There is no record in Crockford's Clerical Directory of Christopher being ordained, nor anywhere else for that matter. Christopher's friend, G. R. Roche, says that Christopher never used any kind of clerical title or made any reference to the possibility of being ordained, but interestingly they met when they were both doing community work for the charity Toc H, an organization started in the First World War that has Christian values at its heart.

Some of the family have speculated that Christopher fancied the social status and the licence to meddle that a churchman enjoyed in those days. In British society there have always been those prepared to use religion as a balcony from which to look down on the rest of the population. There may have been something in that notion, but it seems only right to give Christopher the benefit of the doubt. One source of his religious impulse seems to have been a much deeper spiritual restiveness. His lifelong friend, the Reverend Ian Mackenzie, a cleric of some celebrity, describes an extraordinarily intense and hallucinatory religious experience that he, Christopher and the distinguished physicist, Claude Douglas Curling,* underwent in the mid-fifties. They were on a retreat to the famous religious community on the Hebridean island of Iona that was founded by St Columba and revived in the twentieth century by George MacLeod, the charismatic preacher. Claude Curling was there lecturing about physics and the perils of nuclear energy. Ian was in his second year there visiting the Abbey, and Christopher had been seconded as a part-time helper (wearing his

---

* Claude Curling died in 1993, but his archives are available in King's College, London. The experience seems to have affected him deeply and he became fascinated by the ontological nature of quantum reality.

probation officer hat) to keep a pastoral eye on the many young volunteers who were on the island helping with the rebuilding work.

The experience they underwent on Iona was too complex to be encapsulated in a few paragraphs here – even if I understood it fully. It deserves a book to itself, and I am grateful to Ian Mackenzie for taking such trouble to recall it, place it in context and describe so carefully what aspects of it can be described . It seems to have involved what a materialist would call a shared hallucination and others a mystical vision. Ian Mackenzie says that what Claude Curling and Christopher Adams endured was so intense and strange that afterwards Christopher found it impossible to talk or write about it in prose, and instead wrote an epic poem in the heroic mode in his effort to convey something of what it was about. Ian himself says that his role was that of the rational man, the bearer of the cool intellect of the Church of Scotland, who kept them all grounded and sane. He's always wondered – unnecessarily, surely – if he might have somehow held back the other two from some greater mystery.

Unfortunately, Christopher Adams's poem is lost. Although the Reverend says it was theologically unsound, the gist seems to have concerned a fusion between mysticism and science and the eternal battle between good and evil. The conflict between reason and mystery is age-old; some commentators have found room for the ineffable in the horribly counter-intuitive ambiguities of quantum physics and the predominant role of the observer in systems on the atomic scale. (The latter is widely misunderstood to justify all kinds of wide-eyed nonsense. It is subtle enough to deserve better. In the everyday world of classical physics, the one we inhabit, observation is still the cornerstone of science.)

Of course, Douglas was just an infant when his father underwent this shattering experience, but Reverend Mackenzie recalls that Christopher was just bursting with it, and could talk about little else:

He talked about it for breakfast, lunch and tea. Christopher had a personality almost too big for his body (and that was enormous). He was not a man to keep quiet about interesting things that happened to him.

It is not difficult to imagine Christopher booming away about his relationship with God while Douglas was still a sprat, and it is possible that Christopher and Douglas discussed Iona when Douglas was more of an age to understand. In its very abstraction it would have been a safer topic than any emotionally closer to home, but we can never know for sure. Douglas had little time for mysticism, but he was fascinated by the problem of how the complexity of the world could have emerged without the need for an Intelligent Designer. The link with his father's mystical experience may not be as direct as their having a conversation, of course. It's hard to see that there could be a Mysticism Gene (where is the reproductive or survival advantage?), but it is less tricky to see that deep curiosity may have a hereditary component.

Of course, ecstasy is far removed from academic theology. Nonetheless this aspect too may have appealed to another facet of Christopher's character, a kind of philosophical jokiness – something later manifested in a hugely stylish form in Douglas. Divinity must be the only subject in which you can not only fail, but commit heresy. ('I'm sorry, Simkins, following your viva we've decided to burn you at the stake . . .') There is almost a crossword-puzzling linguistic playfulness to the subject. Think of Anselm defining God into being by starting off with a definition (the greatest possible object of thought) and showing how the existence of the deity must follow. If it didn't, you would face a logical contradiction; for you could imagine a being with all the supreme attributes, but if it lacked that of existence it would not be the greatest possible object of thought – and thus be inconsistent with the 'agreed' definition.* Christopher, clever and complex, enjoyed the niceness of such argument; he also cared about precise usage. With a pedantic friend, he formed the Amateur Syntax Club into which his many children and stepchildren were press-ganged. He was never slow to correct anyone's grammar – including Douglas's.

Christopher was a restive spirit. To the extent that theology entails a search not just for God but for meaning, this trait was one of the many he passed on to Douglas. Certainly at 6'4" he was the origin of his son's

---

* This is a crude simplification of Anselm's Ontological Argument, a dodgy trick for smuggling God into existence by linguistic sleight of hand.

prodigious size. Great height was more unusual then.* Christopher had a long face, ample nose, high forehead and thick, black-rimmed specs. He was bearded in a way that gave him a wicked, piratical look. He wasn't particularly handsome, and he had a short temper and could be appallingly rude, yet his aggression and vitality made him nonetheless attractive. His friend, the Reverend, describes him as looking like the actor James Robertson Justice, especially as the irascible medical consultant in the series of British films, based on books by Richard Gordon, that started with *Doctor in the House*. Christopher could also be charming and sociable, and his evident willingness to take charge must have been appealing to a woman if she were feeling vulnerable or insecure.

He also had a huge appetite for luxury – whatever his financial circumstances – and regarded the good things in life as his by right. He was an excellent cook, though a firm believer in the maxim that whoever cooks does not do the clearing up afterwards. He liked smart restaurants, rich food and fine wine – and this high living may have been a factor in his early death from liver cancer at the age of fifty-seven. Often amusing in company, but more morose in private, he was capable of intense and tenaciously sustained sulking if he did not get his own way. Sue, his first daughter, reports that 'Dad could sulk for England'. Years later Douglas's sister, Jane, used the same expression about Douglas.

Susan Adams, Douglas's sister, was born three years after Douglas, in March 1955, at a time when her parents' marriage was already under great strain. Sue is a pleasant, intuitive woman who has had her share of sadness; she is fiercely protective of her mother.

By the time Douglas was five, his parents' marriage had fallen apart. The family was quite hard up. Janet, as the practical one, routinely faced choices that most of us, thank God, do not have to consider today. Food or shoes? Our generation is seldom put to this test, and we can scarcely imagine the unremitting preoccupation with making ends

---

* Demographically we've all got bigger – especially the Japanese. Even in the West you need only look at the seating in old theatres or buses. Shops for large people now sell sneakers like snowshoes and underpants on which you could show iMax movies.

meet. It's the drip, drip, drip of the Chinese water torture with each little increment of anxiety – not huge in itself – adding to the agony. Christopher was indifferent to such trivia. He would order his expensive pipe tobacco mixture from Dunhill because he liked it – and it was the kind of stylish eccentricity that marked a gentleman. Damn it, it was his due. Janet must have been in torment. Eventually their relationship deteriorated to such an extent that she was unable to endure matters any longer. Feeling that something needed to be done to bring home to Christopher the severity of the crisis, she walked out, taking the two children. So Janet, with Douglas (five) and Sue (two), moved in with Janet's mother and father in their house in Brentwood, Essex, the dark interior of which had not been changed since its Edwardian construction.

Her mother, Grandmama Donovan, was born in 1900 and lived to be nearly ninety-two. She was a woman with a good heart, but she was not overly interested in the children and it must have been a strain having them in that house. She and Janet sometimes argued about whether Janet indulged them too much. Granny Donovan loved mankind in the abstract while nurturing a healthy animus towards people in particular. In many ways she preferred animals to human beings, and her house in Brentwood was an official RSPCA refuge for hurt animals and the distressed pets of gentlefolk. Rather like Poe's Raven, for years the household had a pigeon that lived above the kitchen dresser – 'Pidge', they called it – who sat with broody, bird-brained patience forever trying to hatch a china egg. All the scruffy animals exacerbated young Douglas's hayfever and asthma. His nose dripped for years. It wasn't until he was in his thirties that he discovered how fascinating animals could be and even started to like them.

Grandpa Donovan was bed-bound and ill, an invisible presence pervading the household. Douglas and Sue scarcely saw him. Sue Adams recalls that, until he died, his bedroom door was always closed at the end of a dark corridor. It was forbidden territory.

Janet had to earn money, and she continued as a nurse in the local hospital, mainly working the night shift in order to see more of the children during the day. She is strong, but she must have been fighting off tiredness for years.

Douglas recalled very few memories of living with his granny, but as he said:

> It's amazing the degree to which children treat their own lives as normal. But of course, it was difficult. My parents divorced when it wasn't remotely as common as it is now, and to be honest I have scant memory of anything before I was five. I don't think it was a great time, one way or another.*

It's true, of course, that children have no way of knowing what is 'normal' and, besides, it's a word that is more useful for statistics than for describing human relations. Only when kids visit their friends' homes or, with very sequestered upbringings, at college, do they find out that what is familiar to them may be unusual in the world at large.

It's hard to judge the effect on the young Douglas's imagination of this gloomy house full of damaged animals and a slowly dying grandfather. He was already a little withdrawn. The family legend is that he did not speak at all until he was four. Since this was when his mother and father were still together, perhaps in some way he felt the tension between them. Janet scoffs at this story of his silence, saying that he exaggerated it to make an amusing anecdote, but she was concerned enough to take him to Farnborough Hospital for an examination. Unsurprisingly, in view of Douglas's later brilliance, the doctor was reassuring.

Janet does recall his first words which were uttered in the presence of some august Canon on a visit to the theological college. 'Da . . . da . . . da . . . ma . . .' Was it going to be Dad or Ma, bless him? Then suddenly it came out: 'Damn, damn, damn!' Later his infant burbling was even racier as he was given to saying 'Bugger, bugger, bugger.' James Thrift, hearing this story, remarked that there was no doubt who Douglas's mother was then.

Inductively speaking, the number of polymaths is too small to generalize about, though there is some research that suggests a connection between late blooming and creativity. Einstein, for example,

---

* Quoted in the Prologue by Nicholas Wroe in *The Salmon of Doubt*.

was said not to have spoken until unusually late, and some commentators think that his slow progress contributed to his genius for he was still asking those fundamental childlike questions about how things work at an age when most of us have ceased to wonder. The great Victorian sage, Lord Macaulay, was also reported to be a slow developer, remaining obstinately silent until an aristocratic friend, enquiring after the infant's recent cold, was surprised to hear a little voice pipe up: 'Thank you, madam, the agony is abated.'

Such correlations are probabilistic at best. For instance, being left-handed, like Douglas, is also a factor that is associated with a greater number of writers, musicians, mathematicians and sporting prodigies than population distribution would predict.* Sinistrality also touches upon the issue of the extent to which we humans are bio-robots, with gross characteristics determined by genetic inheritance, or free agents capable of rational choice. This immensely complicated question fascinated Douglas in later life.

Back in the early 1950s in Ridley College, it became obvious both to the teaching staff and to Christopher that he was not suited for the clerical life. They parted company without rancour, and Christopher took up teaching locally. But this was a calling for which his energy, sarcasm and impatience disqualified him temperamentally, and eventually he found a better role as a probation officer. Some of his family have speculated that it gave a degree of authority over his errant clients that appealed to his appetite for control, but whatever the motivation of this complex man he seems to have done the job effectively. Both Heather, Christopher's daughter by his second marriage, and Sue recall that he communicated well with Borstal kids. Though he failed to apply the same skill to his own life, he brought to their problems a professional clarity. Towards the end of his life – for like all the Adams men he could speak well in public – he also gave lectures on probation work, and on that basis described himself as a management consultant. As Douglas himself remarked, 'Dad and management [were] concepts that do not belong together.'

---

* Leonardo da Vinci, Napoleon and Jimi Hendrix were all sinistral. Left-handedness is on the increase (now 13% of males, 11% of females). Professor McManus of UCL believes that the genes that code for left-handedness also have a role in the development of the language centres of the brain.

In July 1960, Christopher Adams remarried. Mary Judith Stewart, born Judith Robertson, was a widow. Her first husband, William Alistair McLean Beardmore Stewart, known as 'B', was unusually also her stepbrother. In 1944, as a Royal Air Force Officer, he had been killed on a disastrous mission to Norway. One of Judith's brothers was killed shortly afterwards. Her mother had died when she was seven; her father had remarried, but had then died in tragic circumstances when Judith was eighteen. In contrast to a society in which many of us reach our fifties without any experience of mortality, Judith had been stalked by death since childhood.

Christopher's new wife was also wealthy. Through family connections her money came from shipbuilding on the Clyde from the days when Britain was once a major shipbuilding power, and the Clyde was lined for miles with cranes and gantries, shipyards and slipways. Under Christopher's influence, Judith came to have less and less to do with her own side of the family. It was if she had to start her life over again with a new set of family relationships put in place for her. From the photographs Judith was a good-looking woman of the Scottish variety – slim, pale, handsome rather than pretty – with a look in her eyes suggesting vulnerability. She lived to be eighty, dying in 2000 only six months before Douglas.

By her first husband Judith had two daughters, Rosemary and Karena. Rosemary, the older, is now a trained therapist practising in Edinburgh. (By chance she also married a Stewart – Quentin, a lawyer specializing in intellectual property.) Rosemary was in her teens when her mother remarried, and she recalls being quite taken by surprise.

The way it happened was that my mother arrived at my boarding school a week before I was due to leave, which was unheard of because days out were strictly rationed. She was suddenly there, and she took me and my sister down to the cottage . . . We must have been in the car – and this chap was there, and the boot was open and there were suitcases in it. [He was] a big chap, dark, bearded. Anyway, hello, hello, who's this? We went down to the cottage, and she sat on my bed and she said, guess what we've done. And I just knew, and said, you've got married. And that was it. We hadn't known about it. So that was quite devastating really, absolutely devastating. It's relatively recently – I suppose in the last fifteen years or so – that I've actually looked at it and dealt with it.

Certainly Rosemary Stewart believes that her mother was dominated by Christopher: 'Mum was Christopher's doormat.' Via their mother's second marriage the girls found themselves inherited by this huge, complicated, overpowering man. As with many stepfather/step-daughter relationships, it had its difficulties.

Karena, on the other hand, who was born after the death of her own father, was not quite so shocked at her mother's remarriage. She recalls that her head was in the clouds for most of her teens. She had suffered badly from anorexia, a condition that predated the appearance of Christopher in her mother's life. Her memory of her stepfather is that when she was very low he would sit and talk to her for hours on end. Of course, there can be an ambivalence about altruism (a means of control? fuel for your own self-esteem?), but it would be ungenerous not to recognize that Christopher helped Karena through her illness.* It was another example of his talent for sorting out other people's lives while being unable to sort out his own. However, Judith's daughters found the relationship with their stepfather tricky, and it is perhaps no coincidence that they both married young and left home.

After their marriage, Judith and Christopher moved to 'Derry', a beautiful house in Stondon Massey. This pretty Essex village – more of a hamlet – is only ten miles up the road from Brentwood, where Sue and Douglas still lived with Mum and Granny. Their nearest railway station was in Brentwood itself and a car was essential. Christopher wanted a sports car, so Judith bought him a Sunbeam Alpine. This was not exciting enough, however, since what he really

---

* Douglas was fascinated by this complex question of altruism, and would recommend Matt Ridley's excellent book, *The Origins of Virtue* (Viking, 1996), to his friends. He bought me a copy after an argumentative lunch one day.

yearned for was an Aston Martin. Also at Judith's expense, he was to have several in turn.*

J.G. Ballard said that we all inhabit an immense novel. In Christopher's version, which he inhabited almost certainly as the only probation officer in the country with an Aston Martin, ownership of a fast car was undoubtedly part of a character he thought of as roguishly charismatic.

Christopher Adams was proud of his driving and intolerant of other drivers. Followed on one occasion along a narrow road by a motorist he considered too close, he stopped and opened the boot and suggested to the man behind that he might like to get in it. Apparently he was quite unambiguous about it. Christopher had passed a high-performance driving course which allowed him to display a HPC badge on the windscreen, and he was keen to point this out to lesser motorists. His cousin, Shirley, remembers how his car was once scraped in an irritating but minor prang in a supermarket car park. Christopher was beside himself with a disproportionate and frightening anger. Once, as a child, Sue Adams recalls falling asleep in the Aston when her father was driving, and waking up to find the landscape was whizzing by at a feverish lick. A glance at the speedometer revealed the truth: 145 mph. (It was partly for drivers like Christopher that Barbara Castle, when Minister of Transport in Harold Wilson's Labour government, introduced the 70 mph limit on motorways – thus interfering with the individual's inalienable right to be hosed away by nauseated firemen.) Sue Adams's memory of the 145 mph moment is that she willed herself to fall asleep again.

All Christopher's children and stepchildren found themselves somewhat displaced when, in 1962, Judith and Christopher produced their own child, Heather Adams. Christopher doted on her. She was the apple of his eye.

Meanwhile, in the other part of Douglas's family life, he and his sister continued to live with their mum, their granny, the slowly dying

---

* For true buffs here's some info otherwise of no interest. But it's so hard won, you're going to be told anyway that the licence number of Christopher's last Aston Martin, a silver DB5, was BLU 119B.

granddad, and a floating population of sick animals. Every weekend, however, Douglas and Sue went to see their father and his new wife.

Stondon Massey is rural Essex at its poshest. 'Derry' was a huge mock-Tudor affair with a sweeping drive, acres of lawn and its own tennis court. At one point Judith also had a flat in Kensington and some domestic staff to help out, a couple called José and Maria. It is odd, given how money expands one's options, that Judith and Christopher should choose to stay in a house only ten miles from Brentwood, and Christopher's first family.

It must have been strange for the kids, commuting between Brentwood and Stondon Massey, so close geographically yet parsecs apart financially and socially. What do you make of breakfast with devilled kidneys served in a silver chafing dish when you are used to cornflakes? Perhaps children do not draw clear conclusions at the time. There is film of Douglas, a tall, gawky schoolboy in dreadful shorts and a tie, with Sue Adams and little Heather, all playing together in the huge garden of the house in Stondon Massey. Douglas runs around, arms and legs all over the place, throwing a ball for the infant Heather, who was round and blonde and smiling, and he shows a touching protectiveness towards the girls from both households. Sometimes, when Judith's two older girls were home from school, all the children were together. You have to wonder if the children quite understood where they all came from. Rosemary recalls her confusion when she first met Christopher's other kids:

> It probably wasn't until after Christmas [1960] that my mother
> would have said to us, oh, by the way, Chris has some children
> and they are going to come on Saturday. It was quite bizarre –
> and I'd said, 'Oh, right,' you know – in those days it was really
> sort of Andy Pandy. 'Shall I make some sandwiches?' And I
> remember the first day we saw them, just looking at them. I
> remember where they were standing – very solemn, both of them.
> I don't know, maybe I was very solemn too. And it was quite
> difficult to know – you know, what is the relationship?

Christopher and Janet could not, or would not, bear to see each other so Grandmama Donovan helped in the mechanics of moving the children around for the weekends. Sometimes she and Judith would meet up at a bank in Ongar for a handover reminiscent of the Cold War spy exchanges, and indeed she and Judith struck up a good relationship. Karena remembers that Granny Donovan was quite often to be seen in 'Derry'. Christopher refused to speak to Janet; their silence endured for decades. (When Sue Adams got married, it took a lot of negotiation to get Christopher to attend.)

Douglas's attitude to money, when he later made a lot of it, must have been influenced by his early knowledge of just how it bought comfort and goodies. Karena remembers her mother once remarked that Christopher and Douglas were far too alike to get on. Certainly Douglas shared with his father an utter lack of pragmatism, along with an awesome appetite for treats. At his memorial service he was retrospectively teased for once being found to have eight horrifically expensive cameras in the back of his car. But unlike his father, Douglas did not let his life pivot around money for its own sake; to him it was just a means to an end. Fun and access to interesting experiences were the main goals – and, being by nature delightfully generous, he was also keen that friends and loved ones should share such pleasures.

Judith's own considerable wealth was deployed unstintingly on behalf of her husband and, interestingly, *all* the children, including Christopher's children by his first marriage. She set up a trust fund for all of them, with Christopher's friend from Toc H, G.R. Roche, as one of the trustees.

One national slander against the British is that we are not very good with children. As generalizations go, this is tosh, but for a certain caste of British society there was a time when some of the emotional complexities of raising kids were thought to be best resolved by sending them to boarding school. Both Douglas and Sue went to fee-paying schools paid for by Judith. Douglas attended Brentwood, starting with its prep school, Middleton Hall. Sue went to Felixstowe College, as subsequently did Heather Adams. Given how eye-wateringly expensive it is to see three kids through the thirteen years or so of education at private schools, it is especially beneficent when two of them are not your own.

Why did Judith do it? Rosemary says her mother had an acute sense of fair play and duty, and by all accounts she was a very decent person.

Perhaps Christopher might also have put pressure on her. You can imagine conversations along the lines of, 'They're my children, but it's you who's got the money, so of course it's up to you . . .' The evidence suggests, however, that Judith paid simply because she felt it was the right thing to do on behalf of all their children. What Janet felt about her kids being educated on the ticket of Christopher's rich second wife is an interesting question. But she is nothing if not practical, and obviously she wanted the best for her children.

In 1964, Janet also remarried, a local vet called Ron Thrift, a man for whom there seems to have been nothing but affection and respect. On his death from cancer in 1991, aged only fifty-nine, the entire community attended a memorial service. When he moved to Shaftesbury in Dorset to set up a new practice, Janet went with him, while Douglas and Susan continued at Brentwood School and Felixstowe College as boarders. Ron, however, took an interest in Janet's kids by her first marriage and did his best to look after their welfare.

Soon after their marriage, Ron and Janet produced a son and a daughter of their own. The elder, Jane Thrift, whom Douglas loved with a fierce fraternal protectiveness, is known in the family as Little Jane, to distinguish her from Big Jane, i.e. Douglas's wife Jane Belson, who's striking for her elegance but also, at six foot, for her height. (Confusingly, while Douglas and Big Jane were tacking, yacht-like, through storm-force seas towards their eventual marriage, there was also a Wrong Jane as opposed to Right Jane.) Years later, Little Jane was to live with them in London where a flat was created for her in the basement of their large and beautiful house in one of Islington's finest Georgian terraces. Little Jane, like her mother, eventually trained as a nurse, before deciding, very much under Douglas's influence, that life had more to offer her.*

---

* There is a story that Douglas, Big Jane, and a small but elite group of media-fashionables including Jon Canter, the film writer, the comedian Lenny Henry, Mary Allen who ran the Opera House at Covent Garden, and several senior telly people, were sitting in the kitchen, trembling into their coffee, after one of the Adamses' awesome parties. Little Jane came in wearing her nurse's uniform. 'Oh, Jane, Jane,' Jon Canter said with self-deprecating irony, 'when will you get a *real* job?'

Little Jane's full brother, James Thrift, now runs a business with his wife, Bronwen, in the West Country bringing the virtues of good design to a local market. His dry sense of humour is very reminiscent of Douglas – which, even allowing for it as a family trait, is not surprising, since Douglas's size and personality must have had a striking effect on a young lad. Douglas saw a lot of his two new half-siblings, dividing the holidays equally between his parents' families. Christopher and Janet at that time were still not exchanging a syllable with each other. Geographically, too, there was now quite a distance between them to be covered. Even these days, Essex to Dorset is not an easy journey – and sometimes it was one that Douglas made as a hitchhiker. (Once or twice he also rode a much too small motorbike with his knees sticking out like parachute brakes.) The sense of commuting between different worlds must have continued as acute as ever.

To recap: Douglas had one full sister, Sue Adams; two stepsisters, Rosemary and Karena; one paternal half-sister, Heather Adams; and two maternal half-siblings, Jane and James. In later life he made strenuous efforts to get them all together as adults – perhaps to recreate a family that he had missed as a child.

As for his relations with his dad, we can only speculate. Heather Adams, who now lives in the Canary Islands with her husband and their two children, is sophisticated and articulate, like all the Adams children of that generation, but a certain caution comes into her voice when talking about her father. She recalls that Douglas's relationship with Christopher was always immensely fraught, but that the two men were never able to talk about it.

Nonetheless, when Douglas was in his teens his father did sometimes take him in the Aston Martin on extravagant holidays abroad. This in itself must have been a bit galling for Rosemary and Karena, since their mother had always been careful with money, not out of meanness but from anxiety. Christopher's love of spending, on the other hand, may have helped to bring him and Douglas together, but it appears that in their anguished, perhaps curiously British way, their conversation always avoided any subject of the slightest emotional importance. No matter how well Christopher com-municated with the delinquents in his professional charge, between him and his only son the tension of things left unsaid lasted all their lives.

Frustration dogged Douglas's relationship with his father even as death finally crept up on Christopher in co-respondent's shoes in 1985, regardless of the fact that, like his son, Christopher was concerned about his blood pressure and started going to a gym in the last decade of his life. When it was clear that Christopher was dying, Judith summoned the family to his bedside in Droitwich Hospital. Douglas had flown back from the States the previous day. The vigil must have been harrowing, and the family members took it in turns to leave the room and lie down for a while. When Christopher chose the moment to depart, it was during his son's brief absence. Douglas was devastated. 'Bloody typical,' he said, 'bloody typical Dad – waited till I was out.'

Christopher Adams and Douglas were so similar in size and appearance that Douglas said that seeing his father laid out in death was like looking at his own dead body. Christopher, returning to his roots, left instructions that his ashes were to be thrown in Loch Fyne.

Five years later, *The Deeper Meaning of Liff* was published. Co-written with John Lloyd, it's a brilliant attempt to save all those unemployed concepts from hanging about and getting into mischief when they really need a respectable word to settle down with. Characteristically, Douglas turns the anguish that he must have associated with Droitwich into a joke about misconstruing intentions:

Droitwich (n)
A street dance. The two partners approach from opposite
directions and try politely to get out of each other's way. They
step to the left, step to the right, apologize, step to the left again,
bump into each other, and repeat as often as unnecessary.

Nobody knows for sure how much his father meant to Douglas. Jane Belson confirms that he always found that relationship very difficult, adding what a pity it is that there was nobody who ever told the young Douglas that he was clever, and that it was all right to be so. In some English households there was a notion – now mercifully extinct – that praising children too fulsomely, or, indeed, at all, might induce personality disorders. It is such a pity that Christopher, a complex man full of anger and unresolved conflicts, who spread havoc through two generations, was never able to say: well done, son, you've done brilliantly, I'm so pleased. Douglas went through his life without ever hearing the words he needed to hear from his father. Some family members think Christopher would have been jealous of Douglas's fame, yet he was without a doubt immensely proud of his son. The trouble is: he never let on.

There has been research that suggests that fathers are important to a child's development of self-esteem. According to these theories, even if the relationship between mother and father is like something out of Strindberg on a bleak day, just having a dad around is good news. This is contentious work, however, and particularly irritating to those for whom the idea that children are resilient is a key component in an ideology that grants a licence to adults to look for happiness where they fancy. In Douglas's case, his father was around, and available – albeit ten miles up the road with a new family in a different universe.

In Douglas's archives there is a complete run of Aston Martin magazines that Douglas either collected at the time or inherited from his father. There's also a black and white photograph of Christopher Adams putting petrol into the unmistakeably elegant flank of a DB5. Douglas must have been playing with an enlarger and some photographic paper, for this image has been printed – sometimes cropped in a slightly different way – again and again and again.

Douglas Adams did not go through life scarred by his childhood. He was fond of his extended, albeit unusual family, and he adored his mum. Yet, sometimes, in later life, he was assailed by profound bouts of insecurity, and he could sink into a kind of dark, inner emptiness for days. He could be quite childlike and mawkishly self-absorbed, but then that is not uncommon with writers whose solitary art can be lonely, especially if they are, like Douglas, people who need company.

To some extent the public Douglas, the wildly creative jolly green giant, was a mask. But in a sense we all play the role of ourselves in the world, so any word that suggests something to be put on and taken off at will is quite the wrong one. Man and mask are inextricably melded together. As a child, Douglas lived a great deal in his head. Fortunately for the rest of us, that turned out a wonderful place to be.

Emotionally, Douglas was as large as his giant frame, and he made correspondingly huge demands on those close to him. Sometimes he wept, a gift lost to many men, and sometimes he displayed the emotional intelligence of a refractory brick on a not particularly sensitive day. But most of the time he was the inventive, funny, extravagant lunk who inspired such affection in those around him. And if there were some psychological itch that he could never quite scratch, the world should be grateful, because it made up part of his genius.

Publishers know that writers with a lot of craft can be counted on to deliver a competent book, but the best books, the ones that shimmer on the page, grow like pearls from some internal irritant. Douglas Adams would always have been clever and funny, but it's doubtful that he would have given the world so much if Mum and Dad had been a happily married nurse and teacher living lives of stodgy contentment in deepest Essex.

Zaphod couldn't sleep. He also wished he knew what it was that he wouldn't let himself think about. For as long as he could remember, he'd suffered from a vague nagging feeling of not being all there. Most of the time he was able to put this thought aside and not worry about it [. . .] Somehow it seemed to conform to a pattern that he couldn't see . . .
Chapter 14, *The Hitchhiker's Guide to the Galaxy*

All writers put themselves into their work – how could they not?

chapter two

Finishing school

'I was at Brentwood School for twelve whole years. And they
were, by and large, in an up and downy kind of way, pretty good
years: fairly happy, reasonably leafy, a bit sportier than I was in
the mood for at the time, but full of good (and sometimes highly
eccentric) teaching. In fact, it was only later that I gradually
came to realize how well I had been taught at Brentwood:
particularly in English, and particularly in Physics. (Odd that.)'
Douglas Adams, *The Best of Days? Memories of Brentwood School**

All boys' schools seem to have their own dire song. Some have verses
that have to be destroyed by controlled explosion. Decades after
leaving, the alumni can only bring themselves to sing the words after
much forehead-smiting and six pints of beer. Brentwood School has a
fine example of the genre called 'The Old Red Wall', a reference to the
handsome brick wall that contains the grounds; it's a truly gruesome
mix of cruelty and sentiment.

According to the song, the institution was founded in the mid-
sixteenth century following a spasm of guilt over the public burning
to death of an innocent lad. Despite these inauspicious beginnings, the
lyrics assure us that there is no question so vexed that it cannot be
settled with a good chat by the stove for 'why we conquered and how
we strove/They tell of it still by the old school stove'. Brentwood was
endowed in 1558 by Sir Anthony Browne, a clever time-serving career

* This book was published by the school in 1999. A copy was kindly lent to me by
old Brentwoodian, Peter Stothard.

lawyer, part-time land speculator and an early prototype of Essex Man.* It was a grammar school in which a boy could learn Latin all day and be beaten for mistaking a declension. He could also be expelled for syphilis or lunacy. There was no namby-pamby counselling in those days.

These days, however, Brentwood includes girls among its 1500 pupils. The school stands in seventy-two acres of its own grounds with an appealing miscellany of buildings, from eighteenth century to modern. The facilities are by any standard – and especially those that prevail in the State sector – excellent. It even boasts that essential accessory, ghosts. Countess Tasker, who lived in Middleton Hall until the turn of the nineteenth century, left that handsome building as a legacy to Brentwood and it now houses the Preparatory School. It is said she occasionally makes a visit, and in her posthumous incarnation she is known as the Blue Lady.

Brentwood School was perhaps the only cliché of Douglas's life. He attended for twelve years, having started at the prep school. His mother recalls that he loved it. When she told him, five years after her divorce from Douglas's father, that she was remarrying, he burst into tears because he thought he might have to leave school. He magically cheered up when told he would be staying.

Brentwood gave him a fine formal education and a grounding in all the odd social and moral apparatus of an English public school. It boasted Praeposters (up-market prefects), a house system (Douglas was in School House), an improving motto ('Virtue, Learning, Manners'), mud, cold showers, rugby, and innumerable societies. Above all, it kept the forces of change at bay and frowned upon tawdry competitiveness – while encouraging it in matters of personal merit and team spirit – by endless regulations.

A host of rules defined the school uniform. Even today school uniforms are the last refuge of the visually illiterate. Perhaps the road-kill ties and staphylococcus yellow and bruise-purple blazers are

---

* Michael Willis, the school's archivist and a teacher of History and Politics, describes 'good' Sir Anthony in these terms in his official history in *The Best of Days?*

thought to discourage vanity, but the worst of contemporary designs are as nothing to the prickly horrors we wore in the fifties. They seemed to have been woven out of cardboard and gravel. Douglas and his fellows were lucky inasmuch as the uniform was designed by one of their famous old boys, Sir Hardy Amies, the couturier to the Queen, who devised an elegant grey check – albeit surmounted by an absurd straw boater for especially embarrassing occasions. Nevertheless the blazer was woven, or perhaps constructed, from intensely scratchy material. Can worsted really be derived from sheep? Or are there herds of wild worsteds with hides of steel wool that evolved to repel the predators of the plains?

One of these regulations obliged Douglas to wear shorts at prep school. To his horror, when he graduated to the main school, the shop had no long trousers with a sufficient length of leg to fit him. For a whole month at the age of twelve he had to wear shorts, despite towering over his contemporaries and most of the masters. It is a fact clear to all schoolboys that to carry on wearing shorts after the age of twelve indicates some profound psycho-sexual confusion or, worse, a tragic yearning to become a scout-master. Douglas describes it as so mortifying that for four weeks he played on the edge of station platforms and forgot the Highway Code when crossing roads.* All his life he was rather clumsy, and at school his uncontainable arms and legs, pumping gallantly but to little effect, made the role of sporting hero impossible. (Most large men know – *pace* American footballers – that well-knit, compact blokes tend to be much better sportsmen than ill-coordinated giants. Alas, they are usually tougher too, as large males, offending merely by an accident of size, sometimes discover in rough pubs.)

In Douglas's day Brentwood was – and probably still is – a very good school in a fee-paying, curriculum-heavy, sport, values, and nicknames sort of way. Is there anywhere outside an English public school or a P.G. Wodehouse novel where so many soppy nicknames are still to be found? Where else can you meet 'Squiffy' and 'Bunny' and 'Spud'? Brentwood teachers included – *inter alia* – 'Tusky' and

---

* See his witty essay on the subject reprinted in *The Salmon of Doubt.*

'Funf'. Such schools, especially for boarders, create an entire world, safely equipped with rules, regulations and the society of peers in the same boat. If the regime is basically fair-minded – as it was in the 1960s under the headmastership of Richard Sale – such worlds can have huge appeal to their inmates. Douglas was a boarder from the age of eleven. Beyond that Old Red Wall lay uncertainty.

For its size, Brentwood has produced a good crop of old boy high-achievers: several bishops, a Home-then-Foreign Secretary (Jack Straw), Robin Day, who broke the mould of abject deference when interviewing shifty politicians on TV, Noel Edmonds, Griff Rhys Jones, some superior journos (Peter Stothard and Brian MacArthur for instance) and a fair sprinkling of senior lawyers, scientists and military men. The teaching itself was very competent. The older teachers were drawn largely from a generation when the Depression drove a lot of people with first-class minds into the profession, and the younger staff were largely men with good degrees and a sense of vocation.

Douglas attended Brentwood for twelve years in all. It wasn't his very first school. That honour goes to Mrs Potter's Primrose Hill Primary in Brentwood town. At six he took the exams and had the interview for Brentwood's prep school. Middleton Hall was not just a machine, like a *foie gras* factory, for stuffing little boys with enough academic learning to cope with promotion to the senior school. It had traditions of its own, lovingly maintained by generations of formidable headmasters. Jack Higgs was the legendary head whose philosophy of character development lived on there. He maintained that it was a school's duty to turn out pupils who were not only adequately briefed with knowledge but who were 'honest, kind and useful'.*

It was while Douglas was still in the prep school that Frank Halford awarded him the legendary ten out of ten for a story. Frank Halford, by then Deputy Head, retired from Brentwood in 1991, and he is still remembered with great affection. In his piece in *The Best of Days?* he records his pleasure that this perfect mark later became such a morale-

---

* Quoted by John Marchant, retired headmaster of the Prep School, in *The Best of Days?*

booster to Douglas when the muse was being capricious. Years later, in 1992, Mr Halford met Douglas again at a speech day celebrating the centenary of the founding of the prep school, and he also attended the secular but nevertheless touching version of a christening for little Polly Adams.*

When Douglas moved up to Middle School, his housemaster was Micky Hall, referred to, naturally, by all students as Henry. Assiduous digging through the well-produced school magazine[†] reveals that for some years Douglas excelled at being tall, but took little part (or at least not prominent enough to be mentioned) in the many extracurricular activities. In 1964, however, he participated in the Sir William Wynne-Finch Award in 'A' camp. It was some kind of privately sponsored version of the Duke of Edinburgh Awards, for it featured orienteering, pitching a bell tent, coastguard training, map reading and various other chunky, practical skills. It conjures up a vision of freezing wet boys, soggy canvas snapping in the wind, and burnt food floating in cold water.

When he was ten, Douglas heard Hank Marvin and the Shadows, and was entranced. His mother recalls that he wanted Hank to come down to Essex and play on Douglas's birthday, and was bemused when she said it wasn't possible. 'But, Mum, it *is* possible,' he said. He knew his geography and could see no physical impediment. 'There's even a plug.' It was the start of his intense love of music. His enthusiasm for the Beatles went almost beyond passion; he was totally besotted. In 1964, Douglas was given his first left-handed guitar, and he taught himself to play it by studying the finger-picking styles of guitar heroes and by practising relentlessly. For the piano he had more formal training, and he shared a teacher with Paul Wickens – aka 'Wix' – who was supremely talented and went on to become the keyboard player

---

* Inspired and inspiring English teachers are the unsung heroes of modern literature. For instance, Raymond Chandler and P.G. Wodehouse – both at Dulwich College though at different times - were taught by the same person.

† *The Brentwoodian.* Douglas kept the complete run of the magazine slowly turning to coal under the weight of a lifetime's kipple stored in giant crates. Later, when he wrote for school publications, he usually missed the deadlines by two weeks – a modest start to a lifelong habit.

in Paul McCartney's band. Later Wix was to play an important role in Douglas's passion for music as an adult. 'Wix and I were both taught music,' he said, 'but in his case it worked.'

Douglas was actually a proficient left-handed guitar player, but his standards in music were as demanding as his standards in writing and he knew that his playing would never catch fire in the way he so admired in great musicians. All his life a streak of perfectionism ran through Douglas like quicksilver, both a boon and a torment.

He was also in the choir, singing like an angel until his voice broke, and he remained an assistant in the chapel, towering over the other choristers. Rather incongruously for one destined to become a militant atheist, he won a Service in Chapel Prize in 1966.

The Beatles, however, were his first love. Douglas used to tell a story of bunking off school on Friday 20 March 1964, to sneak into town to buy 'Can't Buy Me Love' from Radiogram in the High Street. He fell over and badly cut his knees on the way back, though he pointed out that knees are self-repairing whereas self-repairing textiles are still decades off. Lacking his own record player, he snuck into Matron's office and managed to play the record three times, bleeding profusely, before being caught, bandaged and slippered.

Such was his passion for the Beatles that the only time anybody can recall Douglas using his awesome bulk for intimidation was when he learned that another boy had heard the latest Beatles single, and insisted that he hum it. In *The Salmon of Doubt*, Douglas is quoted as saying the song was 'Penny Lane' from the Magical Mystery Tour, so it must have been 1967. He added: 'People now ask if Oasis is as good as the Beatles. I don't think they're as good as the Rutles.' For Beatles fanatics who would like to compare judgements, there is an appendix listing his favourite Beatles' tracks in order of preference in the form of an elaborate document devised by Richard Curtis and others on 25 May 1999.*

In fact Douglas seems to have been a gentle boy, and well enough liked if sometimes a little lonely. His mother recalls that he had a good

---

* My thanks to Richard Curtis for letting me have a copy. You can forget Proust and those stupid cakes. Beatles' songs are more potent.

friend called Steven Prosser, whose surname he appropriated for the jobsworth character from the local authority whose plans to knock down Arthur Dent's house for a bypass were frustrated by the end of the world.

The question of Douglas's great height is easily over-egged. We're all aware of our bodies and conscious of how conspicuous, attractive or grotty we appear to others. In a closed order like a school he must have been aware of it all the time. When you are over six foot tall at twelve with legs like a wading bird, and you blush easily, it is hard to hide in assembly. Looming over masters, not fitting easily into uniform, or beds, or desks, or team games, tolerating the incontinent trickle of schoolboy humour ('Meet me under the Adams') – all would contrive a feeling of difference that must have contributed to his sense of looking at the world from an unusual angle.

The first documentary evidence of Douglas's time at Brentwood was in a sixth-form debate. The motion was that 'This House should shave its head'. Skinheads did not grace the streets until the seventies, so this was more of a contemporary allusion to the long-hair moral panic (druggy threat to the social fabric) than the later short-hair moral panic (*brutal*, druggy threat to the social fabric). Using a remarkably sophisticated idea for a schoolboy, Douglas proposed the motion. The argument went like this: let's invent a character, Johnny the Happy Skin, whose bonce looks exactly like everybody else's. How can he express his individuality? Not through follicular fashion, clearly – only by his life and work. Axiomatically this is a Good Thing. Motion carried.

In the course of that debate Douglas did also commit in public a terrible pun that would have had all those smart public schoolboys groaning. Johnny the Happy Skin, he observed, is part of the 'aggro-cultural revolution'. Hold my aching sides. But even as a schoolboy, he could write with considerable wit. Sue Adams, a county away in her boarding school in Felixstowe, recalls that Douglas would write to her regularly, and that his letters were so funny that she would read them to her schoolmates. After a while the arrival of a letter became a source of some joy to the girls, Douglas's very first fans. Unfortunately, the letters are lost.

Later that same year, 1968, Douglas appears again as an author of spoof reviews in *Broadsheet*, the boys' cyclostyled and stapled arts magazine. (There was another, more literary, magazine called *Green Wood*, a superior miscellany, for which Douglas also contributed the odd piece.) Douglas's parodies were in a chirpy tabloid style, not bad for a schoolboy.

> *Hamlet*: Feeling depressed? Read this account of life before
>   Yeastvite and think how lucky you are.
> *Oliver Twist*: Tale unsuitable for those with a social conscience in a
>   starving world: glutton makes good.

And so on . . . The magazine was edited by a sixth-former called Paul Johnstone. It contains much good material, but possibly the most remarkable thing about it, something shared with many of the extracurricular activities of Brentwood, was the sheer confidence it displayed. The sense that the boys could turn their hands to anything, and expect to succeed, was the most valuable of all the school's gifts to its students.

There follows a brief diversion for serious *Hitchhiker's* fans.

Do you remember when Arthur and Ford stow away on the Vogon starship, get captured and are taken into the bowel-churning presence of Prostetnic Vogon Jeltz? Of course you do. The Vogon subjects them to ordeal by poetry before, with characteristic meanness, throwing them out of the airlock into the icy vacuum of space. The book comments that Vogon poetry is only the third worst in the universe. The second worst is by Poet Master Grunthos the Flatulent. Douglas notes that during the recital of Grunthos's 'Ode to a Small Lump of Putty I Found in My Armpit One Midsummer Morning', four of his audience died of internal haemorrhage, and that the President of the Mid-Galactic Arts Nobbling Council survived only by gnawing off his own leg. The very worst poetry of all, according to the first edition of *Hitchhiker's* and the original radio broadcast, was written by one Paul Neil Milne Johnstone of Redbridge, Essex.

Subsequently the name of the universe's worst poet was changed to Paula Nancy Millstone Jennings (note the initials) and that now appears in all but the very first edition of *Hitchhiker's*. After *Hitchhiker's* was published, Paul Johnstone wrote to Pan Books objecting to the gratuitously hurtful insult to his literary talents.*

To the alarm of his friends, family and publishers, Douglas did have a tendency to put private jokes into his work.[†] It amused him, spared him the agony of cudgelling his brains to invent something *ex nihilo*, and – in all innocence – he thought that either people would not notice (unlikely) or that they would be amused. The improbability drive, for instance, in *Hitchhiker's*, published a friend's real Islington phone number as it lurched its sickening way towards so-called normality. That number rang and rang.[∞] In the case of the dire poetry, I am sure he did not intend any unkindness to Paul Johnstone. Just occasionally, Douglas's emotional intelligence – to steal Daniel Goleman's useful term – was not as sparkling as his high intellect.

The most famous advice in the entire canon – 'Don't Panic' – was something his mother, Janet (a nurse, don't forget), was wont to say quite often. Yet more characteristic utterances of his mum are attributed to the censorious alternative personality of Eddie, the shipboard computer. 'Right! Who said that?' and 'It'll all end in tears' are expressions which to this day the Adamses cannot hear without an inner chortle.[§]

Meanwhile at Brentwood in 1968, the next Adams sighting is in the school's Winter Theatricals. Douglas played Julius Caesar in Shakespeare's

---

* Douglas and I discussed this at the time, and we expressed surprise that the poet did not regard it as a kind of off-beat tribute. In fairness to Paul Johnstone, who I hope did not have a budding career as a poet blighted by Douglas's reference, I suspect that he would now smile about this. If not, and you *are* Paul Johnstone by chance reading this biography, I apologize for having dragged this up again.

† Rather as Ian Fleming found the name of James Bond on the cover of *Birds from the West Indies and Other Caribbean Islands*, Douglas is said by some scholars of Adamsiana to have named Arthur Dent after an obscure puritan who wrote *The Plain Man's Guide to Heaven* (1601). Douglas always denied this, but who knows what lodges in writers' brains?

∞ PLEASE do not call it. The number now belongs to somebody quite unconnected.

§ *The Hitchhiker's Guide to the Galaxy*, pp. 105–6.

tragedy. Brentwood stage productions were nothing if not ambitious. Griff Rhys Jones appeared in the same play as a mere servant to Octavius.

Caesar, you will recall, gets murdered about halfway through the play. That may have been a blessing, for Douglas was not one of the world's natural thesps, even though he loved to perform. He was so big and clumsy that there was always the fear that he would fall off the edge of the stage by mistake. (Even his mum said of Douglas running that it was best to be charitable and not talk of it at all.) He spoke Shakespeare's verse with understanding and intelligence, but his stage timing was off.

History does not record a review of Douglas's acting, but one can't help imagining him being stabbed by lots of schoolboys in togas, and then falling with the slow grace of a combine harvester toppling from a bridge. In the following year's Winter Theatricals his imposing stage presence was exploited in a role for which a certain disjointed other-worldly quality was an advantage. He played the ghost of Hamlet's father in a production featuring Anthony Jacques as Hamlet and Griff Rhys Jones as Rosencrantz.

The Christmas House Dinners were another opportunity for the stagestruck. Lesley Hall, the daughter of Micky 'Henry' Hall, remembers Christmas vividly in her piece in *The Best of Days?*:

> House suppers were always a highlight of the year. A huge Christmas tree was erected in Old Big School and house residents and invited guests were entertained with musical interludes, comic sketches and the odd play . . . I remember the Hare Krishna movement infiltrating one such performance, courtesy of Douglas Adams. I had not come across anything like it before and thought both the concept and the individual rather weird. I accept now that it is OK to be weird.*

Despite not doing all that well in his A Levels, in 1970 Douglas won an Exhibition to St John's College, Cambridge. The setback with his A

---

* My thanks to Lesley Hall and John Kelsall for permission to quote this from *The Best of Days?*

levels he attributed to having met Helen,* his first girlfriend, with whom he was deeply in love, in an Economic History class. However, Douglas blagged his way into Cambridge largely on the basis of an essay on the rise of interest in religious poetry. This had enabled him to perform that trick of the clever but desperate student of taking what little he could remember and wrenching it into a whole new critical perspective, thereby pretending that a great body of knowledge (in reality forgotten or never learned in the first place) had been discarded as a matter of intellectual policy. In this case he recalled some religious poetry he had sung in the choir, much of it from Christopher Smart's *Jubilate Agno* (in college he went on to study this strange poet in more detail). He added a pinch of Gerard Manley Hopkins to a good portion of William Blake, the wild pet of the supercultivated (as T.S. Eliot called him), whose revolutionary verse has – among its many qualities – the virtue of being memorable. Then he managed to work in some Beatles lyrics, all of which were engraved on his heart.

Decades later, when he was awarded that very British accolade of an appearance on BBC Radio Four's *Desert Island Discs*, he told Sue Lawley that his essay was egregious bullshit. In fairness to the academics at St John's it was probably dazzlingly clever egregious bullshit with more than a sediment of genuine insight. St John's happened also to be the college from which his father had graduated, but it is unlikely that this was much of a factor for the admissions committee though it may have loomed larger in Douglas's mind.

When he won a place at St John's on the strength of his brilliant essay, Douglas was certainly aware of his long ancestry of formidable Scottish doctors, and said that he had toyed with the idea of studying medicine. Fortunately his father had broken the line. Douglas was rather fastidious and the thought of peering up the diseased sphincters of the public all his life filled him with dismay; emotionally he certainly would not have been tough enough. Besides, he always knew that his talent was for writing. On the page he was staggeringly good. It was

---

* Readers, the role of biographer is that of licensed nosy bastard. Douglas squirreled everything away in great crates, including Helen's touching love letters. Are they our business? I think not. Do they cast light on Douglas? No.

as if his fierce intelligence had nowhere to hide when he was faced with an exam on a topic that he knew demanded no invention. He performed just as remarkably when he took a test paper for the Philosophy and Literature course at the University of Warwick. Indeed, the admissions tutor there, M.M. Warner, wrote to him – clearly in response to a letter from Douglas – to say that his paper was one of two outstanding ones in the year, and that he certainly would have been offered a place.

His school days had given him a sound education and the beginnings of a useful network (Griff and Wix, for example, stayed in touch). Cambridge, with its beauty, the society of the brightest and the best, and its ready-made matrix of contacts that would make a Freemason sick with envy, was to change his life utterly.

chapter three

St John's, smokers, networks and friends

'Like all the really crucial things in life, this chain of events was completely invisible to Ford Prefect and Arthur Dent . . .'

The Restaurant at the End of the Universe

In the full, panting tabloid sense of the term, the 1960s did not really start in 1960, nor did they waft to a close in 1970. History is not as neat as our decimal notation. The Vietnam War was still going, and in May 1970 US forces invaded neutral Cambodia in an attempt to deny the Vietcong access through that country. 'Interdict' was just one of the era's many bullshit words that attempted to lend a spurious sense of precision to a bloody and chaotic conflict. That same month, the National Guard shot dead four American student protesters in Ohio's Kent State University. Nixon and Kissinger, after a bombing campaign in North Vietnam the devastating scale of which is still not widely understood, agreed a ceasefire in 1972. It was signed in early 1973 and the Fall of Saigon, watched in palsied fascination on telly all over the world, followed in 1975.

The hippy movement – if anything as uncoordinated and woolly could be said to be a movement – was already in retreat. Roland Barthes, the French intellectual, was keen to inform us about the semiotics of clothes. In 1968 flared jeans, bandannas (God help us), and those appallingly whiffy Afghan coats, that somehow we wore without laughing, sent a whole range of signals about politics, social change, attitudes to soft drugs and so on. However, by 1970 it was possible to buy a designer hippy suit – all white – and wear it to Royal Ascot.* At some indefinable moment such gear had ceased to be a sandwich board bearing a message about societal change, and had become fancy dress.

When Douglas went up to Cambridge in 1971, Intel had only just made the first integrated circuit on a silicon chip, so there were no personal computers for Douglas to buy even if he could have afforded one. He had taken on a series of twit jobs which, as Neil Gaiman observes in *Don't Panic*, later served him well in potted biographies on dust jackets.† But there was something important he had to do before going up to Cambridge, something urgent that every restless young man, yearning to feel grown-up and a bit wicked, knew he had to achieve. It was a deed that leaves young blokes feeling as if they'd lived the blues, tunnelled out from a Kerouac novel, sung rambling-on songs through their noses, endured the romance of the bleak, and generally suffered a bit. It was a rite of passage, and one destined to be an essential part of the great canon of anecdotage that surrounded Douglas like an ornate herbaceous border.

No, not sex. It was less fun and much more unhygienic. Hitchhiking around Europe – even to its very edges in Istanbul.

Hitchhiking was far more common in the sixties and seventies than it is now. These days a hitchhiker is regarded as a potential psychopath fully equipped with a delusional system and a twelve-inch Sabatier in the outside pocket of his squillion-litre orange rucksack. Every motorist is an amateur rapist or nutter seizing the opportunity for random malice. These fears are largely nonsense, but we live in un-innocent times. The only hitchhikers routinely spotted on the roads of Britain are stern men in tweedy jackets who have just been delivering somebody's new Jaguar and have the red, trade number-plates under

---

* See the delicious photograph in *Fashions of a Decade – the 1970s* by Jacqueline Herald (Batsford, 1992).

† Chicken shed cleaner, hospital porter . . . Neil Gaiman's witty book, *Don't Panic* (Titan Books, 1987), is an excellent companion to Douglas's work.

their arms to prove it. But thirty years ago hitchhiking was an accepted means of getting about, especially for students and the less well-off. The fact that you could spend a day being poisoned and half-drowned on the *Einfahrt* of some rain-lashed Autobahn was part of the mythology and the appeal of hitchhiking.

Douglas later confessed that he had told the story of getting the idea for *Hitchhiker's* so often that he could no longer recall whether it happened the way he said it did, or whether he was just remembering his many retellings – in which case he would have to trust himself and accept that at some point his original Ur-account had a basis in fact. Most of you will have had a similar experience with a favourite yarn, and you have to be quite tough-minded to be sure that you know whether it really happened or whether repetition, and the desire that it jolly well *ought* to have happened, have induced conviction. We live in linear time (unlike a dog, happy creature, that seems to inhabit an eternal present). Memory on the other hand is not sequential; you can't count backwards to find the moment when you learned the name of the capital of Chad. Memories seem to be stored using a variety of mysterious principles, so that you have to circle around and around, through misty clouds of association, before you can relocate some missing piece. It is easy to persuade yourself of the truth of something for which the only evidence is a strong urge to believe.

Douglas had a repertoire of anecdotes that he used to great effect on the promo circuit and at conventions and conferences. He always told these stories in exactly the same way, right down to the comic hesitations as he appeared to rummage around his cortex for exactly the right word. Before you scoff, this is not something to elicit cynicism, but admiration. Douglas was a frustrated performer with a perfection-ist streak. The appearance of effortless wit is not effortless at all. He liked to entertain, and if he had polished a yarn to the point where it could not be improved he felt he owed it to his listeners to treat them to the best version. The danger of this approach is that a kind of unreality about the original experience creeps up on the teller.

The bare bones of the anecdote are these: hitching round Europe in the summer of 1971, between school and university, with guitar, full of yearning, sap and whatnot rising, looking for adventure, Douglas arrives in Innsbruck,* consumes a bit too much of that sneaky Austrian beer, and lies in a field looking at the stars.† In his bag is a copy of *The Hitchhiker's Guide to Europe* by Ken Welsh.∞ Hmm, thinks Douglas. Someone ought to write that book on a larger scale. *I know!* The whole galaxy. Wow.

He always claimed he never imagined that he would be the one to do it.

Happily, Douglas survived the rigours of the road, and the apocalyptic scenes you can witness in the gents of the cross-Channel ferries when the early autumn gales are blowing, and got back to England in good time for Ron and Janet to drive him to his room in college (D1 in Cripps Court) for the start of the Michaelmas term. He was to read English under the direction of Hugh Sykes Davies and Dr George Watson, the latter remaining a friend after Douglas graduated.

Janet recalls that the first person he met was Nick Burton, a scion of the house of Burton, the high-street tailors, who was to share some rather splendid rooms with Douglas in his third year. Nick was 6'4" tall. Douglas and he just grinned at each other, near as damn it eye-to-eye, with that heady mix of emotions that marks leaving home properly for the first time.

Cambridge was – and is – beguilingly beautiful, a paradise of exquisite buildings and civilized traditions, a veritable theme park of education. St John's College is the largest in the town. It was founded in 1511 by Lady Margaret Beaufort, the mother of Henry VII, a monarch known to generations of schoolchildren for being miserable, Welsh, greedy and having a Chancellor, Morton, who invented a fiscal rather than physical Fork. St John's reminds all visitors that it is a place of work, and not a museum, but you might be excused for thinking

---

* He stayed in the Youth Hostel in Reichenauer Strasse so he wasn't living the blues all that desperately.

† Some documentary film-makers have identified the actual field, but I can't help thinking, even with my tenacious grasp of the trivial, that the field is about as relevant as the number of the tram young Einstein thought in as he made his daily journey to the Patent Office.

∞ Ken Welsh, an Aussie, wrote a book full of good research and sound advice, but it hasn't been updated since 1993 for reasons that probably have to do with the decline in hitchhiking.

otherwise. The college is a delight. From its Tudor gatehouse you pass through what seem like endless courtyards handsomely faced in grey stone, all on an intimate human scale, with windows looking inwards on to lawns so perfect you can scarcely believe that they are vegetable and not extruded from a machine in Allied Carpets. Where the college reaches the river, it hops over with a romantically soppy replica of Venice's Bridge of Sighs, and then continues with more courtyards, accommodation and tutorial rooms on the other bank.

Of course, academic standards are rigorous; doubtless students manage to get fraught and desperate even in this blissful environment, but, compared to the average blocky, wind-blown university campus, St John's is fairyland.

At the time the university was not strenuously political. The economy was not as forgiving as in the previous decade, and the students of the seventies were by and large getting their heads down and working. They were no longer angry, only a bit miffed.

Douglas was not politically radical in any conventional sense, for he was far too intellectually subversive to trust any set of ideas organized enough to be called an ideology. Later in life he wrote with polemical zeal about conservation, but he seldom ventured explicitly into Politics (with a capital 'P'), though the reader can often sense him shaking his huge head at human folly, as if saying to himself 'dumb, dumb, dumb'.

Douglas's short story 'Young Zaphod Plays It Safe' is as strident as he ever got about matters as parochial as the hierarchical arrangements on our local planet. It is a little beauty, by the way: Zaphod and two creeps from the Safety and Civil Reassurance Administration are on a salvage mission to recover a fearsome cargo from a starship wrecked by its captain's foolish diversion to collect a lobster dinner. Unfortunately, one of the creatures in the ship's hold has escaped. It's a charming but simple hominid that is one of the most dangerous creatures that ever lived because there is nothing that it will not do if allowed, and nothing that it will not be allowed to do. It's called a Reagan.*

---

* This story was written in 1986 for the *Utterly, Utterly Merry Comic Relief Christmas Book* and republished in *The Wizards of Odd*, edited by Peter Haining (Souvenir Press, 1996).

Cambridge is famous for many things – including, but, as the lawyers say, not limited to, academic excellence, Ludwig Wittgenstein, astronomy, exquisite but irritating novels about spoilt gits, privilege, parties, pubs, pleasure, punting, spies, and Footlights. Of these, pubs, parties, pleasure and Footlights featured largely in Douglas's life.

Footlights, or more properly the Cambridge Footlights Dramatic Club, was born in 1883 and given its name by a Mr M.H. Cotton. At first the atmosphere in the club was bracing – quite foreign to that naughty aura of sophistication with which it was later associated.* It wasn't until 1924 that the format settled down into the revue style for which it became famous as a showcase for bright young talent. A large share of famous names in writing and acting first trod the boards in Footlights revues. Performers in those early years included Norman Hartnell, Cecil Beaton, the actors, Jack and Claude Hulbert, and Malcolm Lowry, author of *Under the Volcano*. Film was used for the first time in 1931; a recording was issued in 1932, and in that year there were women in the cast. The 1933 revue was called *No More Women*.

Many of the best people in British theatre are Footlights graduates. They were known as the Oxbridge Mafia, even though Cambridge had a far bigger influence than Oxford (which boasted Alan Bennett as a notable exception). The 1954 Footlights revue, with Jonathan Miller, Leslie Bricusse, Frederic Raphael and John Pardoe, transferred to London, as did many other productions from 1963 onwards. Michael Frayn and Joe Melia performed in the late 50s as did Bamber Gascoigne, Timothy Birdsall, Eleanor Bron, John Bird and Peter Cook. Even David Frost. By the sixties the escapees from the club formed a thunderous roll-call of names that were to dominate the revue scene for a generation. Trevor Nunn, Humphrey Barclay and Clive James all directed, and the actors included John Cleese, Graeme Garden, Miriam Margoyles, Bill Oddie, Graham Chapman, Eric Idle, Tim Brooke-Taylor, Russell Davies and many others who went on to be strategically placed

---

* Roger Wilmut, in his scholarly and enjoyable book *From Fringe to Flying Circus* (Eyre Methuen, 1980), quotes a source as describing the club at that time as 'decidedly hearty'. For earnest historians of Footlights, the potted history by the club's treasurer, Dr H.C. Porter, published in the programme for the 1974 revue, *Chox*, is invaluable.

in theatre, telly and other media. Footlights' first big success was in 1963 when its revue, much adapted for its new venue, transferred to London under the name *Cambridge Circus*. Theatre producers and TV scouts started to attend Footlights shows on a regular basis. The annual show turned, by degrees, into an audition for Shaftesbury Avenue and, almost invariably, the Edinburgh Festival. In response, the club exerted itself to put on shows of ever greater professionalism.

This tradition was well understood by undergraduates with histrionic leanings. By the time Douglas arrived in Cambridge, Footlights was not only the place to have astonishing fun with like-minded young thesps – it was a career move.

But Footlights was not a club open to everyone, and, besides, not everyone talented was attracted to it. Among Douglas's contemporaries, John Lloyd was studying law – or, as he concedes, not studying law – next door at Trinity. He and Douglas struck up a complex and competitive friendship, and John later became a collaborator on – *inter alia* – the radio series of *Hitchhiker's* (as well as evolving into the UK's most successful TV comedy producer). He recalls that his nickname for Douglas was Vast Creature. John Lloyd was a good-looking young man whose floppy blond hair made him rather resemble Anthony Andrews, the actor, playing Sebastian Flyte in the TV adaptation of *Brideshead Revisted*. His view of Footlights is less than awestruck:

> Footlights was going through a rather louche and decadent patch
> at the time when a lot of middle-aged or even elderly dons in
> velvet smoking jackets got young, handsome undergraduates to
> do song and dance routines with them . . . Footlights was a joke.
> None of us worth our salt would have gone near the place. People
> who ran the stall at the undergraduate fair – the Freshers' Fair –
> we thought were a bunch of wankers. I'd honestly never heard of
> Footlights before I got to Cambridge, so it was a year or so before
> I got round to thinking about it. And in the meantime I got a part
> in the Trinity revue which had been famous the year before for
> Charlie [Prince Charles] being in a sketch about a man in a
> dustbin . . . In my second year, with my friend Richard Burrage,

we ran the Trinity revue and this is when I got to know Douglas
as we both had college revue backgrounds.

Mind you, John Lloyd did eventually audition for Footlights at the
prompting of a girl he was in love with at the time, the actress, Mary
Allen. Naturally he was accepted and enjoyed a vintage year when Jon
Canter was president of the club. Jon was at Gonville and Caius not
really studying law, like John Lloyd. After graduation, Jon Canter,*
Mary Allen and John Lloyd were all important in Douglas's life.

Douglas auditioned for Footlights in his first term, but was rebuffed
and a little hurt. Footlights was quite tightly controlled at the time by
those who had risen up through the ranks; besides, Douglas's writing
talents had not yet been honed by performance. Long, haranguing
monologues did not work for the languidly witty Footlights committee.
Douglas told Neil Gaiman years later (see *Don't Panic*) that he found
them 'aloof and rather pleased with themselves', so he joined CULES
(the Cambridge University Light Entertainment Society) instead. This
organization literally had a captive audience when it took its shows
out to prisons, and in hospitals its audience was usually too decrepit
to do a runner; Douglas looked back on the experience with some
embarrassment.

Such was Douglas's appetite for performance that he joined the
ADC (Amateur Dramatic Club) where he played Sir Lucius O'Trigger
in Sue Limb's production of Sheridan's *The Rivals*. Opposite him was
Jonathan Brock, another friend destined to play an important part in
Douglas's life a few years later. Jonathan (Jonny to his pals) went on
to become a barrister, and then a QC.† His recollection of their stage
swordfight was that Douglas 'had the coordination of a mastodon. We
did five performances in which the result of the fight depended on

---

* Buffs might like to know that Jon Canter, a lifelong pal of Douglas, came up
  with Marvin's line - 'Life, don't talk to me about life' – in a revue in 1972.
  Douglas always gave Jon the credit for it.

† When I interviewed him for this book in his chambers, he talked about
  Douglas warmly, with appalling energy and perfect clarity of diction, for an
  hour without appearing to draw breath. Sometimes personalities and jobs
  seem well suited.

whether Douglas could get his weapon out of his scabbard.' Jonny in fact had been at school with Jane Belson, later to become Douglas's wife, but she went to Oxford so he met Douglas ten years before she did. At the memorial service he commented that it was 'ten years of chaos before she sorted him out'.

However, Douglas did eventually get into Footlights. It was a little hubristic of him to think that he would be welcomed in his first year; it was considered that to perform in Footlights one had at least to have acquired the jaded sophistication of the second year, and the attainment of earthly paradise (being on the committee) was more or less reserved for third-year students. As Footlights' personnel changed with time, Douglas was encouraged by one committee member who was 'friendly and helpful, all the things the others weren't, a completely nice guy named Simon Jones' (later to play Arthur Dent so brilliantly).* Douglas and his pal Keith Jeffrey were elected together – but not before a minor running skirmish and clash of egos within Footlights.

But even if Footlights in 1971 was full of aesthetes exchanging wickedly inexplicit understandings, there was another path to messing about theatrically that in many ways was much more fun. This was the college revue, or 'smoker', a relatively informal affair in which histrionic undergraduates performed frivolous sketches for the amusement of themselves and their peers. The term derives from an earlier era's 'smoking concert', one in which the chaps were allowed to smoke and from which women were excluded, probably on the daft grounds that many of the sketches featured relentless sexual *double entendres*. ('Your ejaculations fill me with surprise.')†

The smoker appealed enormously to Douglas. He got together with two friends, Martin Smith and Will Adams, to write sketches for a revue of their own. Martin and Will were at Fitzwilliam College studying Economics and English respectively. Martin is neat and clever, and Will is beardy and clever. Martin and Will had been writing together when they met Douglas, but they immediately clicked as a team. The three

---

* Quoted in *Don't Panic*, p. 10.

† Quoted by Ben Duncan in a review for *The Times Educational Supplement*, 17 March 1973.

of them created some brilliant material. Will and Martin continued to write together, but Douglas wrote on his own – a lifelong preference, though rather perverse for a man who needed company as much as he did. On the other hand, his painstaking drafting and redrafting could only work with one creative intelligence in charge. Martin describes their method of working like this:

> The thing was, Douglas and Will and I write very differently. Will and I always wrote together. We were the classic Galton and Simpson, Clement and La Frenais type of combination. We were always stultified into inaction unless we were together. Douglas always wanted to write on his own. What he would do is write three sentences of brilliant introduction, and then he'd be so thrilled with them he'd run up Castle Hill, to where Fitzwilliam was, and he'd sit down with us and say, 'Listen, listen, listen . . .', and he'd try not to laugh all the way through his reading. Will and I would then take it away and write a sketch beginning with those lines. It was like a game of consequences. Will and I would share the lines out, but I think our ability to self-edit wasn't there. So we would turn out stuff that was quite funny, but wasn't very different, so then Douglas would take it back again, and take what we'd done and make it funnier and better. And then we'd take it back off him and make it work, because if you left it to Douglas everybody would be delivering each sketch in Serbo-Croat while riding on roller skates . . .

It's interesting that even then Douglas had a compelling need for approval, and he found it almost impossible to wait before asking for it. Sue Freestone, the editor of many of his books, would later experience this to a degree unusual even among writers, a notoriously demanding lot when it comes to emotional neediness. Douglas was always innocent about finding his own jokes funny; they *were* funny and nobody had ever taught him that Brits should only allow themselves a self-deprecating little smile over their own achievements. Besides, he would hoot with merriment at other people's jokes. Making Douglas laugh, all his friends agree, was one of the great delights of the world.

With his naughty magpie instinct, Douglas later immortalized Martin when Zaphod Beeblebrox says 'this is *Zaphod Beeblebrox* – not bloody Martin Smith of Croydon'. (When Martin evolved into a senior manager in advertising he used to have clients ask him if by chance he came from Croydon.) Will went into publishing and became a book editor and quiz compiler. Martin and Will were – and are – engaging and funny men.

Their first revue was staged on 14 June 1972 in the School of Pythagoras, the theatre in St John's. It started at 11 p.m., a moment not only past cocoa and pyjamas time but also – significantly – pub closing time. The Lady Margaret Players and Adams, Smith, Adams presented *Several Poor Players Strutting and Fretting* (30p, tickets from the Porters' Lodge). Oddly the programme inside was called 'Fruttin' in Streatham', though perhaps it's just that after a few drinks 'strutting and fretting' (a reference to Shakespeare's unmentionable Scottish play, of course) started to transmogrify.

The cast was Martin Smith, Stefanie Singer, Rachel Hood, Will Adams, and Douglas, and the scripts were written by Adams, Smith, Adams with additional material by John Parry, Jon Canter, Jerry Brown and John Cleese of *Monty Python* fame. Douglas's roommate, Nick Burton, managed the house. 'Look around for him,' the programme notes advised, 'he'll be the one who isn't laughing.'

Whether strutting or fruttin', the revue was well received. Who did what in the writing is an enigma, but comic writing is often a team effort because it is so hard for one individual to know what is funny and how it will play. The three of them deserve equal credit. They had become good friends, but Will Adams says that their conversation was largely banter as they batted words and jokes back and forth, enjoying the occasional rally. 'We liked to amuse each other,' he recalls, 'by topping each other's jokes or running with the fantasies. We very rarely talked about anything personal, and I rather regret that now.'

The programme for Several Poor Players was replete with ads for Trinity's *A Big Hand on Your Opening* and *The Budgie* by Tony Chekhov and various bits of spoof biography, but the sketches themselves are listed with minimalist detail. Mary Allen recalls that there was a wonderfully funny one about a structuralist analysis of a railway timetable. (Railway timetables meant more in those pre-privatized days.) Structuralism was fashionable at the time, but not as big as irony. Irony was enormous. Everybody wanted it in quantities that a roomful of French intellectuals could not deconstruct.*

Douglas made friends easily in college, but at first he missed Helen. Although that relationship eventually faded away, in the meantime he visited her. She had also gone to university, to Warwick (which, despite the name, is not in Warwick but lies between Coventry and Kenilworth). Douglas, who loved anecdotes for their humour and cared not if they made him look daft, told the story of hitching there with that essential prop, his guitar, to see her. During his visit he met the long-haired bloke from along the corridor, also with guitar. They jammed together, with the other man trying to direct Douglas to lay down a good rhythm line around which he, the other bloke, could take flight. This was an affront to Douglas's guitar hero ego and it goaded him into venturing the odd and, as he believed, dazzling improvisation. 'No, no,' the hairy one said, 'if you don't mind, I'll do the fiddly bits.' And he did. What's more, he was dauntingly good. Only years later did Douglas find out that the other man was the young Mark Knopfler, later of Dire Straits.

It was during his first summer holiday from university that something happened that retrospectively seems spooky, but isn't. What happened was this: Douglas had a summer job in Dorset in a local warehouse. Shaftesbury and its environs boast some of the most beautiful countryside in Britain, but it is quite hilly. Douglas had to drive a tractor for this job. Until you get used to them, tractors are surprisingly difficult to master with their bewildering gear changes and high centre of gravity. These days, just to prove that the EU is not exclusively about the curvature of bananas and creative expenses, there are sensible regulations that enforce roll-over bars on such vehicles.

---

* The reader might enjoy a very helpful little poem on the subject of structuralism. It goes like this:

This is the creed o' Jacques Derrida
There ain't no author.
There ain't no reader, eeda.

That summer, at the bottom of a hill, Douglas had an accident. He was in an open tractor towing a trailer full of iron girders. He tried to change down as he started down the hill, but he just could not get the lower gear to engage. The tractor careered downwards in neutral, getting faster and faster. Seeing a log across the road, Douglas steered to avoid it, but the tractor turned over. Douglas, the tractor, the trailer and the girders tumbled down the hill, roughly in that order, with Douglas keeping just far enough ahead to avoid being killed. Instead he broke his pelvis and spent three weeks in Yeovil District Hospital while he mended, flat on his back staring at the ceiling, bored out of his mind, and, rather to his doctor's surprise, recuperated enough to start the next term at Cambridge on time. Here's the coincidence: exactly twenty years later, on the same spot, another man turned over a tractor – and died of his injuries. His name: Douglas Adams.

It must have been partly Douglas's accident that inspired Adams, Smith, Adams to run the following credits in the programme for their next revue, *The Patter of Tiny Minds*:

Mr Adams's (D) pelvis by Yeovil District Hospital
The shape of Mr Smith's feet by Start-Rite
Mr Adams's (W) disposition by Yeastvite

The Patter of Tiny Minds, staged from 15–17 November 1973 in the School of Pythagoras, was more ambitious than the trio's first effort. They even did some marketing with a small flyer put in bicycle baskets, and a largish poster featuring Will in some very odd shorts, Martin all in black looking like a hit man, and Douglas wearing his chicken suit complete with real cockscomb. Douglas was always game to get into this preposterous garment; endearingly he never minded making an arse of himself for a good cause, and he liked being in disguise.

The show boasted a director, Tony Root, sound and lighting engineers, John Fassnidge and Jim Besley, and a musician, Andy Thurston, whose violin added its own musical commentary. John Lloyd is credited with writing additional material, and there is script advice from 'Otto'. It turns out that Otto was a reference to John 'Otto' Cleese, who had given them one sketch, but whom they felt should be obscured – perhaps for fear of appearing precious. Even more importantly, the cast included a woman, Margaret Thomas, a talented thesp and singer whom they all apparently fancied something terrible. The spoof copy in the programme was not entirely a matter of invention:

> MARGARET THOMAS is getting fed up with the improper advances that are continually made to her by the other three [members of the cast], all of whom are deeply and tragically in love with her. They are often to be seen offering her tokens of affection – dried cockroaches tied up in ribbon, bits of paper smeared with gum and back copies of *The Farmer* and *Stockbreeder*. On a clear day it is just possible to discern which of the three she detests the most.

The Patter of Tiny Minds was deliciously funny and regarded as a big success. The timing was deliberately designed to be one in the eye for the chaps in velvet jackets over at Footlights. Competitively scheduled just a few days before the Footlights revue, it started late so that if you were bent on an evening's frivolity you could go to the pub and attend the Adams, Smith, Adams revue afterwards. Douglas, Will and Martin reckoned that people could not fail to make judicious comparisons between their revue and Footlights – and that their effort would be regarded as by far the funnier. And so it came to pass. Nearly all the reviewers enjoyed it, though there was one slightly superior review in the *Eagle* – not the great comic, but St John's subscription-only college magazine, a wonderfully eclectic mix of cricket news and analysis of foreign literature (read in the original, naturally). The reviewers, Keith Jeffery and Felix Hodcroft, praise the acting of Martin and Will (Martin's 'searing' Leonard Cohen parody sounds too good to be lost) and relish Margaret Thomas's singing, but are sharp about Douglas himself ('he has the biggest pose'). Their principal criticism of the whole piece is that it contains stereotypical workers with stock prole accents – undergraduates impersonating Pete and Dud imitating the working classes.*

---

* Peter Cook and Dudley Moore had a popular TV series on at the time, *Not Only . . . But Also*, which often featured the two of them in ominously blotched macs pretending to be members of the proletariat.

This review was a typically polished Cambridge put-down, even though co-written by a mate, Keith Jeffery, and not intended to be read entirely seriously. Nevertheless, it reflected a preoccupation with class that was not only of its era but has never really gone away. The great John Cleese wrote and performed one of TV's most enduring sketches around that time with his illustration of the class system in which the diminutive Ronnie Corbett played the token prole. Cleese's Upper Class Twit of the Year has also lodged like a burr in the collective memory of the nation. Left-leaning public schoolboys are often guiltily hung-up about their privileged backgrounds, which may explain why there are so many of them in the media who dissemble about their origins and dress like undercover policemen. All societies have a class system, but perhaps it is only in Britain that we are, as Orwell said, branded on the tongue so that a single vowel sound is enough for the educated ear to place a speaker's origins. This is preposterous, and thus endlessly funny. Adams, Smith, Adams were using staple ingredients by way of shorthand (the upper-class buffoon, the tea-making builders and so on). Admittedly these are comic stereotypes, but not portraits of individuals to be sneered at. Certainly Douglas cared not a whit about social credentials; creativity and brains were what he rated most highly. Adams, Smith, Adams's biggest crime here was not snobbery, but cliché.

Adams, Smith, Adams had another outing with *The Patter of Tiny Minds* in January 1974, this time in the Bush Theatre, above a large pub in West London's Shepherd's Bush (an area well away from the bright lights of the West End). They added another Smith and another Adams, so the line up read Adams, Smith, Adams, Smith, Adams. In fact, the extra Adams was Mary Allen, who joined Equity (the actors' union) as an Adams, and the additional Smith was John Lloyd. It was a hoot to do it in such an intimate and boozy venue. Martin remembers:

We were on as a late night show – we came down from Cambridge to do it. The main performance of the evening was Lindsey Kemp's pantomime to the work of Jean Genet. We were sharing a room with Lindsey Kemp, who of course is as camp as a row of tents, and it was quite a laugh. One evening we went to the cinema and watched – in the days when you'd see two main movies together – *The Wicker Man* and *Don't Look Now*. And in *The Wicker Man*, of course, Lindsey Kemp's playing the publican. And so it was extraordinary, watching the film and seeing the man I'd been avoiding all week.

Sharing the minuscule changing rooms must have been the stuff of sitcoms, with the youngsters exquisitely anxious not to give out any of the wrong signals. Douglas was thrilled that the review made a profit of £25 for each of them.

For the second time in the history of comedy (and possibly for good reason, the last), the show introduced the odd notion of shaving a cat. This entailed no harm to any moggy; it was a thought experiment rather like Schrödinger's unrealistically ambiguous cat of quantum mechanics fame. Both were used to suggest absurdity. In the surreal Adams, Smith, Adams, Smith, Adams version, shaving a cat weaves in and out of the programme – rather cat-like in fact. Does it mean anything? Does it stand for the impossibility of romantic yearning, hem hem? Is it just a daft idea that appealed to their undergraduate imaginations? Here are a few examples:*

THE ROMANTIC TRADITION
Mike and John sitting, facing audience
John reading newspaper, or Freud, or *Usage and Abusage*

[Lots of Pinteresque pinging words across the void in fraught but inconsequential fashion. Then:]

J: Look, Keats was a romantic, wasn't he?
M: May have been . . .
J: Well, he didn't shave cats.
MICRO PAUSE
M: Yes he did.

---

* I am grateful to Mary Allen for finding these sketches and to Will Adams and Martin Smith for letting me reproduce them here.

J: No he didn't.

M: Yes he did!

J: No he didn't!

M: Look, cleverdick, do you know the 'Ode on Melancholy'?

J: Yes . . .

M: The one that begins: 'No, no, go not to Lethe/Neither get your knickers in a twist.

J: That's not what Keats wrote.

M: Yes it is, and he went on to say: 'But when the melancholy fit shall fall,/Sudden from heaven like a weeping cloud/Go and shave the cat.'

J: You're making that up, Mike.

M: I am not!

And so on . . . Or there's this song:

SHEER ROMANCE
Well, babe, it often seems,
I've always known you in my dreams,
You came to me beneath the moon,
That starry night in early June.
Well, babe, I think I love you,
You make my heart go pitterpat,
Feeling so romantic,
Think I'll go and shave the cat.

The final scene in the three-part sketch has a man and a woman talking with hopeless desire about doing it (no doubt in the audience's mind that it equalled sex at this point) before dashing off stage in some excitement. Then there are sound effects of – you've guessed it – cat shaving. Describing this in prose is a vivid reminder about why you have to see sketches performed; yanked out of their natural medium they flop about like distressed goldfish.

Incidentally, about this time, in his second year at St John's, Douglas met Michael Bywater, who was in his first year at Corpus Christi. Michael, a dauntingly bright man, was studying English, having switched from Medicine, although he had originally planned to be there on an organ scholarship. His interest in the theatre was rather more conventional than the Footlights approach, but he sometimes contributed to their musical interludes. He recalls that what brought them together was that they both fancied (with that terrible urgency of nineteen-year-olds) a lovely woman called Isabel. Later she married Michael (and much later they divorced). He was destined to reappear in Douglas's life in the early 1980s.

But for now, Douglas was seldom so happy as when he was on stage performing. He often remarked that he really wanted to be John Cleese – he was tall enough – but was disappointed to discover that the job had already been taken. This did not stop him from being in some ways a rather Pythonesque character – mercurial, funny and given to occasional attacks of ill-coordinated panic. Then Douglas actually met John Cleese. Douglas had come down to London to see a show at the Roundhouse and found himself in the interval standing in the bar, by happy coincidence, right next to John Cleese. Please, please, he said, for since he was seventeen he had been a fervid admirer of *Monty Python, please* could I interview you for *Varsity* magazine? Perhaps John was taken by surprise – or it was difficult to say no to someone so earnest who could look you straight in the eye – but he was kind enough to assent. Indeed, it was an exceptionally long interview with the kind of searching questions and intelligent dialogue that have now become alien to media complicit in the celebrity game.

Douglas treasured his interview with John Cleese and kept a bound copy in the great crates of stuff that biographers are pleased to call 'archives'. He marked one passage in biro that is perhaps the bed-rock of a lot of surreal humour. In response to a question about the development of his particular style, John Cleese said this:

> Some people have said, like Marty Feldman, that it [a Cleese sketch] has got a very strong internal logic . . . That despite the fact that it's mad, the rules are laid down at the very beginning and the rules of the madness are followed very carefully. It is not a conscious thing. I think it comes from the fact that I was a scientist and a lawyer by training . . . The nearest simile I can find

to actually writing a sketch is that you dig around a bit in the top soil and all of a sudden you hit something, a vein of something, and you follow it, and sometimes you lose it, and you have to track your way back to where it last was.*

Years later, Douglas was one of only two writers – other than the Pythons themselves – who ever got a writing credit on *Monty Python's Flying Circus*. (Neil Innes was the other one.)

Monty Python occupied a special place in Douglas's affections, as it did for an entire generation of British students. It was a show that turned the map upside down, an anarchic convention-shatterer that was always stimulating even when the viewers winced rather than laughed. Blokes of a certain age can voice such classics as the dead parrot sketch with word perfect synchrony. For the students who were kids in the sixties, *Monty Python* had a place in our hearts rather like the one occupied by *The Goon Show* for those growing up in the fifties. You still come across men who only need put on an Eccles or Bluebottle voice to fall about pole-axed with mirth.[†] Decades later, Douglas provided the same service for his own fans. Douglas was in that great tradition of the *Goons* and *Monty Python* – he wrote something that became the special property of a generation.[∞]

Despite that tone of 'we're adults now, and damn hard to please' from Douglas's college mates, *The Patter of Tiny Minds* had been greeted with delight. The three principals, according to John Lloyd, were 'easily funnier than anything in Footlights'. They were in demand but like the three musketeers, so several informants have assured me, they had in

---

* John Cleese also adumbrated the Three Laws of Comedy: NO PUNS, NO PUNS, and NO PUNS.

† Spike Milligan's genius was hugely influential on a generation of funny young men. However, the pain of writing the Goons was not dissimilar to the agony experienced by Douglas when struggling to fill a page with apparently effortless drollery.

∞ The backlist sales of Douglas's books bear witness to the fact that the next generation loves his work too. At the age of nine our daughter could recite chunks from memory. 'Those kids will pay my pension,' Douglas once remarked.

a moment of passion formed a pact. According to this legend, they would all audition for Footlights, and it would have to take all of them or none of them. All for one, and one for all. This understanding was put to the test when Martin Smith was recruited by Crispin Thomas to perform in a Footlights May revue without the other two, though as a sop they were invited to be script consultants. For a while there were apparently some dislocated noses. Douglas could certainly sulk, though Will is recorded by all as being insanely good-natured. The only other trouble with this story is that neither Will nor Martin can remember their lives being blighted by any such incident. In any event, all ended well. By 1974, under the presidency of Jon Canter, Martin Smith was the secretary and Douglas and Will were both committee members, though they did not perform on stage.

As a performer Douglas was largely frustrated, but as part of Adams, Smith, Adams, he helped to write great chunks of *Chox*, the 1974 Footlights show. The intermission divided the show into the top layer and the bottom layer (chox = chocs). The production was a knock-out. The cast was particularly talented: Jon Canter, Sue Aldred, Jane Ellison, Griff Rhys Jones, Martin Smith, Crispin Thomas, an improbably hairy Clive Anderson and Geoff McGivern. (Geoff was later to become Ford Prefect in the radio version of *Hitchhiker's*, and – to great effect – also did the voices of Deep Thought and the Frogstar Robot and Traffic Controller.)

But amid all that brilliance, there was still no spot on stage for Douglas. He was disgruntled about it at the time. There is a suggestion that the committee struck a deal with him whereby as compensation he could write, with Will and Martin, many of the sketches, so that the team almost became in effect the principal scriptwriter. Years later he was still a little bitter. 'Footlights was becoming a producer's show,' he said, 'in which the producer calls the tune. I think it should be a writer-performer show.'

By the way, one sketch by the trio, 'Beyond the Infinite', prefigured some of the best-known lines of *Hitchhiker's* by four years. Consider this from Adams, Smith, Adams (1974):

Far out in the depths of the cosmos, beyond the furthest reach of man's perception, amidst the swirling mists of unknown

Galaxies, where lost worlds roll eternally against the gateway of infinity, inexorably on through millions of light years of celestial darkness we call Space – Space – where man dares to brave indescribably elemental horrors, Space [there follows a Star Trek split infinitive joke now too familiar to be reproduced] . . . I can't begin to tell you how far it is – I mean it is so far. You may think it's a long way down the street to the chemist, but that's just peanuts to Space . . .

Why this unwillingness on behalf of his fellow thesps to let Douglas act? It wasn't deliberate unkindness. Mary Allen, an actor with impeccable stagecraft,* thinks he tended to unbalance the general performance:

Douglas was never in a Footlights revue, and I think that was because he was such an idiosyncratic stage presence. In a group revue you have to have your own presence, but also be able to lose it. Sometimes you have to play second fiddle to other people so you have to be able to blend in with the group. You need a fluid stage presence that you can either crank up, to be someone wild and weird and eccentric – a character – or you can crank down, to get lost in a supporting role. Partly through physical size Douglas wasn't able to do that. He wasn't able to lose his identity . . .

He was huge, and he always looked as if he was about to burst into laughter. And you felt that was partly because what he was doing was extremely funny, but you also felt that it was a sort of cosmic laughter if you like – that the whole thing was absurd. It wasn't that purely ironic, parodic approach to absurdity. It was an affectionate, comic approach to absurdity.

Douglas was a talented actor, but Mary's comments chime with other sources. He was not good in ensemble pieces. His timing was not

---

* Ben Duncan in a review in *The Times Educational Supplement* said that she occupied that 'borderline between beauty and oddity where great women comics occur, she steps forth confidently, a complete original'.

perfect, he was as conspicuous as a double-decker bus, and he could not do deadpan if you stood poised over him with red-hot scrotal shears. He was just too easily amused – especially, as one slightly envious friend remarked, by his own jokes. A 6'5" giant grinning wildly in anticipation of a line yet to be delivered is distracting for the other actors on the stage, and it telegraphs what is to come to the detriment of that notoriously tricky art of comic timing. The axiom of thesps is this: don't act with animals or children – to which might have been added, nor Douglas Adams.

But, you must be wondering, was Cambridge all fun? Didn't the damn students ever do any work? Where did he live when he wasn't in the pub or on stage? Well, in his first year he had a room in college (the less glamorous 'new' bit of St John's). In his second year he was in digs in Sydney Street in a house for which Douglas could not muster an atom of sentiment. But in his third year he shared palatial rooms back in college with Nick Burton and a chap called Johnny Simpson, handily located near the student bar. This accommodation subsequently became the model for the rooms of Dr Chronotis of *Dr Who* and *Dirk Gently* fame. They were book-lined and comfortable, with a distinct ambience of erudition and naughtiness, a film set in which you could practise feeling very grown-up indeed – especially if you were asking someone back for a drink, or even tea, with or without an option on your body. Perhaps there is no such thing as true adulthood, only better and better impersonations of it. On second thoughts, that may only apply to men.

As for academic work, Douglas ended up with a BA degree, class 2.2. His tutor, Mr K.J. Pascoe, wrote to inform him that his compulsory dissertation earned him a high 2.1, his other essays were of 2.2 standard and that he had actually failed his tragedy paper. Douglas seems to have done just enough work to wing it, but nevertheless seemed to have got on well with his tutors if the amiable tone of their correspondence is a guide.

With his true passion always lying in non-fiction science, it is interesting to see what he made of the traditional liberal arts syllabus. In *Don't Panic* he told Neil Gaiman that he was proud of the work he'd done on Christopher Smart, the subject of his Part 1 Tripos English

Dissertation. Having unearthed this document, I suspect that Douglas's gift for parody didn't stop short of literary criticism. He could do scholarship, but he was jolly well going to make sure that that's how it sounded. Try reading the chunk below as if you were Alan Bennett doing his steeple-fingered academic ('Very few people who knew Kafka as I did, that is to say, scarcely at all . . .'), and you will see what I mean:

> It was only after W.H. Bond's discovery of its antiphonal structure [of Smart's *Jubilate Agno*] that it began to be recognized as something more important – a fragment of a failed literary experiment, gigantic, perhaps bizarre, eventually out of control, but nevertheless the product of a rational and coherent idea – the transplantation of the rhythms and structure of Hebrew poetry into an English religious poem.

Does this remind you of anything? Arthur Dent and Ford Prefect bullshitting to the Vogon captain about his execrable poetry perhaps? 'Oh, yes, I thought that some of the metaphysical imagery was really particularly effective . . .'*

Christopher Smart was an eighteenth-century poet who had also been educated at Cambridge. From the student's point of view he had two virtues: he only produced two poems of significance and he was sufficiently obscure for there to be no body of knowledge with which one's opinions could be easily challenged. He was the perfect choice for the clever student keener on the pub than the library. There is a legend that Douglas only wrote three essays in his entire time at St John's. Cambridge is good at accommodating eccentrics as long as they are talented, and St John's (which is rich from investments and makes no call on the public purse) clearly recognized something of value in Douglas. However, one essay a year would have tried the patience of even the most detached academic. It is difficult to track down the actual output, but the most likely explanation is that Douglas was delinquent about getting his work in on time but he was forgiven on the grounds that when it finally arrived, it sparkled.

---

* Fit the Second, *The Hitchhiker's Guide to the Galaxy*.

Despite simulating the voice of scholarship, Douglas was never-theless genuinely intrigued by Smart. Most of Smart's life had been spent drunk and debauched until, quite suddenly, in 1756 he suffered an extreme attack of religious ecstasy that left him under a compulsion to pray in the streets. This led to his eventual confinement in a loony bin in Bethnal Green. (How much did Douglas know about his father's experience on Iona?) On leaving the asylum Smart wrote a long poem, *A Song of David*, but he is better known for *Jubilate Agno* ('Rejoice in the Lamb'), an immense manuscript of which only a fragment survives, that was rediscovered in 1939. The poem consists of an interminable call and response pattern, like a parallel text in which many hundreds of lines beginning with the word 'Let . . .' are matched by an equal number that relate to them beginning with the word 'For . . .'* Only thirty-two pages of this remain, but for all its oddness and the rigour of its construction, it feels positively Homeric in length. Fortunately some of it, though celebrating the mystery of God, is about Smart's cat, Jeoffrey (*sic*), and it is quite droll to learn about this beast's fleas in such a feverishly spiritual context. Those keen to trace the provenance of the answer (forty-two) might be interested to know that line nineteen of *Jubilate Agno* reads: 'For there is a mystery in numbers.'

Douglas would have grinned at this over-egged connection. Nevertheless, Smart liked his cat ('For the English cats are the best in Europe') and his line forty-two – quite by chance the antiphon to another overexcited observation about the moggy – reads: 'For he is a mixture of gravity and waggery.'

This is an apposite comment on Douglas himself, for the time was upon him when a young man – albeit one fortified by a network of the brightest mates – is flushed down the plughole of the educational system into the world of possibilities.

In the summer of 1974, he left Cambridge and set out upon three rather bleak years.

---

* *Jubilate Agno* has also been set to music by Benjamin Britten. Religious music can be wonderful, even the exquisite sounds of monks in prickly underwear singing about death, but this piece by Britten is an acquired taste.

chapter four

The seedy flats

'Was this really the Earth? Was there the slightest possibility
that he had made some extraordinary mistake?'
So Long, and Thanks for All the Fish

'What good are brains to a man? They only unsettle him.'
The Adventures of Sally, P.G. Wodehouse

After Cambridge, so far from reaching the 'commanding heights' of
the economy, Douglas embarked upon an era of seedy flats. The first
was in a classic location for transitory accommodation. Every city
must have such a place where no names are ever put on doorbells
because the turnover would make the task tiresome. In London it
is Earl's Court, an area of cliff-like red-brick Edwardian terraces
known then as Kangaroo Valley because of the favour it found with
itinerant Aussies. (The Aussies have moved on to colonize the whole
city, but the extraordinary density of flats remains.) Douglas and
Martin Smith shared a large room in a flat in Redcliffe Gardens that
was owned by two upmarket and grimly constipated Sloaney
women who needed help with the rent but who hated Martin and
Douglas being there (and possibly also Martin and Douglas as
people).

The second was a sprawling but affordable house in Fordwych
Road, Kilburn, or, as it is known to estate agents, West Hampstead. In
addition to Martin and Douglas, it contained a randy collection of

bright recent graduates, including Nigel Hess, a Man Called Phil,* a floating population of bed-partners, and Mary Allen, who was appearing in *The Rocky Horror Show* in the West End.

Douglas had come to London determined to make it as a sketch-writer, but soon found that the world was not poised waiting for him. A series of twit office jobs helped him cope with the tyranny of paying the rent. According to Neil Gaiman's *Don't Panic*, one of these was as a filing clerk. It is hard to imagine anyone less suited than Douglas to the chore of filing. He would have been tempted to redesign the whole system from scratch, side-tracked by the philosophical complexities of information storage and the arbitrary ways in which we organize the world into discrete categories. Putting bits of paper into files *physically* was foreign to his nature. It must have been a torment. He could have filed everything under 'S' for stuff or 'P' for paper; alternatively he might have plunged into minute subdivisions of semantic nuance accessible only to himself.

When not running the gauntlet of those temporary jobs we all tend to do after leaving university but before settling in our packets like detergent, Douglas persisted in writing sketches. One target was *Week Ending*, a weekly radio programme on BBC Radio Four. It was probably the most subversive thing to be found on the airwaves, not excluding TV. The Light Entertainment department, as it was then, had an admirable record of producing wonderfully funny and anarchic programmes. The tradition continues to this day, possibly in part because the excellent David Hatch, then a performer and producer, is now Managing Director of BBC Network Radio.

Back in the seventies there was a lot to be subversive about. The Yom Kippur War between Israel, Egypt and Syria was the latest of a series of bitter conflicts that continue even now. This particular one erupted in October 1973 with a surprise attack on Israel across the Golan Heights and Sinai. Much futile blood-letting ensued, and was followed swiftly by an energy crisis as the OPEC countries imposed an oil embargo. As the prices of just about everything shot up, they

---

* Not an escapee from a Western, but Phil Buscombe, a musician who had been the drummer in Footlights and was then working in *Jesus Christ, Superstar*.

passed the economies of the West going the other way. Harold Wilson's Labour Government was elected in March 1974, and wily old 'Wislon', as he was known to readers of *Private Eye*, ducked and dived, trimmed and fudged, to hold his party and the government together while the graph of the British economy plunged like Shirley Bassey's cleavage. On the popular culture front, Jimmy Page of Led Zeppelin appeared at Earl's Court in satin flairs large enough to house a family of refugees, fashion victims wore cork-soled shoes four inches high, digital watches had just appeared,* and a certain gloom prevailed. Recent university graduates no longer enjoyed the heady sense that they could mess about and still land on their feet.

With a pace almost too fast for the establishment powers at the BBC to clock the full extent of its satirical rudeness, *Week Ending* excoriated the topical follies in the news with all the inhibition of a hand grenade. It was extremely funny, and boasted terrific writers like David Renwick, Andrew Marshall and John Mason. Andrew Marshall recalls the pride this wildly talented bunch had in their ideas, and how they had to wind down at the end of a frantic day by comparing notes in the local pub near Broadcasting House, The Captain's Cabin. The programme's pace made great demands on the cast. This included David Jason, Nigel Rees and Bill Wallace – all of whom went on to become well-known in other spheres – so *Week Ending* was also fertile ground for new acting talent. Its breathless speed was a fearsome consumer of material, a fact reflected in the writing credits. Even enunciated quickly by a professional with precise diction, they went on and on: everyone who contributed a snappy one-liner was entitled to a credit. But Douglas's name rarely featured among them. The only piece accepted was the Adams, Smith, Adams Marilyn Monroe sketch that the three of them wrote in their last year at Cambridge and phoned down to John Lloyd – by then working as a producer on *Week Ending* – from a St John's phone box.

---

* They were expensive until Clive Sinclair's company made a cool black one. Despite Douglas being satirical about us ape-descendants who still thought digital watches were a pretty neat idea, he did later get to know Sir Clive Sinclair who (let's forget the risible C5 'car') made some sophisticated electronics available for the first time at affordable prices.

The radio producer, Simon Brett,* whose faith in Douglas was to be so strategic a couple of years later, said that Douglas and *Week Ending* was one of the worst marriages between writer and subject because the latter was specifically based on news, and Douglas's mind just didn't work like that.[†] I can see why. In photography, in order to compose the image and get everyone with their feet and heads in the frame, you often have to take a step or two backwards. Douglas's view was huge and odd; organizing a picture, he would have started a lot further back than that. It would be tricky for him to take topical politics seriously enough to find them ridiculous – for his perceptions had already expanded to the point where he found man's place in the universe absurd. It would have been like finding your way across Birmingham using a globe. Besides, as a writer, Douglas was a slow, compulsive polisher. Keeping up with the output of *Week Ending* would have frazzled him to a crisp.

Geoffrey Perkins, who as a talented young producer was destined to produce *The Hitchhiker's Guide to the Galaxy*, says that at the time Douglas was 'a particularly strangely shaped peg trying to fit into a variety of round holes':

> He was one of many honourable examples of people who were actually very good writers who couldn't get their stuff onto *Week Ending*. Some very good writers like Andy Hamilton and Alistair Beaton came through it, but there are others, like Douglas, who did not have a great deal of topical or satirical interest and whose natural style was far from a pointed piece that played for a minute and a half. He didn't have that sort of mind. He'd write five-minute sketches which meandered off on some amusing tack.

However, Douglas did get a break. *Chox*, the Footlights revue, had transferred, heavily revised, to London's West End. Dennis Main

---

* Not only was Simon an important telly and radio producer, but he has also written many enjoyable crime novels featuring Charles Paris, a so-so actor but a brilliant detective.

† Quoted by James Naughtie interviewing Douglas on BBC Radio Four's *Book Club*, 2 January 2000.

Wilson, a senior producer from the BBC, was sent to look at it, and as a result the show was televised. Douglas was paid £100 for TV rights to his contributions, a sum not to be sneered at in 1974; it might be a fifteenth of a young graduate's annual wage. The TV version was not a great success. But the BBC's David Hatch and Simon Brett had also seen the live show, and quickly commissioned a radio version of it which fared much better. 'It was a good deal crisper,' John Lloyd recalls, 'and very well received – and this despite being called *Every Packet Carries a Government Health Warning*. It had nothing to do with *Chox* except for the fact that Jon Canter and Griff [Rhys Jones], who were still up at university, were both in it.'

A number of the Footlights aristocracy from a previous age went to see *Chox* in its West End incarnation, among them Graham Chapman from the *Monty Python* team. Graham was enormously taken with Douglas's work, and invited him over to his place in Highgate, North London, for a drink. One sketch, by Adams, Smith, Adams, about the Annual Meeting of the Crawley Paranoid Society, was one which Graham always said he would have liked to have written himself. Douglas and Graham both enjoyed a sense of the surreal, and despite Chapman being outrageously camp,* and Douglas being joyously heterosexual, they got on well and decided to enter an informal writing partnership.

In 1974, *Monty Python* was at a crossroads. It had entranced the public for half a decade, but the last and fourth series of only six half-hours, broadcast from 31 October 1974, was a bit patchy. The links between the sketches – in the past so often witty or deliberately undermining of telly conventions – were getting perfunctory, and the sketches themselves sometimes trailed away without any attempt at a conclusion. Not even another violently funny giant foot or weird visual pun from Terry Gilliam could quite come to the rescue. The Pythons had changed TV forever, but the format, once so liberating, was becoming restrictive. The individual team members were looking to

---

* John Lloyd recalls going to Graham's house and being asked if he fancied a snog. He declined. John recalls that Graham, when very drunk, once emphasized some conversational point by brandishing his willy on the bar.

branch out on their own, and as a team they yearned to make more movies (and did).

Graham Chapman had trained to be a doctor* before being led astray at Cambridge by Footlights. At 6'3", he wasn't as tall as John Cleese or Douglas Adams, but he towered over the other Pythons, with a persona that came across as a decent Englishman at bay – really *awfully* reasonable, but indignant and bewildered that the world could be so strange and cruel. He and John Cleese shared a strong sense of the ridiculous. Graham was the eponymous antihero in *The Life of Brian* (1978), a thoughtful film in a polemical kind of way that is also achingly funny. He died far too young (at about the age when Douglas himself was to die) of cancer of the spine, but at the time he was an established aristocrat of comedy. *Monty Python's Flying Circus* had recaptured a generation of viewers for the BBC; it had achieved international fame, won several awards (including the Silver Rose of Montreux for a compilation programme), and transformed the Beeb's image of slightly censorious aunty to something more like an inventive harlot, the sort that beckons from doorways and asks if you'd like to try something unusual. It would not be a grossly daft exaggeration to say that at the time Graham could have done whatever he wanted.

Another Python, Terry Jones, had seen Douglas in revue and he too particularly remembers the Crawley sketch that had so struck Graham. At first he had been impressed more by Douglas's size than his comedy, but he soon recognized an authentic talent. He recalls that Douglas, as Graham's collaborator, attended some Python script meetings:

> He started working with Graham, because Graham had stopped writing with John at that stage. And so Douglas started coming to script meetings for the fourth series . . . Douglas was full of ideas – I remember he had lots of ideas – and was keen to get writing. We just got on very well. We had the same sort of

* Graham was always rather guilty about giving up medicine. He and his partner had informally adopted – in the sense that they looked after his interests – a young Greek Cypriot boy. Graham had a laboratory in the basement of his house where he tried to educate the boy about medicine. I believe the lad grew up to be a theatrical impresario.

mindset; we enjoyed chatting and having drinks. We were both interested in real ale, so became ale chums, if you like. And, of course, he appeared in that fourth series as well, in a couple of cameos.*

So the portents looked good for Douglas, finding himself conjoined with a star at only twenty-two. Unfortunately, the collaboration with Graham Chapman produced little, and even less was actually screened.

Graham was not an easy person to work with. Terry Jones says that his contributions were intangible; he was a man who could come in with very odd ideas which were great fun, but for a lot of the time he was an 'off the wall reactor'. Of course, feedback – even of the vehement 'Good grief, that sucks' variety – is invaluable for any writer, especially one trying to be funny. It is a good service to refine somebody else's ideas by pushing them to the breaking point. Douglas said that Graham would sit there, puffing on his pipe and looking tweedy, but thinking very, very naughty thoughts – occasionally interjecting one that would turn everything around.[†] But Graham was also boozing very heavily, and that made life much more difficult for all those around him.

Terry, who is one of nature's generous spirits, is not sure that Graham hadn't stopped drinking by then. 'Certainly he sort of tried to stop drinking when we were doing *Holy Grail*, and was firmly on the wagon well before we made *The Life Of Brian*.' Everybody else, however, says that during this period Graham was struggling with potentially severe alcoholism. Andrew Marshall recalls Graham as a man of great sensitivity, and this may in part be why he drank. Sometimes alcohol serves a function like the control rods in a nuclear reactor; they damp everything down and keep the system from going

---

* Once he was a surgeon and once one of those squeaky-voiced androgynous women that the Pythons called Pepperpot Ladies. Later Douglas's American publishers – desperate for a credential that would mean something to the student market – described him as one of the Python team to the embarrassment of all.

† See *Monty Python Speaks* by David Morgan (Fourth Estate,1999) – a must for the serious Python buff.

critical. Graham had a particular taste for gin; his large house in Highgate featured a cavernous cellar lined on one side with an enormous wine rack – except that instead of wine it held bottles of gin with strategic reserves of tonic. It was a wall of gin.

The collaboration between Douglas and Graham entailed a great deal of going to the pub, amusing each other and drinking a lot. Some of their colleagues at the BBC were a bit miffed about this, and it was not a life that Douglas could afford to sustain for long, if only financially. Besides, Douglas was not a heavy boozer.

Martin Smith remembers that Graham was very generous. Sundays (rather like Thursdays which Douglas never got the hang of) were dull in London in the 1970s. The dank shadow of the Lord's Day Observance Society still lay across the land. 'Six days shalt thou labour, and on the seventh thou shalt have no fun at all' was the effect it wrought. Nothing much was open apart from the pubs, and the licensing laws gave you a narrow window, as they say now, for drinking and at ten minutes before closing time you were chivvied to stop by a publican with a voice like a KGB interrogator. Graham, knowing that Douglas and Martin were broke, would often phone them on Sunday and ask if they fancied dinner. They always did, and would either go up to Highgate to Graham's house or out to a restaurant where they would eat and drink too much. Graham liked Helepi, a jolly Greek restaurant in Bayswater, a lot.

Graham Chapman wasn't their only *Python* contact. Martin recalls how Eric Idle also tried to help them onto the screen:

Sometime in 1975, when Douglas and I were living in Fordwych Road, Eric Idle suggested that he would be able to get us into *Rutland Weekend TV* (which was about to go into production) as extras . . . Sadly, this was the time when Equity [the actors' union] was run by Corin Redgrave and there were strict rules of entry into the profession. You almost had more chance of getting an equity card by contributing to the freedom fighters of Mozambique than you did by flashing a BBC contract. But for a leftist thespian regime, Douglas might have made it as a performer, after all!

One of Douglas and Graham's collaborations was an SF comedy intended to be an American TV special and a vehicle for Ringo Starr, though it never crept as far as the pilot stage. It is a pity as Ringo the space-going chauffeur sounds a nifty idea. A programme that did appear – if that is not too positive a word for an unannounced late-night screening on BBC2 – was a miscellany called *Out of the Trees*. One very funny sketch, which Douglas wrote with Graham and Bernard Mackenna, started off with a romantic man picking a peony for his girlfriend and advanced, in inexorably escalating steps, to thermonuclear war. Another, that became quite famous, focused on the domestic life of Genghis Khan. Genghis has been so successful that bit by bit he has been transformed into a harassed business executive juggling his diary to see if there is a window for his financial advisor. All that pillaging, sweeping across the steppes with golden hordes and whatnot, was just too fatiguing. One has one's people for that kind of thing. It appeared again in a slightly different form in a Comic Relief anthology, and years later the idea was recycled and expanded in a short story in *The Salmon of Doubt*. Neil Gaiman quotes Douglas as saying that it was inspired by Graham's mutterings about the other members of the Python team.[*]

A sketch that did get made (the producer was Bernard Thompson) showed that exhilarating zoom-lens lurch from the cosmic to the local that was one of Douglas's favourite tropes. It started like this:

STOCK FILM OF GALAXIES ETC. FOLLOWED BY PLANETS
FOLLOWED BY THE EARTH

Voice Over
The universe, a multitude of mighty galaxies, within each galaxy
a myriad mighty star systems, within each star system a
multiplicity of mighty planets – and in just one of these mighty
planets the mighty British Rail electric train . . .

Of course, the Pythons' smashing (and perversely cheering) Galaxy song does show that they too had a sense of the ridiculously oppressive

---

[*] *Don't Panic* by Neil Gaiman (Titan Books, revised edition 2002).

scale of the universe, so that vertiginous drop from the cosmic to the particular was just as Pythonesque as Adamsy.

After graduation, two Adams, Smith, Adams revues were produced. *So You Think You Feel Haddocky* was staged with Gail Renard, the Canadian comedy writer and performer, in the Little Theatre (now, alas, Stringfellows) in St Martin's Lane in London's West End in the autumn of 1975. *Cerberus* was put on a year earlier at the ADC in Cambridge. The title could have been a self-deprecating reference to the show being a dog looking in all directions at once, but in fact it was because Douglas, Will and Martin were photographed in a clump with their three heads, like some ghastly recombinant DNA experiment, projecting from an improbable tangle of body. The profits were almost imperceptible, and Douglas still had to pay his share of the rent.

Another Adams, Smith, Adams sketch bought by the *Monty Python* team was the infamous one about Dead Marilyn Monroe that had enjoyed a brief outing for *Week Ending*. The Marilyn cult was going strong at the time (and hasn't abated) and the writers thought it was time that the relentless recycling was given a bad taste Swiftian spin. The basic idea was to get her in everything. A director wanted her in his next movie even if it meant digging her up. Cremation was a problem here, of course. Martin recalls that they each got £25 for the rights. It was satisfying to be appreciated, but hardly lucrative.

Douglas also worked with Graham Chapman on an episode of the established TV comedy series based on the *Doctor* books by Richard and Mary Gordon. The novels used to sell in considerable volume and there was quite a reservoir of affection for them. There were fifteen – *Doctor in the House, Doctor in Clover, Doctor in the Nude* . . . – on which a series of engaging British comedy films had been based with Dirk Bogarde starring as an ingénu medico. These were fun, though by modern standards quite old-fashioned, and charmingly innocent: having a flutter on the horses and sliding off to play golf were considered deeply wicked.

Graham and Douglas mapped out the *Doctor* narrative in some detail, devising the cliffhangers, playing with the deadly hospital rivalries, inventing the cringe-making surprises and working out how many sets would be needed. For causal antecedent buffs (wherefore the derogatory use of the word 'anorak'? – it is a perfectly useful garment), the elaborate clockwork of the plot features a bookie's runner who has to pretend to be a medical student in front of a particularly frightening Senior Consultant – a James Robertson Justice figure greatly resembling Douglas's father. Unluckily the bookmaker's runner is asked a medical question. The script states that the answer is a number which the real student has to communicate from behind the Consultant's back using tic-tac (the hand signals that bookmakers use to convey odds across a race track). History does not record if the number was forty-two.

When John Lloyd had come down from Cambridge, he had been promptly snapped up by the BBC which scouted the universities, especially Oxbridge, for graduate trainees. Nobody is as engaging as John Lloyd when he's trying to exercise charm. John Hardress-Lloyd hails from a rather grand Anglo-Irish family, though he says that his branch was the poor one. He went to Kings School, Canterbury, dropping the hyphenated bit from his name – as was fashionable at the time.

John's career took off like an ICBM. (After his glittering start in radio, he went on to become the most significant TV comedy producer of his generation with *Spitting Image*, *Not the Nine O'Clock News* and *Blackadder* to his credit.) Soon he was producing *Week Ending*, and was involved with a host of other radio programmes, becoming frantically busy. A friend of John says that at the time, whenever two or more of his contemporaries were gathered together, they tended to practise a nice line in Lloydie parodies. They went along these lines: 'I'm so, so jealous that you have time to offer me a beer. If only I could. Such an enviable quality of life – a moment to oneself to think. Oh God. I have *at least* a hundred programmes to produce, and three attractive women to juggle. Shit. Is that the time?' Somehow John was also able to direct the 1975 Footlights revue *Paradise Mislaid*.

John and Douglas had been fairly close pals in Cambridge, but once established back in the big city, they became what John calls 'utterly best friends'. Indeed, Douglas had a number of extraordinarily close friendships in which he often invested more than they could bear. Jane Belson reckons this was a recurring pattern in his life: intense friendships that sometimes died away or ended in hurtful schism. His friendship with John was like one of those deep best friend relationships that one has at school, founded not just on personal sympathy but as an alliance against the world, and thus in a sense it depended on the world treating them both equally. It was also made more complex by a needling bone-deep competitiveness, the suppressed premise of their friendship, and the mirror image of their great personal warmth. The tension of things left unsaid was to erupt eighteen months later over the writing of the first *Hitchhiker's* novel.

Douglas and John used to hang out together, particularly in Tootsie's, a hamburger joint in Notting Hill Gate, witness to numerous long conversations about just about everything. Eventually too, Douglas moved from Kilburn, and shared with John a rather pokey flat owned by Bernard Mackenna, the actor and writer (whose name he almost appropriated in *So Long, And Thanks for All the Fish*), not far away in Greencroft Gardens – a location which in Real Estate Speak also purports, just about, to be in West Hampstead. This was the first of their various shared lodgings; Douglas would often squat in John's tiny office at the BBC, and John would sometimes go up to Highgate to drink with Douglas and Graham Chapman in the pub. These marathon drinking sessions tended to begin the same way, with the three of them doing the crossword in every national paper within half an hour. This could have been just fun, a kind of intellectual limbering up, or a more self-conscious advertisement of cleverness.

Sharing a flat with the awesomely successful John Lloyd must have induced moments of tristesse, especially when Douglas was trying to write and the fickle muse refused even to flirt. Consider this useful definition from *The Deeper Meaning of Liff*:

Boinka (n)
The noise through the wall which tells you that the people next door enjoy a better sex life than you do.

Mary Allen describes an episode, in Corfu, of what she calls an all-time terrible holiday. Douglas and John planned to go out there and write, all on their own with no friends, visitors or other accretions.

Nothing would distract them from the Zen purity of the beach and the discipline of the typewriter. But somehow, this was not to be. The rented villa filled up with mates. Douglas, far gone in love, made elaborate plans for a female friend to come and join them – and, without consulting her, to sleep with him. The trouble was, he set about it with the subtlety of a brick. There was much anticipatory juggling of the bedrooms.

In time, blokes attain sufficient sophistication (please God) to know that women hate being taken for granted, but at twenty-three you are blinded by hormones. You are quite sure that if you don't have sex soon, you will die. What's more, many women – though they want chaps to care and try hard – find it unappealing if men come across as desperate. Their anxiety puts too much freight on a relationship too soon. The woman in question, who by all accounts was sensitive and quite lovely, ended up getting off not with Douglas, but with John Lloyd. Later she and Douglas did get together, but it ended unhappily. Thereafter Douglas was never entirely on an even keel on the subject of John Lloyd and women.

In 1976, the collaboration with Graham Chapman was drawing to a close after eighteen months. He and Douglas had enjoyed themselves, and drunk prodigious quantities of alcohol, but their partnership had produced little of a concrete nature. Their relationship became strained when Douglas was drafted in to help with Graham's autobiography, called, with disarming frankness, A Liar's Autobiography (1980). There is no evidence that Douglas's rôle was as big or as formal as that of a ghostwriter – indeed there were several co-writers on this book, so Douglas's involvement seems to have been small. However, as any publisher can confirm, the relationship between biographical subject and ghostwriter is often horribly vexed. If there is one thing over which people are entitled to feel proprietorial, it's their own life, and they hate describing it in somebody else's words. The ghost wants the book to be a good book, but the subject wants to present a good life, however that may be construed. The two ambitions are not always compatible.

Absurdly, both Graham and Douglas are now dead, so we may never know why their cooperation was not more fruitful. Dorothy Parker said that the world is stacked against comic writers because the rest of us – not excluding those who would rather be dipped in sump oil than risk literary judgement – exercise the right to say 'that's not funny'. By the time a writer has looked at a joke sixteen times, rotated it through ninety degrees, changed the context twice and tweaked the punchline, it is genuinely difficult to tell if it *is* funny. There are many reasons why so much comedy is written by teams (company, personal chemistry, complementary skills, live dialogue practice . . .), but certainly one of them is having somebody around to confirm that the gag actually works. However much Douglas and Graham must have felt they needed each other, with the clarity of retrospect two such distinct talents were never likely to be compatible.

Later that year, Douglas was invited back to Cambridge to direct the annual Footlights revue, *A Kick in the Stalls*. But Footlights had changed, starting with the sale of the clubroom for redevelopment as a shopping centre. Instead of a queue of the brainiest young extroverts, poised on one foot, breath held, yearning to strut their stuff upon the stage, there was a feeling abroad that perhaps the club was a bit up itself, to use that useful idiom, and not entirely the thing to do in the grim mid-seventies. Douglas had to beat the bushes looking for talent. The show itself had a generally mixed reception* until it was overhauled by Griff Rhys Jones, who took it to the Edinburgh Festival and made it work. John Lloyd remembers it as overly complicated and thinks it was a mistake to get Douglas to direct. 'He didn't have a single director or producer gene in his whole gigantic genome. Griff, on the other hand, is a born director.'

John and Douglas also worked on another idea, *Sno 7 and the White Dwarves*. (A white dwarf is an astronomical term for a smallish star with a high surface temperature but low intrinsic brightness.) A superior intelligence was planning to use supernovae for advertising purposes, and mankind was doomed because our sun was destined to be the full stop under the exclamation mark of the slogan. John Lloyd was told by the BBC that SF was 'very fifties' (this was the year before *Star Wars*) and that there was no market for it. It sounds as if it would have been a blast.

---

* 'Mixed' is showbiz code for snotty.

Later that year Douglas had another rebuff when he and John prepared a film treatment based on *The Guinness Book of Records*. Mark Forstater had acquired the rights, and John and Douglas invented a race of maniacally competitive aliens ('not unlike the Vogons', John points out) who threaten to destroy the Earth unless humanity could beat them in a kind of inter-galactic Olympics. The aliens were unassailable at anything that needed a talent for violence, but were not so hot at walking backwards and eating pickled eggs. John and Douglas were promised a trip to the West Indies to meet the mighty Robert Stigwood, he of the eponymous organization, to discuss this further, but at the last moment it all fell through.

Douglas and John then moved again, this time to Roehampton, an affluent but somewhat inaccessible West London suburb famous for its estate of Le Corbusier-style blocks of flats that win prizes but are horrible to live in. John, his then girlfriend, Helen Rhys Jones, and Douglas moved into a house full of doilies and china knick-knacks (they were the landlord's and they had a high mortality rate). After a while they were joined by a neurotic American who was prone to attack the garden vegetation on the grounds that it was untidy.

Like the bear, Horace, in the kiddies' story, every day Lloydie would go out hunting – or rather to the BBC – and Douglas would moon about in his room, which was full of wardrobes,* and sleep. Andrew Marshall recalls David Renwick telling him that Douglas actually slept a hell of a lot, and, though we should be wary of glib judgements, this can signify a kind of chemical depression. He also took many baths, partly for pleasure and comfort. The baths helped him to think, and it was something to do. John reports that occasionally he would come home after a day forging and cleaving at the BBC and find Douglas exactly as he had left him that morning – in bed or taking another bath. He must have entered the bath like a plum, and emerged as a prune – a very clean prune.

Douglas can't have been a tremendously jolly flatmate for John Lloyd. Writing is a solitary craft, and writers are self-absorbed even at

---

* There were seven wardrobes, according to legend. It must have felt like the set of one of Beckett's absurdist dramas.

the best of times (just one of the many personality disorders to which they are prone, alas). Authors who know they have talent, but who are failing, are entitled to feel dark. Once John – out of exasperation and not cruelty – suggested to Douglas one evening that he really ought to go out. John was having friends round, and Douglas was so miserable that he would have cast an effluvium of gloom over the proceedings.

Poor old Douglas must have been in a state. His self-esteem was always as fragile as a soap bubble. To pay his way he took a series of silly jobs, subsequently immortalized by anecdote. His favourite from this period was when he was single-handedly holding back the drilled hordes of terrorists, creditors, disgruntled bookmakers and general ne'er-do-wells from an inconceivably wealthy Arab family (not that a single miscreant turned up). After answering an ad in the *London Evening Standard*, he had been taken on as a bodyguard to a sheikh. He must have been employed on the grounds of size alone; many professional guards are wiry, quick and neat. Douglas would have been appalled by violence and would not have been much cop at dishing it out, but, in terms of pay per unit volume of guard, the clients got their money's worth. Douglas had to sit for twelve hours at a time in the corridor of the Dorchester Hotel, just in case. According to myth, his employer had an income of £20,000,000 per day, a figure that seems improbable even by the standards of oil-rich sheikhs. Even divided by ten, however, this would still not have been a family on the edge of the abyss. Douglas used to tell the story of them going to the dining room and ordering from the stunned waiter everything on the menu – the whole lot *à la carte* – so as to ascertain if there was anything that piqued their jaded fancy. It was a thousand pounds' worth. Nothing really did it for them, and they later sent out for hamburgers.

Another pleasure available on a personal delivery basis also appeared while Douglas was keeping his vigil in the hotel corridor. One evening there stepped out from the lift a truly spiffing prostitute – a top-of-the-range model of such sexiness that strong men had to bite their knuckles to stop themselves whimpering. Douglas looked up from his book, and between the two of them a complicit look was exchanged, one that acknowledged the fundamental similarity of their position. 'It seemed to say we're both tarts,' said Douglas, 'and she wasn't wrong.' When she left an hour later, she looked down at Douglas sitting at his post and said in a pleasantly modulated voice: 'At least you can read while you're on the job . . .'

Despite his low morale, he did get it together to go with some friends to that year's Edinburgh Festival Fringe in August with a show called *The Unpleasantness at Brodie's Close* – a wry allusion to Dorothy L. Sayers' *The Unpleasantness at the Bellona Club*. Brodie's Close is the actual location of the venue in Edinburgh; it's a Masonic hall. John Lloyd recalls that the lighting was a switch on the wall. (If you are unfamiliar with the Edinburgh Festival, it's worth going at least once for a manic tour of the culture. The Festival was relatively sane in the 1970s, but it has got bigger and bigger ever since. Once a year it takes over that highly respectable albeit tourist-wracked city. The range covers everything from Wittgenstein's doorknobs to installation art.)

The show was a series of sketches written by David Renwick, Andrew Marshall, John Lloyd, John Mason and Douglas. John Mason, who oscillated between sketch-writing and the high-level teaching of mathematics, had organized the venue and kindly (recklessly?) underwritten the cost of hire. Typically, Douglas's contribution was the last to arrive, and there was some doubt that he would make it at all, for guarding the sheikh paid £100 per week – even without occasional colossal tips, that was serious money if you were broke.

What tied the show together, more or less, was the running gag of a couple in a railway station (akin to *Brief Encounter*) urgently trying to move their relationship forward, but being forever interrupted. The couple's frustrations anticipated the touching scene in *So Long, and Thanks for All the Fish* when Arthur Dent is hopelessly trying to convey his love to Fenchurch in the teeth of a relentlessly attentive lottery ticket seller. Like every writer, Douglas was wont to recycle good ideas. Does this detract from his creativity? Not a bit. It is worth printing this in bold and italics: *execution is all*.

The revue starred the 'Brodie's Close Rollers' (the egregious Bay City Rollers were dominating the pop charts at the time). The Brodie's Close Rollers were Douglas, John Lloyd, John Mason, Becky Fanner and Geoffrey Farrington (both performers rather than writers), and David Renwick. Andrew Marshall had been obliged to scuttle back home to a teaching job before he could get on stage. Douglas claimed him as the model for Marvin, the Paranoid Android,* though Marvin, for reasons too involuted to be described here, was also the nickname of Martin Smith. From the literary point of view Marvin was closer to Eeyore in *Winnie the Pooh*. Douglas confessed that he found this melancholy animal inspirational. Years later, when he read *Winnie the Pooh* to his daughter, Polly, he was struck again by how very similar Marvin and Eeyore were in tone. Andrew is now a successful TV writer. David Renwick went on to become one of the country's top screen writers with the likes of *Jonathan Creek* and the creation of *One Foot in the Grave*. Lloydie himself is no slouch, especially at crisp one-liners. It was a formidably talented team.

They even produced a promotional T-shirt. Two in fact. One bore the enigmatic commercial message: 'I have been Unpleasant at Brodie's Close'. The other one carried the surreal legend: 'So have I . . .' The plan was to walk around Edinburgh side by side. They must have attracted some attention either walking in formation, or singly.

David Renwick, who had first met Douglas in the writers' room at the BBC's Aeolian Hall in New Bond Street, recalls :

> There was also an odd sketch of Douglas's about a cereal manufacturer who put dead jellyfish in cereal packets as a giveaway, and was surprised when it didn't help sell more cornflakes. The stage was so small that we had to hide behind the two curtains at the sides of the rostrum in order to change. I remember Douglas's large bottom protruding from behind the curtain when he had to dress up as Long John Silver . . . Douglas and I had to share a room, too. He was reading *Dombey and Son* [Dickens was one of his favourite writers], and he used to talk in his sleep sometimes. It's a pity I cannot remember what he said.

---

* Andrew has affectionate memories of Douglas, but at the time felt that being identified with Marvin was a little over-personal. We are complex creatures, not cartoony caricatures, and – though he knew Douglas was entirely without malice – Andrew was just a bit cheesed off to be carrying this sandwich board advertising his identity around the media world.

John Lloyd remembers those curtains behind which they had to change. 'Just ordinary window curtains,' he says, 'designed to prevent people on cherry pickers looking in on secret Masonic rituals.' He adds: 'Douglas got terribly upset one night in a bar because he just wasn't getting any laughs. Every time he spoke, the audience fell respectfully mute. At the time Douglas was sporting a huge, black, piratical beard, and after a few lagers we worked out that this was the problem. Enormous man with very loud voice in tiny cramped hall preceded by tenebrous efflorescence of follicles . . . He was simply terrifying the audience into silence. That night he shaved off the offending item, and after that everything was fine.' Andrew says that Douglas's almost uncontainable joy in performing was quite infectious, and that made his occasional lapses in stagecraft forgivable.

Brodie's Close was a huge success. It filled the Masonic hall every night and the run was extended for another two days by popular demand. Unfortunately, the hall could only hold seventy-five people, though they squeezed in ninety, so the revue made no money – not that that's the reason why people take shows to the Edinburgh Fringe. They hope not to lose too much, enjoy themselves and, perhaps, to garner enough smart attention to take their show on to a more commercial incarnation. The Brodie's Close Rollers succeeded in two of these ambitions: they had enormous fun and did nothing to their bank balances.

Mary Allen recalls Douglas as listless and broke at this time. She felt sorry for him, but she never went to bed with him. ('We once came very close in Cambridge,' she remembers, 'but talked about *Macbeth* all night instead.') Douglas was indeed broke by this time, and his overdraft was growing with the kind of inexorability that one hopes is too gradual for the bank manager to notice.

Andrew Marshall possesses an acute if slightly lugubrious sense of humour. He and Douglas got on very well. Andrew remembers going all the way out to Roehampton on one occasion and finding Douglas in poor spirits. He sat up all night with him while Douglas cheered up and they talked about Ideas. Douglas enjoyed ideas; he liked to sneak up on them, like a mugger, from unexpected directions. But he had little small talk, something that was both endearing and rude, for sometimes the small change of human discourse is as important as the big stuff. Andrew thinks that what came across as rudeness was sometimes fear. For all Douglas's Cambridge dazzle, he could find confident, clever people a bit daunting. Andrew recalls that they talked hugely until the sun came up. They had both recently read Robert Sheckley's classic of stoned, witty SF, *Dimension of Miracles*, and they were exhilarated by it.

Douglas's writing career, despite *Brodie's Close*, was still wretched. The opportunity of working with one of his heroes from *Monty Python* had dissipated in a cloud of gin. The script-writing was going nowhere, the sketches were inconsequential, his love life was non-existent, he was broke. What's more, he shared a flat with a golden boy whose life on the sunlit pastures was a mocking reminder of his own lack of achievement. Despite knowing he had talent, he felt pretty washed up.

That summer, 1976, had been the second of the worst drought in living memory – the upper reaches of the Thames dried up completely, and there was even an unfortunate Minister of Drought. The countryside was parched brown and gasping for a drink of water. Finally, as autumn crept into winter, it started raining again – and more or less did not stop for a year. For Douglas it was the pathetic fallacy writ large. His spirits had been falling month by month; he was later to describe that year as the worst of his life.

In 1991, looking back at his misery with the perspective of one who knows he moved on, he gave an interview to Danny Danziger of the *Independent*:

> I totally lost confidence in my ability to write, or to perform, or to do anything at all . . . and went into a catatonic spiral of depression. I suppose because of my background, having grown up as the child of divorced parents, a typical sort of shuttlecock kid, when I get depressed I tend to feel superfluous, that the world is actually better off without me, and that the world is not interested in my welfare at any level. When I was in this state of depression, I kept trying to find activities that would stop my brain going round and round and round. One day I decided to learn German, and went and got myself a pile of Teach Yourself

German books, and spent every single waking hour poring over those books. And by a strange coincidence, at the end of the month I happened to wander into the garden, and there was a woman looking for someone who used to be in the flat, and she was a German. So I sat and talked in German with her and discovered that I had done incredibly well. But since then I've never spoken German, and I don't think I remember a word.*

Despite the morale-lifting effect of learning German, by November he was close to nervous collapse. In a spasm of impatience and general misery, he decided that he was never going to succeed as a writer. A complete existential upheaval would pick him up and put him down again somewhere else – somewhere happier. He applied for a job, 'a proper job', with Jardines, the well-known finance and trading house in Hong Kong, and he was accepted. Fortunately for his millions of readers, he must have reconsidered.

His subsequent retirement to the countryside was very much a retreat, and one in which he felt a failure. Churchill's 'black dog' of depression may not have been a constant companion, but it was certainly sniffing around and looking for a good time with his trouser leg.

Meanwhile in Stalbridge, Dorset, his old room was waiting for him, rent-free. At any time his mum was glad to see him and extend the comforts of home-cooking and family life. Ron, Janet's second husband, the vet, was kindly and always took an interest, and Douglas was fond of Little Jane and James, his half-siblings, then aged ten and eight. (Once, many years before, during the school hols, Douglas had been in the house working while infant James had been upstairs, asleep. Leaving Douglas in charge, Janet nipped out on an errand. When she returned, young James was sitting on the sofa looking at Douglas with wide-eyed fascination. 'Oh dear,' she said, 'did he disturb you?' 'Not at all, Mum,' replied Douglas. 'I thought he might be a bit lonely up there and brought him down.' It is debatable who needed whose company the more . . .)

---

* Douglas Adams talks to Danny Danziger, 'The Worst of Times', the *Independent*, 11 March 1991.

Douglas's room was even rural enough to offer a view of a pigsty, though at the time this was being knocked down in order for the site to be redeveloped as an old people's home. Young James Thrift was fascinated by the JCB which was knocking the stuffing out of the pigsty (though for once the more robust idiom would be literally accurate). The driver of this impressive machine apparently kept a load of porno mags under the seat. Douglas would have been staring out of his window at this while cudgelling his cerebrum for a really good idea. The 'ah-ha!' critical response is to be distrusted, but one can't help thinking of the opening scene of *Hitchhiker's* when Arthur Dent's house is flattened by the local council's bulldozer.

Following his strategic withdrawal to Dorset, Douglas planned the odd raid on the metropolis to deliver work that would be irresistible to producers, and to network. In the media parish you have to remind people that you still exist. That was the plan – and that, amazingly given the success rate of most existential grand designs, was more or less how it worked out.

Mercifully, in the new year Douglas was indeed rescued. Jon Canter, his witty friend from Cambridge and a man of kindness and sensitivity, had visited him over Christmas and helped to cheer him up. Janet remembers Jon with affection. At first she was not sure if he could join in the festivities (Jon is Jewish), but Janet soon discovered that there is not much that will keep him from a party. Jon was sharing a house in Islington with another Cambridge pal, Jonathan Brock, who had played opposite Douglas in the ADC in Sheridan's *The Rivals*. Why not, suggested Jon, come back to town, kip on their vast sofa, kick out the black dog, and lay siege to the BBC once again?

At this point there re-enters into Douglas's life another figure of legend, Simon Brett, then a Light Entertainment Producer at the BBC, a bloke for whom the word 'urbanity' could have been coined. Comedy at the BBC was in a state of change. It was only in 1967 that the programme designations had changed from the Home Service, the Third Programme and so on, to Radios One to Four. (Radio One, the pop station, had occasioned much soul-searching about whether it was *really* the kind of thing the BBC should be doing.)

In fact Simon remembers that the whole institution was poised between the generations. A whole stratum of producers who had joined the BBC after the war was in the process of retiring, and he spent a lot of time going to their parties and wishing them well. Perhaps they were a bit tweedy, but by and large they were a decent and humorous lot. 'There were still a lot of chaps with cravats,' Geoffrey Perkins recalled, 'and I had one producer who, with the arrival of stereo, turned the studio floor into a numbered grid and moved actors around from square to square as if they were on manoeuvres.'

Some brilliant comedy, particularly the *Goon Show*, had emerged from National Service and army life in general, and a generation of producers had shared the advantage of a similar background.* (Mind you, not all of them were up to speed: one nice old chap asked Simon rather anxiously: 'What is this 'go on' show that I keep reading about?') Simon quotes John Peel, the DJ with taste and now a Radio Four presenter, as observing that BBC comedy was all run by ex-bomber pilots. By the mid-seventies the bomber pilots were hanging up their headphones and the BBC was pursuing a policy of recruiting clever young graduates, mainly from Oxbridge.

Simon had always liked Douglas's work as well as Douglas, the man. 'He was energetic and funny, and a delight to have lunch with.' Despite the desert of 1976, Douglas had written a couple of pieces for *The Burkiss Way*, a deliciously funny radio show that Simon produced. One of them, the Kamikaze Briefing, became a bit of a classic[†] and was much enjoyed by John Simmonds, the Senior Producer, so Douglas now had two strategically placed managers ('heavy dudes' in movie speak) poised to support him.

In the course of interviewing Simon for this book, he and I had lunch at the Groucho Club in London's Soho. At the corner table a tanned

---

* 'Advantage' may seem an odd word for risking your life and the sacrificing of years of it for the common weal, but in the context of black comedy they do say there is nothing like the armed services for teaching you how to play the system.

† The sketch has been reproduced in *Don't Panic.* It's horribly funny. Somehow this particular Kamikaze pilot has been on *nineteen* missions, always finding some extraordinary rationale for not completing the mission. Missing the sea altogether figured at one point.

Norman Wisdom, hero of Albania, was being lionized by three fashionables. Douglas would have chortled to think of us discussing him in such a venue. Simon has been asked many times to tell the story of commissioning *The Hitchhiker's Guide to the Galaxy* and must be weary of the repetition, but courteously he did it again:

> Douglas was coming up from Dorset to have lunch with me [4 February 1977] and had promised me three ideas. He was very enthusiastic, curious and funny – very much a social animal. He hated being on his own. So what if he was sometimes depressed. When judging the work, it's the quality that matters.
>
> In some ways I felt he was a talent without a niche. He had struggled to find his voice, but at one level I don't think he was that surprised by fame even though he felt the pressure of success very acutely. Douglas knew that he had something . . . We went out to a Japanese restaurant to discuss his three ideas. I can't for the life of me remember what the other two were – and afterwards Douglas claimed that neither could he – but one of them was a comic SF idea. It had started life as *The Ends of the Earth*, but it became *The Hitchhiker's Guide to the Galaxy*. Everybody liked it, though I remember one of my senior colleagues, a lovely man called Con Mahoney [one of the bomber pilots], asking me: 'Is this funny?'
>
> I assured him it was.

Douglas was on his way.

chapter five

The origin of the species

'"You're very strange," she said.

"No, I'm very ordinary," said Arthur, "but some very strange things have happened to me. You could say I'm more differed from than differing."'

The Restaurant at the End of the Universe

On 1 March 1977 – three weeks after Douglas's lunch with Simon Brett – the BBC approved the making of a pilot of *The Hitchhiker's Guide to the Galaxy*. Then, before committing to the whole series, it sat on its hands for six months. In those days, before the icy fist of commerce had surprised the BBC with its grip, the decision-making process moved at a speed that reminds one that glass is said technically to be a liquid. Many of the individual producers had vision and energy, but further up the hierarchy a committee system reigned whereby all that was required for another month to pass was for one member to look judiciously into the middle distance, express uncertainty and suggest that more research and/or consideration might be wisely invested. That was always an irrefutable position. Then, each summer, much of the top echelons would depart *en masse* for warmer climes. Tuscany was awash with BBC executives.

On the other hand, the BBC – free from the immediate imperatives of budget, ratings, and advertising revenue that command other broadcasters – made programmes of undoubted excellence.

Competition may keep industry 'lean and mean' – often a euphemism for subjecting the workers to unimaginable stress or moving manufacture out to exploitative low labour-cost economies – but there's no evidence that making programmes under that kind of pressure improves them. Besides, as anyone will tell you in an organization making something creative, going like the clappers is not always in the best interests of the project. Management books may employ a ghastly jargon drawn largely from American recreations like sport or hunting ('getting your ducks in a row', 'stepping up to the plate'), but they are unanimous on the virtues of taking the time to get all the machinery on your side.

In any event *Hitchhiker's* was so different that nobody in the BBC could have been poised on one foot, breath held, waiting for it. Geoffrey Perkins says that if anyone had been asked what kind of programme they were looking for, nobody would have said:

> 'I'm looking for a sort of strange SF thing about when the world ends to make a by-pass – and it will take an age to make every programme.' I mean, it was just absolutely not on anybody's radar at all. There were lots of discussions about whether to have an audience. [It was the received wisdom in the BBC at the time that an audience was needed to tell the listeners when to laugh.] I think I won this point when I said, 'Look, they'll have to sit there for a week because it will take us about a week to make these programmes.' Actually half the actors aren't there at the same time anyway.

In any case Douglas was thrilled to get the commission and his morale shot up asymptotically to the cheerfulness axis. He was still hard up, of course, and living off his parents, for the BBC paid him £1000 for what turned into nearly six months' work. (Mind you, if you run inflation backwards to 1977, £1,000 is worth five to six times more in today's terms.) But at least he had a real project, and the promise of income and friendly faces in London – and not just anywhere in London, but Islington, which was to become the centre of Douglas's metropolitan universe.

As the pigsty outside his window was demolished, his mum fed him and brought him cups of tea and peanut butter sandwiches for which he had a particular weakness. Young Jane (Little Jane) and James were quite entertained by their big brother groaning piteously, and then typing furiously before scrunching up sheets of paper and throwing them away. But although rejects filled the wastepaper basket, within a month the pilot was complete. Neil Gaiman says rightly that the first version owed a lot to *Monty Python*, and it certainly took a while for Douglas to find his voice; nevertheless the pilot contained much that was as sparky and brilliant as the final form. (Buffs should look to *Don't Panic*, revised edition, for the definitive exegesis of the differences.)

His mum's cups of tea inspired one of Douglas's inventions – the Infinite Improbablity Drive which uses tea as a Brownian motion generator. His hero, Arthur Dent, is saved by it, but 'he no more knows his destiny than a tea leaf knows the history of the East India Company'.[*]

There follows a short digression on the subject of tea.

Douglas wrote an uncharacteristically finger-wagging essay[†] – aimed at improving the American quality of life, and thus forgivable – about how to make the perfect cup. Warm the tea-pot well; spoon in an adequate supply of tea (preferably loose, but bags will do); pour in roilingly boiling water; infuse properly; pour the milk into the cup first. OK? He points out that it is not considered socially correct to put the milk in first, but on the other hand in England it is generally considered socially incorrect to know things or think about things.

As Arthur Dent is blown uncontrollably around the galaxy in the company of someone infinitely more hip than he is, he devotes much of his time looking for a decent cup of tea, a drink often accorded miraculous powers of comfort by Brits in adversity. Leg amputated? Ship torpedoed? Nice cuppa will soon put you right. Indeed there is something pathetic about Arthur, a bewildered young/old man in his

---

* The Narrator's preamble at the very beginning of *The Hitchhiker's Guide to the Galaxy*.

† In *The Salmon of Doubt*, p. 67.

dressing gown, his entire world wiped out behind him in an unnecessary cock-up, whose ambition is limited to finding a hot, herbal infusion.

Once Arthur nearly causes his own death, and that of his companions, by rhetorically asking Eddie, the shipboard computer with the irritating *faux bonhomme* American primary personality, why Eddie thought that he, Arthur, wanted a cup of tea. The computer, grimly literal-minded as only a machine can be, devotes more and more processing power to the question – imperilling them all.*

Douglas's most repeated anecdote was also set around a cup of tea and is believed to have started life as a real-life incident on Cambridge station. It has been repeated so often you will probably all know about the battle of silent British willpower when the stranger across the table in a station café started eating Douglas's biscuits – or so it appeared. In fact, Douglas's biccies emerged from beneath his newspaper after the other man had departed. In Douglas's hands, this tiny incident was polished to a comic gem suffused with cringe-making English social containment. Shamelessly, he even used the anecdote in *So Long, and Thanks for All the Fish*, when Arthur is wooing Fenchurch. In *The Salmon of Doubt* the story is reprinted in an American context, with tea changed to coffee. However, any other beverage would not be credible; railway coffee is an insipid hot brown liquid that only resembles the real thing inasmuch as they both take the shape of the vessel they're in. (Incidentally, a railway guard of long standing tells me that the pork pies are also a thing of wonder. Every 50,000 miles a trained engineer gives them a tap with a special hammer.)

The biscuit story has since reappeared in many guises, and may in some off-beat viral way still be replicating in saloon bars and over dinner tables. Over time it has picked up accretions of plausible detail. The paper was the *Guardian*. The biccies were Rich Tea. It actually happened to somebody else, and involved the *Daily Telegraph* and a

---

* Serious SF fans might recognise this idea from a Gordon Dickson short story, 'Computers Don't Argue' (a 1965 Nebula winner), in which, after a foolish bet, a computer is set the task of solving a logical paradox, and is thus disabled from maintaining the environmental systems in a Martian colony. The paradox is truly ancient, being a version of Epimenides's old chestnut about all Cretans being liars. (Epimenides was a Cretan.)

Kit-Kat. It stems from Jeffrey Archer's short story with the same plot device, except that in his version the biscuits were cigarettes. (Bit of a long shot, that one, as an explanation of origins, given Jeffrey Archer's eclecticism and the fact that his collection was published some years after Douglas started telling the story.) The BBC's *Home Truths* programme (a radio magazine, hosted by the affably unshockable John Peel, about our oddities) has broadcast an honest-sounding account from a woman who also had a silent clash of wills with a stranger over a packet of Garibaldis. People have looked me in the eye and told me that this self-same amusing incident befell them.

Urban myth? Possibly, but no earlier telling than Douglas's is to be found. Although this is circumstantial, there are stories, jokes and indeed nifty turns of phrase that seem to sweep through society like an epidemic. My theory is that many of them originate with creative users of the language, some of whom are unsung people who just happen to deploy their mother tongue with some pizazz, but a substantial proportion will emanate from professional wordsmiths – copywriters, authors, scriptwriters, Douglas Adams and so on.

Back in Stalbridge, Douglas found it frustrating waiting for the gears to turn in the BBC, so he also sent his *Hitchhiker's* pilot to Robert Holmes, the script editor and occasional writer of *Dr Who*. He was hoping to get a commission to write a *Dr Who* storyline that – if it followed the usual practice – would last for four half-hour episodes. He succeeded. Bob Holmes liked what Douglas had done a lot, and on that basis called him in for a meeting with Anthony Read (who was just taking over from Bob) and the producer, Graham Williams. They encouraged him to have a go. Douglas's resulting *Dr Who* script had great promise, but it needed a lot more work that he undertook with grace. It's been suggested that Douglas's original overdid the humour to the extent that it may have come across as forced or, even worse, frivolous. But then the story still needed a smidge more to tweak it further, and finally just a nuance here and there to get the tone absolutely spot on. Even after the refinement, some hardcore *Dr Who* fans maintain that his episodes are too jokey.

All this editorial tuning was educational for Douglas, and improved the script. But it consumed a great deal of time, with the result that when Douglas was commissioned to write a four-part *Dr Who* story in August, it coincided within a week or two with his commitment to write the *Hitchhiker's* radio series. Thus, between 1977 and 1978, Douglas was to undergo a metamorphosis, from listless aspiration to nerve-end-shredding overwork.

Douglas had always enjoyed *Dr Who* and, unlike some English Literature graduates, never looked down his nose at it on the grounds that it was genre. (Mike Simpson in his invaluable *Hitchhiker's Guide**** says that Douglas originally submitted a script for *Dr Who* in 1974, but that it vanished beyond hope of retrieval somewhere in the BBC. Alas, there was no sign of it in Douglas's papers.)

'The Pirate Planet', the first of the episodes written or co-written by Douglas, is rated as one of the best by the many *Dr Who* enthusiasts who have analysed every episode and, thanks to the Internet, are keepers of the flame. It's full of cortex-mangling concepts – transportable hollow planets, time dams, cybernetic control systems and even a high-tech bionic pirate complete with eye-patch and robotic parrot. ((Douglas had played Long John Silver, don't forget, and was keen on the comic potential of parrots; one features strategically in *Starship Titanic*.) The pirate – typical human being – uses all the breathtaking power and technology at his disposal for trivial self-aggrandisement, belting round the universe stealing other planets' resources like some cosmic shoplifter.

Tom Baker, the actor playing the Doctor, spouted the scientific arcana with total conviction. He and Mary Tamm, as his gorgeous assistant, Romana, breezed through Douglas's adventure with panache, brilliantly supported by Andrew Robertson as Mr Fibuli and Bruce Purchase as the waffling Captain. (There was no spite in Douglas, but he could sometimes be inadvertently cruel in his desire to be funny. One of the leading ladies in *Dr Who* provoked him to say that 'her idea of acting was to point her eyes in one direction while swivelling her hips in another'.)

Even in this early work Douglas's playful approach to science is apparent. He invents travel tubes in which the people are stationary

---

* Published by Pocket Essentials, 2001.

and the tube races past them like there's no tomorrow. Douglas had read his Relativity, and understood that in an inertial frame there would be no distinguishing between the moving and the static, so he was chortling knowingly in the direction of Einstein.

SF fans have wondered about the provenance of Douglas's ideas, and there is a minor scholarly industry in tracking them down as if we cannot credit him with being so startlingly inventive. But Douglas wasn't steeped in the genre and he was always mildly put out if he learned that some original thought had occurred to an SF writer already. A hollow planet, for example, might be traced to Isaac Asimov who, decades earlier, had posited such a planet, Trantor, in his exhilarating *Foundation* trilogy (later, unwisely, racked into a tetralogy for a large advance). Making a planet – or at least cities – moveable at will had been suggested by James Blish many years before in his *Spindizzy* stories. But Douglas was not particularly well versed in SF (apart from Sheckley), unlike his wife, Jane Belson, who had read everything. Apart from the *Eagle* comic, he had – in my partisan view – misspent his youth reading Charles Dickens, when he could have been immersed in Ursula Le Guin, Robert Silverberg, John Wyndham, Philip K. Dick, Theodore Sturgeon, Fred Pohl and, to pinch Kingsley Amis's useful expression, many other dazzling cartographers of hell.*

Dr Who is – or rather was – a great national institution. 'Cult' is a word people reach for too easily, but *Dr Who* qualified. With the exception of the wretched *Star Trek*, whose longevity has been unnaturally prolonged by its transformation into an industry, *Dr Who* was the longest-running SF series ever produced. It was first screened in 1963 and didn't go off the air until 1996 – and even then it continued for a while when the rights were sold to Fox for a one-off.

Dr Who himself was a Time Lord from the galactically central planet of Galifrey. Despite the strictures of their non-interference code – and the deeply laid plotting from another powerful but more malign Time Lord called The Master – Dr Who whizzed about the space-time doing good and righting wrongs in the company of a resourceful and attractive female assistant who helped to keep the dads watching. One

---

* Kingsley Amis, *New Maps of Hell* (Ayer Co Publishing, 1975).

of these was played by the actress, Lalla Ward, who, introduced by Douglas to Richard Dawkins at one of Douglas's wicked parties, subsequently became Mrs Dawkins.

For transport, Dr Who employed an old-fashioned British police telephone box called the Tardis (allegedly an acronym for Time and Relative Dimension in Space). Though finite on the outside, this vehicle had as much space inside as the largest studio could accommodate, and its ability to roam through time and space provided a wonderfully flexible narrative device. The special effects were always a bit clunky, with wobbly sets and acres of Bacofoil; later Douglas grieved about the TV adaptation of *Hitchhiker's* on the grounds that it reminded him of *Dr Who*. But the good thing about a budget limited by time and money is that you have to fall back on old-fashioned virtues – in this case the wit, inventiveness and story-telling ability of the writers who, by and large, delivered the goods for over three decades. Among Dr Who's implacable foes were the Daleks, created by Terry Nation, creatures with totalitarian views whose nasty little bodies had mutated to the extent that they moved about in motorized containers. Conveniently these were about the size of a vacuum cleaner. On top they carried a rotatable dome fitted with an all-purpose sensor device, and projecting from their bodies a death ray and what looked suspiciously like a telescopic drain plunger.* Douglas had always been a fan of the Daleks who were such a charismatic cross between Iago and a kitchen appliance that they had to be revived every few years by popular demand. He had even written an episode of *Dr Who* while at Brentwood School, but could recall little of it beyond the fact that his Daleks were powered by Rice Krispies.[†]

It was a risk commissioning an unknown writer to tackle *Dr Who*. Even as a relatively out-of-sight freelance, writing for it was like being given a paintbrush and being told to nip into the Tate to touch up a Turner. There were also lots of rules designed to avoid inconsistency

---

* Even today if you waggle a hand in front of your face and croak 'EX-TERM-IN-ATE! EX-TERM-IN-ATE!' with a voice full of grit, people (Brits anyway) will instantly recognize a bad Dalek impression.

† *Hitchhiker's Guide*, p. 80.

or boxing writers in for the future. Legions of knowledgeable and dedicated fans were poised to tell you if you made a botch of it. It is a tribute to Douglas that he always took *Dr Who* seriously, devoting particular care to devising concepts that were at least theoretically workable (unlike magic, for example, which suspends the rules and is just a cop-out). As in writing a sketch, Douglas understood that SF must have an internal logic. In this context – though it was a principle to which he cleaved in general – he said that the expression 'tongue-in-cheek' was often an excuse for laziness. 'It means it's not really funny, but we aren't going to do it properly.'*

Dr Who, the Time Lord, was able to regenerate his body after death a total of twelve times – and this was just as well as the actors playing him were prone to anxiety about typecasting.† By the time Douglas was writing for the series, the fourth Doctor was in place, Tom Baker: an engaging, larger than life, former monk with an extravagantly outgoing personality. He loved the part so much that he stayed with it for seven years. Douglas once told me that Tom was then the randiest man he had ever met – and he had encountered one or two in whom the balance of power had never moved even slightly northwards from the gonads to the cerebrum.

Douglas went on to write two more *Dr Who* episodes: 'The City of Death' (co-written with the producer, Graham Williams) and 'Shada'. He also wrote *Dr Who and the Krikkitmen* as a film treatment, featuring one of those sickening time loops. This never got very far, but the ideas were subsequently put to good use in *Life, the Universe and Everything*. 'Shada' unfortunately got caught up in a strike at the BBC and was never transmitted, though I believe that for serious buffs it is available on video.∞ However, Douglas did recycle part of this when Dr Chronotis, a retired Time Lord whose rooms in Cambridge so

---

* *Don't Panic*, revised edition, p. 81.

† OK, for the buffs, in order, the Doctors were: William Hartnell, Patrick Troughton, Jon Pertwee, Tom Baker, Peter Davison, Colin Baker and Sylvester McCoy.

∞ The *Daily Telegraph* (16 November 2002) reports that it will now be remade with Paul McGann as the Doctor.

resembled Douglas's own, appeared in the first Dirk Gently novel, *Dirk Gently's Holistic Detective Agency*.

In this story Douglas once again scratches away at the time-travel paradox – on this occasion with literally cosmic ramifications – like some terrible intellectual itch. What happens if you go back in time and waylay your grandad with a quick beer, thus preventing him from meeting your grandma? (There are more Freudian expressions of this notion involving killing your mum, but the paradox is the same.) If you succeed, you no longer exist so could not have succeeded – in which case you do exist, so round you go again in a logically impregnable circle. This conundrum was something that clearly fascinated Douglas for he came back to it frequently. Remember Zaphod Beeblebrox summoning up his grandfather, Zaphod Beeblebrox the *Third*? An accident, Zaphod explains, with a contraceptive and a time machine.

'The City of Death' was a four-part script started by David Fisher, a regular and reliable scriptwriter who had been suddenly waylaid by family problems. Douglas and Graham Williams finished it off under immense time pressure, a director and a studio slot having been booked only days away from the realization that they had no script. Douglas was locked up in Graham's study where he lived on black coffee and whisky. Because of Writers' Guild regulations, the departmental name of David Agnew was used for the credits.

Despite the rush, or possibly because of it, 'The City of Death' story is splendidly inventive. It prefigures that somewhat disturbing *Hitchhiker's* idea that life is not only inadvertent, but possibly – thanks to time-travel – circular. Dr Who has to ensure that an explosion on Earth actually happened because the resulting chemical chaos kick-started the whole improbable business of evolution that ends up with sentience, chartered accountants, geraniums, ants, whales and all our planet's astonishing biodiversity. This again is the horror of the time-travel paradox, but writ large. In *The Restaurant at the End of the Universe*, Douglas posits that the entire human race is a logical absurdity as it is descended from those who returned to the Earth and became their own ancestors. Teleologically speaking, it's teeth-grindingly up itself.

Christopher Douglas Adams in his mid-forties.

Douglas Adams aged
seven months.

Douglas, already six feet tall at twelve, pointing out the dangers of money at the village fête in Dorset.

Douglas, aged thirteen, in the chemistry laboratory in Brentwood School.

School House, Brentwood. Douglas, to the left of his house master, was conspicuous due to his height.

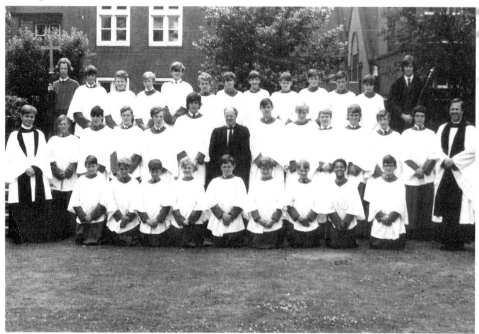

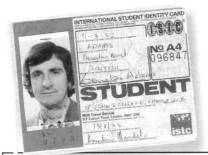

Main: Strutting and Fretting in a student revue.
Top: Douglas's student indentity card showing him sporting a classic seventies haircut.
Bottom: Douglas's Footlights membership card.

Lady Margaret Players/J.T./Adams, Smith, Adams
Presents a Revue in the School of Pythagoras

TELEPHONE

Way out
Travel centre

Several Poor Players

Strutting and Fretting

11pm June 14th, 15th, 16th, Tickets 30p
From St. John's College Porters Lodge
and at door.   Cheap day return 50p.

PRINTED BY CAMBRIDGE INSTANTPRINT LTD. 64017

Footlights Dramatic Club

This is to certify that
Douglas Adams
of St. John's   is
an official member of Footlights

John Parry
Secretary

Members Signature Douglas Adams

Douglas, looking bashful, with Jon Canter and Lucy Parker in Cambridge, 1971.

John Lloyd on a fraught holiday in Corfu.

Douglas with the cast of the *Hitchhiker's* radio series in November 1978. From left to right: David Tate (various roles), Alan Ford (Roosta), Geoffrey McGivern (Ford Prefect), Mark Wing-Davey (Zaphod Beeblebrox) and Simon Jones (Arthur Dent).

Taking some time out from recording. From left to right: Douglas, Geoffrey Perkins, David Tate, Geoffrey McGivern, Mark Wing-Davey, Simon Jones and Alan Ford.

Douglas on the set of the TV series of *Hitchiker's* which was first broadcast in January 1981.

Marvin the paranoid android.

Mark Wing-Davey wearing his extra head with panache as Zaphod Beeblebrox.

David Dixon and Simon Jones as Ford Prefect and Arthur Dent.

Douglas on set again. He was not happy with the TV series, which he felt lacked the magic of the radio version.

Douglas's first Golden Pan, presented in January 1984 for one million copies sold of *The Hitchhiker's Guide to the Galaxy*.

The *Dr Who* plot also embroils the viewer in the stealing of the Mona Lisa (there are multiple copies, some of which are marked 'fake' in felt-tip pen). Eleanor Bron and John Cleese provide delicious cameos as art-lovers who believe that the Tardis is a gallery exhibit.

Meanwhile, Douglas, encouraged by Jon Canter, was commuting back and forth from Dorset to London, gradually relocating in the city as his morale improved and he had more work. Jon, who had studied law ('a mistake'), now had a job as an advertising copywriter and was sharing a house in Arlington Avenue with trainee barrister, Jonny Brock, and his wife, Clare Gorst. Jonny, you will remember, was the aspirant thespian from Douglas's days of amateur dramatics, who eventually became a QC. The house boasted a large sofa on which Douglas was invited to crash, and he frequently did when in town. Jon, Jonny and Clare offered friendship, warmth, digestive biscuits and stability in addition to somewhere to sleep. Douglas was very fond of them, and dedicated the first *Hitchhiker's* novel to Jonny Brock and Clare Gorst, and 'all the other Arlingtonians for tea, sympathy and a sofa'.

Their house in this particularly leafy early Victorian part of Islington overlooks a section of the Grand Union Canal, now recreational rather than mercantile, which circles London to the east and west before joining the Thames. Where it runs through Islington, its tow-paths are compacted by massed joggers from the law, telly, advertising and journalism. During his intermittent spasms of physical self-improvement, Douglas too used to jog along the canal, and continued to do so when he had his own place in nearby Upper Street.*

In 1977, things were distinctly looking up. Douglas had his *Dr Who* episodes to write and supportive friends in town. Finally he even got a real job. He was delighted. It was the world's lowliest job in radio, as a producer so junior that even the cleaners could boss him about, but it was still a *job*, one on the staff and not just a freelance contract –

---

* Sue and I met him on the canal once in 1979 looking very ragged and sweaty in jogging gear. 'Every generation will have its characteristic ailments,' he gasped. 'Ours will have great cardio-vascular systems, but terminally buggered knees and tendons.'

and at the BBC no less, a national treasure with correspondingly huge cachet. David Hatch, then the Head of the Light Entertainment Department, had given it to him. Like Simon Brett, he believed in Douglas, and Douglas may have felt under some obligation to show that their confidence was not misplaced.

Apparently though, Douglas was not much cop as a producer. John Lloyd had seconded him briefly to the *News Quiz** when the usual co-producer, Danny Greenstone, was away. But it did not work out. John Lloyd:

> Trouble was Douglas was *never* any good at all with anybody else's formats. He could *only* do his own stuff. He really, really wanted to be able to write one-liners for *The Two Ronnies*, or sketches for *Week Ending* or whatever, but he just *could not do it*. You might as well have asked him to write thank you letters in Korean. None of it made the slightest sense to him. So I daresay we called it a day after getting nowhere.

Of course, John Lloyd – as later events are to make clear – has a complex view of Douglas. Writers may be pals, but there is always an element of rivalry.[†] Gore Vidal once memorably remarked that he could not hear of the success of a friend without dying a little. Affection, envy, irritation, admiration, hurt – all go into the rich stew stirred by Douglas and John. Douglas may not have been all that hopeless a producer, but there is little doubt that he could not resist endless fine-tuning of a work in progress – and that sits uneasily with schedules that, once published, march with no nonsense to a drill sergeant's beat.

---

* A topical quiz in which some funny and fearless people are scurrilous about the preceding week's events. It sounds a bit naff, but in fact is brilliant. The format makes for variety, and the personal chemistry between the team members is a hoot. They are selected not just for their personalities and quick wits but also for their willingness to elaborate one another's fantasies. They get away with comments that in a more solemn context would have the libel lawyers reaching for their writs. The programme is still running, and is well worth a listen.

† OK. This is a generalization for which I can only offer 'anecdotal evidence' (sociologists' code for no grant), but it is based on thirty years of observation.

To do their job, producers need to get a lot of people together, charm them, organize them, and bully them with a judicious mixture of tact and steel, while simultaneously making them all feel good about themselves. The task is to turn a collection of disparate and sometimes highly strung individuals into a team. It's a difficult trick, and one which did not serve Douglas's strengths. He was too vulnerable to cope well with stress and, despite being a social animal with a need for company and stimulation, as a creator he preferred to be solitary.

Whatever his virtues as a radio producer in the Light Entertainment department, Douglas did not stay at it for very long. Early in 1978 he was offered, and he accepted, the job of script editor of *Dr Who*, where Anthony Read was moving on. David Hatch was said to be a little narked as Douglas had not really paid his dues in the current job and his haste in transferring appeared unseemly. Simon Brett had left to go to London Weekend Television (leaving Geoffrey Perkins as *Hitchhiker's* producer). But, as Douglas remarked, David himself moved on shortly afterwards so Douglas did not feel so badly about it. Radio people are always sensitive about the talent leaving them for the glamorous but blowsy tart called television. There is an inferiority complex at work that's entirely unnecessary, especially as radio is often braver than the telly, more intelligent and less tyrannized by market expediency.

One collaboration with John Lloyd that did work out well was when the two of them, by then in adjacent offices in Langham Street behind Broadcasting House, wrote the script for a Dutch cartoon series called *Dr Snuggles*. They were paid £500, a very generous fee when you consider that their annual salaries would have been between £2000 and £3000 at the time. *Dr Snuggles* was designed to be one of the very few non-violent cartoons for children. John says it was huge fun to do: 'With animation the only limit was our own imaginations. We also loved the fact that the Dutch producer was called Joop Visch, his assistant was a young man called Wim Oops, and his secretary was Veronica Plinck.'

Douglas's life was threatening to go from torpid to flat-out faster than a Porsche 928S. The BBC approved *Hitchhiker's* at the end of August 1977. He also had the *Dr Who* commissions. Then he got a job. It seemed like a sensible time to find an agent.

He became a client of Jill Foster, to whom he had been recommended by Graham Chapman. Jill was small, quick, no-nonsense, good-hearted and rather sexy. She had recently declared independence from a larger agency and set up on her own with her husband, Malcolm Hamer, an agent specializing in sports. She looked after all the Pythons apart from John Cleese and Eric Idle, and she knows what's what. Jill has always tried to do what is best for her clients as people. If this means they should not take on something unsuitable, despite cabbage-sized wads of cash waved under their noses, Jill will tell them.

She recalls that Douglas was hugely amusing and had a talent for lunch. He often rang her at ten in the morning and chatted, despite the fact that she was very busy. Jill always forgave him because he was so funny, 'like a giant puppy with a sense of humour'. She recalls that he wrote a sketch about two lighthouse keepers who had fallen out. (They drew a diameter line through their lighthouse and could not infringe on each other's territory.) 'It was a brilliant sketch,' she says. 'The market for sketches was very difficult and I could not find a buyer for it. But it was exceptional and I realized then that he had something very special.' Even after Douglas had left her for a new agent, Ed Victor, following publication of *The Restaurant at the End of the Universe*, they remained on good terms and would enjoy the occasional lunch. 'I think he fancied me a bit,' says Jill, 'but he gave up flirting after I gave birth to my daughter.'

These days we live in a post-*Hitchhiker's* world in which references to forty-two, life, the universe and everything are greeted with a smile of recognition. It's hard to think back to the time before our sensibilities were skewed forever by Douglas's work. Of course there had been humorous SF by Bob Shaw, Robert Sheckley, Theodore Sturgeon amongst others, though it was not widely read outside the parish. Even Isaac Asimov liked jokes, and a lot of his short stories were witty explorations not of who done it? but of what done it? and how was it done?

But before Douglas nobody had been *cosmically* funny. He loved philosophical ideas, and had a natural grasp of them, but he knew that plonking them unadorned into the text would induce instant tedium followed by the heterodyne squeal of a million radios being retuned.

For instance, Douglas describes the creator of the universe as a curmudgeon with a disagreeable cat and a mucky shed.* This decrepit old git has lost all confidence that the universe actually exists because his sense data could be doing the dirty on him. ('Contingent' is the word philosophers use in this context.) It's a nightmarishly solipsistic idea. You cannot know for sure if anything is real. That's why Descartes's famous observation, *cogito, ergo sum*, is such an important test for existence because even if the 'I' that seems to be experiencing the world is in the grip of some hallucination, at least it can be sure there is an entity that is conscious, even if cruelly deluded. The fact that the Supreme Being is prepared to deal administratively with the world on the assumption that it *might* really be there is an empirical accommodation with phenomenalism – and rather a bleak joke. Besides, philosophical notions described in this way would be pretty dull. Douglas's genius was to sneak them into the reader's brain camouflaged as a series of extremely good jokes. It is this serious underpinning of dazzling notions and intellect that made *Hitchhiker's* so extraordinary.

Lest we forget, the work was quite amazingly innovative. He spoke to the reader directly, even – especially – to readers unfamiliar with the conventions of response that come from being a regular consumer of literature. When Douglas died, it was poignant to see so many heartbroken teenagers leaving their tributes on the website created for the purpose. Alienated youngsters in small towns in Alaska knew that he was talking to them personally.

The pilot for *The Hitchhiker's Guide to the Galaxy* was recorded in the BBC's large West London Paris Studio in June 1977. Simon Brett was the producer of the pilot, almost his last task before sliding off into telly, and then for the rest of the series Geoffrey Perkins took over. Although he self-deprecatingly says that he had no idea what he was doing ('that's all right,' said Douglas, 'neither do I'), it was clear from the beginning that Geoffrey got it, as they say, perfectly. He was also confident enough about his own humour and sense of narrative construction to chivvy Douglas when things got too incoherent. It's

---

* *The Restaurant at the End of the Universe*, Chapter 29 (Pan Books, 1980).

partly as a result of Geoffrey's nagging that anything resembling a plot emerged at all.

Much has been written about the casting of the show, and for completists the full credits are included in an Appendix. The reality was that Douglas and Geoffrey were well served by the cast, many of whom were mates from the Footlights days. (This old-boy networking would be harder to accept were it not for the fact that the cast was brilliant.) The actors performed to perfection, even those who found the whole thing bewildering. Don't forget that they did not all have to be present during the recording, so some of them had their parts spliced in later. The script tells a picaresque, strange and discontinuous story at the best of times – even if you listen to it all, and pay attention – so it is not surprising that some of the actors, like Roy Hudd for instance, who played the compère in the restaurant at the end of the universe, found it all a bit weird.* All the actors liked playing their parts, which says something for the lilt of the writing and the huge grin that shines through the text. Similarly, all the engineers and studio managers relished making it all sound seamless. (See Chapter Seven.) The fun they had was communicated in every broadcast moment.

The story of Peter Jones as the Book has become part of the many-volume Chronicles of Adams that embrace the first broadcasts. Peter Jones was an experienced radio performer with exquisite comic timing from a lifetime behind the microphone and treading the boards. He'd starred in *In All Directions* (with Peter Ustinov) and was frequently on *Just a Minute*, a BBC radio show in which the panellists have to talk for sixty seconds without hesitation, deviation or repetition. (It's not so easy.) His tone was just right for the Book. Like some autodidact in a bar telling you all the species of woodlouse to be found north of 50° latitude, he was terribly matter-of-fact, slightly sententious and utterly

---

* Geoffrey Perkins tells a story of how Roy Hudd met Stephen Moore (Marvin) for an interview for the BBC World Service, and told him that he'd just been in this really strange thing with the universe ending in some kind of cabaret act, and that he had to do about five minutes of ad-libbing as well. He had no idea what it was about. Stephen said to him, hmm, that sounds like the thing that I'm in. It was Geoffrey who called the android Marvin by the way. Douglas's original was Marshall, but it sounded too military somehow.

uninterruptible. Douglas and Simon Brett were casting about for someone with a Peter Jones-type voice. Mike Simpson reports that they had approached Michael Palin and one or two others, but were frustrated.* The classic anecdote goes like this: they were having a meeting over BBC tea and digestive biscuits, but getting nowhere.

'We definitely need a Peter Jonesy sound,' opined Douglas. 'Damn, damn, damn . . .'

There was much gnawing of knuckles and sudden starts of 'How about . . .? Oh, bugger, he's dead' or 'Thingy might do it, but is he too expensive now?'

Simon's secretary, losing patience with the high-octane ratiocination of the chaps with their V8 brains, then came in and said: 'Do you think it's possible that Peter Jones himself might have a Peter Jones-type voice?'

Lights flickered in Broadcasting House, daffodils erupted from the earth in nearby Regent's Park, suddenly the sun shone. Of course, why *not* get Peter Jones himself? Women, eh? Dauntingly pragmatic . . .

Douglas now set about writing the *Hitchhiker's* radio series in a tremendous spasm of creativity. These days we are so used to computer technology that it takes some imaginative effort to understand the discipline of the typewriter. It was quicker than longhand and, God knows, in most cases more legible, but it was not more flexible. No copy and paste, no scrolling up the screen to add an afterthought or transpose a sentence so the rhythm was better. Every word had to be pounded onto paper where it sat as immovable as a pyramid. The whole page had to be jettisoned, and clean-typed after an amendment or two. And, of course, quite apart from the mechanical problems, comic writing is just astonishingly difficult.

The Paris Studio in Maida Vale was, despite the name, geared up for an audience. Without one, it was dark and empty. It wasn't the easiest space to work in, but any gloom was quickly dispelled by the energy and enjoyment of the team making *Hitchhiker's*. Relays of actors came in to do their bit, and left chortling. Geoffrey and his brilliant team of technicians had to invent effects on the spot, sometimes singing

---

* *Hitchhiker's Guide.*

them themselves (creating a vast choir of off-key robots, for instance). It was all huge fun. In order to get proper voice separation, Geoffrey hid his actors all over the building, even stuffed into cupboards. He recalls:

> Richard Goolden, a little guy who played Mole in *Toad of Toad Hall*, must have been about eighty then. He was a sweet little actor who was absolutely bent over double. [He was Zaphod Beeblebrox the Fourth.] I'd put him in some cupboard to do his bit, and it must have been about half an hour after we'd finished that sequence when this little voice said, 'Is it all right if I come out?' I said, 'Oh, so sorry, Richard, I forgot about you . . .'

When Douglas had written four episodes, he had to break off to write four episodes of *Dr Who*, 'The Pirate Planet'. Geoffrey Perkins empathized:

> It wasn't that Douglas was too bloody lazy to get down and do it. He was sweating over every word. And he had this strange technique of writing backwards. He was actually typing the thing on a typewriter and would come in with about twelve pages of script the week before the show, and I'd say, OK, so this a third of the script – all right, we'll keep the studio, and keep the actors because if he just keeps going at this rate he'll finish it soon. But then he'd come in four days later and say: 'I've got eight pages of script.' And you couldn't quite work out how he'd gone down . . .

The reduction of twelve pages of effervescent copy to eight was characteristic Douglas. All his life he would ruthlessly self-edit his work, pruning and pruning it down to its nerve ends. Just as poetry is more intense than prose, the result of all this compression was frequently brilliant, but it must have had the production team sighing and groaning. It's not a handy technique when the clock is running and there is time to fill. 'Dead air' – or silence – is anathema to radio producers; thirty seconds of broadcasting nothing is an eternity.

Hitchhiker's and *Dr Who* left Douglas exhausted.

I had simply run out of words. Since John Lloyd always beat me at Scrabble I reckoned he must know lots more words than me and asked him if he would collaborate with me on the last couple of scripts. 'Prehensile', 'anaconda' and 'ningi' are just three of the words I would never have thought of myself.*

Douglas was always the kindest of men, but sometimes he found it difficult to acknowledge creative debts. He was scrupulous about the attribution of particular lines to their authors and generous in his public praise of the work of other writers and thinkers whom he rated, but when it came to personal assistance he wanted to be the sole creator; Doctor Adams with the crash cart paddles would kick-start the heart of the beast. There is a kind of child-like 'look what I've done! And all on my own!' in all authors, hence their hunger for admiration no matter how established they are. In Douglas's case his desire for approval went beyond the familiar and forgivable promptings of ego; it was a desperate need for reassurance. Pragmatically too, his perfectionism and idiosyncratic voice would have been hard to impose upon a writing partner without Douglas coming across as capriciously difficult, if not incipiently bonkers. Besides, he knew he would be judged on the work. He well understood just how much he craved emotional support, encouragement, cups of tea and all-purpose round-the-clock unconditional love. But when it came to hearing the music within his own words he needed – as with his sketches with Will Smith and Martin Adams – to work on his own. Help with the actual text was something he couldn't bear. This left some of his fellow scribes, such as John, and later Michael Bywater, feeling, as Wodehouse said, not exactly gruntled – an emotion doubtless exacerbated by the huge commercial success of the work. It's one thing to help an anguished friend in the creative process if the result is one smart mention in the *TLS* and the sale of three copies (two to the author's mother). In those circumstances you're pleased to have been of use. But you might be more ambivalent when the work in question had sold over several million copies and made your pal famous.

---

* *The Hitchhiker's Guide to the Galaxy: The Complete Radio Scripts*, footnotes to Fit the Fifth.

In the end it is hard to assess the degree to which Douglas was helped. Having someone simpatico fizzing away creatively on the same wavelength is an invaluable service. On the other hand, Douglas had invented the context and the characters into which the remaining episodes had to fit. The voice and the template were already established. However, John Lloyd is a very talented man, and Geoffrey recalls that at least one long Narrator's speech in episode six was entirely down to John, who also dreamed up the Haggunenons, the fast-evolving creatures with the undisciplined chromosomes. Without wanting to get too fruitlessly preoccupied with who did what -- for a co-written script is like one of those irreversible chemical reactions which cannot be sorted back into its original components – Douglas appears to acknowledge John's contribution with the Narrator and the Haggunenons as those passages include the aforementioned words, 'Ningi', a galactic currency unit, and 'prehensile', that he reckoned were essentially Lloydie. It is interesting, though in the light of later events hardly surprising, that when Douglas wrote the first novel of *Hitchhiker's* based on the radio scripts, he did not rely on John Lloyd's contributions at all.

In his introduction to the compendium of the trilogy (in four parts) published by Pan in 1992 and also in his preamble to the third volume of the Byron Preiss graphic novels of *The Hitchhiker's Guide to the Galaxy* (published in 1993), Douglas makes it clear that his first book was a substantially expanded novel version of episodes one to four of the radio series, i.e. he did not use any material from the co-written episodes. In the same introduction, Douglas explains that his second novel, *The Restaurant at the End of the Universe*, was based – with heavy revision and editing – on episodes seven through twelve, and then also five and six 'in that order'. Douglas may have been concerned about copyright, although he never had a legalistic turn of mind (indeed, he could be quite innocent in such matters), but when he was writing the first novel there had been such a major falling out with John Lloyd that Douglas would have been alert to the dangers of using any of John's ideas. By the second book, relations with John had settled down to a state that in hospital parlance might be described as critical but stable. Douglas felt able to return to episodes five and six, but even then he largely wrote John's contributions out of the novel.

So Douglas's assessment of John Lloyd's contribution is misleadingly flippant, for he needed help urgently. What's more, episodes two to four were recorded in the Paris Studio in November and December of 1977, so the schedule was rapidly catching up with his rate of production.

By the time the first episode was broadcast (8 March 1978), they were still recording the last episode, cutting things fine given post-production editing and the lead times for publishing the programmes. Later that year there was a 'Christmas Special' broadcast in December that had nothing at all to do with Christmas, and which Geoffrey succeeded in prising out of Douglas by moving in with him and zapping him with pathos on an hourly basis.

John Lloyd's account of working with Douglas on the last two episodes of the first series is not as cool as Douglas's. He reckons that by the time Douglas had reached episode five of the radio series, he had proved to himself that he could create something completely original, and that he just wasn't enjoying the process any more. John himself was in the throes of writing notes for a comic SF novel called *GiGax*, a term that meant the greatest area that could be encompassed by the human imagination (so everything from a nutshell to the cosmos). Douglas, says John, got completely stuck around the beginning of episode five, and was very distressed about it. John came to the rescue and plundered some of his own ideas from *GiGax*:

> The ghastly trauma for me with Douglas was that he got stuck, and said, 'Look, we've got to write these last two and I'm under terrible time pressure now, but if you could help me out if there's another series, we'll go back to our old system of writing together.' I was living in Knightsbridge at the time, in the flat of a rather well-off friend.* There was a kind of garage that had been converted into a rough and ready office where we worked. And although it had taken Douglas almost ten months to write the first four episodes, the last one and a half/two we wrote in three weeks.

---

* Alex Catto in William Mews, Knightsbridge. Years later Alex, by then a venture capitalist, was one of the investors in The Digital Village.

Actually, though the chronology is hard to reconstruct, it looks as if Douglas was not quite as dilatory as John suggests. He did not get down to writing seriously until August when the series was commissioned. However, there's no doubt about the deadlines. Time, tide and the BBC wait for no man. Bringing John in gave the whole process an enormous boost.

> We laughed a lot. What happened was that I gave him hundreds of pages of my novel, *GiGax*. I can't remember why I called it that, but I do remember that the guy who created Dungeons and Dragons was called something like it, and I thought I'd invented the name. Anyway, I gave him these hundreds of pages and said, take anything you want. Mine was a rather pretentious book, I suppose, but there were quite a lot of crucial ideas in it and Douglas had this wonderful way of taking the kernel of an idea and turning it around to make it much funnier. He always had a way of putting a gag on the end, whereas my natural inclination was to go forward with the basic idea to try to find a solution rather than a gag. It was in that garage that we jointly came up with the number forty-two and the Scrabble set, which even at the time seemed the most wonderful, striking, simple and hilarious idea.

Apropos of forty-two, by the way, Griff Rhys Jones, a friend since their schooldays, remarks that there was always a precision to Douglas's writing. Griff is sure that Douglas would have first toyed with the comic potential of eighteen, and mulled over the possibilities of thirty-seven. Five always seems a perky little number, but is it funny?

By now forty-two has been the subject of a great deal of arcane speculation; Douglas was always amused and diverted by just how abstruse and inventive some of the explanations could be. It is appreciably more droll than forty-one – though perhaps not such a ribtickler as seventy-eight.

Bizarrely, once you become sensitized to forty-two, you see it everywhere. It seems to come up more often in the National Lottery than it should (no, no – that way, madness lies). There's a giant office building in the City of London with an illuminated forty-two, lighting up the night sky, across its upper floors. Most appropriately there is a wonderful book called *Powers of Ten** which explores the whole universe by starting with, roughly, the human scale (one metre) and working upwards and downwards in powers of ten, from the quark to the greatest known extent of the cosmos. The number of base ten exponents? Forty-two. It says a lot for the power of the idea that it can be invoked without any need for context in the confident expectation that people will get the reference.

Douglas's background as a frustrated performer was a great help to him in writing the dialogue for *Hitchhiker's*. Geoffrey Perkins says that it all read very fluently because Douglas would have heard it spoken in his mind before committing it to paper. On the other hand, Geoffrey sometimes had to remind him about consistency, for Douglas, understandably reluctant to abandon a hard-won good bit, would sometimes move lines from one character to another. The whole experience, says Geoffrey, was enjoyable, but not without *angst*.

While all this was going on, there had been developments over in Arlington Avenue. Clare was pregnant, and sooner or later she and Jonny would need Jon's room for the forthcoming child (a Sam, as it turned out). Douglas could not camp on their squashy sofa forever. So when Jon Canter, one of nature's gentlemen, suggested that they share a flat together, it was timely. Jon had found a flat up a narrow flight of stairs redolent of departed cats in Kingsdown Road, N19, just off the Holloway Road.[†] Though this major thoroughfare leads directly into Upper Street in Douglas's beloved Islington, in the late seventies it was pretty grim – a wasteland of garages, downmarket bargain stores, dodgy-looking minicab companies, unbelievable traffic, and curry houses where for peace of mind it was best not to ask exactly what creature went into the vindaloo. Near the junction with the Seven Sisters Road, another major traffic artery despite the lyrical name,

---

[*] *Powers of Ten* by Philip and Phylis Morrison and Charles and Ray Eames (Scientific American Library, 1982).

[†] Apropos incontinent moggies, Douglas once remarked that underground car parks all smell of the same thing: impatience.

pubs – warehouses full of huge men drinking with Celtic determination – offered detumescent strip shows. Jon recalls that there was
nothing erotic within miles of the Holloway Road.

Jon and Douglas moved in to Kingsdown Road in January 1978, in
the teeth of a miserably wet winter. The kitchen was so narrow that
they could not both be in there simultaneously, and, if they were, they
could not get past each other without the kind of compromise alien to
both their natures. It was, says Jon, 'a bit Desperate Dan-ish. In fact,
the flat was a real shithole.'

It was in this unlikely environment that Douglas was to write the
novel of *Hitchhiker's*, but in the winter of 1977–78 that commission
would have been inconceivable. Writing the radio scripts and the *Dr
Who* episodes was more than enough. Douglas had only tentatively
emerged from the despond of failure and was still quite fragile inside,
however much superficially he may sometimes have appeared to be a
confident Cambridge graduate. Moreover nobody anticipated that
Hitchhiker's would explode in so many directions so quickly. Geoffrey,
who has a sharp instinct for such things, reckons that he knew they
had something very special by about episode four, but it's fair to say
that by and large the world was taken by surprise.

It's worth pointing out here that the second radio series – scheduled
to start pre-production in August 1979 for transmission beginning the
end of January 1980 – was if anything even more fraught than the first
even though everybody knew by then that they had a mega-success
on their hands. Once more the deadlines came excruciatingly close to
the wire.

Geoffrey was again the producer. He is now Creative Director of
Tiger Aspect, one of the best independent production companies. When
interviewing him in his office in London's Soho for this biography,
there were moments when he sighed as he went into a trance of
recollected pressure. Deep in his bones, Geoffrey understood that being
the producer of any show written by Douglas was a bit like being a rat
in a stress experiment of frightening subtlety.

This time Geoffrey allowed plenty of room for authorial dilatoriness
by starting the whole process early, the very moment he returned from
his summer holidays. It was just as well because things went very

slowly, with false starts and scripts going back and forth. By mid-October they had only recorded one episode, but with transmission of six starting at the end of January, at the rate of one per week, Geoffrey thought that, though tight, the schedule was feasible. Surely they had until the middle of March to prepare the last one?

Then David Hatch, now Controller of Radio Four, fired a starshell. You can imagine the scene from one of those naval war movies with Kenneth More – klaxons going whoop, whoop all over Maida Vale, and stiff-upper-lipped chaps saying things like, 'What a bore. The balloon has gone up.' David wanted to award *Hitchhiker's* the ultimate accolade in terms of the BBC: the cover of the *Radio Times*. Despite the magazine's title, the front cover was seldom devoted to radio; telly had the glamour. (Back in the seventies, before everybody was allowed to publish extended programme information, the *Radio Times* was easily the biggest selling magazine in the country. It's still huge, with a print run that looks like the population of a country, and an even larger readership. But as part of his negotiations with the *Radio Times* and the BBC hierarchy, David had agreed to make the second series more of an event by running the episodes consecutively in a single week, an arrangement known in the humid world of broadcast scheduling as 'stripping'. This decision, though flattering, suddenly consumed all of Geoffrey's carefully contrived Douglas fudge factor. The shows took months to write and a week to produce. The race was on.

It is remarkable how polished the final production sounded given its close shaves with disaster. Geoffrey recalls Douglas writing the script with actors actually in the studio:

> I can remember being in a taxi going down to the Paris Studio. Douglas had given me the script and I'd read half the penultimate episode, and I'd brought the second half with me to read on the way down, which is only a five or ten minute journey. And I'm getting very excited as we got out of the cab when Douglas said, 'Do you realize that this script is now actually too long, and this six or seven minute scene can come out and go into the start of the next episode – so you've now got seven minutes of the next episode.

So that was great. Hurrah. But when we got to the studio for the final recording, Douglas must only have written about half the script. We talked, very roughly, about what it was going to be – there was this ruler of the universe, the man in the shack, who was going to be dubbed in. So I booked Jonathan Pryce to be the ruler of the universe, and when he turned up in the studio I said, 'I'm very sorry, but the ruler of the universe hasn't been written yet,' because Douglas is now in the back room typing away on these things which gave you six carbon copies and which looked like toilet paper – sort of rather flimsy, slightly hard toilet paper. That led to the myth of people thinking the scripts had actually been written on toilet paper. Anyway, I said to Jonathan Pryce, 'It's not been written yet – do you mind being another character called Zarniwhoop?' And he said, 'Who's Zarniwhoop?' And I said, 'I'm not sure, he seems to be sort of vague – a bit like you in fact.' So he did Zarniwhoop, and I said, 'Well, while we're waiting for the ruler of the universe, do you mind being a tannoy announcement?' This was right at the end of the series on this flight where they'd all been becalmed for hundreds of years waiting for the supply of lemon-scented paper napkins. Jonathan had to do this whole thing about 'Return to your seat, return to your seat'. So he did that, and it was about five o'clock, and he said, 'I'm really sorry, but I'm due in the theatre' – he was doing something rather major at the time – 'and I've really got to go.' So I said, 'Well, of course, that's OK.' So by the time Douglas emerged with this bit of script, the only person left to do it was Stephen Moore. So he did it.

When we came to make the programme, we just about managed it. But Paddy Kingsland and I had been up for two nights at the radiophonic workshop. We started episode six and got most of the way through it, and then Paddy said: 'I'm really sorry – I'm just hallucinating . . .' But we sort of just about finished it when Lisa [now Geoffrey's wife] came round with some champagne to celebrate the end of the show. We hadn't quite finished the editing, but we had no time to put anything behind that last five minutes – no time for music or effects. So I

just put wind behind it because it sounded sort of eerie. And a
cat. Wind and a cat.

Geoffrey winced as he described the mechanics of getting the last
episode done and off to the BBC. His P.A.'s husband had been on stand-
by for hours with his car, but had been obliged to leave. A messenger
was waiting.

I just had to listen to the tape for a final check, so we played it.
There was a retake that had been in the programme, so we cut it
out – Lisa cut the retake out – but the tape wrapped round the
capstan head, so the two of us were just cutting bits of tape and
sticking them together. It left Maida Vale at about a quarter past
ten, and had to get to Broadcasting House by half past ten. I got
back to where I was living, only ten minutes away, and turned on
the radio fully expecting to hear an announcement saying, we're
very sorry, we cannot bring you the advertised programme. But it
got there with two minutes to go.

Douglas was out of all this. After the first two shows I
remember he phoned up on the Wednesday night – we were in
the studio – just saying, 'I thought I'd phone and find out how
things were going.' And I said: 'It's a bit frantic, but we sort of got
there.' And he said: 'Oh good. What did you think of the show
last night? I didn't hear it actually.' We were really, really angry
with Douglas – after all that, he fucking didn't listen to the
fucking programme go out!

Meanwhile, however, back on 8 March 1978, at 10.30 in the evening on
Radio Four, and with no publicity perceptible to human sense, the first
episode of *The Hitchhiker's Guide to the Galaxy* was broadcast. The BBC's
monitoring service was not sensitive enough to detect an audience for
it, so it recorded a listening figure of zero – none at all.

Then something unusual happened. Douglas had naïvely asked
Simon Brett some months beforehand what the reviews would be like.
Simon had chortled kindly in order to save Douglas the disap-
pointment. 'This is *radio*, Douglas. We'll be lucky to get a mention

anywhere.' But the programme *was* reviewed that very week in two of the quality broadsheet papers, *The Times* and the *Observer*. (In the latter, the shrewd Paul Ferris, who loved it and who was particularly taken with the Babel Fish, remarked: 'This just might be the most original radio comedy for years . . .') What's more, the programme was promoted by the most powerful mechanism known to man, one which marketing people try hardest, and with least success, to manufacture: word of mouth. The first happy listeners were stunned; they told their mates who in turn told *their* mates. Like neutrons hitting nuclei and producing more neutrons, a great demographic chain reaction cascaded through the population. By the second week, most of the students in the country were tuning in. By week three word had got out to the world at large, even as far as publishers in London. Simon Brett says he knew something extraordinary had happened when his squash partner, an engineer, started talking about it. By week four, the production office was receiving an unprecedented twenty to thirty letters a day – one addressed simply to The Hitchhiker's Guide to the Galaxy, Megadodo House, Megadodo Publications, Ursa Minor. Someone in the Post Office had written 'try BBC' on the corner of the letter. You would have had to be living up a pole on a small island not to have heard of the series by week five.

When the final episode was broadcast, 12 April 1978, Douglas was famous, though as yet he did not know it. There was an identifiable moment when the penny dropped – but that's for the next chapter.

chapter six

Making it

'I awoke one morning and found myself famous.'

Lord Byron on the instant acclaim for *Childe Harolde*

All over the West End, in restaurants where even the starters are in French, you can spot men in crumpled corduroy suits and beautifully turned-out women toadying abjectly to smug-looking media trendies. These are publishers lunching TV producers (on expenses, God forbid otherwise) in the hope that they will be persuaded to make a huge-budget, multi-part, prime-time serial based upon one of the books in the publisher's catalogue. The so-called TV tie-ins are all over the bookshops, sometimes to bizarre effect. Some classic title, repackaged with so much foil the book looks oven-ready, as the old joke goes, and sporting the *embonpoint* of some currently hot actress, will look as if it had just sprung into being that very season. It may have been selling for a century or more. 'Powerful' and 'searing' are two adjectives to watch out for when some fat, magnificent but stodgy nineteenth-century novel is given the tie-in treatment. The original was probably written in serial form for a market so tragically bored and desperate that length was a virtue in itself.

But, in fact, the radio, though not nearly as huge as telly in terms of rating numbers, is in many ways much more reliable. The Radio Four listeners are particularly valuable. Demographers and market researchers at the BBC will have to forgive the simplification: Radio Four reaches the concerned and educated middle classes via unerring self-selection. Its audience is pretty well the book-buying public. Radio should never be underrated as a means of selling books just because, as Dennis Potter put it, TV is the occupying power of our culture.

When Douglas Adams's *The Hitchhiker's Guide to the Galaxy* burst upon the airwaves in 1978, publishers took note. BBC Publishing had been given an early look at the property, as was their right, but had passed (something about which they felt immensely sick thereafter). In fairness to them, comedy and SF had always been a commercially vexed mix, and being invited to make a judgement early is not always an advantage. The world was, after all, taken by surprise. To those of us who tuned in with increasing enthusiasm every Wednesday evening, Douglas, with his wild verbal panache and wit, was clearly a wordsmith with all the instincts of a writer. It sounded so wonderful, it would surely work on the page. Pretty soon editors were beating a path to Jill Foster's door. Dot Houghton of NEL was one of the contenders, and Nick Austin of Sphere wasn't far behind.

It is odd to be writing a biography in which I, the author, have a small role. Other people's lives are at least as complex as one's own – and much more so in the case of Douglas. Just getting it down seems to do some of the subtleties a mischief. You cannot help tidying things up a little. So how should I describe myself? 'Nick Webb, debonair, decisive, destined to be played in the movie by the young Clint Eastwood, swept down on the rights like a marsh harrier snatching up a vole'?

Alas, that would be a lie. The truth is that I bought the rights in *Hitchhiker's* and then, at the end of 1978, left Pan for what I (mistakenly) thought was a grander job. I took no further part in Douglas's astonishing publishing success.

In researching this book, I have found that a few people tend to overclaim about their relations with Douglas – maybe to be close to the glamour of fame – so perhaps it's time to come clean and tell you that my part in the story is modest. I liked him a lot – and still do, despite becoming his biographer. We remained mates until he died, but we did not have one of those extraordinary and intense friendships in which Douglas invested so much. Instead we would meet up every so often, usually for lunch, and argue about science. Douglas's voracious reading and piercing intelligence usually left me labouring along in his wake, but I knew enough to say from time to time, 'Hmm, I dunno if that's not bollocks, Douglas.' We always hugely enjoyed the ensuing argument.

At the time of the first broadcasting of *Hitchhiker's*, I was the Fiction Editor at Pan Books whose staggeringly fashionable offices were above the Pan bookshop in the Fulham Road, opposite a wine bar where strangely beautiful women would lunch with each other after a heavy morning in the shops.

Pan was then owned by a consortium of three large publishers, Heinemann, Collins, and Macmillan, and this ownership helped give it access to some of the most desirable paperback rights in the market. Paperback companies were distinct from hardback companies in those days, and most of what appeared in paperback was published under a licence, usually of eight or ten years, bought from the first publisher of the work. Back in the seventies, before the era of conglomeration, there were many of these independent hardcover publishers. Only a few remain. One of the tasks of a paperback editor was to scout these houses and negotiate for the mass-market rights in books that looked as if they would have a robust second life in paperback. Because at that time paperbackers did not originate as much as the hardcover houses (something that changed markedly over the next decades), they were often patronized ('not real publishers, old boy') while at the same time being treated as chequebooks on the hoof whose sole purpose was to underwrite some hardcover publisher's dodgier investments.

Ralph Vernon-Hunt, Pan's Managing Director, just like the retiring generation of BBC producers, genuinely was an ex-bomber pilot.* He

---

* There is a story of Ralph being interviewed at the Frankfurt Book Fair by *Die Franfurter Allgemeine Zeitung*, not a frivolous paper. 'When were you last in Frankfurt, Mr Vernon-Hunt?' asked the earnest young reporter. 'Not *in* exactly, old boy,' said Ralph. 'Over . . .'

was a charming man with a long, bony face, a roguish smile and a salty no-bullshit manner – very brisk and no-nonsense when it came to business. Sonny Mehta, a handsome, aristocratic Indian with good taste and intuition, was the Editorial Director. He is now President and Editor-in-Chief of Knopf, and one of the industry's élite. Sonny is often credited with starting what became the trade paperback revolution when he launched the Paladin list. and published Germaine Greer's *The Female Eunuch*. (Trade paperbacks are larger, more expensive and usually more literary than the mass-market variety.) Simon Master, a clever, somewhat cool man with family connections to the firm, ran the systems, and there was a legendary Sales Director, grey, streetwise and tough, called Bob Williams, who ruled a formidable bunch of representatives with steel beneath a steel gauntlet. There were many others in what was a very competent team highly regarded within the publishing parish.

If they buy a winner, editors always shrewdly maintain it was their judgement and not luck. On the other hand, if they buy a complete dog, it's invariably because some idiot in the art department failed to package the book properly, the reps never understood it and the big chains suffered a pusillanimous courage bypass by failing to order enough copies (or, in extreme cases, any). I was lucky enough to be tipped off. My soon to be brother-in-law in darkest Norfolk had told me to listen to *Hitchhiker's* on the radio; I was completely overwhelmed by the humour, its bleak philosophical jokes and its sheer verbal dexterity. This bloke Adams, I thought, must write a novel. In all honesty I had not the slightest inkling that the book would go as bananas as it did.

But first, through the good offices of Jill Foster, I met Douglas and John Lloyd in a pub in Argyll St, near the London Palladium. It must have been about the end of May 1978. The Argyll Arms is one of those noisy pubs, a great rectangle of a room divided into smaller bars by Victorian glass, and full of youngsters flirting urgently. Despite this, Douglas and I, being much the same height, managed to talk above the hubbub. We discussed Wittgenstein and quantum physics. Actually that's a fib. I could bluff and report what we said in immense detail, but all I can remember is that we talked about *Hitchhiker's* and SF in general, and that he surprised me by not having a philosophy degree. Instead, much more valuably, he possessed a philosophical turn of mind. I thought he was rather wonderful. John Lloyd was also on good form, but harder to hear in this ill-chosen venue. I do recall how the women in the pub instantly clocked him even though Douglas and I did not register on their radar at all.

The three of us got on tremendously well, and I remember thinking, as I made my slightly unsteady way home that evening, that if the offer were not too mean, we would be successful in acquiring the book.

Sonny Mehta recalls what happened:

> You came in [that's me] in your usual shambling way, saying there was this radio series you'd been listening to that you thought was really something, and that you figured we ask the writer of the scripts if he could turn it into a novel. That's roughly what happened. You gave me some of the tapes – I remember listening to them. It was a small contract, but when we published, it just went through printing after printing.

Editors are not sovereign in most publishing houses; they have to get the blessing of the right forum in order to spend the company's money. They do this at the editorial meeting, an institution that authors have learned to dread. Suppose, they fret, not entirely without reason, the committee gets around to my book, in which I've invested years of toil and anguish, after a long, fractious meeting, *and it's time for lunch.*

At the editorial meeting (nomenclature may vary), the editor makes a pitch about a book to his or her colleagues, usually with the sales director or some professional hard-nose also present. Publishing is a business to some extent concerned with managing failure (axiomatically most of what's published does not become a bestseller), so the people around the table are pretty cynical. They've heard it all before, and regard its repetition as an unnatural act. You might think this is a tough test for the work of a delicate author to endure, but it's not unreasonable. The editor can get the benefit of the pooled experience of those present, and if he or she cannot sell the book in-house, is it fair to expect the sales team to sell it to the trade?* After all, if you think the editorial meeting team sounds blasé, let me tell you its members are sweetness itself compared to the professional buyers in the big bookselling chains like W.H. Smith. These world-weary, etiolated people are so gorged on publishers' hype that they could scarcely raise a flicker of interest if a mile-high silver starship landed on their Swindon warehouse; they rank as amongst the most jaded on Earth, possibly in the entire history of the species.

But at the Pan editorial meeting, in an airless room in the middle of the building, Sonny Mehta and the rest of my colleagues smiled at my enthusiasm. After some haggling with Jill Foster over royalties and sub-right splits,† Pan acquired the world rights for an advance against all earnings of £3,000, half payable on signature of the agreement and half on publication. Douglas and John Lloyd were the original parties to the contract, but John Lloyd's name was later deleted – and thereby hangs a tale.

Although not a huge risk for Pan, in 1978 £3000 was a decent sum. John Lloyd says that at the time he was badly in debt, with an overdraft.

It seemed like a fortune. Writing together was perfectly natural. We'd written lots of things together – a pilot for the BBC, a film treatment, a cartoon series for that Dutch company. We'd tried lots of things and we were very close friends, we'd shared a flat together. We got on very well as writers because we weren't the same sort of writer, so there was very little competition; it was just a sort of cooperative thing. We laughed a lot; we had great fun.

---

* Publishing is a confidence game. The editor must believe in the author's work, and transmit that confidence to the rest of the organization that in turn must convey it to the trade. It's only after the trade has agreed to display the work that the public has a chance of buying it. It is possible to sit in a meeting and see the chain of confidence broken under one's nose, in which case it must be repaired quickly or else the book will probably fail.

† These define the percentages of the income from the sale of rights that flow through to the author's account.

Douglas, living in squalor with Jon Canter off the Holloway Road, was also thrilled to get an advance. He embraced the possibilities of having some spare change with childlike glee. Jon recalls Douglas nipping out to the local off-licence to buy some Coke, and coming back with an almost unmanageable crate of the stuff – because he could. He'd woken up to the realization that he could afford to buy in quantity if he wanted. Douglas, literally and figuratively, was never a single bottle purchaser again.

But when Douglas sat down to write the novel, he felt – as with his script and sketch writing – that he should do it on his own, without John Lloyd. He wrote to John suggesting that he alone wrote the book, and that he was sure that John would see the sense of doing things that way.

For all the complexities, John and Douglas were friends, and for many months they had been the thickness of a brick away at home and at work, so the fact that Douglas put all this in a letter was particularly hurtful to John. Why not talk, for goodness sake? It may suggest that Douglas found it a difficult subject to broach, but it is just as likely that he did it in all innocence, not anticipating that it would be a problem, but only knowing that one had to be formal about such under-standings. It was, as he explained in an interview with Neil Gaiman, his project. Although he had felt it might be fun to collaborate, when he realized he could do it himself, he changed his mind. He was within his rights, but as he admits:

> I should have handled it better. John Lloyd and I are incredibly good friends, but on the other hand we are incredibly good at rubbing each other up the wrong way. We have these ridiculous fights when I'm determined to have a go at him and he's determined to have a go at me.*

Douglas was taken by surprise by the vehemence of their row. But John was furious. Being fired off the book was a burning coal in his heart. He was humiliated. Years later, when both men were reconciled, it was

* *Don't Panic.*

still a subject that had to be stepped around as delicately as a sapper probing for a mine. Douglas, by then fully aware that he had been a clodhopper, rationalized that it had been good for John, for it had pushed him into telly where he became hugely successful. John, suffused with the benignity that follows the passage of decades and the extinction of a friend, says that Douglas's need to write the book on his own was vindicated by results. Nobody else could have captured his voice or done it so well. Of course, John explains, he sulked for a while, but now he understands that Douglas did the right thing.

However, at the time it hurt deeply. We tend to lie to ourselves about our friendships because such fibs reflect well on our own resources of emotional generosity. What's more, facing up to the possibility that friendships can sometimes be a matter of convenience requires us to be unflinchingly clear-sighted about the fallibility of human relations and the horror of loneliness. John and Douglas's relationship was a planet in a highly elliptical orbit. Sometimes it would be close to its star and basking in the warmth. Other times it would be remote and frozen – and at all times it would have a ferocious precession as it wobbled around an axis of envy and competition.

John was driven to find an agent to represent his interests. As a staffer, his creative work at the BBC was the property of the organization, but ventures out of house belonged to him. Besides, agents are enormously useful to serve as a toughie ('my partner, Mr Gradgrind') when you would find it embarrassing to fight a particular battle yourself. Mark Berlin, of London Management, had admired John since seeing him in revue at Cambridge, and was happy to take him on. Mark is tidy-minded, courteous, and steely when required. He has a filing system of an efficiency unparalleled in the history of the industry and can even find notes of telephone conversations that occurred a quarter of a century ago. John, Mark recalls, was hurt by Douglas's decision and said 'that he was not prepared to be Douglas's emotional football any longer'.

Mark and Jill Foster haggled as only agents can. It was all very civilized. Mark's advice to John was to ask for 15% of the income from the book in perpetuity, a better long-term bet in Mark's view than a more substantial share of the advance. The calculation of 15% was based on John's help with two episodes out of twelve, i.e. one sixth, rounded down to a more convenient number. John says that he would not hear of such an arrangement and chose instead the enhanced share of the advance. Perhaps he just wanted to draw a line under a painful wrangle by settling for a payment that would close the subject forever. Of course, he may have figured that a cheque in the hand is worth several in the future if you're broke, but he was also concerned with doing the decent thing. In the many complications of their relationship John and Douglas were adept at inducing subtle guilts in each other. In the end, after some toing and froing, John Lloyd's interest in the contract was bought out for half the advance, but with no continuing participation in any subsequent royalty income.

This is an interesting wrangle from the point of view of what m'learned friends have taught us to call 'intellectual property'. If John's contribution in the two episodes he co-wrote (out of twelve) had been to help devise the essential furniture of the narrative, then he would have been entitled to a small but proportional share of all the subsequent incarnations of the work. Even if he had wholly written two episodes, but without creating the infrastructure of the narrative, he would be entitled to share pro rata in any direct use of his material. But Douglas was careful not to use anything from episodes five and six in the book. This would have rendered the argument for continuing participation untenable. On the other hand, if you were prepared to be really bloody about it (which, to his credit, John wasn't), it may have been possible to negotiate some more money in order for the proprietor not to be troubled by any further encumbrance. Given that *The Hitchhiker's Guide to the Galaxy* went on to sell a million copies in record time, this must have been a bit galling for John, but he wasn't the victim of unfairness. Money was not the whole issue in any case. In the febrile world of dauntingly bright Cambridge smarties, it was fame, and especially the recognition of creative excellence, that were the spur.*

---

* Despite working for many years in a feral American corporation which prided itself, for some perverse reason, on its killer corporate culture, I have never come across such competitiveness – usually unstated – as that which prevails among the clever Cambridge media set that graduated with Douglas.

John was deeply cheesed off for years. Douglas may have needled him in a peculiarly sensitive spot. As a producer John has been inspirational, but it must be frustrating to be the nurturer of talent, forever out of shot when the public makes stars of those in front of the camera. As he said:

The thing is, Douglas was the first in our circle to make it. He was a rich person long before anyone else. Then Mel Smith got rich and put £3000 on a horse, and that seemed mad. Now lots of people one knows in the comedy snakepit own strings of racehorses so nobody thinks twice about bringing a bottle of champagne or ordering one. [Douglas had ordered a bottle of champagne in a Chinese restaurant to the bewilderment of the waiter and amazement of his friends.] But Douglas was always a step ahead, and it's more evidence that he went through life with a bag over his head; he didn't realize that people would be hurt. And yet, he used to say the same about me. Years later he said, 'I remember going to dinner once at your house, Johnny, and you said to me: "Pass the salt, you failure." And he'd carried that inside him for fifteen years of multi-millionaire success – this canker inside him saying, he hates me, he thinks I'm a failure. I think anyone who knows me will understand that I am just not capable of that kind of blatant cruelty. It was probably said as a joke or something . . .

Once, after Not the Nine O'Clock News [the huge TV hit produced by John], Sean Hardie, the producer, and I went for a rather miserable week to the South of France to invent a new project. We didn't really come up with anything – we'd been working too much together and too closely and had run out of things to say. But we did come up with this idea for a sitcom. It was called Rich Bastard. It was about this writer who's very rich and rather clodhopping in the way that Douglas was. It was slightly about him. [In the sitcom] he had this friend, who was a radio producer who he was always terribly, improbably jealous of – which was slightly the relationship we had. Whatever Douglas did, he always seemed to feel I'd bested him, including the business of having children first. He used to go around saying that bastard Lloyd's beaten me again.

The plan had been for Douglas and Lloydie to fly to Corfu (again). There they would write the book, and at the end of a righteous day at the word-face they would totter down through the cool of the evening and the scented, balmy air and reward themselves, while the stars came out, with a jolly meal and a bottle of retsina in the local taverna. With any luck they might be able to offer an option on their bodies to any passing female Scandinavian tourists . . .

Instead, Douglas repaired to the flat off the Holloway Road, a long way from the Greek islands in every sense. There he set about writing with what was (for him) grim method. This is what he took to his room: lots of Coke (the drink), a typewriter, several reams of A-4, a gramophone, and 'Wuthering Heights' by Kate Bush (for trance induction). He played it until he wore the needle out. Jon Canter, heroically good-natured, was worn out as well.

Alistair Beaton, the author and playwright, identifies four stages in the collapse of an author's self-esteem. They go roughly like this:

1) This is bloody difficult. I may be blocked.
2) Oh no, oh no. I can't manage this bit at all.
3) Gloom, gloom. Bloody hell. If I'm honest with myself I can't write any of it.
4) The truth is, I just can't write at all. I'm a fraud, and finally I have been found out.

Douglas did not get very far down the Beaton Scale for this first book, but he was a man who needed company. In solitude he could easily fall into a kind of gloomy vacancy. Writing, as well as all its technical challenges and its brain-bruising calls on invention and talent, is lonely, and the writer's world tends to shrink to just a room and the keyboard. John Lloyd says:

Douglas was determined to prove himself because he'd been a cooperative writer with Adams, Smith, Adams, Graham

Chapman, Ringo Starr and me. He'd never done anything, except for the famous sketch about the Kamikaze pilot, on his own. And so he was determined, when he got the contract to do *Hitchhiker's*, that he would do the damned thing himself and prove he was a proper writer.

Characteristically, Douglas delivered late. In his introduction to the compendium volume of the *Hitchhiker's* novels, he describes his delinquency like this:

> After a lot of procrastination and hiding and inventing excuses and having baths, I managed to get two thirds of it done. At this point they said, very pleasantly and politely, that I had already passed ten deadlines, so would I please finish the page I was on and let them have the damn thing.
>
> Meanwhile I was busy trying to write the second series and was also writing and script-editing *Dr Who*, because while it was very pleasant to have your own radio series, especially one that somebody had written in to say they heard, it didn't exactly buy you lunch.

Certainly the first novel judders to a halt with every narrative strand in suspension. At the time I imagined – naïve git that I was – that his abrupt finish was a deliberate literary device, a kind of playful suborning of the convention whereby fiction is so much tidier than life. Also the final page, in which the characters set off to the restaurant at the end of the universe, looked like a shameless means of whetting the market's appetite for a sequel. But no. Pan's fiction editor Caroline Upcher and Sonny Mehta had just got annoyed by being strung along by Douglas, who was not guilty of deliberate lies about delivery so much as optimistic and sincere self-deception. In *Don't Panic*, Neil Gaiman reports that Pan executives spoke with Douglas along these lines: 'How much have you done?' then, 'Oh dear, well, it will have to do – we'll send somebody to collect it.' Caroline does not remember such a conversation, and it would go against any publisher's grain to publish something incomplete. It's more likely that Douglas estimated that he would have rounded the story off more satisfactorily by the time the motorcycle messenger arrived – but he hadn't.

Pan's paperback had been catalogued, presented to the chains and a witty one-page flyer had been distributed all over the environment. The cover had been designed (Hipgnosis artwork with Pan's Ian Wright doing the layout) and printed, and was waiting on the binding line at Clays, the big book-printer in Bungay, Suffolk. The reps had subscribed the book to the trade, and the turnover anticipated in the annual budget. Just about everything that could be done had been done short of having the actual text. The point had been reached when they just had to have the book.

John Lloyd reported that to him at first the novel read rather too much like the work of the great Kurt Vonnegut.* The reviewers also picked up on this, though it has to said that the more Douglas wrote and rewrote, the more the voice became his own. He and Vonnegut do have much in common. Vonnegut is less explicitly comic, more darkly sardonic and more artful about narrative construction. Both writers have a sense of the absurd – though Douglas's is more cosmic – and they have mastered an immediate and conversational style that is easy to read, but hell to write. Vonnegut is a humanist; as he puts it so well in *God Bless You, Dr Kevorkian*, he has tried to behave decently without any expectation of reward or punishment after he's dead. He always seems melancholy about the human condition and the horrific things we can do to each other. After all, he witnessed the firebombing of Dresden, something so unspeakable that it took him over two decades to find a way of writing about it (*Slaughterhouse Five*). You can imagine Vonnegut banging his head on his desk and sighing with a blend of sarcasm and sadness at mankind's antics. Douglas, on the other hand, is less satirical; with the exception of *Last Chance to See*, he finds humanity not so much tragically graceless as comically odd.

Bizarrely, Vonnegut, despite pre-dating Douglas by a generation, was once reviewed by someone who said he had written a very

---

* If you haven't tried him, start at once. *Slaughterhouse Five*, *Player Piano*, *God Bless You Mr Rosewater*, *Breakfast of Champions* and *Galapagos* are essential reading.

Adamsy book, *viz* his superb novel, *Galapagos*.* That novel does indeed share Douglas's preoccupation with evolution. Vonnegut points out that in the long term big brains are not all that desirable from the evolutionary point of view. In a fragile world the possessors of them can use their intelligence to ruin the planet in ways unimaginable by a less intellectually endowed species (and, he asks, is intelligence an adaptation that makes for happiness?). Vonnegut's character who uses high explosives 'as a branch of show business' is a trope that Douglas would have been proud to devise. But in the literary antecedents game beloved by critics, it's clear that this had always been Vonnegut's voice – and he started writing when Douglas was scarcely taller than a dachshund.

The novel of *Hitchhiker's* was not the first reincarnation of the radio series. Ken Campbell, of the Science Fiction Theatre of Liverpool, had heard the series and had immediately thought it could and should be staged. He was very quick off the mark, and sought out Jill Foster to license the dramatisation rights. His was to be the first of many theatrical versions of *Hitchhiker's* that continue to this day. Including the amateur productions, these must number into the hundreds by now. There has even been a stage version of the horribly complex *Dirk Gently's Holistic Agency*, directed by Arvind David in Oxford, that Douglas liked very much.

Ken Campbell may only be familiar to people under twenty-five as a character actor on the box. He is a small, quick-witted baldy with bulging eyes and a manner so belligerent and fizzing with energy that if he were ever to take stimulants he would probably explode. His voice, still with Liverpudlian cadences, screeches with indignation. It can penetrate a bank vault door at a hundred yards and has the strangulated quality of a man who just a moment before has stopped screaming. But if we were ever to have Heroes of the British Isles (as they had of the Soviet Union), he would get many votes for services to theatre, fun and general subversion. In some ways, Ken Campbell is a similar spirit to Douglas – inventive, funny, somewhat amazed by it all.

---

* Published in the UK by Jonathan Cape, 1985.

The Science Fiction Theatre of Liverpool, founded in 1976, could not have been further from the luvvie world of the West End with all those nicely observed plays with sofas and French windows. Ken was not interested in miniatures; he liked a bigger canvas. One of his first projects was a 'Discordian production' ('We're Discordians – We Stick Apart'), in which anybody could take part. This was based upon the *Illuminatus!* trilogy by Robert Anton Wilson and Robert Shea. These books may be a fruitcake, but they are the giants of the fruitcake world – indigestibly rich, spanning thousands of years, and containing every possible paranoia-inducing or arcane ingredient you can imagine. The Illuminati are the ultimate conspirators with their octupoid fingers in a plenitude of pies – the Cathars, the masons, the Catholic Church, the great Pyramids, the Knights Templar, Atlantis . . . One seductive angle to the conspiracy is that the lack of evidence to support it, supports it, for surely only *they* – the Illuminati themselves – have the resources to cover their tracks up so completely. Fearing that *Illuminatus!* did not require sufficient commitment from its audience, being a mere eight hours, Ken's next production was *The Warp*, a twenty-two hour cult epic with breaks for food, hygiene and alcohol. According to Robert Anton Wilson, it also achieved the distinction of winning the prize for the greatest number of simulated blow jobs in one drama in the history of theatre.

Ken's approach to *The Hitchhiker's Guide to the Galaxy* was characteristically imaginative, quick and energetic. He says he had never heard of the programme until some fans rang him up and told him to listen. 'That seemed great,' he said. 'I mean, here was an audience demanding a show.'

The production took place with dazzling promptness (the end of May, 1979) in the Institute of Contemporary Arts, in Carlton Terrace, London. This elegant Regency building on the Mall (the wide avenue that runs from Trafalgar Square to Buckingham Palace) is possibly the poshest bit of real estate in London. The drama starts with the destruction of the Earth so, in order for the audience to feel fully engaged, Ken decided to take them off-planet. Proceedings began with the sale of Pan-Galactic Gargle Blasters, a cocktail that Douglas described as having an effect like being hit over the head with a slice of lemon wrapped around a gold brick. The performance kicked off in the foyer with the audience – only eighty or so per performance – sitting down on a raised dais. In fact this was a platform, devised by a man called Mike Hurst, mounted on industrial skates. These were designed to move massive bits of plant by floating them on a millimetre or two of air pumped under pressure through thousands of tiny holes.* Despite the weight, the result was almost frictionless, so the whole audience – with the platform, all seventeen hundred tons of it – could be moved around smoothly from set to set rather than sitting there like non-participant potatoes while underpaid ASMs changed the scenery in front of them. It was a radical and innovative idea, and the production was a huge success.

The show was also stunningly noisy, but *Tribune* magazine said in a review that 'the actors resisted the temptation to overreact against the din'. The two-headed Zaphod problem was solved by having two actors in a single suit. You couldn't get a ticket to save your life. More people were turned away than were let in.

It was a complete sell-out. Douglas was thrilled.

Inspired by the success of the first outing, Ken Campbell decided to restage *Hitchhiker's* the following year (July 1980) at the Rainbow, a huge, rather gloomy building in Finsbury Park, north London, that had started life as a confident 1930s cinema, suffered from a changing market for it was just too big to make economic sense, and eventually transmogrified into a funky venue for rock concerts. (More recently it was home to charismatic Christian evangelists, something that Douglas would have grieved about.) The Rainbow production was brave, but doomed. As Mike Simpson says in his *Hitchhiker's Guide*, the most charitable thing that can be said about this production was that it featured lasers, and was long. The critics excoriated it. The subtlety and wit of the original did not survive the big treatment happily. The most successful theatrical versions, like the Theatr Clwyd show directed by Jonathan Petherbridge, are quite intimate.

---

* For the borderline obsessive fan, I can report that the platform was supported by 22" diameter blue disc-skates from Rolair Systems and that Motivair supplied the compressed air from a 152DS Hydrovane Compressor. Even the *Stage*, the professional thesps' magazine, said it was technically brilliant, but added that the seating was insufficiently raked.

Another deal executed before the publication of the first book was for the recording rights. Perversely (for surely they knew what they had by now?), BBC Enterprises had once again passed on the audio opportunity, perhaps on the grounds that in record form the unabridged radio series would have required a three-album set – we're talking big vinyl platters here, don't forget, not CDs – or a double tape cassette. Both would have been expensive and daunting for the market. With the wisdom of retrospect the BBC feels nauseous about this now.

In 1979, Geoffrey Perkins had talked to several record companies that had expressed interest in issuing *Hitchhiker's* commercially. He was on the point of signing with one of them when the proprietor insisted on showing him a hardcore porn film, a hopeless misjudgement of the culture of his potential business partner. In the end, Geoffrey and Douglas decided on a small company, Original Records, that seemed in sympathy with the nature of the project and had specialized in comedy.*

Geoffrey assembled much of the original radio cast with a few minor changes. Susan Sheridan was on a Disney film so Cindy Oswin from the ICA production played Trillian. Deep Thought was not played by Geoffrey McGivern but by Valentine Dyall, the owner of a famously chocolatey voice.† Some of the radio music could not be replayed on a record for copyright reasons (for instance, it had come from albums already licensed exclusively to a record company). The new music, by Tim Souster, was regarded as a triumph. All in all, Geoffrey was pleased. The cutting had sharpened the narrative line and there were a number of improvements to the voice treatments and the effects. Some slightly more high-tech equipment was available and this time the team were better able to draw breath and think about what they were doing.

The double album sold remarkably well (over 120,000 units), especially as it was initially available only through mail order at £6.99 (including postage and packing) via a coupon, ostensibly written by

---

* This company has nothing to do with the present Original Records, a reggae music specialist.

† He'd been *The Man in Black* for a celebrated Home Service radio series.

Zarniwoop himself, at the back of the Pan paperback. The cheque had to be made out to Megadodo Publications. This coupon was taken out of later printings after Pan received complaints about fulfilment, and indeed Geoffrey Perkins reported that he and the cast never got paid for the first recording, something that made the second recording of *The Restaurant at the End of the Universe* 'a lot less interesting'. In fact there was a major problem with the royalties, with the result that Ed Victor, who became Douglas's agent pushed the company into bankruptcy when it defaulted. Original Records seem to have hurried the making of the second album to the extent that the quality suffered, but the first is superb, and if you have a copy, hang on to it. It is now a collector's item and quite valuable.

Douglas now was starting to make some money. It was not a tsunami of cash, but enough for him to buy a blue MG sports car. He went everywhere in it, possibly the ten yards to the pillar box at the end of the road and certainly down to Dorset to show it off to his mum and all the family.

Douglas was not one of nature's drivers. It's not so much that he was clumsy, it was more a matter of attention. He loved to talk, even in the car. He'd be making some fascinating point but he would not be focused on the six-axle forty-ton cement lorry with the pneumatic brakes that had improbably just stopped on a sixpence in the lane ahead. 'For God's sake,' you wanted to say, 'stop your mind zooming and pirouetting about the stratosphere and come down to road level.' When Douglas was driving a manual he would change gear from time to time as if he remembered that that's what drivers did.

When he became successful, and before he settled down with large, sensible, automatic saloons, he had flings (so reminiscent of his father's romance with Aston Martins) with several Porsches. The first one, a 911, he crashed into the Piccadilly underpass at Hyde Park Corner just outside the Hard Rock Café where a huge queue of people applauded with satirical cheeriness; nice Jacqui Graham, the Press Officer of Pan, had to come out in her little Renault and rescue him. He walked away from the car and never saw it again. He said he hated the car anyway: 'Going for a drive was like setting out to invade

Poland.'* Nevertheless, he bought another one of which he said: 'It was like taking a Ming vase to a football match.' (Buffs might note that an obnoxious Porsche driver features in *So Long, and Thanks for All the Fish*.) This second car he sold when he was in a militantly anti-smoking phase and Stephen Fry smoked in it – but he may have just fancied a new one anyway. The third was stolen and never seen again. The final sports car, like the ritual scene of cleansing at the end of a Hammer Horror movie, was totally consumed by fire at the Porsche garage when it was in for a service. After this, Douglas took a brief car holiday. In Douglas's account of the story, the garage still asked for their awesome bill to be paid on the grounds that they had completed the service before the fire broke out. Once Douglas took me for a ride in this last absurd vehicle. It was a 928 turbo. 'When you put your foot down,' Douglas explained, 'there's just the teensiest delay: it's the car asking you – do you *really* want to do this?'

All through 1979, the momentum of *Hitchhiker's* fame went on gathering. Douglas gave more and more interviews from his squalid flat, for it would have been bad form to invite journos to his workplace in the BBC. In August, he was Guest of Honour at the world annual SF convention. That year it was 'Seacon', held in the Grand Hotel, Brighton. There is a degree of contact between the writers and readers of SF that is not matched in any other literary genre. The writers get a weekend on expenses, a welcome boost to their egos and a valuable opportunity to get feedback straight from the market. In a sense all writing is talking to the readers, but it is – as far as I know – only SF that has formalized the process of turning the monologue into a dialogue via so many large and well-organized conventions. What's in it for the fans? They get to meet authors they admire and to enjoy the society of those with a similar interest. They also have fun and frequently drink too much.

In fact it was not long before *Hitchhiker's* spawned its own dedicated conventions. Only the year after publication there was 'Hitchercon' in the Albany Hotel in Glasgow (26–28 September 1980). Douglas – or the Big D as he was known – was guest of honour. There were many

---

* *Don't Panic.*

subsequent conventions and the Big D attended when he could in order to perform as himself – and receive a tremendous boost to his *amour propre*. An official fan club, ZZ9 Plural Z Alpha, with its own nifty and well-written magazine, *Mostly Harmless*, started in 1980. This was available on subscription for enthusiastic 'ZZ9ers', the nomenclature based on the coordinates at which Arthur and Ford are plucked from the icy vacuum of space by Zaphod's stolen Improbability Drive.

Usually at conventions like the one in Brighton – 'worldcons' to give them their slightly surreal title – there is no prize for radio. However, there is an award for the best SF representation other than in artwork or words. Rather to everybody's disappointment in Brighton, it was won by the film *Superman*, which received a polite round of applause. *Hitchhiker's* came second; the audience stood up and gave it a standing ovation, a fact not lost on the producers of *Superman* who were gracious enough to suggest that the order should have been reversed.

I was at that convention in the line of duty, but I'm embarrassed to admit that in a moment of weakness I met up with someone who thought a sound strategy for appreciating the Best SF Creature Costume Competition was to take illegal drugs. Alas, I remember very little. However, before being led astray, I had a date with Douglas for a beer. An incident that sticks in my mind was being displaced at the bar by a female fan (seriously enthusiastic as well as seriously female) who had pointed her bosom at Douglas with the kind of graceful singleness of purpose that one associates with naval guns swivelling for a broadside. Tactfully I departed, leaving Douglas with a huge, uncontrollable priapic grin on his phizzog. History does not record whether he kept himself entirely pure that weekend.

By the time Pan published *The Hitchhiker's Guide to the Galaxy*, Douglas was already in great demand. Jacqui Graham nevertheless did a relentlessly professional job of promoting him. There was no radio or TV station so obscure, no magazine or journal so esoteric that it did not get a letter, a copy of the book and a follow-up call. The list of interviews could be mistaken for Brad's Press Guide. From the *International Herald Tribune* to *Miss London*, Douglas did the lot. His signing session in Roger Peyton's celebrated Andromeda bookshop in Birmingham sold over 450 copies, a record unbroken to this day. On the road, being made a fuss of, on expenses, and performing the role he knew best, that of himself – he adored it, and was always a complete trouper. Autographing books until his arm ached, listening politely to the same question that he'd heard only thirty times that day and chortling appreciatively at its insight, telling jokes on cue, not over-running his allotted time, tailoring his anecdotes to the preoccupations of the interviewer, it was like days and days of stand-up to an audience that loved you before you even got on stage.

Even better for his morale was that he and Jacqui became, as we used to say in those days, an item. Jacqui Graham was an unattached, brainy, very elegant blonde who still looks much as she did then (though now happily married with children). She speaks of Douglas warmly but with a certain cool clarity. He was, she recalls, romantic, amusing, relentlessly self-absorbed, spoilt, vain, emotional, entertain-ing, given to extravagant gestures, unpragmatic, exasperating, and fun to be with most of the time. Theirs was not a relationship destined to last forever, but they enjoyed themselves while it did and remained friends.

The Hitchhiker's Guide to the Galaxy was published on 12 October 1979 as a Pan original, price 80p, with an initial run of 60,000 copies. That disappeared instantly. They reprinted, and reprinted again (this time at 85p), then again. Within three months the book had sold quarter of a million units, the first hundred thousand in only four weeks, and it had been number one in the *Sunday Times* paperback bestseller list since publication. It was reviewed everywhere. Philip Oakes interviewed Douglas at length in the all-important *Sunday Times*. There was a large picture of Douglas looking cool with the caption: 'Higher absurdity strikes it rich', and a chunky headline: 'Cultists find a guiding light'.

In the same paper, *Hitchhiker's* was selected as one of the Books of the Year by Philippa Toomey ('I am deeply grateful to Douglas Adams for *The Hitchhiker's Guide to the Galaxy*, just as good as the radio serial . . .'). Her choice was a welcome relief as most of the literati had plumped for Mary Soame's biography of Clementine Churchill, Volume Two of the Lyttleton Hart-Davis Letters (no, honestly) or the *Memoirs of Shostakovich* edited by Solomon Volkov. Douglas was sensitive about the fact that he did not often get considered alongside mainstream 'literary' – for want of a less tendentious word – material, so he was particularly pleased to be graced by that ultimate accolade of respectability: four intellectuals discussing him on Radio Three's Critics Forum.*

Five months later there was a hardcover edition of the work – now a collector's item – licensed by Pan and published by Arthur Barker, an imprint of Weidenfeld and Nicolson that specialized in library editions. (Library suppliers employed legions of nimble-fingered women on piecework who would prepare books exactly as local librarians preferred. There was a glorious inconsistency about this among librarians in different authorities.)

But on Wednesday 10 October, two days before the publication date, something happened that brought the reality home to Douglas like nothing else. By the evening of that day, when by chance he was having dinner with Terry Jones, the Monty Python, he was crazy with exuberance, quite incandescent with the knowledge of it.

As Douglas recounted this story (so it may have gained a little in transmission), Pan had arranged a signing session for him at 12 noon in London's premier SF specialist shop, Forbidden Planet, which was then in Denmark Street in the West End. Using their usual and very reliable car service, Jacqui Graham had arranged for a driver to pick Douglas up from his ghastly flat. But as they approached the venue, the going got very slow. There were people thronging the streets in unnatural numbers. 'I'm sorry, guv,' said the driver, 'but we're having trouble getting through. I don't know what's going on. I haven't heard of anything on the radio. Must be a bloody demo or a march or something.'

But it wasn't a demo, or a march. What had caused congestion in the West End that day was the huge crowd of people enthusiastically converging on Forbidden Planet to meet Douglas. A proposed one-hour signing session had fans queuing round the block, and it lasted so long into the evening that he was late for dinner. He had stopped the traffic.

It was the day that Douglas knew he was condemned to everlasting fame. He had made it.

---

* *Critics' Forum*, Radio Three, broadcast 26 January 1980, with Robert Cushman, Benedict Nightingale, Claire Tomalin and Richard Cork. They loved it.

chapter seven

Hearing the Music

'When I hear Mozart, I understand what it is to be a human
being; when I hear Beethoven, I understand what it is to be
Beethoven; but when I listen to Bach, I understand what it is to
be the universe.'

Douglas Adams, on BBC's Radio Four, *Private Passions*

Hamish Hamilton, the publisher, used to count Raymond Chandler
among his friends and authors, two categories of humankind then
more likely to overlap than in the current era of corporate media cartels.
He once wrote to Chandler asking for a pre-publication quote for a
book that Hamish Hamilton was about to publish. Publishers were
pretty shameless, even in the era of urbane gentlemen who thought it
bad form to poach each other's authors.

Chandler wrote back a wonderful letter about life in California, the
perils of alcohol and the state of his marriage. He didn't ignore the plea
for a quote. Instead he wrote something that has such profound
relevance to publishing then as now that it should be carved on every
editor's desk in 72-point Arial Bold. This chap, he observed, can
construct a perfectly grammatical and efficient sentence, but *he just
doesn't hear the music.*

Douglas heard the music. Writers often worry that they are losing
control of their prose, and are just letting it ramble on and on, with lots
of proliferating subordinate clauses, like that one, which take on a

momentum of their own, so by the time the readers have laboured to the end of a sentence, the main verb – a locomotive pulling a great train of carriages along the rails of grammar – has been quite forgotten. It's the kind of prose that is all too easy to write, but painful to read. One of the traditional correctives for this nasty literary complaint is to read aloud what you've written. When a sentence can only be read in a single breath if you happen to be a skin-diver or an orchestral flautist, it's too long.

Douglas Adams understood this deeply. He felt the rhythm of words, the lilt of a well-tuned phrase. His ear was acute, and this is something particularly important in comic writing when a clumsy word can drain the humour from a sentence. P.G. Wodehouse (to whom Douglas's work often pays homage) had the same gift; he would polish and polish his prose, pinning his pages of text to the wall of his study and editing them vertically so that gradually the pages moved higher as they improved. Plum, as Wodehouse was known to his friends, only promoted his text to his eye-line when it was perfect. Unlike Douglas, however, he loved composition and regarded life as a regrettable series of interruptions to writing. With Douglas it was the other way around.*

Douglas's style – funny, fluid, conversational and full of amusing tropes and inventive images – is clearly influenced by Plum. Is this Adams or Wodehouse, for instance?

He slid gracelessly off his seat and peered upwards to see if he could spot the owner of this discourteous hand. The owner was not hard to spot, on account of his being something of the order of seven feet tall and not slightly built with it. In fact he was built the way one builds leather sofas, shiny, lumpy and with lots of stuffing. The suit into which the man's body had been stuffed looked as if its only purpose in life was to demonstrate how difficult it was to get this sort of body into a suit. The face had the texture of an orange and the colour of an apple, but there the resemblance to anything sweet ended.

---

* Douglas describes his love for Wodehouse in his introduction to the Penguin edition of *Sunset at Blandings*.

This monster is Hotblack Desiato's bodyguard in *The Restaurant at the End of the Universe* (Hotblack, you'll recall, is taking a year off, dead, for tax reasons) but there's an affectionate nod in the direction of Wodehouse's description of the Reverend 'Beefy' Bingham, the massive Oxford rower who so nearly lost the heart of Gertrude, Lord Emsworth's niece, to the weedy but dangerous crooner, Orlo Watkins. Compare the rhythm of Douglas's piece, for instance, with this account of Lord Emsworth being saved from drowning by 'Beefy'.

> If there was one thing the Rev. Rupert Bingham, who in his day had swum for Oxford, knew, it was what to do when drowning men struggled. Something that might have been a very hard and knobbly leg of mutton smote Lord Emsworth violently behind the ear: the sun was turned off at the main: the stars came out, many of them of a singular brightness: there was a sound of rushing waters: and he knew no more.*

Douglas described his rediscovery of Wodehouse in an article in the *Guardian*.†

> I suddenly realized, with goose-pimples rising all over me, that I was in the presence of a great master.
> Since then I have devoured his work repeatedly and voraciously, not merely because he is a great comic writer, but because he is arguably the greatest musician of the English language I have ever encountered. He may not have anything to say about Real Life (he would hoot at the very idea) but art practised at that level doesn't have to be *about* anything.

Norman Mailer once said that Hemingway was a son of a bitch, but that as a writer he was one of those rare people who 'can write

---

* 'Company for Gertrude' from *The Collected Blandings Short Stories* by P.G. Wodehouse (Penguin Books, 1992).

† Quoted by Frank Muir in his smashing introduction to *The Collected Blandings Short Stories* by P.G. Wodehouse.

sentences that are impossible to change'. It's a good test. Take your favourite piece from one of Douglas's novels and try to substitute your own words for the ones he used. Nothing else works so well. Mailer was spot on about Hemingway, but of the other 'mainstream' writers, perhaps only Nabokov, at his most excruciatingly lapidary, placed words on the page with the same precision as Douglas or Plum at the height of their powers.

In many ways comedy is more difficult to write than 'serious' literature. The word 'serious' above is in inverted commas not because of any doubt about the quality of authors like A.S. Byatt and Iris Murdoch, with their fine observations of the velleities of human relations, but because it is possible to be serious *and* funny. Douglas's books are witty about big questions (the existence of God, what it is that can be said to be real, man's place in the universe . . .) but not so hot on the existential burdens of being an unhappy civil servant with a constipated love life. The reader can choose of course . . .

Douglas's sensitivity to the rhythms of a sentence was intimately connected with his love of music. His ears were opened back at school where he sang in the choir and had piano lessons. He did not have many opportunities for escaping from Brentwood and going to concerts, but in 1969 he did hear Jacques Loussier and his Play Bach band doing their subtle jazzy versions of Bach, and he was completely won over.

Douglas was admirably strong-willed about mastering technique. He had a finger-picking guitar style and would practise relentlessly until he had something off accurately. Usually he chose tunes that appealed to his romantic and complex nature, lyrical tunes you could lose yourself in. Douglas was no three-chord wonder; he would study all the trickiest guitar parts – Pauls Simon and McCartney were favourites – until he could play them fluently, twiddly bits and all. When he heard Procul Harum's *A Whiter Shade of Pale* in 1967 he pestered all his relatives to buy him the album for Christmas, and set about learning many of the tracks.

Sue Adams remembers that, as an adult, he took his binoculars to a Dire Straits gig at the Birmingham NEC and spent much of the concert, indifferent to the odd looks from those nearby, peering closely at Mark Knopfler's fingers. Then he had to mentally adjust what he saw to make it work for a left-handed guitar, which is strung so that the pitch of the strings is in the reverse order from a guitar tuned for a right-hander.

Interestingly, as a musician Douglas suffered from the same complaint that made all those clever Cambridge thespians reluctant to act with him on stage: for him ensemble playing was difficult. Ken Follett, the author, whose wife, Barbara, is the highly effective Labour MP for Stevenage, is famous for bestsellers like *The Eye of the Needle* and *The Pillars of the Earth*. He is less well known as a funky bass guitarist in the band Damn Right I Got the Blues. He jammed with Douglas a lot. Douglas's agent, Ed Victor (a man whose address book must encompass most of the known media world), had suggested that they might enjoy playing together – and they did.

Ken is one of the most articulate human beings on Earth.* He says:

I'm not a virtuoso – quite the reverse. The pleasure of music is sharing it with other people, usually guys. The buzz is making something collectively. So I like that, and I have – astonishing though it will be to my friends and family – not much of an ego when it comes to music. I'm happy to be the background guy playing the bass guitar. So when Douglas and I played together, I was really his accompanist. He was the virtuoso.

He could certainly play very complicated things on the guitar, and on his own he was fine, and with an accompanist who was willing to follow his tempo and his pace, he was fine. It was partly a matter of skill, and partly determination. He would spend time learning things. Wonderful, wonderful musicians like

---

* His interview for this book was the easiest to transcribe because he talks in well-rounded sentences without hesitation, an 'um' or an 'er', or changes of direction. His band, Damn Right I Got the Blues, would strut their stuff in a subterranean bar at the Frankfurt Book Fair. The group consists of writers and publishers who deep down want to be rock'n'roll heroes, and not media fashionables. They are really quite loud and urgent, and they play with enormous attack. All in all, pretty good. Douglas would occasionally perform with them as a guest artist.

Paul McCartney and Paul Simon make them up, and if you want to copy them you have first to figure out what they are, and practise a lot. Douglas was willing to do that. He could play very nicely. And he could play with one other person, so he and I were quite good together. We enjoyed ourselves. We performed in Miami at an American Booksellers' Association convention* to some applause, and we performed in a club in London called L'Équipe Française, once again to considerable applause.

But he had one serious flaw which prevented him from being a really good musician, and that is no sense of time . . . When you perform with a real band with a drummer, you have to listen to the drummer. The drummer in a rock band is like the conductor of an orchestra who sets the pace and keeps it. You must listen to him and play on his beat. Douglas, bless his heart, was not able to do this. So when he did appear with us he would play a brilliant guitar solo, but would finish it half a beat before the rest of the band.

Before reading too much into the observation that Douglas was just a smidgen out of time with the rest of the world, this is a good moment for a brief anecdote about Paul Simon.

Douglas nearly had a close encounter with Paul Simon, a musician he admired without equivocation. When Douglas became famous and loaded, he spent a lot of time in New York. During one sojourn in Godless Gotham he decided that he would like to meet Paul Simon. Douglas could be quite no-nonsense about approaching celebrities, and, such was his own fame and his infectious enthusiasm, he usually ending up meeting them. In case you imagine this was a severe attack of status chasing, he was just as assiduous about tracking down the less famous as long as they fulfilled the one vital criterion – doing something interesting. His joy at other people's achievements was engaging, and his generous admiration acted like a magnet.

Initially through Paul Simon's record label, and then onwards via

---

* They were the support band to the dangerously funky Rock-Bottom Remainders with stormin' Steve King on lead guitar.

his management company, tentative contact was established. The rich and famous have 'people', as in 'have your people call my people'. These people have hard eyes, careful haircuts, and easy smiles; they are paid to protect the privacy of their masters. Phone numbers are guarded by those whose jobs would not be worth a moment's purchase if they divulged them to the wrong sort of reptile. Soundings are taken, bona fides are checked and the supplicant's status and/or desirability are calculated, yea unto several decimal places. In short, getting access to the rich and famous is a gavotte with many tricky steps.

The vetting process was nearly complete. Douglas was adequately famous and clearly an abject fan of Paul Simon. A meeting was on the very point of being fixed when one of the aides asked, in a tone that did not appear to place that much freight on the question, 'By the way, how tall are you?'

In all innocence Douglas replied – probably with an amusing riff on the subject (Mount Rushmore may have featured) – that he was very, very tall, quite ridiculously tall in fact. There followed what Hollywood calls a beat. Time stretched like chewing gum. 'Umm,' said the aide finally, 'I'm sorry, but your meeting with Paul will have to be postponed . . .' The encounter was never rearranged. It is possible, of course, that they had just missed the moment, or that Paul's assistants were overly alert to the dangers of a photo opportunity. Paul Simon is five foot three.

Ed Victor, who is well over six feet tall and always elegantly turned out, commented on hearing this story that it was naïve of me to be surprised. 'Nick,' he said, 'surely you must have noticed along the way how much small men hate us. What's going through their minds, which you can almost see like a subtitle on a French movie, is: why him, why not me? *Why him, why not me?* Why does he have the height? Why was he given this gift?'

Douglas's mum, says his interest in music started early. From the time he was a chorister at school, his love of choral music was life-long. Mercifully he never sang in public after his voice broke.

Paul Wickens, aka Wix, also went to Brentwood, though a couple of years behind Douglas. Although they were not particularly close as schoolboys, James Thrift reckons that the relationship gave Douglas access to a lot of contemporary music. There was a family connection too; Wix's father, John Wickens, was the vet who looked after Grandma Donovan's many animals so the links between the two families go back to the 1950s.

Wix and Douglas were reunited in a way that is characteristically Douglas. Wix's partner, Margo Buchanan, the singer, describes it like this:

> I met the Big One [an affectionate nickname for Douglas used by family and close friends] after a Paul McCartney gig. He actually went to the same school as Wix and they shared a music teacher. Douglas used to sometimes come round to Wix's house and play with Wix's older brother, David, when he was a boy. They do go back a long way, but I think there was a four-year age difference – something like that – between them. Anyway, Douglas went to a Paul McCartney gig one night – you know what he was like [about the Beatles]. He'd got hold of a ticket – he was someone's guest, Robbie McIntosh's I think. And he was reading the programme and had got to the part about Wix. And Wix actually mentioned his music teacher in the little blurb about him. So Douglas went, hang on a minute, that was my music teacher. That can't be the same Wickens I used to go and play with as a child . . . I must find out . . .

Following this happy coincidence, Douglas and Wix became friends and went on to collaborate on a variety of music. Wix ended up writing much of the music for the *Starship Titanic* computer game.

Margo Buchanan, as well as singing with heart-piercing clarity, brings a gift of intuition to her friendship with Douglas and Jane. This is her recollection of how, after the McCartney concert, they all ended up in Soho at the Groucho Club.

> Douglas was at our table at the Groucho. He was extremely exuberant after the McCartney gig, sitting talking to McCartney . . . He loved the Beatles and Paul McCartney, he really did . . . Douglas was one of the nicest people I've ever met, once you got through that protective shell that he had. You know

the way some people could use intellect as a shield? I don't think he ever did that because his intellect was just too magnificent and interesting. But he did have a protective front which could be typically upper-middle-class Cambridge graduate, you know . . . And I think the reason for that was because he had a very tender side. Very tender, very vulnerable. And I think that sometimes the world used to bewilder Douglas. I think that when he heard stories of cruelty and war he was genuinely hurt and bewildered . . . There was an innocence – that's the word I'm looking for – there was an innocence about him that he was very adept at camouflaging. But if you knew him well, you saw it. It was an innocence, and he never lost it.

In his childhood Douglas was also exposed to the wonders of the classical canon. Judith Adams, his stepmother, was musical; she had studied in Paris and played the piano beautifully, as well as singing in a Bach choir. There was a grand piano in 'Derry' (the house in Stondon Massey) on which Douglas messed around. (One of the first things he did when he started making some dosh was to buy a good upright piano. By the time he moved to the permanent family home, in Duncan Terrace in Islington, this had become a concert grand.)

Sue Adams also recalls Douglas spending a lot of time as a boy with a local blind man, David James, who played the guitar with the passion of a man possessed. Sue says that he was a big influence. 'David was really into the guitar. He and Douglas used to play together for hours and hours.'

The romantic possibilities of music had not escaped Douglas either. Sue also recalls:

We had a young woman at my stepmother's house – I think she was Austrian and might have been an au pair. Douglas was completely and utterly smitten, and he would spend hours at the bottom of this massive great garden which had these great big circular flowerbeds in it. Down the bottom left-hand corner was this great big tree – and Douglas would spend ages down there serenading her on his guitar . . .

Such was Douglas's passion for music that it was around this time that he attended a lecture in Vienna by the great Hungarian composer, Gyorgy Ligeti,* despite the fact that he could not understand a word. This probably happened on the same legendary hitchhiking frolic that took him to the field in Innsbruck, but it is possible that it was during one of his high-speed holidays with his father in one of the Aston Martins. Ligeti, one of the most innovative modern composers who extended our sound palate in the most extraordinary way, is best known to the non-specialist public as the man whose *Lux Aeterna* was deployed to such mind-mangling effect in the film *2001: A Space Odyssey*. Ligeti, though Hungarian, gave his lecture in German, a language of which Douglas knew little more than *Ja, Nein*, and *Achtung! Engländer!* from his *Eagle* comic days. Nevertheless, Douglas caught something of Ligeti's meaning, and certainly understood the musical language. Afterwards Ligeti, who had spotted this huge youngster in the audience, apologized to him for being unintelligible. (For tonto buffs, Ligeti's *Volumina* provides the final dramatic chord of the first episode of *Hitchhiker's*, and the *Kyrie* from his *Requiem* plays quietly at first, but with gathering urgency, as Slartibartfast takes Arthur Dent into the heart of Magrathea in the third episode.)

Douglas's passion for music and the sensitivity of his ear were manifest in the way he and Geoffrey Perkins, the producer, put together the soundscape of the radio series of *Hitchhiker's*. From the first seductive sounds of the opening theme (the Eagles' superb track 'Journey of the Sorcerer' from the album *One of These Nights*), the care with which the sound effects and the music were married to the spoken voice was clear. The brilliant execution owed much to Paddy Kingsland (the boss), Dick Mills and Harry Parker of the BBC Radiophonic Workshop and the studio team led by Alick Hale-Munro, whose joy in their work is obvious. They all deserve a mention: Max Alcock, Lisa Braun, Colin Duff, Paul Hawdon, Martha Knight, John Whitehall and

---

* It's difficult to confirm the time and place via Ligeti. He was a professor at the College of Music in Stockholm at the time, but had been in Vienna (after leaving Budapest in 1956) before going to Darmstadt and he returned to Vienna quite often.

Eric Young. On one occasion, recounted by Geoffrey Perkins in his introduction to the radio scripts, they insisted on keeping going *without claiming overtime* because the budget was so limited. (In the industrial climate of the time, BBC technicians waiving their right to overtime is rather like saying that the speed of light is not constant. It shows a love that passeth all understanding.) Every bit of *Hitchhiker's* often irritating technology had its own distinctive acoustic signature, from the leaky steam-valve clank of Marvin to the whosh of those bloody Sirius Cybernetics Corporation doors with their centre-fold voices and relentless cheerfulness. The sophistication of the sound picture had come a long way since 'Door Slam, sound of running feet, AAGH'.*

Douglas said:

> I wanted *Hitchhiker's* to sound like a rock album. I wanted the
> voices and the effects and the music to be so seamlessly
> orchestrated as to create a coherent picture of another world –
> and I said this and many similar sorts of things and waved my
> hands around a lot, while people nodded patiently and said 'Yes,
> Douglas, but what's it actually about?'[†]

He was certainly aware of how to create a universe in sound – how sound can be used to model the world, and what it must be like if that model breaks down. Breaking down our model of the world is in a sense what a lot of his work is about.

As an easily disoriented mammal, Douglas himself had an ear like Jodrell Bank. The radio series of *Hitchhiker's* created the sense of inhabiting a three-dimensional world through the use of sound. (Later even the TV series – despite its clunky effects and the tension between Douglas and Alan Bell, the producer – won several Bafta awards, one of which was for best soundtrack.)

---

* The hugely influential Goons were the first to understand how much humour could be wrung from special effects. Remember the thunder of the artillery barrage? 'What is happening?' asks Eccles. Reply: 'They're shelling peas in the kitchen . . .'

† See Douglas's introduction to *The Hitchhiker's Guide to the Galaxy: the Complete Radio Scripts* (Pan Books, 1985).

'Too much Mozart,' Douglas was fond of saying, 'is an oxymoron.' But among composers, Bach, he believed, was a genius almost off the scale. His quote about seeing the universe in Bach is interesting. There are so many harmonies and periodicities in the cosmos at large (and at the microscopic scale) that once you see them, you also see their beauty. Every bit of information stands in some relationship to every other bit, and this can be expressed – as Pythagoras believed – in the divine dance of numbers. In *Dirk Gently's Holistic Detective Agency* Douglas suggests that the erosion patterns of the Himalayas might make a flute quintet. Numbers can describe the movement of galaxies, the replication of cells, or even – according to one of Douglas's engagingly wild ideas on the lecture circuit – corporate accounts. Every corporation could enjoy its unique tune.

A love of mathematics and of music often go together. In Douglas's case it wasn't so much the maths that fascinated him, as the patterns – patterns that he found both in the lilt of a sentence and the fractal shapes of the Mandelbrot set. His enthusiasm for scientific connections knew no bounds, and this related to the way he thought. Some people seem to have better pattern-recognition abilities than others. Einstein once described Niels Bohr's speculations about quantum mechanics as 'the highest form of musicality in the sphere of thought'.[*] Incidentally, have you ever wondered if Albert Einstein was any good on the fiddle? 'Perfectly correct, totally uninteresting', apparently.

The *Voyager 1* and *2* space probes, launched in 1978, are both currently beyond the orbit of Pluto. They are by far the most travelled artefacts ever made by mankind – at distances now measured in light hours. *Voyager 2* is almost out of the heliopause altogether. For any alien that may chance upon them, welded to the sides of both craft is a gold-plated copper data disk that contains sounds and images of our species and its outstanding achievements. Along with an eclectic collection of African percussion, aboriginal chants, Chuck Berry's 'Johnny B. Goode', a message from Kurt Waldheim of the United Nations (inadvertent truthfulness there about mankind) and so on, Carl

---

[*] Quoted by Charles Flowers in *Instability Rules* (Wiley, 2002). It is the same source for Einstein's anonymous accompanist.

Sagan's team included some Bach – the first movement of the Brandenburg Concerto no. 2 and the Prelude and Fugue no.1 from The Well-Tempered Clavier. On hearing about the Bach, Douglas remarked, apropos of the potential extraterrestrial investigators: 'Won't they think we're boasting a bit?'

J.S. Bach fascinated Douglas. For one thing, Bach's prodigious output of music was limited only by the physical process of getting the notation down. It is scarcely imaginable that something like the Agnus Dei from Bach's B-Minor Mass (surely the most exquisite noise ever to penetrate the ear of man) could have been composed as fast as Johann could move his scratchy quill over the parchment. Douglas, who could spend a day in anguish over a single line, was in awe of such creativity. His own genius on the page was much more hard won. For all his skill on his guitar, he could not improvise easily like those to whom musical fluency seems to come like the gift of grace – and in the same way he could not spontaneously invent text.

With success, at the improbably early age of twenty-six (just like Dickens with whom there are several parallels),* came fame, and this opened up a new dimension to Douglas's passion for music. The massive and sudden success of the first book (in 1979) also provided lots of money, and one of the first appetites to be indulged was music. It was at this point that Douglas embarked upon a lifelong quest for the perfect guitar. Ken Follett says:

> Don't forget that guitars are very beautiful. People buy them for their looks as well as for what they sound like, and the last one Douglas told me about was a bass. Because I play the bass he thought I'd be interested, so he said: 'I've bought a left-handed Hohner bass.' And I told him it didn't have any significance for me at all – which was of course stupid because that was what Paul McCartney bought in Hamburg in 1961 . . . So Douglas had

---

* Douglas and Charles Dickens had much in common. They both loved performance, they both made it big when they were only twenty-six, they both toured America getting knackered, they both wrote women characters who were deeply soppy. Dickens, with his prolixity and emotional manipulation, is better on telly than on the page, whereas Douglas is the complete opposite.

bought one of these – it can't have been very long before he died and he was very pleased about it. He was going to learn to play the bass. I'm sure he would have actually.

Douglas ended up with twenty-four left-handed guitars and one right-handed one for visiting right-handed musicians like Dave Gilmour of Pink Floyd. Once, on a lecture tour in the States, he made a special diversion to Austin, Texas, where there is a famous guitar emporium, solely in order to gawp, and then buy another. Undoubtedly he knew a lot about the instrument. He even interrupts the slow mutual seduction of Fenchurch and Arthur Dent for a teasing, but accurate, aside about Dire Straits: 'Mark Knopfler has an extraordinary ability to make a Schecter Custom Stratocaster hoot and sing like angels on Saturday night, exhausted from being good all week and needing a stiff beer . . .'* (And he names one of his characters, Kate Schechter, in the Dirk Gently novels, after a guitar.)

All these instruments, many mounted in custom frames, led Douglas's friend, Jon Canter, to describe the top floor of the family home in Islington as Guitar Henge.

All his life, Douglas succumbed to gadgets; forever telling himself that one more Sharp IQ, PDA, Casio databank or, above all, a laptop computer would really get him organized. Objectively he was too intelligent to believe this, and he knew that the rate of obsolescence was such that if you dropped the new toy it would probably be out of date by the time it hit the ground. Nevertheless, a new electronic gizmo, murmuring 'buy me, buy me, big boy' was hard to resist. He had a special weakness for Apple Macs, and in fairness he understood the implications of Information Technology years before the rest of us. There is something child-like in many men, but most of us do not have the money to be put to the test. We therefore pretend that when we do not buy toys, it is a sign of maturity.

Another of Douglas's indulgences was all the more seductive because it combined his love of music with his love of gadgets. He bought stereo systems the way Renaissance popes made chapels –

---

* *So Long and Thanks for All the Fish* (Pan Books, 1984).

expertly commissioned, horrendously expensive, shoehorned precisely into the available space. His sound systems were a thing of wonder, finally achieving perfection in Duncan Terrace.

Duncan Terrace is strikingly light and handsome with some spectacular rooms for parties. On the first floor (the second for Americans) is a rectangular room, maybe forty feet long, with three floor-to-ceiling sash windows at the end facing the street. It's an elegant space with excellent acoustics. This room was to become home to squashy sofas and a TV large enough for one to expect a woman selling choc-ices to appear in every commercial break. It was also to house one of the world's great stereo systems.

When Douglas and Jane Belson finally had the family home sorted, after years of building and architectural tweaking, they specified that the loudspeaker leads must be integral to the extent that they run under the polished wood floor.

The first system to be installed had half-inch-thick, vacuum-sealed double-insulated loudspeaker cables, gold-plugged at each end, popping up from the floor boards into the back of two seven-foot-tall, austerely elegant Japanese screens. Only they weren't Japanese screens at all, but large, flat, state-of-the-art Magnaplanar electrostatic speakers that produced sound by warping and vibrating their entire surface, thus producing, as any buff knows, 'a quasi-omnisphere, figure of eight, bi-directional out-of-phase dispersion pattern'. Douglas loved the technical copy, but before spending a small fortune, he thought he'd better listen to the actual speakers first. He, Jane and Rick Paxton, the charming architect of Duncan Terrace, went off to a house in Wimbledon to hear the Magnaplanars *in situ*. The security in this mansion was so tight that allegedly wild animals selected for their unfriendly dispositions roamed the estate. Anyway, Rick is sure that it was something more exotic than your usual Alsatian.

Douglas and Jane had a fierce spat over these speakers. Douglas fancied them something wicked, but Jane, burdened as she is with taste, thought they dominated the room. It was not quite a matter of choosing between Jane and the speakers, but Rick recalls that the atmosphere became distinctly gelid before a compromise on location was reached.

These monsters required a hefty signal to drive them. Douglas was persuaded that valve-amplifiers produced a warmer sound than solid state machines. Just possibly his ear was acute enough to hear a difference. When he turned the system on needles flickered in distant power stations and there was a slight whoompf, like a far-off mortar, from outside the room. This was the automatic extractor fan coming on to vent the heat from two thousand-watt valve amplifiers, one per channel, that lived in the specially designed cupboard under the stairs. The whole system cost – and this was the eighties – just a tad over £30,000. I remember we had some badinage on the subject:

'Fucking hell, Douglas,' I said wittily. 'Thirty grand for a stereo. That's pretty decadent. Our house in Hackney cost that.'

Douglas blushed, a pretty effect on a surface so large. 'Actually,' he said, '*honestly*, the system was a bit of a bargain. You can spend much more at this end of the market. Besides, the suppliers threw in the phono cartridge – twenty-five hundred quid's worth – for free.'

How Douglas spent his money was his choice, after all. He was not a man for floating tupperware gin-palaces or shared legs of race-horses; nor did he belong among the affluent who invest in art so that it can advertise their taste while increasing in value. It was because he genuinely loved music that he wanted the best possible reproduction of it. He possessed an ear (his right actually, as he was a tiny bit deaf in his left) educated enough to appreciate the nuances.

But, you will be wondering, what did this thirty grand's worth of equipment *sound* like? Does the law of diminishing returns apply with a vengeance here, as in other areas of conspicuous consumption? A £20 meal may be twice as good as a £10 meal, but can a £100 meal be ten times as good?

In this case, however, the sound was astonishing. It might not have been as loud as the noise made by Disaster Area, the heavy metal band in *The Restaurant at the End of the Universe*, for which the ideal listening position was in a concrete bunker thirty miles away, but it approached the pain threshold if wound up to maximum. It also boasted amazing definition and clarity. Beatles albums that I thought I knew acquired new colour. Not a scrap of information imprinted on the original vinyl or CD was lost. In classical music the sheer physical effort of playing was apparent even to the musically uneducated. The friction of the strings, the movement of the bodies, the scrape of chairs moving on concert platforms, the sigh of the conductor making some athletic Guilini-type gesture – all the ambience of live performance somehow materialized around you, only better, for no concert hall boasts acoustics as brilliant as absolutely top-end stereo equipment. You wanted to look behind the sofa to see if Douglas and Jane had cunningly hidden an orchestra somewhere in the room.

Douglas's record collection – both vinyl and CD (that saviour of the record companies which reissued the back catalogue at twice the price) – was stunning both in number and the catholic eclecticism of his taste. It was large enough to be housed in bespoke CD cupboards of blond wood the length of the wall in that half of the drawing room nearest the street. He could have stocked a medium-sized record shop.

Incidentally, his next generation stereo went solid state. Douglas got irritated by the frequency with which he had to replace valves, and the nearly ubiquitous use of a digital sound source had come to favour amplifiers specifically designed to cope with it. The speakers changed to the large Nautilus design whose intriguing tapered rear-facing cones and snail-like Fibonacci coils mop up the reaction energy from the speakers so completely that the sound emerging from them suffers almost no interference, and is thus exceptionally unmuddied. The amplifier, CD player, turntable and radio were all housed in a large free-standing cabinet of considerable stylishness and incorporating every imaginable technical goody. The CD player looked as if it was carved out of a solid lump of slate and titanium.

But none of this kit could match the delight of live performance. Douglas wanted to hear live music in his own house and so set about getting to know some world-class musicians. One of them was Robbie McIntosh, known in the music world as the guitarists' guitarist. His touch combines precision and passion. Here's what Douglas said about him:

Robbie McIntosh is one of the world's best guitar players, and also one of its most incompetent human beings, as anyone who has watched him trying to buy a shirt will tell you.

We first met years ago when he walked up to me in a bar and said that one of his best friends knew my grandmother very well. Good opening. It was Wix he was talking about, or Paul Wickens as I knew him when we had the same piano teacher at school. Robbie and Wix were both in Paul McCartney's band at this time (no, not that one).

Before that, Robbie had been lead guitarist in The Pretenders, and has also played for Talk Talk, Tears for Fears, Paul Young and even Cher. When he's not jetting round the world playing vast stadiums, he tends to sit at home in Dorset looking after his goats and chickens, and tinkering. Actually, let me correct that last sentence. When he's not jetting round the world playing vast stadiums he tends to sit at home in Dorset being looked after by his goats and chickens, and tinkering.

I asked him what he'd been tinkering at, and he showed me. I should mention at this point that I am myself a passionate, though not very good, acoustic guitarist, so Robbie decided to play me some of the acoustic guitar pieces he'd been tinkering with down in Dorset. I was transfixed. It was some of the most mesmerizing music I'd heard in years. Most of the pieces were original, but some of them were arrangements of old folk tunes, Elvis Presley, Chopin, blues . . . What they all shared was an apparently simple melodic surface with a wonderfully rich internal life of harmony and counterpoint, which meant that each piece grew and grew in your mind with every listening. It's technically complex, but there's no showing off. All the technique is there just to serve the music. It's not folk, it's not jazz, it's not pop, it's not classical, it's just pure, pure music. The real stuff. Complex. Simple. Breathtaking.

I played the tapes Robbie gave me incessantly, and it quickly became one of my favourite-ever albums. People would sit in my care and say 'What is this?' Over a period of years I gradually coaxed and nudged Robbie into making an actual CD of it and letting my company, The Digital Village, release it. It took an astonishingly long time, but it is astonishingly good. The reasons for both of these things are contained in my opening paragraph.

There's one more thing I should add. Robbie McIntosh is one of the nicest people in the world.*

Another famous rock musician that Douglas befriended was Procul Harum's Gary Brooker, now a drily amusing silver-bearded chap in his fifties. Margo Buchanan, who knew him well, had arranged an introduction following a meal during which Douglas had banged on about how much he loved Gary's music. Douglas had played Procul Harum's *Grand Hotel* again and again while writing *The Restaurant at the End of the Universe*. This was a pattern with him: whenever he was chained to his keyboard with a book, Douglas would play certain pieces with demented repetitiveness, almost as if he were deliberately trying to induce some state of fugue or trance in which he would be exulted enough – or mad enough – to write without pain.

For those of you under a certain age, Procul Harum was a band famous for a song called *A Whiter Shade of Pale* which dominated the singles charts (a Deram label EP – remember those?) in the summer of 1967. It was music to get stoned to; it was slow enough to smooch to if you were lucky. It's a great song, with strange, poetic, slightly anxiety-inducing lyrics by Keith Reid and a piercingly atmospheric, almost hymnal melody that Gary Brooker admits to having been inspired by Bach's Air on a G-String. The song is so evocative, so arcane, so downright enigmatic, that there is a minor scholarship industry, active on the net, dedicated to working out what the hell it means. Procul Harum, though some of its personnel changed, went on to produce a lot of good music, but *A Whiter Shade of Pale* just caught a moment. (Once, indeed, it was used in a Dr Who episode, but not one written by Douglas.) *AWSoP*, as it's known to the buffs, is a classic that will always haunt them, and by and large there are worse things to be haunted by than a song.

From time to time Gary Brooker reformed the band, and he also had his own group, The Gary Brooker Ensemble, that played with many of the biggest names in the business (Stevie Winwood, Eric Clapton and

---

* Douglas's note on Robbie McIntosh, written in Santa Barbara 1999, from the WholeNote website.

178 Wish you were here

so on). Rather than attempt to encapsulate his career, here are Douglas's own words from a speech he made introducing the sell-out Procul Harum and London Symphony Orchestra concert that took place in the Barbican on 8 February 1996:

> I have loved Gary Brooker and Procol Harum ever since nearly thirty years ago when they suddenly surprised the world by leaping absolutely out of nowhere with one of the biggest hit records ever done by anybody at all ever under any circumstances. They then surprised the world even more by suddenly turning out to be from Southend and not from Detroit as everybody thought.
>
> They then surprised the world even more by their complete failure to bring out an album within four months of the single, on the grounds that they hadn't written it yet. And then in a move of unparalleled marketing shrewdness and ingenuity they also actually left *A Whiter Shade Of Pale* off the album. They never did anything straightforwardly at all as anyone who's ever tried to follow the chords of *A Rum Tale* will know.
>
> Now they had one very very particular effect on my life. It was a song they did, which I expect some of you here will know, called *Grand Hotel*. Whenever I'm writing I tend to have music on in the background, and on this particular occasion I had *Grand Hotel* on the record player. This song always used to interest me because while Keith Reid's lyrics were all about this sort of beautiful hotel – the silver, the chandeliers, all those kind of things – suddenly in the middle of the song there was this huge orchestral climax that came out of nowhere and didn't seem to be about anything. I kept wondering what was this huge thing happening in the background? And I eventually thought, it sounds as if there ought to be some sort of floorshow going on. Something huge and extraordinary, like, well, like the end of the universe. And so that was where the idea for *The Restaurant at the End of the Universe* came from – from *Grand Hotel* . . .

Given a choice of venues, Margo says that musicians love small, intimate ones like pubs; you can see the whites of the audience's eyes and get instant and gratifying feedback. There's nothing like it. But pubs don't pay anything, and hiring a van to move the equipment means that the musos are often out of pocket. It's not worth the hassle. She was lamenting this one day in Douglas's company, and he just went quieter and quieter while the cogs turned. 'Well,' he said eventually, 'I've got this great idea. You should come and play in my house. It's a good room, and quite feasible . . .' And so began a legendary run of parties.

All through the nineties, until their departure to California, Douglas and Jane threw some wonderful parties in Duncan Terrace. Once or twice a year they'd organize the added draw of live music, and these were called Douglas and Jane's Partially Unplugged evenings (a reference to Paul McCartney's 'Official Bootleg' *Unplugged* album).*

These evenings were magical. First there would be champagne – lots of it, gallons and gallons in fact. Jane Belson has a rule to serve only champagne or white wine. Though they wreak havoc with the higher cognitive functions, they do less mischief to the surroundings than red wine. A suave local caterer would provide delicious little nibbly things on sticks; this company made superior party food and seemed to have a policy of only employing sexy young things who looked good in black. Douglas and Jane were exceedingly generous hosts; that kind of entertaining is expensive.

The guests were the brightest and the best from the media and the law. The term 'élite' is frowned upon these days. Some people find it to be triumphalist and implicitly snotty, but this useful little word undoubtedly describes the guests at the Partially Unplugged parties. You couldn't move for actors, film people, writers, stand-up comedians, barristers, telly presenters, scientists, technology billionaires, even a publisher or two . . . You found yourself forever on the point of greeting someone as a long-lost old friend, one whose name had just slipped through a lacuna in your brain, until, waking up, you'd realize that the

---

* There was one for Polly Adams's birthday, a near Saturday anyway, on 24 June 1995, another on 30 March 1996, and 16 November 1996 and, of course, one for Douglas's forty-second birthday on 12 March 1994. A truly amazing party also – a Farewell to Britain, off to Hollywood debauch – on 10 July 1999. This list, not exhaustive, courtesy of Sue Webb's addiction to diaries.

familiarity of the phizzog was not friendship blurred by time but the spurious intimacy of telly. Jonathan Porrit would be chatting to Stephen Fry, Richard Dawkins to Clive Anderson, Clare Francis to Lenny Henry, Kathy Lette to Terry Gilliam, Melvyn Bragg with Ben Elton. Salman Rushdie was often there, radiating intelligence and looking very dapper for a man under siege from a *fatwah*. His Special Branch minder would blend in almost invisibly. There was the odd, very rare spliff, but dope was not a feature of Douglas's parties. Douglas said that he'd tried it once and didn't like it very much and Jane would not countenance the house being used for anything illegal. When the guests were truly warmed up, the lights would dim and the music would begin.

Of course, there were people present who would not have stopped flirting, or talking shop, even if Horowitz had been playing a duet with God himself. This was a crowd of people quite pleased to be in each other's company. Fortunately the house was quite big enough for the party to continue on different floors with people drifting in and out as the mood took them.

For those who favoured the music the evenings were bliss. It was a privilege to hear musicians of the calibre of Robbie McIntosh, Wix, Margo, and Gary Brooker doing their stuff in a setting of such warmth and intimacy. Sometimes Michael Bywater would show off his virtuosity at musical parody on the big piano. Dave Gilmour of Pink Floyd would occasionally join in, improvising with Robbie McIntosh with the ensemble precision of Charlie Parker and Dizzy Gillespie on a good day. (Douglas knew Dave Gilmour through two connections: Nick Mason's wife, an actress, who was working on a show produced by a friend of Douglas's, and Dave's wife, the writer Polly Samson, knew Jane.)

Hearing such musicians enjoying themselves in a friend's front room was like being allowed to eavesdrop on something very special. The music was intimate and lyrical; the sort of music to liberate the imagination. The musicians performing in Duncan Terrace were not just a bunch of mates having fun; they were the rock aristocracy having fun. You had to pinch yourself sometimes to remember that these were the finest in the business. It was as incongruous as having some violinist bear down upon you in a Hungarian restaurant – and realizing it was Nigel Kennedy.

Dave Gilmour was famously able to return the favour. Douglas and Jane held a particularly extravagant party for Douglas's forty-second birthday in March 1994. This had a special significance – though Douglas's tongue was lodged firmly in his cheek on the issue – because of the cultish preoccupation with the number forty-two.

Dave Gilmour's imaginative present to Douglas was in the form of a permit that, with suitable flourishes and calligraphy (is there a font called School Diploma?), empowered Douglas to appear in concert with the Floyd and play one guitar solo. As the Pink Floyd had a gig coming up in the giant Earl's Court venue in the autumn, this was a gift of more than academic relevance. Douglas was thrilled beyond measure. When the time came (28 October 1994), Dave Gilmour invited him onto the stage to warm applause, and Douglas played a solo at Earl's Court with Pink Floyd backing him artfully and atmospherically as only they can. By all accounts he had practised and practised this number until the household could scarcely bear to hear it again. On the day itself he did not participate in any of the high-spirited backstage messing about beforehand, but holed up rather anxiously in a corner, and practised again. He was good, and played the piece with great skill. He finished – not that anyone minded – just half a beat behind the band.

The following year Douglas gave an interview in which he reported that he'd heard that someone in the audience had asked: 'Which one is Douglas Adams?' His companion had replied: 'The old, fat, balding one.' And the first bloke said: 'But *which* old, fat, balding one?'[*]

At this time the Floyd had just recorded what was to be *The Division Bell*, one of their most subtle albums; as yet, however, they had not decided what to call it. Dave Gilmour was agonising over this; nothing struck the musicians as quite right. Even when you are as big as Pink Floyd, so the name of the band rather than the album is the brand, you still want an engaging title.[†] According to legend, Douglas told Dave

---

[*] Interview with Duncan Fallowell,1995.

[†] Oddly much the same applies to books. Bestselling authors, whose names on their books are huge and embossed (and whose titles are mere footnotes), still twitch in case they come up with something so doggy that it inhibits potential buyers at the point of sale.

Gilmour that he had the title, but that Dave had to write a cheque for £25,000 on the spot made out to the Save the Rhino Foundation before Douglas would tell him. After some muttering, Dave agreed. 'The title's right there in the lyrics,' said Douglas – hence *The Division Bell*.

Those musical evenings in Islington, surrounded by family, friends and celebrities, gave Douglas enormous joy. He'd sit close to the musicians with an ecstatic grin, moving only to fetch someone whom he felt should share the pleasure. He always felt bereft if someone he loved was missing out on something wonderful. Sue Adams tells a story of staying in the house in Santa Barbara when Douglas and Jane had driven down to Los Angeles for a Paul McCartney and Dave Gilmour concert. In high excitement, Douglas phoned her from the auditorium. 'Listen to this,' he said, holding his mobile phone above his head. 'Just listen.' And Sue listened to a wall of sound relayed through the tiny microphone of a mobile.

Of course, it was gratifying to Douglas's ego that he could persuade such artists to come to Islington. He would have to have been exceptionally free from vanity (he wasn't) not to have felt at such times like a patron of the arts, the Cosimo di Medici of Islington. But anyone who saw him could not doubt that his was the joy of genuine musical appreciation.

He felt music deep in the heart of him, and his sensitivity to it was inextricably linked with his sensitivity to the cadences of language. Music was a passion that lasted all his life.

chapter eight

Whooshing by

'**Farnham** (n)
That feeling you get about four o'clock in the
afternoon when you haven't got enough done.'

The Deeper Meaning of Liff

'You write with ease to show your breeding,
But easy writing's vile hard reading.'

Clio's Protest, Sheridan

When *The Hitchhiker's Guide to the Galaxy* went straight in at number
one in the charts (number one with a bullet, as they say in the music
world) and stayed there, two things happened. First of all Douglas,
laughing hugely at his own self-indulgence, went out and bought his
short-lived Porsche 911. The second was that, unsurprisingly, Caroline
Upcher and Sonny Mehta at Pan wanted a sequel, and soon agreed
terms, for much, much more money, with Jill Foster and Douglas for
*The Restaurant at the End of the Universe.**

Meanwhile the success of *Hitchhiker's* had attracted the attention of
publishers around the world. They all keep an eye on the charts and a
lot of them in major markets, especially London and New York, employ
scouts whose literary noses are trained to sniff out goodies for their
clients. You can be sure that the phones were humming, and dear old
postie was burdened with much excited correspondence. (The fax
machine was not in general use in 1979 even though it is quite old-

---

* In many ways this is the most satisfying of the *Hitchhiker's* books.

fashioned technology.) Germany,* France, Italy, Scandinavia, Japan, Spain, Greece . . . all the major markets of the world bought translation rights, followed smartly by the smaller ones. Estonia, Bulgaria, Czechoslovakia (as it was then), Hungary, Israel, Poland, Serbia . . . Pretty soon there was scarcely a country in the world with a local publishing industry in which Douglas didn't appear. (For a complete list, see Appendix One.)

A blessed by-product of all these deals was, of course, a trickle, then a stream of money. Yen, Deutschmarks, francs, drachma, zlotys and whatnot, all came sloshing through the system in Douglas's direction – but quite slowly. (Actually the smaller markets usually have to buy in US dollars.) Those of you unfamiliar with publishing might imagine that if, say, a German publisher buys the rights in a work for 100,000 Euros, then the author fairly promptly receives 100,000 Euros, perhaps minus the agent's fee of 10%. Not a bit of it. First of all the acquiring publisher will disburse the advance using a schedule of payment that usually divides the total into at least two stages (signature of the contract and publication). Then a sub-agent in the relevant territory will take a 10% commission for executing the deal and deploying his or her local knowledge. Sometimes tax-exemption procedures can be glacial without someone on the spot. Then the proprietor – in Douglas's case it was Pan handling foreign rights sales – will take the agreed percentage from the sale of those rights (typically 25%). Only if the original advance has been earned out will the balance then be passed on to the author's agent, and probably not until the next royalty accounting date of which there are two per annum. The agent will deduct the 10% or sometimes these days 15% for his or her services. Only after the money has been transmitted down this long chain (no single link of which is motivated to be very speedy) does the author receive a share. It can take many months.

You can see that Douglas would not have been overwhelmed by spondulix, and this is just as well as he would only have spent it

---

* Douglas was always huge in Germany which, despite the stereotype, seems to have a weakness for surreal British humour. They even made a German version of Monty Python's *Fliegender Zirkus* once, with all the Pythons learning their lines phonetically.

instantly. However, he now had a significant income from foreign sales, and in March 1980 he would also have received his first, and rather awesome, royalty cheque from Pan.

Douglas, frankly, loved the money when, in the eighties, it finally started rolling in like Pacific breakers. He'd tried not having money; not unreasonably, having money had the edge. His approach was innocently simple. He divided his income into three. One third was Monopoly money for play and pleasure. One third he put aside for a pension or a time when the wellsprings of creativity might dry up. One third, destined – as he believed – for the taxman, he gave to his accountant (about whom there is a macabre story to be told in a later chapter).

Douglas's accommodation was still pretty cheap. Jon Canter was working as a copywriter in advertising, though his heart was in screenplays and sketches, and Douglas was bringing home veritable sides of bacon, so they decided to escape from the Holloway Road. The flat there may have had a kind of romance of the bleak, but by comparison their new digs near St Mary's Church in leafy Highbury New Park were heaven. Those versed in the geography of London will notice that each move was taking Douglas closer to Islington, though he did not buy any property there until 1981. Jon says it was strange to come home after a hard day writing fizzy selling copy to find Douglas being interviewed by some bright-eyed journalist.

Two snapshots of their life there: the first cordless phones, about the size and weight of a brick, had just been manufactured. Douglas just had to have one, and took to wandering about the flat with it making calls, even taking it to the loo. 'Blimey,' or words to that effect, said one caller, 'reception is not so great on those gadgets. The interference sounds like someone having a piss from a great height.' Another detail Jon remembers was giving a dinner party when Douglas wandered in and rather commandeered it by deciding the theme for the evening would be the greatness of Ringo Starr's drumming. Jon was not angry about his party being hijacked. 'It wasn't anarchic,' he says, 'and it wasn't intended to disrupt. It was just ingenuous to a fault . . .'

But more often than not, Douglas would eat out. The restaurant trade in London in the early eighties has a lot to be grateful for: Douglas did much to sustain it. He was wildly hospitable about taking friends out for exotic meals; sometimes, though, his mates resented it. Douglas had never intended his wealth to be seen as triumphalist and, when he was accused of a lack of sensitivity, he was mortified.*

Douglas himself had little envy in his make-up and liked to see his friends succeed, and this could lead to a certain naïveté about money. He was recklessly extravagant. It did not occur to him to feel jealous of those with more (though much later, in California, he came to lose his innocence in that regard) and he could be taken by surprise by those who were jealous of him. Other writers who knew Douglas at the BBC could be a little satirical. There is a writers' room at the BBC, in a grim office block in Langham Street just behind Broadcasting House, where the writers of topical comedy are housed in uncomfortable chairs and fed all the daily papers. Once Douglas was spotted on the pavement from the window of this retreat. Several scriptwriters yanked open the window, and one of them, believed to be a witty, short, scruffy git with a beard, yelled out: 'Oi, Douglas, toss us up some dosh!'

Douglas's love of computers, he said 'gave a whole new meaning to the term disposable income'. Once he was extolling the virtues of the new Apple laptop to me, and urged me not to delay. 'Nick,' he said, after a brilliant exposition about the superiority of its operating system over that of the PC, 'You simply must get one immediately.' It was about £2,000. I pointed out to Douglas that he had simply forgotten what it was not to be wealthy. He went quite pink.

But he was not unaware of the apparent contradictions of having passionate views about the state of the world while not being put to the test by his privileged life in his beloved Islington – famously the home of 'champagne socialism' and, at one time, Tony Blair. 'Apparent'

---

* Jonny Brock tells a story of being a house guest with a large party when Douglas had his place in Provence. Towards the end of the holiday, Douglas suggested that they all go to one of the world's most famous and expensive restaurants on the Swiss border. There was much gulping and surreptitious wincing, until Jonny took Douglas aside and explained that most of them could not afford it and would feel uncomfortable about being feasted so extravagantly. The solution was for everybody to buy their own food, but Douglas would treat the party to the fearsomely costly component – the wine.

should be in quotation marks because it is hard to see why having money in the bank *ipso facto* disqualifies you from caring about the planet, especially if your opinions are supported by well-informed and rational argument. Later Douglas gave unstintingly to such causes as the Save the Rhino fund. In *So Long, and Thanks for All the Fish*, Douglas teases those suffering from subtle liberal guilt by inventing a prostitute who provides an intimate and specialized service: she tells wealthy people that it's all right to be rich.

Initially, though, amid the welter of foreign rights being sold, the biggest English language market of them all, the United States, did not go for the book at all. Within five years, however, the US was to become Douglas's biggest source of income.

The publishing industry in America is largely based in New York, though there are pockets of publishers in California and Boston. New York is an exciting city, but the problem is that it knows it. New Yorkers are convinced that they are the pivot around which the world turns; in many ways, they are right. Think of that famous cartoon by Steinberg on the front of the *New Yorker* magazine. It was captioned 'The view from Fifth Avenue' and three-quarters of the image went as far as Eighth Avenue. Almost out of the frame, on the horizon it said California and Japan.

Certainly in publishing it is New York and not London where the major deals are executed, and there is a vitality and buzz about the business there that is hugely exhilarating. The native wit is wonderful, but it's the humour of people under fire. Even buying a sandwich is combat. 'We've got the money, we've got the smarts, we've got the style, and you're a bunch of Brits who are, by and large, charming but useless – and not invariably charming either' is an attitude often encountered when doing business over there.

Back in 1979, publishing in New York was madly fashionable (and still is, despite having become much more corporate). At the time it was set mainly in mid-town Manhattan; all the publishers knew each other, many of them socially, quite a few had slept with each other, and a fair number had places on Long Island in the Hamptons (the right Hamptons as opposed to the wrong Hamptons), where the hierarchies of office life would continue in different form. God help us, New

Yorkers use expressions like 'restaurant culture' without laughing and worry about getting a table *by the pool* at the Four Seasons. In that tough city it matters if the sneakers do not quite go with the jeans. It was a hothouse full of clever people working in a debauch of self-regard. Yet for all its gloss, New York can be very parochial.

'It's far too British . . . British humour does not travel. We cosmopolitan city slickers from Gotham City understand it, but how will it go down in Oshkosh, Wisconsin?' Such were the sentiments employed by American editors to keep their chequebooks inviolate when faced with *The Hitchhiker's Guide to the Galaxy.* In fairness, America is the dominant culture of the world and it exports its entertainment in such extraordinary volume that the industry is up there with armaments and agriculture as one of their big three foreign exchange earners. There must be kids in villages in North Wales or rural Japan who are more familiar with Los Angeles police procedural slang than they are with their own culture. Innumerable TV series and movies have made the American landscape known to us, but the reverse is not true. Why should it be when the United States manufactures a home-grown product that is so seductive that it sells all over the planet?

Douglas was beside himself. He so wanted to be a success in the USA.

'Bloody, bloody publishers,' he would snarl, 'they always say that stuff is too British. They said that about *Monty Python.* The sophisticated media people say it. They all bloody say it. The only people who don't say it are the audience. You know, the readers, the actual public. I've met some of my American fans, lots of them, and they get it. They are very much like my British ones.' You had to tease him to nudge him out of his Tourette-ish riff. And, of course, eventually the rights were sold.

Sonny Mehta remembers the process:

I was on a trip to New York [the winter of 1979], right after we'd published *Hitchhiker's* and it was number one in the charts. I was actually rather hooked on Workman Publishing in those days. They only did non-fiction of a very specific sort. They were a small, very focused publishing house, and I just loved the type of things they did and the energy with which they did them. Then Bruce [Harris, of Crown], who was a friend, happened to come by and take me out to lunch or something. I said I had this extremely odd novel . . . It's not exactly science fiction; it's very eccentric. So he said: 'Let me see it,' and I said, 'Well, actually another publisher has it.' I kept waiting but [name deleted to save embarrassment] has had it for a week or ten days, and hasn't come back to me. So Bruce said: 'I'll send someone to pick it up.' And the very next morning the phone rings at about 7.30 and I'd been getting wasted the night before. It's Bruce Harris. I said: 'Bruce, do you know what time it is?' And he said: 'Now listen, I just want to tell you that last night I read that manuscript you gave me, and I really want to do it.' And I said: 'You call me at 7.30 to buy a manuscript? – forget it.'* Bruce must have thought it was a negotiating ploy, because he rang five times.

Anyway, they did see it immediately, and actually Bruce was the other person I wanted to read it, so he bought it straightaway.

Bruce Harris is an affable, civilized editor of the old school. Now the Publisher at Workman, he was then the Publisher at Harmony Books and Marketing Director of Crown, a feisty independent house, with the memorable address of 1 Park Avenue. Crown has long since been absorbed by a pseudopod from one of the industry's giant cartels. Bruce says that when he read *Hitchhiker's* he laughed out loud. (You should appreciate that it takes a lot to produce this response in a publisher for whom the joys of reading have often been crushed by routine.) It was, he says, the proverbial light bulb going off in his head . . .

And the fact that I could pick up two books for a sensible advance of only $15,000 in total, when smarter publishers than I had passed, was helpful. I had to clear it with my boss, for Crown did

---

* Sonny is a supremely civilized man, but he is not a person in whom the blood reaches the higher cognitive functions before around 10.30 a.m.

not publish much fiction. We always tried to do good stuff, and Douglas Adams proved to be helpful for the imprint.

I remember Douglas with great warmth. When he first came over to do promotion, we went out to lunch and we got on famously. Then I took him to a bookstore, Colosseum Books, and said: 'Go ahead, buy what you want. I'll pay.' I always found it interesting to see what authors choose, and it's a gesture they appreciate. We once did a deal with Maurice Sendak after giving him the run of our warehouse. Anyway, Douglas was modest at first, but eventually bought about $200 worth of books. Right on top of the pile was a title on how to overcome writer's block.

Our first edition of *Hitchhiker's* was a neat little hardback priced at $9.95. It had an illustrated jacket of the rings of Saturn making a rude gesture, and largely on the strength of that we got floor displays from Walden Books [a large, powerful chain]. Douglas enjoyed the promotion tours, too. A lot of authors find them arduous, but he seemed to like the travel, the hotels, the pretty girls, and doing the signings. He got a kick out of reading his work and liked meeting the audience.

I'll miss him. He was always jolly, a gust of fresh air. He was terribly prescient about Information Technology and all that stuff. He foresaw its implications years before the rest of us. Once I was on a panel with him in Cannes to discuss the impact of the CD-Rom on publishing, something about which I knew little. Douglas rehearsed some it with me before we went on, and then he gave a dazzling performance himself. I still recall him describing how it would be possible to view the ceiling of the Sistine Chapel as if walking along just a few feet beneath it.

It is interesting that Bruce mentions Douglas's love of travel, because later in his life, when he found it excruciatingly difficult to write, he would use travel as an anaesthetic. The succession of airports and endless lonely hotel rooms, with their identical lay-out, mini-bars and anxiously polythene-wrapped plastic mugs, the jet lag, the permanent hum in the ears, the homogeneous malls, his polished production of the same speech – all this could induce a kind of hypnagogic trance, like lucid dreaming. It was flight – flight from deadlines and some of the responsibilities of home.

Bruce wasn't the only American publisher to adore the book. Back in London, Marty Asher, Editor-in-Chief of Pocket Books, also loved it. Pocket Books was a large paperback house, part of Simon & Schuster (itself then owned by Paramount, and now part of the even more unlikely media cartel, Viacom). Marty is a modestly sized man with a quick wit and engaging manner. He was in London on a mission that was the reciprocal version of Sonny's on the other side of the Atlantic. Marty was searching the British market for goodies,* and had seen a copy of *Hitchhiker's* in Pan's office and scrounged one for consideration of its US potential.

It had been a wintry day. Marty had just got back to his room at the Savoy Hotel, suffused with the honourable fatigue that comes after trawling publishers all across London, and from being politely non-committal when offered complete dogs. He decided to take a bath. The baths at the Savoy are very comfortable for they are constructed on such a heroic scale that you have to swim to reach the plughole. Also they come equipped with stainless steel art-deco accessories for holding loofahs, sponges, soap and recent British bestsellers. Marty Asher (nothing if not professional) relaxed in the hot bath, reading Douglas Adams and laughing like a drain.

This book, he thought, is a must-have. He was disappointed to learn that he had just been beaten to the post by Bruce Harris, but as Pocket was a mass-market paperback house with considerable clout, Marty was able to buy the US paperback rights from Crown. In many ways this was an ideal combination. Crown was quirky, independent and trying hard, and still small enough to have the personal touch, while Pocket was a big marketing machine with powerful distribution across the US.

---

* These trips are fun. You charge around the industry seeing old mates and usually being treated to a great deal of lunch, but after a week of three or four meetings in the morning, lunch in the line of duty, four meetings in the afternoon, early evening drinks and sometimes dinner, your hotel room is ankle deep in manuscripts and you're in such a state of fugue that you would not recognize a bestseller if it bit you on the bum.

Crown's Harmony hardcover sold out, but *Hitchhiker's* did not become the huge bestseller that it had been in the UK. The radio series had been picked up by some of the cooler stations in the American National Public Radio network, but it wasn't until March 1981 that all the stations took it and gave it a national airing. Pocket's promotion for the paperback was quite inventive. They pitched the book squarely at the college crowd with lots of advanced reading copies given away at university and college bookshops. Douglas was embarrassed that more was made of his connection with *Monty Python* than was really the case, but he partly had himself to blame as he had solicited spoof quotes from all the Pythons. ('A lot funnier than anything John Cleese has ever written' – Terry Jones – gives a flavour.) Besides, from the publisher's point of view, *Monty Python* was exactly the right button to press, something quintessentially English that worked commercially in America.

Pocket ran a large ad in the *Rolling Stone*, a magazine with some excellent journalism and impeccable street cred. The first 3,000 respondents who could bear to write to the Hyperspace Hitchhiking Club (c/o Pocket Books) would receive a freebie copy.

Marty recalls that when they published the paperback in August 1981, the initial impact was not huge but that the pattern of sales was very encouraging. He recalls:

> It went out in the hipper independent bookshops, especially where there was a big student market. It was culty. We sold 50,000 and then reprinted, and kept on going back to press. By the time his second hardcover was published we knew we had something. The series kept on looping round on National Radio too.
>
> I met Douglas at the ABA [the American Booksellers' Association, a huge trade convention] in Los Angeles that year. We had a large, amusing lunch. He was wonderfully lunatic, and I was surprised at how much he loved California. He was like a kid in a gigantic toy store. He loved it even though there was another deadline imminent.

Meanwhile, back at Pan, publishing Douglas was both pleasurable and irritating. Publishers' editors, for example, will often buy their authors lunch. It's one of the perks in an industry that is not well paid. It is easier to establish a rapport with someone while sharing such a basic human appetite as food. From the professional point of view it also has the virtue of putting a frame around the encounter; even a really long lunch is not as dangerous as inviting an author to the office where he or she can hang about all day peering resentfully at other authors' point-of-sale material.

But the margins in publishing are as thin as the paint on a French car, and editors do not have unlimited expenses. Inevitably the exes get scrutinized – sometimes with appalling rigour – by a clerk in the accounts department who cannot grasp why some spoilt media-trendy should be entitled to so much free lunch. So the deal, though inexplicit, with authors is that they do not trespass too much on the editor's privileges. It's just bad form always to order the most expensive thing on the menu and wash it down with wine that may cost a week's wages. Dear old Douglas had no such inhibitions. It was partly that he inherited his father's appetite for luxury. Also, though in many ways he loved fame, he could never quite believe it. Insecurity gnawed at him all the time: am I really a star? Perhaps if I act like one, and people clearly treat me like one, it will by some process of magical thinking become an unassailable truth. But, one has to concede, sometimes he was just thoughtless. His editor, Caroline Upcher, who combines emotional sensitivity* with an uncompromising determination never to be a corporate drone, was not amused when he ordered, not checking with her first, a bottle of champagne in a smart restaurant with breathtaking smart restaurant-type mark-ups. There is a legend, still whispered in lunching circles, that she told him he could pay for it himself.

As anybody who has worked in an office for more than a minute will appreciate, internal memoranda are more often a vehicle for politics than for information. The ease of email has only exacerbated the problem. Caroline is a fine editor, not a tactician; it is hugely to her credit that she could never be bothered with the nuances of the blind copy to the CEO; life is too short. Companies have their own style, and Pan's idiom was racy and no-nonsense.

---

* Much later, when she had turned into a fine writer herself, she wrote for GQ magazine one of the most insightful pieces about Douglas ever published.

Here's a memo from the Pan files that speaks of Douglas's some-times exasperating need for attention.

To: Sonny   From: Caroline
cc: Jacqui [Graham]   29 October 1979

Re: DOUGLAS ADAMS

Douglas is under the impression he is having dinner with you and Jacqui on Wednesday, 31 October (Halloween). He had assumed I would be there but I told him (quite truthfully) that I had a date for dinner that night but, if asked, I would be happy to be around here for a drink earlier on. I was actually intending to wait until we had tied up terms for the second book before getting him in for a drink with you, but now he has hooked onto you via Jacqui I guess it makes no difference.

BUT he is now PESTERING me about the fucking evening. Approximately three times on Friday and twice already today. I can't dine with him on Wednesday and I'm sure poor Jacqui has had her fill of him for a while, but maybe I'm wrong. Do you or Jacqui want to finalize what you want to do with the fucker on Wednesday and let him know – or let me know so I can give him an answer next time he calls . . .?

Thanks.

Underneath Caroline wrote in longhand: 'Bet you ten quid he gets on to either one of us by noon today! C.'

However, coping with Douglas's stupendous talent for restaurants was the least of any publisher's problems with him. The shatteringly stressful vexation was getting the text out of him in the first place for Douglas enjoyed *being* a famous writer, but he loathed the process of becoming one. That entailed writing.

The stories of his delinquency about deadlines are, sadly, all true. Famously he said he loved deadlines because he loved the sound of them whooshing by. The reality was that his dilatoriness was just not funny. It caused a deal of grief for his publishers, but for them it was just a matter of professional inconvenience and commercial pain. Poor Douglas suffered agonizing despair when he felt he just could not do it. He was known to fall to the carpet and weep.

Publishers are used to authors running late; over the years they have evolved a nicely judged scale of responses. When an author confesses to lateness, as a publisher you cannot afford to be too urbane ('Don't worry . . . par for the course . . . get it right rather than do it now . . .'), even if you haven't scheduled the book in question and it's not particularly time-sensitive. Many authors are so chronically insecure that they interpret a forgiving response as indifference ('Oh no', they think, 'My publisher doesn't appear to want it'). This may legitimize further dilatoriness on their part. No, you have to be distinctly disappointed, but not so narked that you induce a paralysing degree of anxiety in your wayward author. On the other hand, if the work in question is a major chunk of turnover, the absence of which will make a noticeable dent in the annual accounts, and the entire trade is geared up for its arrival on a particular date, your need to get the work on time acquires an unusual sincerity. Even more so if you have paid a large advance for it.

With his third book, *Life, the Universe and Everything*, Douglas had decided to change agents. Jill Foster is smart, but Douglas felt that he needed representation from a high-profile heavy. Ed Victor is such a man; with his mellifluous mid-Atlantic voice, he is one of nature's great salesmen. He is celebrated in the media world and was once listed as the man who, with his wife, Carol, a lawyer, went to more parties in London in one season than any other human being. (Henry James is supposed to be the all-time record-holder, having attended more dinner parties in one year than there are days in the year.) For Douglas's third and fourth books, Ed had negotiated a lorry-load of money.

Now Douglas loved serious money and all the options that it could buy, but at the same time he told his friends that he felt trapped by the huge advances that imposed a pressure all of their own. If someone is paying £5 a word, they had better be bloody well-chosen words. He found it terribly difficult to get down to any work. Being preternaturally smart, he understood what he was doing and then despised himself for being so weak-willed. His crude subterfuges for not writing were never convincing, least of all to Douglas himself.

It was with *So Long, and Thanks for All the Fish,** Douglas's fourth book (and the first not to be based on his radio scripts) that matters took a drastic turn.

Sonny Mehta recalls what happened:

There was always the problem of when the manuscripts were going to be delivered. I don't think it was writer's block so much as he hated doing it. I'm sure he always meant to write, it's just that more interesting things came up. Either thinking, or going to the pub for a drink, or meeting some mate for lunch, or something like that. I can understand it entirely – I'm much like it myself when you come down to it. I did have a great deal of sympathy for him.

But I did lock him up in the hotel room – that is absolutely true. We were really up against the wire. We had the jacket done and all the rest of that kind of crap. Then, of course, I speak to Douglas. 'How's it going?' I say, and he says, 'Oh, pretty well. You should have it in a couple of months.' This used to go on and on and on. Then I'd phone Ed, and Ed would say, 'Listen, I think Douglas is working. He said you should have it in a couple of months.' And as I recollect, Ed finally said, 'I think we ought to have a meeting about this.' So we all turned up at Upper Street, where Douglas and Jane were, and we sat down and had a long talk, and it became clear, actually, that Douglas had only written about twenty-five pages. So then I went back to the office, and I spoke to Simon [Master] and I said, 'Look, you're not going to have the manuscript.'

This was important, because we'd made a big fuss about the fact we were publishing it in hardcover[†] and all the rest of it –

---

* The critics were harsh about this one. For instance, Tom Shippey, the academic SF expert and reviewer, found it 'too cool, as Adams is now edging down from Vogon poetry to mere satire of British Rail sandwiches . . .'

† *So Long, and Thanks for All the Fish* was Pan's first hardcover edition. They had been licensing library editions to Arthur Barker, but they realized they were missing a trick. It was a very elegant book, all black, designed by Gary Day Ellison with an odd lenticular image on the front that alternated between a walrus and a plesiosaur depending on the angle. David Bleasdale, their Production Director, had picked up a job lot of these images in Hong Kong. It didn't have much to do with the text, but somehow it worked and the book is now a collector's item.

apart from the fact that we were counting on it, just in financial terms. So I had a long talk with Ed the next morning and I said, 'Look, Douglas has got to finish this book, and if we just wait, we may be waiting eighteen months, two years . . .' Clearly I was enormously concerned, and I'm sure Ed was too, because there was money in it for him too. So I said, 'Why don't I put Douglas in an environment where he's really *got* to work?' Ed said, 'It's an interesting idea.'

So I came up with the wheeze of putting him in a hotel room someplace. But it was no good putting him in a hotel room if he wasn't going to be supervised. So I said, 'Look, I'm going to do this: I'm going to get a hotel suite and I'll move in myself and *make* Douglas churn out pages.' Everyone thought it was a good idea if I was prepared to do it. We found the Berkeley – fucking great terrace outside, I might add . . . It did cost a few bob. I phoned Bruce Harris at Crown, and said, 'Listen, this is what I'm going to do,' and it turned out those guys were even more anxious than we were at Pan, so I said, 'But you're going to have to pick up half the tab for the hotel.' There was a big silence and then they agreed.

And so I went to look at the suite, and I told Douglas that we'd better be there at 3 o'clock tomorrow, and he agreed. He and Jane talked about it. I said, 'Bring clothes and whatever else – there is going to be a routine, I'll spell it out to you when you turn up.' And we sent a cab around to pick him up.

So he turned up with a typewriter, his clothes, a guitar or two – I didn't mind at all. [Douglas was in a Dire Straits mode at the time.] I was just so relieved the fucker turned up. The office shipped across a case of wine for me and boxes of manuscripts, so that I would be able to work. And I moved in. There were two bedrooms – I remember putting Douglas in the smaller one because I was extremely pissed off.

The reason we hit the Berkeley was he wanted to swim, and there was a pool upstairs. The other reason was that it was close to my house, so I could nip out from time to time and say hello to my wife. So I explained the routine was that I'd get him out of bed; he'd go up for a swim; we'd have breakfast; finish by 8.30 a.m. Then Douglas would sit down at this small desk with a typewriter, and I would sit in an armchair at forty-five degrees from that, my back facing him, and I'd read a manuscript. I'd wait for the sound of those fingers on his typewriter keys – which sometimes would happen, sporadically, and then there'd be long periods of silence, and I'd turn around to check him out and see that he hadn't croaked on me or something. He'd be sitting up, staring out the window at this roof terrace. Every now and then I'd say, 'How's it going?' And he'd say, 'Fine, fine.' And you'd hear paper being crumpled and thrown into a bin.

It was quite macabre, looking back on it. Gradually the pile of manuscripts that I was reading would grow on the floor as I went through yet another submission. At the end of the day I would gather together whatever pages Douglas had written, and we'd talk about it and then I would phone the office. My assistant, Jenny [Gregorian] would turn up and collect the pages and take them to the office. Room service would come down for lunch, and in the evening we would go out to some restaurant round the corner, have dinner, and then I'd bring Douglas back, and say, 'Okay Douglas, you'd better get some sleep,' and he would be sent to his room.

That is roughly what the routine was. Every now and then he would get up and play the guitar. And we'd talk a little bit . . . you know. That was about it. Occasionally I'd go through the bin to see what he'd chucked away – you know, discreetly, when he was gone to have a piss or something – and it would say things like, 'Who the fuck does he think he is?' There was one page, I remember, of very choice abuse, which I actually kept and had on my notice board for quite a while – even in New York, actually. During one of the refurbishments it kind of vanished, along with other memorabilia.

This kidnapping of Douglas has entered publishing legend. Sonny and Douglas are so unlike each other that at times it must have been like some dodgy hostage siege.* Sonny was extraordinarily patient, but he has always had the capacity to concentrate on a manuscript and, being incarcerated in a hotel with coffee and room service, he probably got through an unusual amount of work.

It says a lot for Sonny's sympathy, and the general affection in which Douglas was held, that this desperate expedient was resorted to at all. Of course, Pan needed the book and you just cannot terrorize an author into creative brilliance. But there are not many industries in which a party in breach of contract would receive such succour.

Every evening in the Berkeley, Sonny would sit and read the day's output under the close inspection of Douglas. All authors need approval. In my experience the best writers are actually or incipiently a little nuts; you have to be slightly mad to pursue such a solitary craft in the first place. Reading an author's work in his or her presence is a kind of agony. No study of your face has ever been so close or unremitting. Was that a twitch? Did you smile? In which case, at which bit of text? Did you get that joke? For Christ's sake, say something. Most authors are content – no, 'content' is not a word that can be applied to writers – are *prepared* to wait until they've finished the book before demanding admiration from their editor. With his later books there were times when Douglas needed love almost page by page.

Sonny, who is not a natural thespian, nevertheless has authority. 'This is fine, Douglas,' would carry as much weight from him as volumes of gush from a lesser figure. Despite their solitary confinement, Sonny and Douglas remained on good terms. When the final page was delivered, they went out for a dinner that was so large and alcoholic that it was erased from both their memories.

Sonny never had to lock up Douglas again. Later, Sue Freestone, first on a freelance basis and then as his editor at Heinemann, took over the role, and discharged it with empathy and compassion.

What of the book itself? It is regarded by hardcore Douglas fans as rather thin. But it is very funny and more emotional than many of his others which tend to be sparkling with intellect, but less sure on characterization and human interaction. *So Long* is in many ways a

---

* Would make a two-hander play?

tender love story, and its construction – which is very episodic – is full of little scenes that are almost self-contained and that show off Douglas's talent as a sketch writer. In *Sputnik Sweetheart*, Haruki Murakami, the wonderful Japanese writer whose work in some ways has been influenced by Douglas, described the story within the story forever being written by one of his characters as 'the best patchwork quilt of a novel sewn by grumpy old ladies'.* *So Long, and Thanks for All the Fish* is also rather quilt-like; it's enveloping, warm, a bit soppy, and the squares of the patchwork alternate between the surreal and the everyday. In places it reads almost as if he didn't want to write the fantastical bits, but could not short-change his readers with their expectations of the weird.

Douglas ends the book on a note that seems both to work within the context of the narrative and to stand outside as a commentary upon it: 'There was a point to this story, but it has temporarily escaped the chronicler's mind . . .' The truth is that he really did not want to write any more if he could avoid it. He was determined to make another *Hitchhiker's* sequel impossible. Unfortunately, he was so inventive that he could escape from any dead-end of plot, as he had proved already by writing around the smashing into atoms of the planet Earth. Like Conan Doyle, forced by public demand to revive Sherlock Holmes after his headlong drop with the evil Moriarty into the Reichenbach Falls, Douglas had been pushed by his legions of fans – and, let's not be ingenuous, by the huge advances – into carrying on hitchhiking.

Heartbreakingly for many of his fans, he killed off Marvin the Paranoid Android, who, after billions of years of boredom and depression mostly spent in a car park waiting to be patronized by dim primates, is allowed blissfully, finally and irrevocably to stop.

'I think,' he murmured at last, from deep within his corroding, rattling thorax. 'I feel good about it.'

It's a message from Douglas: no more. He yearned to move on.

_____

* Haruki Murakami, *Sputnik Sweetheart*, translated by Philip Gabriel (Vintage Books, 1999).

chapter nine

Hippodust, films
and the telly saga

'Nobody knows anything.'
Adventures in the Screen Trade, William Goldman

'California is a great place to live if you happen to be an orange.'
Fred Allen

Californian evenings . . . As film people sit round their great oak-effect fires, and chronicle their adventures in the movie business, many are the tales told of the agent kings, borne on the heroic bodies of starlets from the field of battle to their Valhalla in the Polo Lounge. There they hold court, enthroned in bar furniture of the deepest plush, toying with their iced mineral water as they talk of fortunes won and lost, and deals that made or broke the names of mortal men. And of all the sagas, sung from rooftops, whispered in corners, few have been so terrible, so extended, so downright capricious as the Great Non-making of Hitchhiker, the Movie.

Shortly before he died, Douglas, with his talent for the telling analogy, said that making a film was like trying to grill a steak by having a series of people come into the room and breathe on it. In a moment's despair, he told Ed Victor how he calculated that he'd wasted five and a half years of his life trying to get the movie made, and that, 'I'm not going to spend another fucking minute on it.'

'Of course,' Ed recalled, 'a month later he was back devoting himself to the film. He just wanted that film so much.'

There's even this bitter definition in *The Deeper Meaning of Liff*:

Spiddle (vb)
To fritter away a perfectly good life pretending to develop a film project.

In part it is the horrific expense of making a movie that pervades the business with anxiety. It may be true that many people in the film world are unsure about their own judgement and frightened of looking like idiots, but in fairness the risks are huge. In publishing, for instance, if an editor buys a book that doesn't sell, total loss will be the advance, the expenditure on manufacture and distribution, and the burden on overheads – tieing up costly machinery with a dog. Unless it were a huge punt on something disastrous, the total loss is unlikely be more than tens of thousands of pounds or dollars. A movie, on the other hand, can burn up $100 million and recover only a few million in theatrical release and video sales. In a tough town like Hollywood you cannot have many disasters on that scale. Fear stalks the studio corridors like a Psycho-killer in Residence.

From the moment *Hitchhiker's* was published in 1979, there was talk of a film. There had been mention of George Lucas, whose Industrial Light and Magic had stunned the world the year before with the special effects in *Close Encounters of the Third Kind*. However, there is no record of any flirtation with Lucas. Given that Douglas squirreled away everything (though in no kind of order), such a rumour was probably just wishful thinking.

But before the film saga could begin, the telly mini-series of *The Hitchhiker's Guide to the Galaxy* had to come, and go.

The series was made at the end of 1980 and broadcast in six episodes from 5 January 1981 to 9 February 1981, about three months after publication of *The Restaurant at the End of the Universe*, which was still riding high in the bestseller lists. These days, TV and film rights are usually sold together on the grounds that if both were to be exploited simultaneously they could interfere with each other. Besides, their markets are so intertwined that it makes sense to keep them linked. For instance, even were it possible to negotiate a non-exclusive contract, whose video would be released first if both a film and a telly company make a version of a particular work? Films consume such prodigious quantities of money that every right with any commercial potential known to man, not excluding stained-glass dramatization and microdots, has to be part of the deal and is factored into the original decision. At the time, however, Ed Victor was able to put the film rights into play without the TV series representing too much of an encumbrance.

The TV version was firmly in the hands of the BBC. The Beeb had been thrilled by its success with the two radio series. Being jealous of its property, it was irritated that the runaway sales of the books were being enjoyed by an external publisher. During this period the institution was emerging from its noble mantle of public service into a harsher world of commerce and it was coming under a lot of pressure from the Conservative government of Margaret Thatcher, a woman suffused with the frightening certainty of one whose electoral prospects had been incalculably enhanced by the bloody war over the Falkland Islands.* She seemed to have an almost visceral dislike of a broadcasting corporation that many of us regarded as a national treasure. In the demonology of the right wing, the BBC was staffed by left-leaning, over-privileged, disrespectful public schoolboys who were insulated from the real world[†] by the public's money in the form of licence fees.

This was the background that predisposed the BBC to keep its goodies in-house. The huge, cultish success of the two radio series would surely translate to the TV. It was John Lloyd who started off the whole process with a memo back in September 1979 to the Head of Light Entertainment. In it, John persuasively listed all the credentials

---

* For those of you too young to remember, in March 1982 the Argentine military dictator, Colonel Leopoldo Galtieri, facing economic crisis and unrest at home, invaded the Falkland Islands, some 300 miles off the coast of Argentina, to which the Argentines had long laid claim. By the end of June, after a bitter 72-day campaign, Britain had retaken the islands by force. Nearly a thousand men from both sides had died. Galtieri was deposed; Margaret Thatcher lasted until the end of the decade.

† Politicians often invoke this philosophically hazy concept when they are arguing some spiteful spasm of policy is a necessity.

that *Hitchhiker's* had acquired by then: radio series that were repeated over and over again by public demand, bestselling books, theatrical productions, even a nomination for a Hugo Award.* John had by then moved over to television where he was riding high on the success of *Not the Nine O'Clock News*, and was looking for another project. Evidently he had forgiven Douglas for firing him off the book, or at least both parties tacitly conspired not to talk about it. In their complicated dance of advance and retreat, they were again best friends. Eventually, however, John did not produce the show. Having started as co-producer on the first episode, he then became – in that exquisitely precise code known only to the initiated – Associate Producer. Several suggestions from him about how to proceed were disregarded, but in fairness creative endeavours like this do often need a single, strong voice. Eventually the demands of John's own extraordinarily successful career took him away from the series altogether.

By this time Douglas had given up his job at the BBC. He had been doing it for fifteen months and was very tired. It was, as Neil Gaiman points out in *Don't Panic*, the only proper job he ever had – and he'd worked at it like a man possessed. He had script-edited many episodes of *Dr Who*, four of which he had also written (three of these, buffs will note, featured a disturbed Captain who, Vogon-like, destroyed worlds). Douglas had also written the entire second *Hitchhiker's* radio series, and created and produced a pantomime, a characteristically odd and parodic work called *Black Cinderella II Goes East*. He had made enough money to declare independence; he was under contract to write more books; and his private life – of which more in the next chapter – had acquired a shattering degree of intensity. The day job had to go.

All through his creative life, Douglas liked to have if not total control then considerable influence on how the different forms of his work would appear. This desire was later to prove a handicap with Hollywood which regards its writers as krill, a species destined to remain a long way down the food chain. It wasn't just the vanity that declares 'nobody can do this as well as I can!' His wish for control over

---

* Named after the legendary editor, Hugo Gernsback, this is SF's highest annual accolade.

his own material was more a response to the quirkiness of what he produced. There's an integrity to it that could easily have been lost if it were emulsified and then poured into the standard formats that the mavens of mass-market entertainment patronizingly misperceive as being what the public wants.

To his credit, Douglas had, after some negotiation, turned down a TV offer from ABC in America where *The Restaurant at the End of the Universe* had made the US *New York Times* bestseller list. ABC had offered a tempting $50,000 for the rights with more to come. But following discussion with the men in suits, Douglas realized that just about everything that made *Hitchhiker's* unusual would not survive the process of rendering it down for the US market. He was proud of his decision ('though I had to get drunk to make it,' he told Neil Gaiman): it showed a respect for the integrity of the work and a refusal not to follow the money slavishly. ABC were, according to Douglas, more interested in special effects than in the script, which was apparently dire.* In any case, the cost of the first episode was estimated at an unacceptable $2 million plus. Perhaps it was this experience that prompted Douglas to say to his guitar-playing pal, Ken Follett: 'The thing it took me some time to grasp, Ken, is that Hollywood is deeply shallow.'

Ed Victor recalls:

There was an American guy called Don Taffner who lived in England and made a very decent living by spotting shows in which he could buy format rights and then sell them in America. I think he did *'Til Death Do Us Part*, and he may have done *Steptoe and Son*. He wanted to make *The Hitchhiker's Guide to the Galaxy* as a television series. He planned to pilot ninety minutes for ABC. I made a deal with him, but it never happened.

One side-effect of the flirtation with ABC was that in late 1980 Douglas was flown out to Los Angeles where, on a colossal daily rate, earning him more in a week than he had been paid to write the series, he hung

---

* See his interview with Neil Gaiman in *Don't Panic*.

about the production office doing very little. This gave him an unfortunate appetite for doing very little in California, a place where the rewards from a deal are so mind-boggling that the investment of years of doing very little (camouflaged, of course, as networking or contractual foreplay) may seem perversely rational.

But back in the real world, Douglas had a BBC television script to write. In his books, he had been sole master. There were no imaginative or budgetary constraints; if he wanted a scene with a million singing robots or to crash a starship into a sun, he could do so – several times if he fancied. Such freedom does not apply to a visual medium. So Douglas couldn't just adapt the radio scripts; he had to re-imagine the whole adventure visually.

There were some delicious bits of invention that were not in the radio series. For instance, the travellers' final meal in Milliways, the restaurant at the end of the universe (and incidentally the biggest set ever made by the BBC at the time), features one of his most disconcerting comic flights of fancy, *viz* the Dish of the Day, a bovine, philosophical animal that actually wants to be eaten. Douglas had originally written this scene for Ken Campbell's theatrical production, and it played so well that he kept it. The Dish, an off-beat creature, was acted by Peter Davison, the fifth Dr Who and husband of Sandra Dickinson who played Trillian. He was keen to join in for less than his usual rate, performing any role, no matter how heavy the disguise (which was necessary for the *Dr Who* office would not have been amused to see him in another SF role).

During the production the cast had a lot of fun. Douglas was by then something of an expert on restaurants and he had just discovered the *Good Food Guide*. With characteristic extravagance, at the close of the day's filming he was wont to take people out to some amusing restaurant he had found in the guide. In his convertible Golf Gti, with its front seats pushed back as far as they could go and the rear passengers squeezed like midget contortionists into a near-natal position, he would lead a convoy. If it was warm, Douglas would have the hood down and, his head almost above the roof line, he'd drive at full speed through the night to the sound of the car's specially installed bowel-vibrating sound system.

Incidentally, in the course of researching this book, I interviewed

Professor Richard Dawkins, not only a great friend of Douglas's but also a world authority on evolution. I asked him about the creature that yearned to be eaten, and whether such a thing could ever evolve. After all, I said, there are many plants that replicate by packaging their seeds in fertilizer collected on their journey through the digestive tract of something ingesting them. Could such a mechanism apply to an animal? 'Hmm,' said the Prof, with the caution of a man who has been too often cornered by nutters with pet notions. 'It is hard to see the reproductive advantages of such a strategy. On the other hand it might be theoretically possible to genetically engineer a creature that likes pain, though such a project would be perverse in the extreme . . .'* The idea of a creature that wants to be eaten is not prescient in the same way as, say, Arthur C. Clarke's prediction of geosynchronous communication satellites. Rather it is another example of Douglas once again taking something so invisibly familiar to us that we just don't think about it – in this case shoving heated lumps of dead animal down an orifice in our faces in order to absorb nutrition – and, by means of a comic trope, forcing us to do so.

For the TV series, the BBC appointed as producer/director Alan J. W. Bell, already an experienced programme maker, trusted by the powers-that-be, who had directed the delightful *Ripping Yarns* and the hugely popular *Last of the Summer Wine*. After *Hitchhiker's*, through the eighties and nineties he went on to produce and direct a dozen major projects in film and TV, winning an Emmy Award in 1999 for *Lost for Words*.

Alan Bell had been approached earlier about *Hitchhiker's*. His first impulse was to say that it could never be televised because the special effects and the large sets would be prohibitively expensive. However, he was persuaded to take the job by John Howard Davis, the Head of Comedy, who described the TV script as one of the best he had ever seen.

On paper, it could have been a good marriage between Douglas the

---

* However, there is now research underway on growing animal tissue in tanks on a collagen substrate in suitable growth medium, perhaps for consumption on long space journeys. Chicken in a pot? See 'Raising the Steaks' by Wendy Wolfson, *New Scientist*, 21–28 December 2002.

visionary and Alan the pragmatist. Alas, right from the beginning they had poor personal chemistry. But given the investment, which was considerable, the BBC must have felt it was prudent to use someone with TV experience.

To his credit, Alan Bell introduced a number of details that were bound to work better on television. For instance he put Simon Jones (Arthur Dent) into that comforting but passion-killing Marks & Spencer dressing gown and devised the air-car that carries Slartibartfast into the planet-making factory. Douglas himself made a couple of Hitchcockian cameo appearances, once as a drinker in the pub bar to which Arthur and Ford repair before the end of the world, and, when the original actor was taken ill, as the man who tears up those absurd bits of paper money and walks naked out to sea. This was a brave move for Douglas and it explains why so many of the crew were buying him drinks the night before. It says a lot for his willingness to perform. It was a closed set, something which instantly attracted the attention of everybody within a half mile radius. Many large men with a passion for food have arses like a white blancmange in a polythene bag.

Douglas had thought hard about the technology of telly. He understood that it could be exploited to produce something so much more than the camera acting as an eye in front of a stage. Multiple images could be displayed, and merge into each other, or show separate narrative strands, and jump cut, and cooperate with or counterpoint the soundtrack. Telly could achieve what was later to be called in the computer world 'parallel processing'. Douglas was only sorry that the human brain had not yet evolved to the point where such a rich mix could be inhaled in one go, but he believed that 'there should be more going on than the viewer can take in'. Such plethora of detail gives a three-dimensional feel that makes the world thus created utterly believable. Just think how much processing power is devoted to the creatures – few of whom have any narrative function – in the space bar in *Star Wars*. In short, Douglas believed TV could offer unconventional techniques as new ways of telling a story.

Alan Bell, by contrast, was a professional who excelled at delivering the product on time and to budget. Already the first pilot had been costed at £120,000 – four times the price of a *Dr Who* episode – an expenditure that John Howard Davis had authorized personally. It was not Alan's role to provide an opportunity for clever young Oxbridge things to explore the possibilities of telly as an experimental medium. Besides, there was simply no time for Douglas to feel his way, with hesitations and reprises, towards some television first. Alan's task was to get the job done, and beneath his urbane exterior lay a grimly tenacious grasp of the relevant. He succeeded despite a work-to-rule by the electrician's union, the ETU, that meant that every day's filming had to stop not one picosecond after 10 p.m.

He and Douglas clashed immediately. Later Douglas, who rarely displayed personal animus, would describe Alan as 'a bone-headed wanker', a judgement that from the perspective of several decades on looks deeply unfair. A tough, albeit occasionally abrasive, pragmatist would be a better description. Alan himself has not gone public on the subject of Douglas. The quality of the TV series in any case undermines Douglas's grievance about the producer. Having watched it again for this book, I found it still fresh, funny and joyous. Being essentially text-led, it was probably a little too wordy for television, but this was the nature of the beast. The sound, engineered by Mike McCarthy, was tight, the actors appeared to have fun, the script was witty, the effects were inventive. The graphics, as many have pointed out, were particularly seductive.

Two kinds of culture clash were apparent from the outset: Alan was not of the bomber-pilot generation of producers, but in BBC terms he was the old guard – not part of the influx of Cambridge smarties. The traditional radio/TV schism ran deep too. Upstart radio people telling experienced telly people how to do their job was not appealing, and Alan could be a little regal.* Douglas was in a fine young rapture of success. It was probably difficult to tell him anything.

In the event, Douglas was never happy with the TV series which he

---

* When the series was completed, Alan made a speech congratulating all concerned. In one of those mock jocular asides indicating some deep feeling that etiquette obliges you to disguise, he said that everybody was happy except the radio producer – and that didn't count.

felt lacked the magic of the radio. He persisted in regarding the radio series as the definitive version. There is a famous remark often quoted in publishing that the difference between a book and a film is that in a book the pictures are better. Douglas felt something analogous about the difference between radio and telly, though he conceded that there were some brilliant TV performances.

Douglas and Alan had their first disagreement over casting. Douglas wanted the radio cast to be translated to telly, but Alan felt that TV had its own imperatives and that a judicious look around would be sensible. They compromised. Many of the original cast did cross the barrier and were just as brilliant on TV. Simon Jones was a shoe-in for Arthur Dent; after all, the role was written with him in mind. But Alan felt he wanted somebody unusual for Ford Prefect and went to audition. Much anxiety and many actors later, he found David Dixon, who understood the humour of the writing perfectly. This actor has an intelligent, elfin face that conceivably could have hailed from Betelgeuse and not Guildford; to make him stranger yet, he wore purple contact lenses. It's hard to imagine Ford Prefect now as anybody else. Trillian was written as the archetypal English rose, but ended up being played by the fine American comic actress, Sandra Dickinson, in her own trilling transatlantic alto.* David Learner, who had played Marvin on stage, took the part on again, though Stephen Moore continued to provide the voice. Slartibartfast, a part originally written with John Le Mesurier in mind, was played with exemplary, languid menace by Richard Vernon, reprising his original radio role.

Money was another source of dissension. Douglas abhorred the papier-mâché boulders and endless recycling of the same corridor shot from different angles to be found in *Star Trek* almost as much as he hated the wobbly plastic sets in *Dr Who*. George Lucas, Steven

---

* Serious buffs are referred to the excellent *The Making of The Hitchhiker's Guide to the Galaxy*, available as part of a double DVD (and also on video) from the BBC. Douglas, with a stupendous effort at tact writ large on his guileless features, remarks on this DVD that he might not have done Sandra a favour when he declined her offer to do an English accent. She has an excellent range of accents. He was, on the other hand, thrilled with her comic timing.

Spielberg, and the grand-daddy of them all, Stanley Kubrick in *2001: A Space Odyssey*, had shown how it was possible to visualize an alien world in which everything looked sharp-edged and real. Douglas, in the grip of his creative vision, knew that he did not have such resources, but within the limits he desperately wanted his work not to look tacky. The obstructions of accountants or corporate footwork artists were not his problem.* Certainly of all the people on the set, Douglas himself was the hardest to please.

In fact, the weird landscapes were remarkably good for the limited budget. Andrew Howe-Davis, the designer, made innovative use of glass painting (beautifully executed by a Frenchman, Jean Peyre) in order to squeeze infinity onto a sound stage at Ealing Studios in West London.

The planet Magrathea, for instance (the site of the customized world manufacturers, you will recall), had to be somewhere alien and bleak. Douglas fancied Iceland. Morocco was also a possibility until, after a recce, Alan was warned off by a melancholy Japanese film crew who had had all their kit confiscated in order to keep them in the country – spending money – for longer. The BBC team ended up in the strange off-white china clay pits in St Austell, Cornwall (now, incidentally, the site of the wondrous Eden Project with its graceful biomes).

Similarly, the prehistoric Earth was filmed in the Lake District. It was bitterly cold and the extras in their animal skins were chilled to the marrow. Aubrey Morris, the captain of the B-Ark with the Douglas-sized appetite for baths, was freezing despite the constant topping-up of the bath with hot water. (Andrew Howe-Davis had found that the nearest source of water was a paper mill 200 metres away, so keeping the bath hot was not easy.) Conscious of his shoulders blotched with cold, he asked, in a voice fruitier than a bunch of grapes, if he couldn't

---

* Some say that the ennobling nature of great art means that it is likely to be executed by decent human beings, but there are many counter-examples that suggest the opposite may be true. You need a certain self-regarding single-mindedness and indifference to others to pursue an idea to the death. Douglas proved an honourable exception as he was - most of the time – a sweetiepie.

have some fake-suntan lotion. But none was handy. Beth Porter, a buxom actress playing one of the scantily-clad hairdressers destined to out-evolve the early hominids, told him not to worry as the audience would all be looking at her boobs.

David Learner, the actor inside Marvin, also suffered for his art. It took him so long to get in and out of his android gear that when it was raining, and the crew took a break, they would leave him there with only an umbrella to stop him rusting solid on the spot. For obvious reasons the poor man had to be circumspect about accepting cups of tea or other drinks with diuretic properties.

Nor were the actors paid a fortune. Mark Wing-Davey, who played Zaphod Beeblebrox with stylish cool, wore his second head with enormous panache. He thinks he may have been cast because of a hippy reputation lingering on from his university days, but Douglas said that it was because he had seen Mark in *The Glittering Prizes*, Frederic Raphael's TV drama. The fake head was heavy, uncomfortable, and radio-controlled by the ingenious technician, Mike Kelt, who had made it. Later Mark Wing-Davey was to discover that it had cost twice as much to make as he was paid (£3000 is the oft-quoted figure). Mark recalled that by contemporary standards 'it wasn't a great head', though its electronic innards had appeared to some admiration on *Tomorrow's World*, the gee-whizz BBC programme about new technology. Whatever the virtues or otherwise of the head, few of the fans minded – we all liked the effort enough that we were happy to suspend disbelief. Douglas, on the other hand, was mortified.

Fortunately, he loved the graphics. These were the ingenious solution to the problem of converting the narrator to television. Peter Jones as the Book worked deliciously on the radio, but what would he have become on TV? An awkwardly protracted voice-over perhaps. But instead, a new dimension was added to the narrator's delivery that, as on the radio, contrived to be all the more matter-of-fact as the content grew increasingly surreal. As Peter spoke, the words appeared – glowing with hectic radioactive colour – one by one on the screen. At the same time, elsewhere on the screen, a graphic image illustrated and amplified the words with tremendous visual flair and three-dimensional movement.* The result was an integrated feast for both eye and ear.

The story of the graphics is one of those serendipitous accidents. Kevin Davies, one of the graphics team, was then a passionate young fan of *Hitchhiker's*.† By chance he overheard the sound of R2D2, the *Star Wars* robot, emerging from an editing suite in the Ealing Studios. It must have been an odd moment. Unable to resist, he went in and discovered Alan Bell trying out different effects for *Hitchhiker's*. Kevin worked for Pearce Studios, an animation house in the same building, and his enthusiasm was such that he persuaded Alan to meet the boss, Rod Lord, who in turn convinced Alan to allow them to tender for the job. This they won on price as well as quality. As many people have pointed out, with heroically suppressed irritation, no computers were harmed in the making of *The Hitchhiker's Guide to the Galaxy*. What Pearce Studios did had nothing to do with computers. It was cartoon animation of extraordinary sophistication: movement was created frame by frame, using a rostrum camera and images drawn on transparent acetates. Rod Lord and his team well deserved the 1981 BAFTA Award they won for the *Hitchhiker's* graphics.

Another source of argument between Douglas and Alan was the laughter track. This battle had been fought and won already in connection with the radio, but nevertheless for TV it had to be put to the test again. The BBC believed that without laughter a comedy show lacked warmth; it couldn't be funny. The viewers at home might laugh along with a studio audience, but they would not laugh on their own in the solitude of their front rooms. Douglas resisted this artifice, but, despite his views, an audience track was added using the laughter from a specially organized showing to committed SF fans at the National Film Theatre. But *Hitchhiker's* was not a sitcom. The audible merriment

---

* I have a soft spot for the creature representing the editor at Megadodo House for, despite looking like a hairy alien polyp, it is called Web Nixo.

† Kevin Davies was in fact more than a fan. Not only did his timely intrusion on Alan Bell help get Pearce Studios the graphics contract, but Kevin produced the props for the ill-fated Rainbow Theatre show and he was closely involved in the creation of *The Illustrated Hitchhiker's Guide to the Galaxy*. He also produced and directed *The Making of the Hitchhiker's Guide to the Galaxy*.

sounded false. Crudely cueing the audience at home to jokes which apparently need that much help is a bit like throwing both ends of a rope to a drowning man. Fortunately, Alan dropped the laughter track after an early showing at the Edinburgh TV Festival.

It is an irony that Douglas and Alan did not get on better. There was so much for the viewer to like in the TV series. It broke new ground creatively. The fans were ecstatic and the series created many more of them who had missed the radio broadcasts. The appearance of the characters on screen was often not as the listener, or the reader, had imagined – but that problem is insuperable with any transfer from a non-visual medium to a visual one. Douglas himself told Jim Francis, the fx (special effects) designer, that he did not see Marvin the way he was on TV.

By and large, the critics liked it too, though some were unkind about the fx. But this is to miss the point. If the fx look a bit clunky now it is because we have been spoiled by computer-generated imagery. That technology was just not available in the era of the BBC micro and the Sinclair ZX81 – hamster-powered by today's standards. Domestic computers came with all of 4k of ram, though for a fancy price an enthusiast could buy another 16k. Mainframes were for business use, and lived in air-conditioned splendour being serviced by white-coated acolytes. Now we have enough processing power to move millions of pixels smoothly with software that calculates the effect of changing light on every one of them. Back in 1980 Jim Francis worked wonders with what he had to hand. As it was, the series consumed so much of the fx budget that this may have been partly responsible for the defection of *The Goodies* from the BBC to ITV later in the year.*

Besides, *Hitchhiker's* was never about verisimilitude. *Close Encounters of the Third Kind* needed the mother ship to be about the size of Pittsburgh as it loomed over the Devil's Tower because the director was trying visually to bludgeon us into awe. *Star Wars* needed teams of ace designers using the world's largest network of Sun RISC-chip workstations to create a sense of reality because the scripts themselves are as subtle as a car crash. But *The Hitchhiker's Guide to the Galaxy* was

---

* *The Hitchhiker's Guide.*

different. It was about wit, philosophical jokes and an underpinning of intellect. You don't care about Zaphod's palsied second head; Douglas should not have tormented himself.

The TV series pulled in excellent ratings and heightened Douglas's already considerable profile. Nor did it do any harm to his book sales. Only a year after publication, the original *Hitchhiker's Guide to the Galaxy* had sold half a million copies. In 1980, *The Restaurant at the End of the Universe* had gone straight into the charts on both sides of the Atlantic and in August 1982, *Life, the Universe and Everything* did likewise, sitting at number one in the *Sunday Times* bestseller list for seven weeks and featuring in the charts for fifteen weeks altogether. The original *Hitchhiker's* had sold a million copies by the end of 1983 and won Douglas a Golden Pan from his publishers. This was the fastest attainment of that accolade in the history of the company, and in January 1984, by way of celebration, Pan threw a stylish party for Douglas in the Roof Garden of the former Biba store in Kensington High Street.

Despite the impressive TV ratings, though, a second series was not commissioned. Douglas's feuding with Alan may well have contributed to the BBC's hesitation. The cost and complexity were also compelling factors; you can imagine them being judiciously invoked at meetings in airless rooms in Television Centre. Given that Alan Bell was one of the BBC's trusted producer/directors, the aura of vexation around the project cannot have helped. Usually if there is a dispute between the talent and a producer the solution is to change the producer in the hope that someone new might have a better personal rapport. It is rare for the BBC to back the producer in such wrangles.

In this case the BBC stuck by Alan Bell. Douglas had wanted Geoffrey Perkins to produce the second series, but the two of them together – with Geoffrey producing and Alan directing – was considered, probably for good reason, an unworkable combination. By way of compensation Geoffrey was offered the job of script editor. He was in New Zealand at the time, touring with the wonderful *RadioActive* comedy show, and he remembers being somewhat drunk very late one night and having a crackly international telephone call about this job offer with John Howard Davis, who was enjoying his early afternoon cup of BBC tea. Not surprisingly – for he is no dope – Geoffrey declined (though it took a few years for the TV people to forgive him). It would have been a classic case of responsibility without power. 'I thought it was the most thankless task imaginable,' he said. He had experienced the agony of getting material out of Douglas already. As it was pretty obvious that Douglas did not want to work with Alan again, the prospects for another series were effectively terminated. In the end, says Ed Victor, the final decision not to make a second series was Douglas's.

The first series was eventually sold to the States and broadcast in November 1982. It was regarded as a dud. American TV does not use the same line standard as British TV (NTSC is 525 lines whereas European PAL is 625) so the resolution was not quite as clear; consequently the American critics complained that the complex graphics were not always legible. It is tempting, though probably facile, to see a cultural difference here. Douglas liked the fact that there was more happening on the screen than could be taken in at once. But some Americans may have found that irritating. Theirs is a society in which entertainment is slick and digestible, consumed wholesale, in giant bites, like a cheeseburger slavered in relish. (A few years later, however, America produced some of the most compelling multi-stranded 'tapestry' TV ever made in the form of shows like *ER* and *West Wing*. Douglas was a major fan of both.) Certainly Simon Jones, who went over to help promote the series in the US, was soon put on the defensive, though he was quick-witted enough to turn apparent vices into virtues. The American scorn about the tackiness of the fx was particularly embarrassing given how these had impoverished the BBC, but, as Simon pointed out, the sophisticated viewer would understand that these were meant to be artfully artless.

It wasn't until the BBC had definitely decided against the second series in November 1981 that the selling of the film rights began in earnest.

Terry Jones, who had co-written and co-directed *Monty Python and the Holy Grail* and *The Life of Brian* so he knew whereof he spoke, was the first in the frame to suggest that he and Douglas make the film together. They had always got on tremendously well and Terry's peculiar imagination would definitely have been right for the job. But Douglas was reluctant. He had seen *Hitchhiker's* through almost every incarnation known to man (including the towel) and he was just a bit overdosed with rewriting it for different media. Initially it would have been fun as they found excuses for getting dangerously twisted on real ale (script conferences, naturally). However, Douglas knew that few relationships survive making a movie together, a process more potent in its ability to induce discord than unwanted sexual advances or stealing your pal's last fiver. After some to-ing and fro-ing, Terry and Douglas agreed that they would like to make a film together one day, but that it would be better to start from scratch with an idea innocent of history.*

Meanwhile Douglas had finally moved to Islington, the district he thought of as home. Jon Canter, his former flatmate, and Douglas remained good friends although, following his pattern, Douglas somewhat disengaged from what had been a very close friendship while he invested new enthusiasm in other people. Jon is too civilized to say whether he found this hurtful.

Through the good offices of Hotblack Desiato (not the rock star from Disaster Area but the respectable Islington estate agent), Douglas bought a wonderfully louche duplex flat near the Royal Agricultural Hall in a tiny sidestreet, more of an alley, called St Alban's Place. The first floor (the second if you're American), reached by a narrow flight of stairs, was mostly one large L-shaped room given over to parties and pleasure. There was a bar well-stocked with the sticky ingredients of exotic cocktails and, always, champagne in the fridge. Bedrooms, bathrooms with giant antique fixtures (from the previous trendy owners), loos and so on were upstairs. At the very top there was a roof garden.

The whole place was distinctly flash. Douglas liked to show off the TV mounted on a wall bracket so that he could watch it from his bed. He was a big kid in so many ways. For an evocative description, you

---

* The nearest Douglas and Terry got to a major film undertaking was when Douglas bought some tickets for Abel Gance's *Napoleon* and persuaded Terry to accompany him. Over five hours of silent movie struck them as such an awful prospect that they simply had to see it.

can do no better than to read his own in *So Long, and Thanks for All the Fish*. Fenchurch's place (minus the TV) was lifted from reality.

Although access was from St Alban's Place, the apartment beetled out over an antique shop in Upper Street, a thoroughfare so preposterously fashionable – in an arty Bohemian sort of way – that it includes roughly eighty restaurants, two theatres, seventeen estate agencies, ten purveyors of stripped pine furniture (some distressed), a mall of antiques emporia, several designer clothes shops, two shops apparently selling Italian wastepaper baskets, a dozen pubs and almost nowhere to buy a tin of beans or a bottle of milk.

It was here that Douglas conducted an intense love affair (of which more in the next chapter) which lasted about a year before breaking up. This left him living with the Black Dog, deeply depressed. Mary Allen, his thespian friend from Cambridge, imagining him rattling around his huge apartment trying despairingly to write and knowing how badly he coped on his own, thought he needed a flatmate. She introduced him to Jane Belson, a tall, good-looking barrister.

Jane is an articulate woman (St Pauls, Oxford, the Treasury and the Law) whose intelligence is of the rigorous, legalistic, linear kind ('if A implies B, and B implies C, then surely the court must agree that A implies C'). She was a useful foil to Douglas's lateral way of thinking. At the bar she specialized in matters matrimonial. All aspects of the law (apart from the existence of the law itself) strike me as not likely to improve your view of humankind, but fighting divorces must be especially destructive of sentimental illusion. Jane is a strong character, though her superficial toughness is belied by a certain look of vulnerability around the eyes. After a while she and Douglas fell for each other and got together – of which again more later – but in the context of the film saga, the important thing is that in the summer of 1982 they went on holiday together to California, the heartland of the film industry and the spiritual home of the slacker. There they rented a house in Malibu. This was the first of many visits for them both. Douglas loved it. He had lots of fans there – especially in the growing techie community – who were always ready to make a gratifying fuss of him. He was becoming fascinated by computers and the extraordinary fever pitch of technological innovation that was centred on Silicon Valley, a description just coming into currency.

His affection for everything American was reciprocated. The Americans were amused by his extravagant manner and his repertoire of excellent anecdotes. Here was a whole continent that hadn't heard his stories already. Douglas's passion for new ideas struck a sympathetic chord with them, and his vast range of interests was seen as admirable. In more rigid societies like Britain, excelling outside your appointed compartment sometimes excites envy. Being a polymath is bad form.

There's an openness about American society that Douglas relished. All societies, they say, have a class structure because of the universality of human nature burdened with all its evolutionary baggage. Put two humans together and they will sort themselves into a hierarchy. Add a third, and there's room for schisms and factions. But at least in the USA the system is based more upon money and success than on antecedents. Maybe Douglas's milieu of clever North London fashionables, eternally competing over their achievements, reminded him of some painfully overdue contractual obligation (there always was one), so there was an element of flight. Whatever the reasons he loved the USA in general, New York a lot, and California hugely.

There is a legend that I have been unable to verify that Douglas even got to meet the president of the USA. In the mid-eighties, when most of Douglas's income came from the States and he was at the height of his fame, the story goes that a group of famous authors were invited to lunch with Ronald Reagan. It is possible that Douglas heard this from one of the actual participants – for he met many fellow writers on the promo circuit – and enjoyed the anecdote. Of course it is dodgy practice to include a yarn of such uncertain provenance, but this one (hedged with a health warning) is hard to resist and has a ghastly ring of verisimilitude.

Apparently this collection of writers (which may or may not have included Douglas) went to the White House for a really long lunch. They did their best to entertain the president who was twinkly and affable. After lunch they moved to the pool room and had coffee and talked some more. Then they had afternoon tea. President Reagan showed no sign of wanting to throw them out. Surely, they thought, he must be busy as ruler of the western world? But it went on and on.

From time to time, men and women would appear with important-looking pieces of paper which the president would sign. It got to be a little embarrassing. Some of them had commitments later that day. How do you tell the most powerful man in the world that you have another appointment?

But America wasn't all just about having fun. On this particular holiday to California in 1982 John Lloyd came out to join them. He and Douglas were working on *The Meaning of Liff*, the collection of place names for which they invented alternative meanings. Jane recalls that although Lloydie sulked a lot, they did do a lot of work on the book. They had sensibly taken a gazetteer with them, and they went through it looking out likely place names and writing down possible meanings on cards. The result is enduringly brilliant.

It was also during this visit to California that Douglas met Michael Gross and Joe Medjuck, former members of *National Lampoon*. This irreverent organ featured some trenchant journalism, a lot of stereo and sports car ads, and a surfeit of sophomoric anatomy jokes. It is often described as the US *Private Eye* though in feel and production values it is quite different. The old Cambridge network might have played a part here, for one of Douglas's pals at university had been Jim Siegelman,* former member of Footlights and also president of the *Harvard Lampoon*, from which in 1969 *National Lampoon* had derived.

Michael Gross and Joe Medjuck were then working for Ivan Reitman, a producer/director with Columbia Studios who had made some successful comedies (*Animal House*, for instance, with John Belushi).† It was through these intermediaries that Ivan Reitman became interested in the film rights. Douglas was hot. His books were in the charts and selling in huge numbers, especially to the all-important college market. (The demographics of the US film market are skewed towards the younger end of the population. There has to be some reason why all those *Police Academy* films get made.)

---

* Jim is an author and communications scholar. Because of Jim's research interests, Douglas once called him a 'massacre expert'.

† A popular legend has it that Belushi's character in the movie was modelled on the early days of George W. Bush.

Ed Victor likes to sell film rights for the sort of money that motivates the purchaser to actually make the movie. This means that the sale is lucrative but permanent, unlike an option sale that typically only brings in a fraction of the money.* Ed is too experienced to discuss the details of a client's deal unless they are already in the public domain. However, in his fascinating book, *The Greatest Sci-Fi Movies Never Made* (Titan Books, 2001), David Hughes describes the sum paid for the film rights as too large for even Zaphod Beeblebrox to leave in a taxi. At the time, with royalties also rolling in from book sales, Douglas could easily afford to relocate to California to write the screenplay – so he did. Of course, you don't actually have to *be* in movie land to write a screenplay, but Douglas always liked being on the set, as it were, and he thought that easy access to the right people would be advantageous.

In early 1983, he and Jane flew out to California again and rented a house in Coldwater Canyon, a pleasant district of Los Angeles with a famous park. He was in heaven – tooling about in open cars,† buying computers, having lunch and 'working' on the movie. Jane, on the other hand, found the combination of sun, orange juice, the beach and the whole open-weave lifestyle a bit stupefying. However, she is not the sort of person to let her brain idle in neutral for long. Realizing that Douglas had fallen for the West Coast in a big way and that they would spend a lot of time there, she decided to take the Californian bar exams. God forbid that the mysteries of the American legal profession should

---

* An option is a short-term arrangement whereby the option holder buys certain rights in the author's intellectual property – in this case, film – for a sum that is an advance against a larger fee. This more serious money only becomes payable if the option is exercised by putting the work into production. Within the agreed time the purchaser has an exclusive lien on the rights, and after the expiry of that term the rights granted revert to the author again. Options are frequently renewed and can evolve into a decent source of income, but it's ultimately frustrating if the work is not filmed. Producers often have a portfolio of options, but they change their minds as often as their socks.

† Though he believed that American cars are only for going in straight lines and not around corners. In *So Long, and Thanks for All the Fish* (Pan Books, 1984) he has a fantasy about this in which he concludes that it's better to hire a car that's already headed in the right direction than attempt to negotiate an American one around a bend.

be impugned by outsiders, but Jane's crisp verdict on the exams was 'a surprising amount of multiple choice questions. You have these questions to which there are four possible answers. None of them is right. One of them is merely less wrong than the others. All my friends at the bar told me I wasn't allowed to fail. They made a terrible fuss about it. It really wasn't very difficult.' She qualified, but in the end did not practise.

Ed takes up the story:

I sold *Hitchhiker's* four times. The first time was to Don Taffner and ABC. Then I sold the film rights to Columbia for Ivan Reitman. Douglas went out there to reincarnate himself in Hollywood. He was thrilled. He had a parking space with his name on it.

They [Ivan Reitman and team] were in the middle of making *Ghostbusters* and were completely preoccupied with that. They just left Douglas alone. Douglas turned in a 250-page script. It was too long.

And then it turned out that Ivan Reitman did not think that forty-two was a very good answer. 'It's just not a great punchline,' he said. 'What does it mean? Will the audience get it?' He's not Sonny [Mehta]. Douglas knew he was in trouble then.

Anyway, they played with it and played with it. They brought in another writer and they told us they were unhappy. It was a miserable experience. Various other people also played around with it. They would buy it and put it into turnaround. David Puttnam became involved. Jeffrey Katzenberg was interested. At one point there was an attempt to bring the film to Disney because Katzenberg had just gone there. Remember Rocky Morton and Annabel Jankel? They developed *Max Headroom*.* They were going to direct *Hitchhiker's*. But then they made a film for Disney which was a remake of a very famous forties love story called *DOA* [dead on arrival]. It came out, and was DOA. So it opened, and it closed – and Katzenberg pulled out.

---

* Max Headroom – a wonderful cyberspace character who appeared in his own bizarre and anarchic TV series in the mid-eighties.

Douglas was dreadfully upset that the second screenplay did the rounds without him having contributed so much as a comma to it. It bore his name and that of the new writer, Abbie Bernstein, who, in an attempt to organize the material into a more movie-like pattern, had cut it brutally, taking out much of the humour in the process. Douglas abominated this version and it fuelled his anxiety about ever losing control of the project again. He also feared that the new screenplay would blacken his name with the movie moguls. In fact, he need not have worried. Producers are so deluged by a tidal wave of material that in self-defence they have developed the attention span of a flea with an amphetamine sulphate habit. Besides, they tend to remember the turkeys that do get made rather than the multitude that don't.

Much more damaging to the movie's prospects was Douglas's desire to have more creative control than Hollywood normally grants to tyros. In this tough town, the power-brokers are exquisitely alert to any foreigner, Brit or otherwise, who arrives with this attitude: 'I'm unspeakably talented, and available – now please give me $100 million and I'll show you how it's done.' Douglas was never guilty of that particular sin, but his protectiveness towards his vision could easily have been misconstrued.

The Hitchhiker's Guide to the Galaxy is a book that borders on being intractably difficult to turn into a film, especially a Hollywood film. The investment is so great that it would be a foolhardy producer who jettisoned the well-tried storytelling structures. Having been written in episodes, *Hitchhiker's* remains stubbornly and indefatigably episodic. It just does not have what the scriptwriting guru, Robert McKee, calls a narrative arc. There's no exposition, the build-up meanders discontinuously, the climax is at the *beginning* for God's sake, and the resolution, albeit funny, is bleak. To work as a film, the whole book would have to be radically restructured, but without losing its essential humour and the ferro-concrete underpinnings provided by its ideas. Of course, Douglas understood this, and his screenwriting craft improved with every iteration. But the lesson was nonetheless slow and painful.

One bonus of being in Hollywood was another terrific friendship. Richard Curtis, now famous for *Four Weddings and a Funeral* and *Notting*

Hill amongst other goodies, had been imported to California like some amusing variety of British grape that Hollywood hoped would graft on to local vines. How things started with him and Douglas is itself movie-like. Richard reminisces:

> The most interesting section of our relationship was the beginning. I think I probably paled into a pretty ordinary friend thereafter, although I did like him a lot. But my first meeting with him was absolutely extraordinary, because I was in Los Angeles, having a very hard time – well, not hard compared to someone in Peru – because I was writing a film which I didn't really understand and I was away from home, which I find very difficult.
>
> What happened was I met an American producer who came up with an idea and commissioned me to write it. I wrote it, but it wasn't an idea I really believed in in my heart. Ever since then I've always written ideas that I've already had for five years. Finally I wrote a draft. He said there was a funny scene to do with slippers, and as for the rest – well, you could see there was a glimmer of something in it. So he flew me over to America to live in his house, work with the director and write it. I didn't know the director, and I've learned to be very fussy about such things these days. I don't think he believed in my script at all. He was just interested in the possibility that it might turn into a script he loved. The producer was a perfectly lovely man, but, you know, living with a person you are working for is a bit odd. After three weeks I kind of cracked and rang Douglas's number, which I'd been given by John Lloyd, because even though I'd been friends with a lot of people from Cambridge, I'd never met Douglas.
>
> And the long and short of the tale is that we went out for lunch – and I left two months later.
>
> We went to lunch, and talked until half past four. At the end of lunch he said, 'Come on back to the house.' Then we had dinner and Jane turned up. She'd been studying for her law exams. He said – or she said – 'Why don't you stay the night?' The next morning they both said: 'It's ridiculous if you're finding it tricky

living with your employer, why don't you continue to stay here?'
And I stayed there a long, long time. That's a remarkable degree
of exuberant hospitality, to take someone from total stranger to
the longest house guest you'd ever had with no intermediate
phase.

Richard is as entertaining and clever a guest as anyone could wish for;
Douglas could have advertised for him. It must have been blissful not
writing on the grounds that you're gallantly rescuing a compatriot from
the claustrophobic embarrassment of living with his employer. They
had a lot of fun together, though Richard winces at the recollection of
Douglas lurching into one encounter with the finesse of an army
lorry . . .

Staying with Douglas was a wonderful way of learning about
America. We went bowling together; we went to the movies
together. One thing I particularly recall – which would only be
one of a string of things – was that I took him out to dinner with
the director I had been working with. It was a bit like the old
girlfriend meeting the new girlfriend. Michael *** came in and I
misphrased my opening remark, so instead of saying 'Douglas,
this is Michael *** who made *Quest for Fire*,' I said: 'Douglas, do
you remember *Quest for Fire*?' And before I could interject, he
said: 'Oh God, that was an *awful* film. I absolutely hated that film.
The make-up was so unconvincing. The anthropology was
rubbish. Who could possibly believe that men would be like that
at that time? What a ridiculous waste it all was . . .' What's more,
he didn't back off with much embarrassment when I told him
who Michael was, and it certainly didn't, as it were, stop his flow.

Eventually it became clear that Ivan Reitman was not the right man for
Hitchhiker's. With the spurious insight of retrospect it seems like a
mismatch in all respects. The broad comedy of *National Lampoon* and
Ghostbusters is perfectly fine: it's full of energy, slapstick and innuendo
that appeal to millions. But it's miles away from the surreal cerebral
wittiness of *Hitchhiker's*. The film rights were returned to Columbia

where they languished, possibly in development hell, or maybe forgotten half to death.

The next deal was a tribute to the role of inadvertence in human affairs and to Douglas's talent for friendship. It revolved around the alliance that sprang up between Douglas and Michael 'Nez' Nesmith – TV and film producer and former Monkee.

Those of you who remember that Ringo Starr was once in a pop group before he became the narrator of *Thomas the Tank Engine* will also know the Monkees ('Hey, Hey, we're the Monkees!') – the rock band and stars of the 1966 TV series produced by Bob Rafelson and Bert Schneider. People tend either to like or loathe the Monkees – and for much the same reason: they were utterly manufactured, which was sickening if you believed that the music was about social change and not just Tin-Pan Alley (this *was* the sixties). On the other hand, the Monkees were utterly manufactured *by professionals* who knew what they were doing. Using a format loosely based on the Beatles' movie *A Hard Day's Night*, each episode followed the high-spirited adventures of a rock group played by four engaging young actors. It was a brilliant piece of multi-media marketing.

Somewhere in Monkee history the balance shifted from a sitcom about a band to a sort of semi-real band using TV for promotion. As rock'n'roll went, they were wholesome rather than dangerous. Commercially, they were huge.

The four actors were Micky Dolenz (the wild-looking drummer), Peter Tork (the funny one with the boy-next-door phizzog), Davy Jones (the cute, jockey-sized Brit who always got the girl), and Michael ('Nez') Nesmith, the cool Texan with the green beanie hat and the dry smile.

Nez has an interesting background. His mother, Bette Graham, worked as a secretary. She was struggling to fend for young Michael and herself when she had a bright idea. Wouldn't it be neat, she thought, if you could fix all those infuriating typing errors that oblige the pernickety (or those working for them) to start a document all over again? (This was decades before word processing.) She invented Liquid Paper in her kitchen and it quickly became essential for offices all over the world. The family fortunes were emphatically made.

In his career after the Monkees, Nez among other things is credited with being one of the founders of MTV. He is a delightful man with a streak of fantasy in his imagination that lent wings to his magical realist novel, *The Long Sandy Hair of Neftoon Zamora*. (Douglas gave it a generous quote: 'It rises in the imagination like a fantastical building in the desert.') Like Douglas, Nez is interested in unconventional thinking. From time to time, using the Gihon Foundation (founded by his mother and dedicated to productive innovation), he organizes the Council of Ideas in which creative people from different disciplines can come together for truly blue sky speculation.

Ed Victor picks up the story:

> I went to a dinner party one night at my lawyer's home. Michael Nesmith was there, and I mentioned that I represented Douglas and that the film rights were free. Michael turned out to be a fan, and he and I talked about doing a joint venture with Douglas. Douglas went out to Michael's ranch in Santa Fe. They got along famously, really liked each other. Douglas was convinced that Michael would help him make the film and that it was going to be a huge high-rolling thing to do. But first we'd got to get the rights back from Columbia . . .

By now it was 1992, and nearly a decade had whizzed past without the movie getting any further. But Douglas was confident that the next deal was imminent, so, with Ed's help, he bought the film rights back from Columbia for $350,000. Not having that much in cash, he had to raid his pension fund. As a general rule, authors prefer receiving large cheques to writing them, and it was painful to stump up the money for rights that were passively marinading in some studio's inventory of intellectual property. It says a lot for his ambition to make this movie.

Douglas went out to Santa Fe, state capital of New Mexico, and stayed on Nez's ranch to write the screenplay for the movie that Michael would produce. James Cameron, no less, was one of the directors who was said to be interested. Nez and Douglas discovered that they laughed incessantly together and had in common a sideways view of the world. (Jane thinks that Nez, who's a kindly man and very grounded, was to some extent one of Douglas's father surrogates.)

Santa Fe appealed to Douglas. It's sunny and affluent, and the altitude and the surrounding desert lend the light a mysterious quality. The town is a mix of the hard-boiled and the dreamy. The Santa Fe Institute (home of Murray Gell-Mann, amongst others) contains some of the brightest brains on the planet. In the bars you might find yourself sandwiched between a Nobel Prize-winner and a mystic local fruitcake. Douglas fondly carried a memento of his time there in the form of a large Native American silver bracelet which he wore all the time. 'It's so heavy,' he told Jane, 'that when I take it off it feels as if my arm should float up to the ceiling.'

One evening on the ranch, at the end of an exhausting day (for there had been a meeting of the Council of Ideas), Nez and Douglas were sitting on the veranda looking at the sun putting on its daily spectacular when, apropos of nothing in particular, Douglas said: 'You know when I was young I didn't know what I would do. Then one day I saw this cartoon. It showed me a whole new way of thinking about comedy. Up till then I confused comedy with sarcasm. Sarcasm is Oxbridge's biggest export, you know.'

'That's strange,' said Nez, 'because when I was a kid I saw a weird cartoon as well that I just loved. It might have been in the *New Yorker*. I've been trying to find it ever since. I've never forgotten it. There were these two hippos . . .'

At this point much head-slapping and cries of 'stone me' ensued, for they realized that they had both been inspired by the same cartoon.* At just the right ages for their young minds not to suffer from sclerosis of the categories, this cartoon had given them a nudge towards the surreal.

---

* The cartoon was by a Brit whose *nom de plume* was Paul Crum. His real name was Roger Pettiward. He was 6'5½", and he died with lots of brave Canadians during the disastrous commando raid on Dieppe in World War Two. The cartoon was first published in *Punch* and then republished in the *New Yorker*. In the history of the genre, Crum is important as he prefigures by decades the kind of humour found in the *Goon Show* or *Monty Python*. I am indebted for this information to Dr Mark Bryant whose encyclopaedic knowledge of cartoons is second to none.

" I keep thinking it's Tuesday."

They were soul brothers. Douglas may have had an echo of the cartoon –
reproduced above – in his mind when Arthur Dent complains that, 'It
must be Thursday. I never got the hang of Thursdays.'

Ever since that day, when Nez and Douglas worried that their
conversation or ideas were getting too sensible or prosaic, they would
say that what they needed was a sprinkling of Hippo Dust, a magical
coating of the crazy.

Douglas worked hard on the screenplay out in Santa Fe. He also
managed to have some stimulating dinners at the Institute with the mega-
brains. Meanwhile, Michael Nesmith opened doors in Hollywood and
inveigled the work under the noses of all kinds of powerful people whose
filtering services would otherwise have assassinated the very idea further
upstream. Nez is streetwise in the ways of Hollywood. He has had the
educational experience of becoming dangerous to know, for he fought,
and won, a famous ten-year legal battle with PBS. There is not much he
does not understand about how Hollywood works, and in part he saw
his role as keeping Douglas out of harm's way.

When the film still failed to appear, Ed Victor was terribly disappointed. He and Douglas had a complex relationship. Its warmth went
well beyond the professional bonhomie between an agent and a bestselling
author. Douglas needed fixed points in his life, and Ed was like a mature
older brother, always there to get him money and dispense wisdom.
Douglas wept with anxiety when a conspiracy of events misled him to
believe that Ed had been on Pan Am Flight 103 that was destroyed over

Lockerbie on 21 December 1988. That's not to say that Douglas never ventured down those minor tributaries of conversational infidelity to which all of us are prone. Remaining expediently silent while someone insults a pal is all too human. Writers are particularly likely to whinge about their agents. This is either on the grounds that their bloody agent never does anything or because their agent has got them into some ghastly commitment that the writer cannot possibly discharge without an incomprehensible extremity of angst. Authors are the original ingrates.

Ed recollects:

> When Douglas had finished the screenplay, Michael Nesmith exposed *Hitchhiker's* here and there, but no one bid. And that was the end of that. You know, the moment just passed. A lot of energy and effort had gone into it. When Douglas was out in Santa Fe, I went out there and had dinner with him. At that time he was working well on the screenplay, and Michael was helping him. On another occasion I remember there was a meeting that took place at Michael's ranch. Alan Schwartz came from LA, Douglas and I flew in from Miami and we all sat round talking about it. We were all quite convinced that it was going to happen.

By October 1993, Douglas told *Mostly Harmless*, the fanzine, that he was sure the movie would finally be made. However, by the following February, there was a hint of ambivalence in his witty response to the eternal film question. 'It's off the back burner,' he said, 'and being singed on the front burner.'

But the film didn't happen. Nobody was interested enough to come up with a budget. Not only had Hollywood realized that *Hitchhiker's* was too picaresque for a classical movie structure, and expensive to make, but there was also little evidence there was much of a market for comic SF. Portentous SF – no problem. Epic, mythic SF – clearly a winner. But *comic* SF had hardly ever been done – and probably for good reason.*

---

* One honourable exception is the hilarious *Dark Star*, an early John Carpenter movie (1974), made on a budget of sixpence with a terrific screenplay by Dan O'Bannon. Like *Starship Titanic*, it also features a talking bomb.

This was the received wisdom for nearly twenty years until something occurred that radically changed the climate of opinion, and enabled Ed to make his fourth and final deal. *Men in Black*, with Will Smith and Tommy Lee Jones, came out. It was huge, what *Variety* calls a 'boffo' – a box-office phenomenon. Suddenly everybody wanted funny SF.

Ed resumes the saga:

We just happened to have comic SF and Disney had the money. At the end of 1997, with the help of my co-agent, Bob Bookman at CAA, I sold the rights to Roger Birnbaum for Jay Roach to direct. He was just finishing *Austin Powers, International Man of Mystery*, which was going to be huge. Jay seemed very committed to *Hitchhiker's*. He wanted it to be his next film. That was the plan. Jay would direct it and Roger Birnbaum would produce it. I've always felt that if you made a halfway decent movie of *Hitchhiker's*, you're on to a huge hit. It was going to be an $80 million movie.

It all looked promising. Douglas comforted himself with the thought that the years in development limbo had enabled the technology to catch up with his imagination. It would be a much better movie made in the late nineties than in the early eighties.

Yet even with all these favourable portents, there was a hiccough. New personnel at Disney had looked in some dismay at the *Hitchhiker's* project and its awesome budget, and felt icy winds wuthering up the corporate trousers. Ed recalls:

I was sitting in a little bar in my hotel with Douglas when the whole Disney thing collapsed. He was in despair . . . The reason Disney took a walk is that they had actually greenlit the movie at $45 million. They told Jay [Roach] to make the film for $45 million and that they'd back it . . . But Douglas and Jay said this film is an $80–85 million movie because we've written it that way. They'd have to reconfigure it to make a $45 million movie. I said to Douglas: 'You're crazy. Grab it. It's still a $45 million movie.' And he said: 'No, Ed, it would be cheesy.' I remember, taking my courage in both hands, I said: '*Hitchhiker's is* cheesy – that's its charm. It's not *Star Wars*. You keep on wanting to make *Star Wars* with jokes. But it's not *Star Wars*. It can be cheesy . . .'

Douglas and Ed did row about that observation, but Ed was right. *Hitchhiker's* is the juxtaposition of jokes about a sandwich and the cosmos, the man in the dressing-gown and the starship crossing the galaxy at superluminal speeds. It's scruffy, but philosophically wild. That's its brilliance.

Briefly, Douglas considered mobilizing his fans to bombard Michael Eisner, the head of Disney, with protests. Robbie Stamp, then Managing Director of H2G2, the successor to Douglas's company, The Digital Village, remembers that:

> Douglas sent this achingly sad email . . . My heart really bled for him. It was copied to everybody. Just looking at it you could see it was sent in the wee small hours of the morning. I knew and loved Douglas and I could just feel him there in the night – because he often couldn't sleep – thinking: 'When is this ever going to happen?' So he sent this email which said: 'Let's organize a writing campaign to Disney to show them how big the market is out there and why they should be doing it.' It never happened – we managed to head it off. I think it was left to me to say that it was probably not the best idea. You can imagine Michael Eisner getting email from some sixteen-year-old in Harlesden saying, 'You arsehole, why haven't you made this film?'*

It *was* daft of Douglas after all those years of anguish not to seize the offer of a $45 million movie. Perhaps having carried the torch for so

---

* Douglas had earlier enjoyed some success with an email to the studio in which he had listed every conceivable number on which he could be reached, not excluding his daughter's nanny's mobile and the local supermarket where he might be shopping. He said if they did not call, they were trying very hard not to. It was funny, angry and powerfully written. There is probably nobody else in the world who could have sent an email like that and got away with it. It is republished in *The Salmon of Doubt*.

long and been so steadfast about preserving the special quality of the work, he thought that it would be crazy now – out of sheer fatigue – to compromise. Maybe he gambled that the offer was the first step in a back and forth gavotte that would culminate in something closer to the desired budget – or that the era of men in suits would pass and be replaced by a period of more sympathetic men in suits. But there are thousands of films looking for money. The great William Goldman estimated the ratio of aspiration to execution as ten thousand to one. Douglas's bluff was called. He felt defeated. His entire family had transplanted to Santa Barbara so he could follow his dream. He was utterly despondent.

It is odd, by the way, that such a super-intelligent man did not have greater clarity of vision about his film, because Ed was spot on. *Hitchhiker's* is not *Star Wars*; it doesn't need $80 million. It's script-led. The fx needed to be credible, but they are not the essence of the movie. There may even have been some demon of the perverse at work in Douglas's complex nature – even so, the hint of fear that he felt at being put to the test would have been far outweighed by his desire to see the movie made.

Then in May 2001, Douglas died.

It is an irony too obvious to labour that the film of *The Hitchhiker's Guide to the Galaxy* is once again on the stocks and looking more probable than at any moment in the last twenty years. At the time of writing (April 2003), Robbie Stamp is pushing it along with a judicious mixture of tact and steel. Jay Roach now has other commitments but Karey Kirkpatrick, whose pin-sharp screenwriting has given us such delights as *James and the Giant Peach* and the blissful *Chicken Run*, has produced an excellent screenplay. The budget may no longer look like the population of a large country, but it will be substantial.

Woody Allen once said that some seek immortality through their work, but that he preferred to achieve it by not dying. Lacking that option, Douglas does leave work behind him that will give many generations pleasure and pause for thought. Personal extinction is something only a few of us, usually in the grip of religious mania, rate highly; the truth is that it's bleak. But however bloody awful it may be, we are not just our bodies. We all contribute something to the world – and this is especially true of creative artists.

Douglas scoffed at superstition. Robert Heinlein, the SF writer, once had a pedantic alien who would not say 'good luck' but insisted on the locution 'benign random variable factors to you'. Benign random variable factors to the *Hitchhiker's* movie then. Millions of fans are hoping it will be added to Douglas's many achievements.

chapter ten

On love

'. . . there was Arthur Dent the smooth and casual, in
corduroys and a chunky sweater. His hair was cropped and
washed, his chin clean shaven. Only the eyes still said that
whatever it was the Universe thought it was doing to him,
he would still like it please to stop.'

So Long, and Thanks for All the Fish

The Hitchhiker's Guide to the Galaxy proves mathematically that there
is nothing in the universe. If the universe is, as many cosmologists
believe, infinite then any quantity, no matter how chunky, divided by
infinity tends to zero. Confusingly there are many different varieties
of infinity recognized by mathematicians, and many physicists
believe that the universe is finite but unbounded, a counter-intuitive
notion that demands instant retreat to a quiet pub for further
pondering. This is just the sort of thing that Douglas enjoyed
discussing.

But there is no doubt that space is big. The basic notion holds. To
put it in more elegant notation: $n/\infty \rightarrow 0$. This simple formula
encapsulates the ultimate triviality of mankind, and life itself, so it is
just as well that we do not think about it all the time. The same dismal
truth suggests that there is no money, and no conscious entities to
spend it even if there were. Continuing the thought, this is what
Douglas had to say about the amount of sex in the universe:

None. In fact there is an awful lot of this largely because of the total lack of money, trade, banks or anything else that might keep all the nonexistent people of the universe occupied.

However, it is not worth embarking on a long discussion of it now because it really is terribly complicated . . .

And here is the authentic voice of Douglas on the subject of human relations:

'Here I am, Zaphod Beeblebrox, I can go anywhere, do anything. I have the greatest ship in the known sky, a girl with whom things seem to be working out pretty well . . .'

'Are they?'

'As far as I can tell. I'm not an expert in personal relationships . . .'

Trillian raised her eyebrows.

'I am,' he added, 'one hell of a guy. I can do anything I want only I haven't the faintest idea what.'*

Like Zaphod, Douglas was no expert at human relations. Sometimes he could be slow on the uptake, as in this story that he told against himself. Here Jon Canter recounts it:

Douglas was in New York, I think on his first promo tour. He met this incredibly beautiful woman in a bar. He talked and talked. You know what writers are like. He talked for an hour and a half – he told her everything about himself, his plans, his book, and what he was doing in New York. And finally he said: 'And what do you do?' And she said: 'I entertain men.' Even then, he didn't pick up on it. He said: 'Oh, that's interesting. How do you do that?' And she said: 'Sexually . . .'

Douglas was a big man with large appetites. He was amusing, hedonistic, wealthy and, for much of his life, single. He moved in

---

* *Life, the Universe and Everything* (Pan Books, 1982).

sophisticated media circles; you may guess that he did not live with austere monk-like chastity all the time. He liked women: he was romantic, extravagant, entertaining, and sometimes a little careless.*

He also did not do things by halves, for, in late 1980, he fell deeply, precipitously, passionately in love. He could no more have resisted than a deckchair could resist a tornado. He was blown off his feet.

He met Sally Emerson at a writer's talk in Sterling, Scotland, when her first novel, *Second Sight*, was published and he was publicizing *The Restaurant at the End of the Universe*. They were both young novelists of about the same age. He was Cambridge; she was Oxford. Sally is a talented writer, and she had been a terrific editor of the literary magazine, *Books and Bookmen*, before its publishers self-destructed. She is slim, dark-haired and with a sexy smile. At the time she was in a state of change; her job had vanished and she had been with the same man for eight years when, just as they were both getting restive, she married him. As it turned out, this was not so foolish since he really was the man for her in the end.

However, at this time, Sally and Douglas were attracted to each other in a way that was all the more intense for their feeling that it was dangerous. She was tremendously drawn to him. She writes:

> He struck me as enormously vulnerable, and the combination of his huge, masculine form and little-boy-lost manner was attractive. The first time we met he was sincere and intense rather than funny. I can see him now, slouched low in a chair late at night talking, with his limbs somehow all over the place like an octopus . . . I remember thinking then on that first evening that Douglas definitely needed me, or someone very like me.

They had much in common, but it was not until they met each other again in New York, where Sally's novel was being published, that they

---

* I'm sorry, readers, there is no list of romantic attachments. Pepys made diary notes about his sexual activities using a primitive code deciphered by scholars for the amusement of later generations, but that was in the seventeenth century . . .

started an affair. They went off to Mexico together. The relationship continued back in London where Sally lived around the corner from Douglas in Highbury. She nudged him to change his flat and his agent and helped him find the duplex in St Alban's Place. It never appealed to her, however, as much as to Douglas; Sally says there was something just too showy about it.

Their relationship was tortured and romantic.

> We understood each other very well, and we were on exactly the same imaginative wavelength. It was the joy of our relationship but it also contained within it the seeds of its destruction. When one of us was upset, so was the other. It was as though there were no walls between us. I would be constantly leaving him, furious at his massive egotism, but would return before I was even at the bottom of the stairs.

Douglas was knocked over by his emotions. Here he was – a material-ist sceptic with a scientific world view – completely, sentimentally, embarrassingly in love. He knew all about the mechanistic explanation – the pheromones, the endocrine system, the unimaginable stretches of time over which our genes, through the blind repetition of Darwinian processes, had tweaked us into sophisticated vehicles for their own propagation. But what was going on? Why did he feel so blissfully soppy? Had his brain gone? (Douglas has Arthur Dent, in a similar state, apologize in a shop for a non sequitur: 'Forgive me,' he says, 'I'm terribly happy.') It just didn't compute. An evolutionary biologist might argue that love has been selected because close relationships make for reproductive success, but couldn't mutual need account for stable bonding just as well? Where does the joy come from? Love is as hard to explain to a materialist as the genius of Bach.

Sally and Douglas lived together in St Alban's Place, both writing. Douglas's writing was getting harder all the time – three on the Beaton Scale of Author Angst, with occasional peaks at four. Sally, on the other hand, wrote fluently and had made a respectable literary debut, gaining some excellent reviews in the sort of papers that Douglas resented. Douglas held Sally up for approval of his prose far more often than vice versa, and she was glad of being in sympathy with him creatively and able to help. The image of these two writers tapping away in different rooms in the large apartment, passing each other on the stairs or meeting in the kitchen for coffee, comparing notes about their output (or lack of it) has a certain sitcom-ish quality, perhaps with a hint of Strindberg. ('I've done a thousand words. How about you?' 'I've done twenty-seven, but every one is placed with the precision of a haiku – so there . . .') It was an intense affair; they were thrown in upon each other.

The book Douglas was writing at the time was *Life, the Universe and Everything*, which recycled some of the ideas in his TV treatment, *Dr Who and the Krikkitmen*. Though it uses the well-loved cast of *Hitchhiker's* characters, it was his first novel not based on radio scripts and it contains some fresh, unearthly invention. For instance, Wowbagger is a creature condemned to eternal life by a bizarre accident. ('Me only cruel immortality consumes . . .' said the ever-aging Tithonus in Tennyson's poem.) Wowbagger, tortured by his infinite longevity, bored to the bone, but unable to be bored to death, makes it his mission to insult personally every conscious entity in the universe. Slartibartfast also reappears in a more active role than in his previous outing. There is a lot of battling in this novel, much inadvertent warfare and accidental killing. It is funny, but quite violent and disturbing. The ultimate question and ultimate answer are proved to be unknowable simultaneously – a sardonic reflection on humankind's stupid yearning to know one or two Really Big Things as opposed to lots and lots of interestingly complex little things. Douglas really didn't want to write any more *Hitchhiker's* and was trying to draw a line under them with this book. He tried even harder with the next, *So Long, and Thanks for All the Fish*.

There are many ideas in *Life, the Universe and Everything*, a book which is dedicated to Sally. She says that he told her in a letter that he had intended to write 'To Sally – who I love above the title', but she had left him by then so he couldn't. Interestingly, it was Douglas's next book which reflects the relationship more than the one being written while the affair was going on. He was hurt by the hostility of the critics who by and large felt that this third outing was veering towards self-parody and repetition. ('Arthur Dent is in danger of being shrivelled in the heat of his author's imagination,' wrote Kelvin Johnstone in the *Observer*.) It is also the novel in the trilogy (all five of them) that many fans find the least satisfactory, for it is a love story in fantasy camouflage, more tender than cosmic. This did not stop the book selling in huge numbers, and it may tell us something about the fans, of course. *Life, the Universe and Everything* was the first book for which Douglas toured Australia, a country that he liked hugely for many of the same reasons that he found California so appealing.

One particularly engaging notion in *Life, the Universe and Everything*, which Douglas developed in more depth in *So Long, and Thanks for All the Fish*, is being able to fly like a bird. It's his metaphor for love and a kind of ecstasy. In chapter two of *Life, the Universe and Everything*, Ford explains to Arthur how to fly. Solitude has so ravaged him by this point in the novel that his social skills and even his vocabulary have fallen into disuse. In all senses he needs Ford to give him a lift:

'The Guide says there is an art to flying,' said Ford, 'or rather a knack. The knack lies in learning how to throw yourself at the ground and miss.' He smiled weakly. He pointed to the knees of his trousers and held up his arms to show the elbows. They were all torn and worn through.

Fenchurch, 'Fenny', adored by Arthur Dent in *So Long, and Thanks for All the Fish*, also has a problem with everyday physics. Her feet do not actually touch the ground, a fine example of Douglas's ability to take the familiar (in this case, a figure of speech) and make us wonder what would happen if it were literally true. Fenny, rather like many of the women in the novels of Douglas's hero, Charles Dickens, is a slightly fey and mawkish character. Arthur loves her dearly – or perhaps he loves the idea of her rather more.

Fenchurch and Arthur learn to fly together, and their flight is sustained by mutual confidence. The shadow of doubt brings them back to earth. As if in some enchanting cartoon, they pirouette and zoom above the London rooftops, surprising the birds and a passing 747. Flying, like love, is an altered state, an escape from ground level and all the gravity of the daily round that imprisons us in the prosaic. Sally says that at first she was flattered to think she was the model for Fenchurch, but that when she read the book carefully she was less so. The novel is all about Arthur's love for her, and not really about her at all.

Despite the fun and the access to smart restaurants, living with Douglas was hard work. Discretion was a quality foreign to his extravagant nature. He was bursting to let on, with the result that he told all his friends (in strictest confidence of course) how happy he was, and why. He might possibly have stopped passers-by on the street and told them too. Soon Douglas and Sally's relationship was common knowledge in the circles in which they moved, and it wasn't long before it was reported in London's daily paper, the *Evening Standard*. Sally was very upset about this, but she says that Douglas was much better at being supported than being supportive. It was, she says, like trying to get comfort from a black hole.

Years later this handy definition appeared in *The Meaning of Liff*:

Tukituki (n)
A sexual liaison which is meant to be secret but which is in fact common knowledge.

Douglas was not only emotionally needy but averse to commitment, attributes to which his odd childhood must have contributed. On top of that he was a creative artist of some genius who had no easy affinity with the art form that made him his fortune. These were the ingredients of an insecure mix. For all his charm and humour, Douglas could be relentlessly self-absorbed. Living with him was emotionally draining.

After less than a year, Sally and Douglas broke up. Sally felt claustrophobic. She had to escape; she missed her husband. Years later, when he felt able to be flippant, Douglas remarked that, 'She went off with this bloke on the to me rather spurious grounds that he was her husband.' For Sally it was a good move. She went back to her husband (who had not been pining at home all the time) and they rediscovered all the reasons why they had got together in the first place. As in all the best stories, they produced two talented kids and lived happily ever after.

Douglas, on the other hand, was plunged into what his mother, Janet, called the Sally Crisis. His family had to rally round. Janet came up from Dorset. Little Jane, then a teenager, turned up occasionally to administer sympathy and cups of tea, and try to take the Black Dog out for the occasional walkie. Douglas drooped about the St Alban's Place flat moping tearfully, feeling wretched and wondering What It Was All About.

Douglas and Sally had exchanged a fair amount of correspondence. Writing this book would be so much less toe-curlingly intrusive if they had been of Pepys's era, say, safely sanctified by history; I could look at their love letters in the sterile conditions of the Public Records Office or the British Library to lift appropriate chunks for the modern reader. As it is, I felt rather like a moist journalist from the tabloids when I chanced upon their correspondence in the bottom of one of Douglas's huge crates of disorganized papers. Wordsworth described a particular variety of nature poet as 'one who would peep and botanize upon his mother's grave'. Biographers must feel like that all the time.

Three things struck me about these letters.

Firstly, as you would expect from two literary talents in a state of heightened emotion and at the top of their form, the letters were beautifully written and suffused with feeling. Douglas was demanding though wildly romantic. At one point he wrote that he would come back for Sally after the bomb fell. In a hundred years' time, like the correspondence between the Brownings, their letters should be published.

Mind you, the utter shamelessness of writers would bring a smile to the face of a reader familiar with Douglas's work. Some of the nifty turns of phrase in his letters were recycled in books – possibly as private references, but also because they were just too good to be lost. For instance, in one of them there's an evocative account of a Victorian picture of anthropomorphized animals, seen with vague unease in childhood and only decontaminated years later by adult perception. It reappears almost unchanged in *So Long, and Thanks for All the Fish*.* This in no way detracts from the emotion behind the original account.

---

* Pan hardback edition (1984), p. 108–9.

Artists use everything, but that doesn't mean they live their lives in what your existentialist would call bad faith. It's just that the well they draw from is themselves; nothing is sacred. The pride of creation is overwhelming; they cannot let the good bits go to waste after one private outing.

Secondly, Douglas's tone after the break-up is full of complaint. He found it difficult to comprehend Sally's viewpoint. He was terribly anguished but self-referential. (How could you do this to *me* with all my creative burdens?) Eric Berne in his classic book on transactional analysis, *Games People Play*, identifies one of the games as 'See What You've Made Me Do'.* The letters show Douglas playing that one at tournament level. Undeniably the poor man was prostrate with unhappiness, but he showed little understanding that Sally had also been put through the wringer. His own emotional needs were so profound that he did not – or could not – always grasp that other people had them too.

Finally, Douglas had neatly fixed copies of his own replies to Sally's letters. For a biographer that's handy, but you have to wonder why. It's not as if, like some villain in a melodrama, he'd promised Sally to make her Empress of India and had to be careful not to contradict or repeat himself in later exchanges. Like all couples going through the pain of break-up, there was a certain amount of epistolary ping-pong of the 'in Paris you said . . . no, you said it first' variety. Anybody who has been through such an experience knows there is no contradiction between trivial point scoring and being racked by huge emotions. However, Douglas attached copies of his own love letters in reply to Sally's for the entire course of the affair, not just the terminal stages. Perhaps here too his writer's pride took precedence over everything. He could not bear to see a good piece of work consigned to the post forever, like a message in a bottle hurled into the sea. Of course, it's possible that he retrospectively organized the correspondence though the closeness with which the two of them responded to each other's letters gives the impression that the admin was contemporaneous.

---

* *Games People Play*, Eric Berne (Penguin Books 1978).

244 Wish you were here

Somehow keeping copies seems rather too efficient for a man in a state of turmoil – but God forbid that too much is read into a stapler. Make of it what you will.

One thing that Douglas did ask of Sally when they had irretrievably separated was that she promise that – though the heavens fall – she would never, *never* ever, have an affair with John Lloyd.

Following the break-up, Mary Allen was dismayed by the state Douglas had worked himself into by late 1981. She realized that what he needed was company. Douglas without society was a lost soul, and a twenty-eight-year-old man cannot expect his mum to be on hand all the time.

Mary Allen and Jane Belson had become friends under unusual circumstances. Jane had been going out with a barrister called Martin whom she took to a party where he met Mary Allen and promptly started dating her too. Mary decided quite quickly that the relationship was not for her, particularly after she heard on the grapevine that she was not quite the only woman in Martin's life. About a year later Martin (who had by then confessed all to Jane) thought it would be entertaining to introduce them to each other to see if they would scratch each other's eyes out. In fact they liked each other immediately and have remained on the best of terms ever since.

Jane recalls her first encounter with Douglas:

Mary felt sorry for Douglas but her capacity for listening to him on the phone for two hours a day was running out. He was desperate in that big flat on his own. She thought a solution would be to provide him with a flat mate. They discussed two or three possibles. One of them was me, and the others were eliminated by Douglas on the grounds that he would only have an affair with them – and that was not what he wanted. I had retrained as a barrister and was doing pupillage at the bar, where you don't have any income at all, so I was stony broke and back living with my parents. So when Mary suggested it, the idea appealed. I had met Douglas a few times by then, but didn't know him at all well. I knew Sally and her husband rather better.

I came to see him and the flat to see if it would work. My first reaction was to be surprised all over again by how much taller he was than me. Most men aren't. He took me up to the roof garden where we sat on uncomfortable metal chairs. He was shy and awkward at first. I think he was comforted by the fact that I knew Sally and her husband so he didn't have to start the story from the beginning. We discovered more mutual friends – Douglas was a wonderfully indiscreet gossip – and started to feel more at ease with each other. Douglas had a curious combination of confidence and shyness, with physical awkwardness thrown in. He didn't know where to put his legs and waved his hands around a lot when he talked. He later told me that when he was little and his mother wanted him to stop talking, she would tell him to sit on his hands. For Douglas, talking without moving his hands around was like trying to eat a sugary doughnut without licking your lips.

We passed each other's tests and I moved into the spare bedroom. It's odd sharing a flat with a man you don't really know all that well. Shortly after I moved in, the Falklands War (sorry, Conflict) broke out, and while it was horrible it was also exciting in a gruesome sort of way. We took it in turns to rush downstairs and get the newspaper every morning and we watched TV news all the time.

Douglas was under great pressure to finish *Life, The Universe and Everything*, which had come to a grinding halt about halfway through when Sally left. He sat in his study with several typewriters switching from one to the other to give the day a bit of structure. There would be bursts of typing punctuated by long bits of guitar playing (acoustic – the electric guitar came later and annoyed the hell out of our neighbours). I'd come home from chambers to find Douglas waiting to read me what he had written, scrutinizing my reactions minutely and checking carefully to see that I was laughing in the right way at the right joke. It was my first encounter with a writer (well, anybody really) who needed that level of reassurance.

When Jane was first spotted by Rick and Heidi, Douglas's architect neighbours in St Alban's Place, they were intrigued. Sometimes she appeared as a tall figure in fuscous barrister gear like some kind of professional *burka*, but off duty Jane sported a minute red leather miniskirt revealing legs that went on and on. 'We wondered what Douglas was up to,' Rick said. 'It looked odd.'

Jane has the sort of brain that takes no prisoners. Douglas would complain about it sometimes – rather unfairly – though he was proud of her.* Of course it would be lovely for any chap if the woman in his life gave him unconditional support and admiration for every notion, no matter how daft, but in the long term she would not be doing him a favour at all. Jane kept Douglas anchored to the ground. In the psychobabble of today, this service is known as a reality check. It's invaluable, and not to be confused with lack of support: it is in fact the very best available.

Jane and Douglas became friends, then lovers, and eventually soulmates.

They were one of the most fashionable couples in London. They knew the brightest and the best from showbiz, the media, technology and the law – and they gave amazing parties in the apartment off Upper Street. One infamous occasion climaxed with a famous woman writer being entertained (in the same way as the woman in the bar in New York entertained men) by two chaps simultaneously while everyone else at first drifted, and then scuttled, into the other arm of the L-shaped drawing room. Douglas's mother attended that party and received a contrite letter afterwards from the woman concerned. 'Oh, *that* party,' Janet recalls with the *sang froid* of a nurse who has seen almost everything, 'that party was really rather naughty. But is it fair? That woman is about my age.'

Jane and Douglas also liked to give dinner parties and enjoyed

---

* Sue and I went to dinner there on Friday 18 June 1982, shortly after they had got together. 'Guess what Jane does,' a grinning Douglas challenged us after some articulate and well-sustained riff from Jane on a subject long forgotten. 'Hmm,' I said, 'doctor, journo, academic philosopher . . .?' Sue twigged it at once because she noticed the formal clothes as well as the orderly marshalling of ideas. [Info courtesy of Sue Webb's addiction to diaries.] It was slow of me not to get it, though Jane managed to keep her professional reflexes contained in the courtroom, unlike one barrister of our acquaintance. If you say 'good morning' to him, he counterattacks: 'I put it to you that it is Not a good morning . . .'

Jane Belson in the early
eighties when she first met
Douglas.

Douglas and Polly.

Janet Thrift, Douglas's mother, at home in Dorset in 1991.

Jane Thrift, aka Little Jane, and James Thrift at an 'Unplugged' party.

The 'Guitar Henge' at the top of the house in Duncan Terrace. Douglas had twenty-four left-handed guitars.

Douglas and Dave Gilmour of Pink Floyd practising at Earl's Court for Douglas's forty-second birthday appearance.

The author, Catherine Webb aged six, Polly Adams aged a few weeks, and Douglas in Duncan Terrace in June 1994.

Douglas and Jane in party mode in November 1996.

JILL FURMANOVSKY

Douglas, ecstatic, at an 'Unplugged' party with Margot Buchanan and Robbie McIntosh in the background.

Some of the 'Unplugged' audience enjoying themselves. Mark Wing-Davey and Richard Harris are visible in the foreground. Richard Creasey, Salman Rushdie and the author can be spotted towards the back.

JILL FURMANOVSKY

The directors of The Digital Village in Ed Victor's office in the spring of 1996. Standing (left to right): Richard Harris, Mary Glanville, Ian Stewart, Richard Creasey, Ed Victor. Sitting: Douglas and Robbie Stamp.

Terry Jones and Douglas in a promo picture for Starship Titanic in 1998.

Douglas's lectures and readings were theatrical performances. In typical thespian mode at the Almeida Theatre, Islington in 1996.

Jane, Polly and Douglas lived here, their second and favourite house in Santa Barbara.

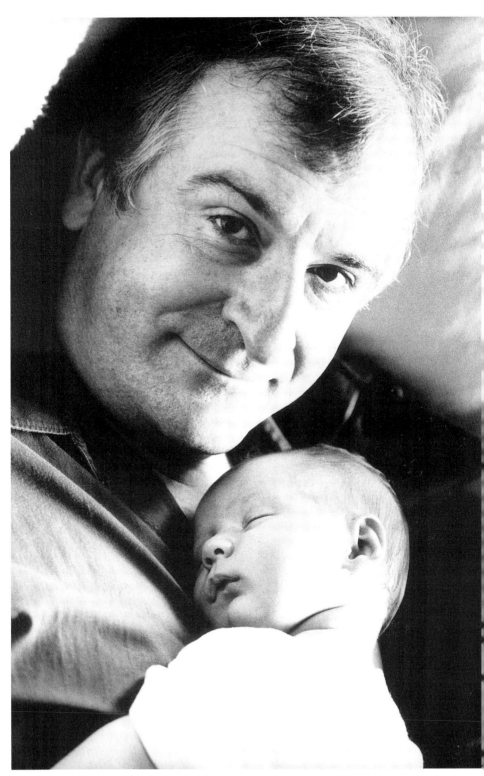
Polly and her proud father in July 1994.

collecting clever people from diverse fields and putting them together. On one lavish occasion they fed over a hundred people and – fearing the conversational constipation of the Brits – managed to find an intriguing fact about every single person that they printed out and placed with the adjacent guest.*

A well-known anecdote from this period concerns Sir Clive Sinclair, he of the eponymous computers, digital watches and calculators, who was having dinner with them (October 1984). He spotted an early proof copy of *So Long, and Thanks for All the Fish*.

'I must have it,' he said, with the unwavering singleness of purpose that distinguishes the entrepreneur from lesser folk.

'Alas,' said Douglas, 'I'm afraid it's the only one, so I must hang on to it.'

'I'll buy it, of course,' said Sir Clive.

'I am sorry,' replied Douglas, 'but it's my only early copy and not for sale.'

'A thousand pounds,' said Sir Clive, taking out his chequebook, 'to the charity of your choice . . .'

Greenpeace made a grand that evening.

Throughout this period the relationship between Douglas and Jane deepened:

We sort of lived together, and we had a lot of fun. When he finished *Life, The Universe and Everything*, we went off for a while and enjoyed ourselves. It was Whitsun, and we toured round bits of France in his open-topped VW listening to very loud music – Paul Simon mostly – and staying at very nice places. He had told his mother he was taking me, so we got visited by his mother and his aunt for an inspection. We both had Aunt Vals as it happened, who lived very respectably with men to whom they were not married. Douglas's Aunt Val was deeply glamorous and enormous fun. She led off the vetting, asking exactly the sort of questions you hope people won't.

---

* Mine said: On your left is Anita Carey. Good thing to ask her about: her grandmother and Bernard Shaw.

Not surprisingly, Jane survived the vetting process.

In August 1983, after their move to Los Angeles, they both became desperately homesick, even Douglas who had taken to California like a walrus slipping into the briny. Returning, they drove all the way east across America in a Saab, listening to music and being impressed by the sheer scale of it all. There's a romance to the size of the States that eludes us in Britain where you cannot drive all day, listening to country and western artists singing sad ballads through their noses, without ending up in the sea. From New York they flew home, and were reinstalled in Upper Street, where Jane resumed her practice as a barrister. Douglas started writing *So Long, and Thanks for All the Fish,* found he had enormous trouble with it and ended up being locked in that hotel with Sonny Mehta.

The relationship between Douglas and Jane did not always float along serenely. As Denis Healey once said of the government, it only looks like a swan on the surface because it's paddling like buggery underneath. Jane sometimes found it tough living with Douglas. He was adorable but egocentric, enthusiastic but indecisive, creative yet repetitive . . . (She bore the word-perfect retellings of anecdotes with great fortitude as any loyal partner must.) But he was never dull. 'I had to do the work on the growing-up side of the ledger,' said Jane. 'I think that's because he thought he'd lose his creativity.'

Douglas had a weakness for toys, Jane remembers, especially electronic and expensive ones.

> He bought them on impulse. He had a complete incapacity for throwing things away – not because he didn't like throwing things away, but because he could not decide *what* to throw away. The process of decision-making was beyond him, so he kept everything. And I think he also felt guilty because he was the first of his contemporaries to make money. So he was stinking rich while they were all grubbing around trying to make a living. I think he did find that difficult. Now, of course, a lot of them are richer.

It wasn't just the jettisoning of toys that drove him into agonies of indecision. Douglas was fearful of commitment, and Jane is strong-willed. They mostly got on, but they had some astonishing arguments on a scale suitable for decommissioning by United Nations weapons inspectors. In 1985 they nearly got married, Jane recalls, but they both backed off.

Jane remembers one fearsomely energetic row (topic now wholly forgotten) they had sitting across the table from each other:

> Douglas would argue with great passion, precise grammar and a lot of sub-clauses. He was in full flow, arms windmilling, when he suddenly stopped. I waited. And waited a bit more, and then the penny dropped. 'Split the fucking infinitive.' I said.

One morning of this interesting time – which happened to be St Valentine's Day – Jane opened her front door to find a large bunch of exquisite flowers. From Douglas. A few minutes later, the doorbell rang and there was another and larger bunch. Both bunches were put in water before Jane left for work. At court she was interrupted in listening to her client's account of the appalling behaviour of his about-to-be-ex-wife by the delivery of another and, by then, ludicrously huge bunch of flowers by an impressed usher. 'You keep that man,' she said. 'He must be a good one.' Jane's client was less romantically touched. A fourth bunch was waiting in the court office as she left. Having struggled back to Chambers carrying the files of an acrimonious divorce and two bunches of flowers, she was greeted by a fifth under her desk. Once home, bunches six and seven arrived. She spent the evening scrounging vases.

All through the eighties they tacked back and forth. Mostly they had fun. They fell out, and got together again for massive reconciliations. They were passionate and cheesed off with each other simultaneously. Both parties took what Jane termed 'time off for bad behaviour' when they lived apart for a while. In the old Chinese proverb sense, it was an interesting time.

But, having been put to the test, their relationship survived. On 25 November 1991, Pan threw a party for Douglas in the Groucho Club in London's Soho. Ostensibly it was to celebrate the recent Pan publication of *Last Chance to See* and the presentation of Douglas's third Golden Pan Award. Douglas faxed the ever-efficient Jacqui Graham, by then a director, an extensive guest list. She was not surprised, though she sighed a little at its length.

In the event, all became clear. Douglas had hijacked the party. All his mates were there (including Sue and me) freeloading remorselessly on champagne and those delicious little edibles. Suddenly there was a pinging of glasses as our attention was requested. Douglas placed himself in the 'Ladies and Gentlemen' position. He looked sublimely happy. Jane stood next to him in a fetching irony-red suit. Instead of the usual gracious author speech, he announced that we were all wrong in our speculation about when they would ever get married because 'after a whirlwind ten-year romance' he and Jane had done the deed that very afternoon. Everybody roared with approval.

On 22 June 1994, Jane gave birth to Polly Jane Rocket Adams. (Rocket for Jane's pregnant food cravings rather than the spectacular but crude device for getting into space.) They adored her from the first moment; Douglas was besotted and would whip out his baby pictures on any pretext despite the fact that all babies look much the same (except one's own). Polly was pretty cute, with her mother's brown eyes, and already at the top of the range for height. Douglas had so many photographs that if he held them by a corner and flipped the edges, there would have been the illusion of movement.

Brian Davies, who as a director of Pan in the UK and Australia, knew Douglas well, once spotted him with Polly in Harrods. It was Christmas 1995, so Polly was still not much more than a babe in arms. She was looking lovely but bewildered. 'What ho, Douglas. Happy Christmas,' said Brian. 'And to you,' replied Douglas, looking slightly sheepish. 'Um, I thought it was about time that Polly met Father Christmas . . .'

Indeed, the happiest I ever saw Douglas was when he was flopping on one of their big, squashy sofas with little Polly resting on his substantial tum. She was half asleep, looking up at her dad from a position that gave her a view up his mountain range of a nose. He was peering down at her with a look of utter bliss on his face.

A year after Polly's birth, Douglas and Jane held a party in her honour. Douglas, as a committed atheist, would not hear of her being dunked by some soggy-minded cleric into an unhygienic stone bath full of cold water. Yet he felt that new life in general, and Polly in particular, needed to be celebrated.

Douglas and Jane devised a sort of secular christening and called upon their formidable collection of mates with histrionic talent to provide some inspiring performances. It could have been funny – all those London fashionables tiptoeing around the forbidden God word – but actually it was touching.

After we'd all got thoroughly mellow in Duncan Terrace on the generous lashings of champagne, about a dozen pieces were read. Sue Lloyd-Roberts, one of Jane's oldest friends, found something funny. There was a double hander too, and some music. Little Polly was either in her parents' arms or crawling about beneath the piano looking amazed. Jonny Brock, also an un-godparent, contributed a deed. The layout, the legalisms, the dearth of punctuation – all show his training in drafting, though the undertakings themselves were less formal, a mix of the deeply felt and the deeply frivolous. The contract went like this:

THIS DEED is made the 24th day of June 1995
BETWEEN DOUGLAS NOEL ADAMS and JANE HYACINTH BELSON ('the Parents') of the first part and SUE LETITIA LLOYD-ROBERTS MARY MABEL ALLEN MICHAEL CALIGULA BYWATER and JONATHAN SIMON BROCK of the second part

WHEREBY the parties intend to contract for the benefit succour wellbeing and support of POLLY JANE ROCKET (sic) ADAMS ('the Child')

IT IS HEREBY AGREED AS FOLLOWS

1. The parties of the second part are intended by the parents each to assume the role of non-denominational guardian or vicarious supreme being substitute but will hereafter for the sake of convenience only be referred to as 'the Godparents'

2. This deed is non-gender-discriminatory and where the context so admits the feminine shall include the masculine and vice versa

3. The Parents hereby covenant with the Child and with the Godparents as follows:

(1) To bring up the Child in a supreme being fearing and sober manner

(2) To lavish her with love and affection

(3) Not to be too horrid to her boyfriends howsoever spotty and malodorous they may be from time to time

4. The Godparents hereby each and severally covenant with the Child and with the Parents as follows:

(1) To be a jolly good chap[ette] at all material times

(2) To commiserate with the Child as to the irascibility and downright curmudgeonliness of the Parents

(3) [Female godparents] To take the Child on bracing walking holidays in Iceland

(4) [Male godparents] To do bugger all until the Child is 16 and thereafter to take her on long weekends to Venice whereat the waiters will ogle the Child and cast admiring and envious glances at the Godparent

(5) [Lloyd-Roberts] To foster in the Child the spirit of independence enterprise and downright rank foolhardiness

(6) [Allen] To teach the Child how to be a very important person indeed

(7) [Bywater] To tutor the Child in the ways of boozing whoring falling down drunk shooting up down and every which way and playing the piano like unto an angel

(8) [Brock] To rant

WHEREAT the parties have this day hereunto signed and affixed their seals
WITNESSED BY

Douglas himself made a short speech about how profoundly his world view had changed for the better since the birth of little Polly. His sense of wonder had been renewed. Though not a man who often resorted to other people's words, the poem which encapsulated his feelings the best was Keats' 'On First Looking into Chapman's Homer'. It's beautiful, so here it is:

> Much have I travell'd in the realms of gold,
> And many goodly states and kingdoms seen;
> Round many western islands have I been
> Which bards in fealty to Apollo hold.
> Oft of one wide expanse had I been told
> That deep-brow'd Homer ruled as his demesne;
> Yet did I never breathe its pure serene
> Till I heard Chapman speak out loud and bold:
> Then felt I like some watcher of the skies
> When a new planet swims into his ken;
> Or like stout Cortez, when with eagle eyes
> He stared at the Pacific – and all his men
> Look'd at each other with a wild surmise –
> Silent, upon a peak on Darien.

Douglas read this well, with tears in his eyes. He loved Polly totally and unconditionally. It was the least complicated relationship of his entire life.

chapter eleven

More books, money and a Sense of Place

'The planet has, or had, a problem – which was this: most of the people living on it were unhappy for pretty much of the time. Many solutions were suggested for this problem, but most of these were largely concerned with the movements of small green pieces of paper, which is odd because on the whole it wasn't the small green pieces of paper that were unhappy.'

Fit the Second, *The Hitchhiker's Guide to the Galaxy*

Douglas was never a man to settle down like an old cat in an airing cupboard, but the 1980s were relatively stable. His fame was considerable, and so was his income. Unfortunately, he was pretty hopeless about managing his money. If there were a shoppers' spectrum of caution, with somebody at one end of the scale who takes six months of reconnaissance before buying a hanky and a tonto out-of-control impulse purchaser at the other, Douglas would have been firmly down the frivolous end. But the fortunes spent in restaurants and computer shops were small potatoes compared to what he spent on places to live. It was paradoxical; he loved travelling, yet he needed to put down roots.

Ed Victor had negotiated an advance of over £600,000 for *Life, the Universe and Everything* from Heinemann bidding with Pan. It was an ideal combination for Douglas: for he stayed with his paperback house that had done so well by him, but he had the kudos of a hardback edition from an established hardcover publisher. He had always been irritated by the distinction in English letters between literary writing and commercial fiction – or perhaps 'successful' or 'accessible' would be better words than commercial. It's a divide which has more to do with snobbery than editorial virtue. Isn't there, as Wilde observed in another context, just good writing and bad writing? Nick Clee, the urbane editor of the *Bookseller* (the publishing industry's trade journal) recalls having dinner with Douglas and Jacqui Graham at the Edinburgh Book Festival in 1983. 'Douglas was charming and funny, but a bit chippy about reviewers. He said that if the opening sequence of *A History of the World in 10½ Chapters* [Julian Barnes] had been submitted to the BBC comedy department, it would have been promptly rejected.' Douglas knew just how excruciatingly hard it was to create his kind of book and could not understand why it merited less attention than the novel of another writer who happened not to employ the conventions and shortcuts of SF.* His deal with a grand old hardcover publisher seemed like critical validation.

Money from foreign rights was also finding its way down the contractual links in satisfactory volume. Douglas was doing well all over the planet. Eastern Europe could not get enough of him, and the Japanese had taken to his Zen humour in a big way. He was particularly successful in Germany, then as now a major market that in those pre-Euro days paid in DMs, a currency solid enough to induce a religious experience in any recipient.† Infocom, the leading Massachusetts-based game company, had acquired the computer game rights (in 1983) in *Hitchhiker's* in a multi-game deal for a sum believed to be one million dollars.

In 1983, Faber and Faber published *The Meaning of Liff* by Douglas

---

* Lisa Eveleigh, the literary agent, recounts how she was once in ZEN NW3 (a restaurant, what else?) with all the agents from A.P. Watt who were making a huge fuss of their client, Graham Swift, the Booker Prize winner. By chance Douglas and some friends were in the same restaurant. Douglas came over and toasted them with these ambivalent words: 'Commercial fiction pays homage to literary fiction . . .'

† Douglas did several tours in Germany, both for book promotion and as a guest speaker at scientific conferences. He enjoyed them very much. The audiences, a sophisticated lot, had no trouble with his English and they very much got his off-beat sense of humour. Why is it that the mischievous stereotypes about national characteristics die so hard?

and John Lloyd (Faber was John's publisher). It was a cute, breast-pocket sized edition quite stuffed with definitions that really ought to exist. Creatively it is a *tour de force.* William Burroughs once defined language as the ultimate control system legislating thought, feeling and what he rather alarmingly called *apparent* sensory perception. It's instant migraine trying to think of a concept for which there is no word in the lexicon. We think linguistically, after all. Actually, there is a whole load of other stuff going on in the brain that could be called thought but which is not linguistic; nonetheless, formal discourse – ratiocination about concepts – does presuppose language. You try thinking of something for which no word exists. Tricky, isn't it? Of course, John and Douglas started with words in a gazetteer, but then they still had to invent hitherto non-existent meanings to apply to them. What's more, those meanings had to be apt and droll. It's a remarkable display of virtuosity, and John and Douglas were exceedingly miffed when an unscrupulous advertising agency pinched the idea in the form of *The Oxtail English Dictionary* to sell chocolates.

The Meaning of Liff is abidingly funny. Most people recognized it as very special, and it sold fairly well, though less so in the USA. There was some minor sniping when it was pointed out that Paul Jennings (in *Ware, Wye and Watford*) had done something similar many years before, though his approach had been suggested by homophones rather than finding labels for unemployed concepts. Douglas was mortified, and wrote to Jennings explaining that no disrespect was intended. The idea may have lurked in his brain from a game devised many years before by Frank Halford, Douglas's English teacher at school, but John Lloyd and Douglas had given it their own remarkable stamp over many a drink in Malibu. Execution is all. *Liff* is a little gem, an opuscule of genius, and one of the few books of Douglas's that he said he could reread without wincing.

The Meaning of Liff also coincided fairly closely with Monty Python's *The Meaning of Life,* and some have suggested that there was some attempt to feed off the marketing profile of the movie. A closer look at the chronology does not support this ungenerous view. The similarity was a complete coincidence though John and Douglas did decide not to change the name of their book when it was pointed out. The authors did not make a fortune from *Liff* – which is a shame because it, and its sequel, should be in every home.

However, in November 1985, in a hotel room in New York, Douglas sat goggle-eyed, oscillating between fear and joy, while Ed Victor conducted the American auction for *Dirk Gently's Holistic Detective Agency* and its sequel (the UK rights having gone to Heinemann and Pan again). Douglas had been yearning to escape from *Hitchhiker's*, and Dirk Gently, a hero so cool that his mind owed more to Heisenberg's Uncertainty Principle than traditional deduction, was the means whereby he planned to tunnel out past the perimeter guards and barbed-wire entanglements of his previous work. But first, the auction.

You may have an image of Ed Victor, elegantly suited, clutching a gavel, standing behind a dais in a roomful of Gotham City's finest publishers: 'Roll up, roll up,' he would say. 'Mix memory and desire [this was a literary auction after all], give me your chequebooks yearning to be free. What am I bid for this great novel and its sequel? Two lovely little copyrights from an author with an awesome record. Once in a lifetime opportunity – do I hear a million? One million two from the gentleman in the corner . . .'

A rights auction is not like that. Ed knew the major players, and he would have established who was interested and able to come to the party with sufficient funds. (Bruce Harris had participated until the price became just too high for a small house like Crown.) The publishers would be given time – typically a couple of weeks – to read the book, do their sums, check the existing sales, take soundings from the bookselling chains, confer with the hard-eyed guardians of the corporate wallet, have lunch, and stare contemplatively into space: in other words, the full rigour of the acquisition process.

Then, on the appointed day, Ed would take bids by phone, and those calls would have to be made by a particular time if the publisher wanted to be in the game. The bawdy hand of time, as Shakespeare put it, would be standing on the very prick of noon, for midday is often the deadline for the first round of bidding. Telephone bids are binding – not because publishers are intrinsically more honest than people in other industries, but because the business is so small, and it operates in such a debauch of self-referential gossip, that villains would become known instantly and then find it impossible to function. There is an etiquette to auctions that Ed would have observed. This dictates that the first to bid is usually the first to be called during the next round, so, in exchange for starting off the whole business before taking the temperature, as it were, from the rivals, the first in enjoys a slight tactical advantage. That's because in later rounds he or she will know that – the other gannets having offered or passed – the sum reached at that stage represents (if only temporarily) the highest offer. There are variations to the conventions; sometimes the auctioneer will go back to the interested parties in the reverse order of the size of the bid so that the best bidder in each round has the advantage of being last out in the following round. Usually the rules are made explicit at the beginning, and all the players are familiar with such nuances.

Of course the proprietor reserves the right not always to accept the largest numerical bid as other components of the deal such as marketing guarantees, royalty rates and schedule of payment may make a lower bid more attractive. But by and large the auction is an effective mechanism for getting the most money out of a market. The bidding will go on through successive rounds, with publishers dropping out when their limit has been reached, and the increments of each bid sending signals about the bullishness of the remaining players. Of course, the psychology of the auction, and the intense desire of publishers within their up-itself parish to win the game, can mean that they persuade themselves to go above the limit that the costings originally suggested was the sensible one. The rationale invoked is that if you've already convinced yourself to offer a million, a risk to bring tears to the eyes of your Finance Director, then the danger of a mere extra five grand seems too paltry a sum for which to lose the book. Not only do publishers, a vain lot, get emotional investment in winning the game, but the market too encourages these big punts, for there is now little middle ground between the bestseller and the modest performer. Nobody gets any prizes for being runner-up.

Ed Victor can conduct an auction with the finesse of Horowitz playing Mozart. (Apparently Horowitz could tell if it was going to rain because the hammers of his Steinway would absorb that little bit more moisture.) Round by round the bidding went up until it eventually stopped when Simon & Schuster acquired the two titles for a smidgen over $2.2 million. Then a division of Paramount, S&S was a powerful force in the marketplace and had never been leery of levering open its giant chequebook for what it wanted. Its only vice as a publisher is that it suffers from a management culture which confuses brutality with efficiency. Despite his stonking advance, Douglas was always satirical about S&S. 'It's one of those companies,' he told me, 'where you know that everybody's lipgloss will be perfect, but you're not sure if they've ever read a book.'

One of the things Douglas did with the money was buy property. By this time he and Jane had become friends with their neighbours, Rick Paxton and Heidi Lochler, who lived a little further down St Alban's Place.* They are now established architects whose energy-neutral offices in a mews off Regent's Park Road are stunning both in looks and function. Then they were starting up their architectural practice. It was a happy coincidence that Douglas and Jane were looking for somewhere else to live, a place they could create together. Eventually they found a magnificent Georgian house on Duncan Terrace, a few minutes' walk from St Alban's Place, and they commissioned Rick and Heidi to design and build a new interior for it.

Thanks to the UK's planning regulations, the handsome exterior of Duncan Terrace was, of course, sacrosanct. The building was not much more than a shell when Douglas acquired it, and, as is axiomatic with any construction work, progress was interrupted by horrid discoveries, and sharp intakes of breath denoting the kind of problem that requires serious funds to fix. On such occasions builders repair the fabric with a specially efficacious form of mortar made of water and scrunched-up, high-denomination bank notes. Duncan Terrace must have consumed at least a UK book's worth of money. One of the many vexations was finding dry rot in the top storey. Rick smiles when he

---

* The architects' converted mews in St Alban's Place was part of the elaborate pun about 'stable events' in the dedication in *So Long, and Thanks for All the Fish*. Incidentally, Huntsham Court was a remarkable, converted country house in Somerset where Douglas liked to retreat in order to write – or angstify (*sic*?) about not writing. This was another part of the stable event in the dedication.

recalls that Douglas wanted 'about two hundred' electrical sockets in his work room on the top floor for all his computers, synthesizers, electric guitars and toys. There would indeed be a heady whiff of ozone in his study, and enough processing power to run an airline.

Years later Douglas was interviewed about the house by one of the glossy mortgage-company magazines.* (He always found it difficult to say no to any interview. He was a complete media tart. Interviews were good for his morale; he could pretend they were work.) He said:

> There had been a rag-trade sweatshop on the ground floor, a picture framer's in the basement and an optician's on the first floor. It had to be completely gutted. At one stage you could walk in and see the sky. The structural work alone took eighteen months.

Rick is an engaging man with a vivid sense of humour. A typical architect, he likes to think with a pen in his hand so he can doodle plans and create graphical networks of ideas. He and Douglas hit it off immediately, and they became great friends, rather on the pattern of Douglas's other intense male friendships. Quite possibly, says Jane, this was the closest of the lot. They saw something in each other's talents that was not dissimilar. As creative activities, writing and architecture both entail a painstaking attention to detail and the elaborate loading of structure onto proper foundations. Douglas was intrigued by creativity and he believed there was a lot in common between the insight of a scientist and the inventiveness of a writer. Douglas admired Rick's talent, and was pleased to think that he was commissioning a building – surely the ultimate in patronage.

They were very much in sympathy intellectually. After all 'architecture is frozen music.'† When architects and writers are on song, they may both experience a eureka moment when something unexpected emerges. Rick remembers a typically foody Douglas analogy that went along these lines:

---

* *Inside Story* published by the Abbey National, spring 1990.

† Friedrich von Schelling, *Philosophie der Kunst* (1809).

It's like cooking roast duck. You check the recipe book, consult the *Larousse Gastronomique*, do lots of research, select the right spices and prepare the duck with exquisite care. Then you put it in the oven for exactly the right time for the very best duck results. When it's ready – there you are. Perfect chocolate soufflé.

They had some visionary plans for the house. Douglas wanted a swimming pool and a gym in the basement, and Rick worked out how he could achieve it by digging out the garden and replacing it on top of the new construction. It would have been preposterously indulgent but quite magical. Unfortunately there was no access to the site for heavy plant except by going over the back wall of the garden. This was also the back wall of the Royal Bank of Scotland complex, a huge bunker of a building with a frontage overlooking the less fashionable (a relative term) end of Upper Street near the Angel tube station. As this happens to be where the bank stores its bullion, security is correspondingly humourless. Douglas and Rick petitioned the bank very charmingly for access, and even went up to Scotland to toady to the managing director in person. But the most they could negotiate was two hours per week, and Rick had to advise Douglas not to go ahead. Instead the basement became an elegant flat for Little Jane, Douglas's young half-sister, who used it while she was training to be a nurse.

Douglas was a wonderful client for a young architect. Architects adore clients with imagination; it is just so much more fun building a house where you are encouraged to show some flair. It's also a useful credential for further work. Douglas, Rick recalls, would always go for the wild idea even if it were more expensive. Jane, however, was better at reading plans and working out what they would mean in practice. But delay can lead to a certain testiness even in the nicest client. All through 1986 and into 1987 the work dragged on and on.

The expense was unimaginable. When the taxi meter is whizzing around in the head of an architect, it makes even a lawyer look affordable. You certainly don't pass the time of day exchanging pleasantries about how clement conditions are for the season.

It was unfortunately just at this time that Douglas suffered a major financial blow. Ever since he started making serious money he had followed his tripartite scheme: a third for fun, a third for retirement, and a third to the accountant for the tax man. (Douglas would have been in the 40% tax bracket, but then what are accountants for? Besides, authors were then allowed to spread their income on the grounds that a book may represent several years' labour, amid lots of genuine and allowable expenses.) This arrangement worked satisfactorily until 1986, though Douglas could never sustain interest long enough to grasp the detail. This definition from *The Deeper Meaning of Liff* gives a clue:

Swanibost (adj.)
Completely shagged out after a hard day having income tax explained to you.

Then things went seriously wrong. Douglas's accountant had used Douglas's money to pay his own debts, having unwisely guaranteed the liabilities of another client. Unfortunately, he was unable to replace Douglas's funds that had been set aside for the Revenue. The loss was at least £150,000. Douglas's own estimate came to £345,000, though as this was in a letter apologising for a manuscript delay, it may have been amplified by pathos. His lawyer, Leon Morgan of Davenport Lyons, and his new accountant, Alan Clark of Nyman Libson Paul & Co, took action against the accountancy firm on three counts: recovery of monies, retrieval of documents, and professional negligence. Meanwhile the Inland Revenue wanted its tax. The Revenue was sympathetic, but as Douglas said in a letter to his friend and collaborator, Mark Carwardine, their sympathy did not extend as far as letting him off. He would be given time, but he would still have to pay the tax and interest on the late payment. In the meantime he was spending awesome quantities of money as the building costs on Duncan Terrace took off like an F-16 from a flight deck. Douglas was bitter about this, pointing out in the same letter to Mark that he only committed himself to the project on the basis of advice from his accountant – who must have known full well that Douglas didn't have the money, having nicked it himself.

Ed Victor and his colleague, Maggie Phillips, say that Douglas was in turmoil about whether to take criminal proceedings against the delinquent accountant (who had children to be considered) or to leave the matter as a civil action. In the end he decided not to involve the police. But he was righteously furious. On the other hand, the practical reality was that he could only hope to recover some of the money from someone earning, rather than doing time at her Majesty's pleasure. Calling in the police, he explained to Mark, 'is a bit like holding a gun on somebody. Once you've actually pulled the trigger, that's it.'

Events took a darker turn when the accountant committed suicide. God knows how complex this affair would prove if his story could also be told. Douglas was very upset at his death, especially for the widow and children. He sobbed, Ed says, and was consumed with guilt. But the truth is that it was just ill chance that there was plenty of handy money in a client account, one that happened to belong to Douglas. The whole experience was very unsettling. Douglas had never been prudent, but he had made enough money not to have to worry about it. When he was married he was relieved that Jane could take over running his financial affairs.

All this *Sturm und Drang* only increased the urgent need to stop pouring money into Duncan Terrace. They say that everybody falls out with their architect sooner or later, and the only reason most of us don't is because we cannot afford one in the first place. Rick and Heidi's costs were based on a percentage of the building budget, so their fees rose as the project encountered ever more difficulties. Mind you, as Jane says, Rick was actually good value in terms of the aeons of time he put in. It says a lot for the affection between Douglas and Rick that they remained friends even though Douglas's fascination faded a little. Eventually, when Duncan Terrace was completed, Douglas saw less of Rick and they drifted apart.

Another property into which Douglas tipped money was in New York where he acquired an elegant apartment on the fourteenth floor of a handsome building on Central Park South. He was by then making more money in the US than in any other market, and was back and forth across the Atlantic like a fiddler's elbow. Driven by his perennial wanderlust and his love of America, Douglas convinced himself that it made sense not to spend money on hotels when he had so much business in New York and enjoyed being there so much.

Douglas loved to travel. He was relentlessly inquisitive, but travel was also, in all senses, flight. However, he did not believe that hardship is good for the character. Rather than being ennobling, discomfort is – if anything – likely to induce a corrupting resentment. On the contrary, he liked to fly first class, partly because that way he met more movers and shakers, but mainly due to the fact that he was genuinely too big for those seats in Economy (or 'World Traveller' – euphemisms vary by airline) that seem to be made for small children. Even the airlines' employees privately call it 'scum class'. Fortunately Douglas had a good relationship with British Airways with whom he spent a small fortune every year. The airline would often try to organise an upgrade to First when he bought his Business Class tickets, if seats were available. Upgrading, a process driven by Kafkaesque subtleties beyond the ken of ordinary men, was later to be a pivotal component in the game of *Starship Titanic*.

Even in New York's volatile property market, it is almost impossible not to make a profit if you just hold on for long enough, but Douglas managed it. He and Jane never used their Central Park South apartment as much as they had anticipated. They freely lent it out to their mates, but for a lot of the time it sat there empty, satirically burning up dollars in service charges. Douglas had bought it at the top of the market. When he sold after a few years, he lost money for he had paid for it when the dollar was weak and sold it when the dollar was strong.

Nearer to home, the third and final property (this was 1989) that Douglas fell for was a villa called La Masure near Gordes in Provence. It was paradise. This part of the south of France has long occupied a special place in the hearts of the English. It is unfairly favoured by nature, being warm and hilly with entrancing vistas. The local vernacular runs to thick-walled whitewashed villas with pinky-brown pantile roofs and shady courtyards full of roses. Bars and, more importantly, restaurants abound. What's more it's accessible within hours from London's airports with direct flights to Marseilles. A Brit can enjoy a transformation as magical as entering a railway tunnel in a grimy industrial suburb and emerging into the garden of Eden. You can even drive there from the Channel ports in a day if you are prepared to be one of the Continent's *très vite* Porsche-owning, white-knuckle crazies.*

Douglas and Jane had many a jolly holiday down there, and had no trouble enticing lots of smart friends to join them sitting on their terrace boozing and talking into the balmy evenings. Phil Pope, the actor, Stephen Fry, and John Lloyd and his wife, Sarah, were frequent visitors. Once, to the terror of all, his friend from Cambridge, Michael Bywater, a qualified pilot, flew a party down in a small two-engined aeroplane. La Masure was bliss, though they must have felt like escapees from one of those quintessentially English novels in which women in straw hats exchange inexplicit understandings in foreign villas. Douglas loved to invite friends there to witness him writing – but then he wouldn't actually write. Conversation and local restaurants were much more amusing.

The house had been owned by a well-known publisher, Tom Maschler, the editorial boss of the famous imprint, Jonathan Cape. Ed Victor had helped to broker the deal. Douglas rang me when he was buying the property. The conversation went something like this:

'Tell me about Tom Maschler,' he said.

'Douglas, I'm intrigued. Why do you want to know?'

'Well,' he said, 'I'm paying him a lot of dosh for his lovely place in France. He's removed the light bulbs, the light fittings and the fire backs. Then he came back and took some of the logs away from the wood store. Is he a loony?'

I chortled. 'No Douglas. Just a publisher, just a publisher . . .'

Douglas's love of this part of France had been ignited by his stay in Juan les Pins, on the Mediterranean coast, where he had rented a villa while writing *Last Chance to See*. La Masure would have been the perfect place in which to write, except that the search for somewhere conducive to the fickle muse is just literary foreplay on an epic scale. Writers play

---

* My experience of driving down to the south of France is that the Germans win the prize of Mad Turbo-charged Bastards of Europe, closely followed by the French and the British. Belgium at that time had such lax licensing standards that one seldom saw Belgians who had lasted that far.

this game in different ways depending on their resources. Some have to go swimming every morning – to oxygenate the brain, don't you know? – because otherwise their lives are dangerously sedentary. Others invest time and money in getting the office absolutely right: the dictionaries within reach, the chair gripping the bottom like a libidinous old friend, the anglepoise with the full spectrum bulb positioned exactly . . .

Michael Bywater, who was then a writer on *Punch* magazine, tells a story of staying with Douglas in France. They dined out almost every night and in one local restaurant, Le Provençal, they were taken 'for a couple of poofs'. He and Douglas used to argue passionately about ideas, and these were regarded as lovers' tiffs by the incorrigibly superior French waiters. On another occasion, Michael and Douglas were rowing furiously about Roman Catholicism in Le Comptoir de Victuailler, a wonderfully decadent restaurant in Gordes where the food is so sensuous that Douglas said the owner was more like a panderer than a restaurateur. ('He looks at you with approval,' Michael remembers Douglas saying, 'as if you were a degenerate who had just ordered a well-greased choirboy . . .') Michael's position on Catholicism was that if you could only accept the first premise (a pretty big 'if'), the rest of the religion was well worked out by generations of subtle Jesuits. Internally it is logically consistent. Douglas was furious about the idea, the loathing of organized religion in all its forms rising in him from his childhood and his overwhelming father. Having just ordered fish, he picked it up and slapped Michael across the face with it. It was a turbot, Michael reports. They ate it afterwards. Delicious apparently. Michael, now a regular columnist in the *Independent on Sunday* newspaper, is the kind of writer who would torture a sentence half to death in order to avoid a cliché like, 'Well, it's better than a slap across the face with a wet fish . . .' Now, at least, he can claim to understand it more deeply than most.

Buying a place in France has all kinds of virtues, but doing so in order to write is not one of them. Douglas soon discovered that, unlike retailing, location is not the secret of writing.

* * *

The deal with Heinemann to publish Douglas's books in hardcover had another virtue. It introduced Douglas to his new editor, Sue Freestone, who was at first drafted in to work with him on a freelance basis, but soon joined the company permanently. Sue was to become an important person in Douglas's creative life. She's a short, blonde, husky-voiced Canadian woman who confesses to being an ex-hippie. Her innate sensitivity, her somewhat rackety life before she settled down with her husband, the television journalist Vivian White, and a certain maternal kindness have given her a particular strength as an editor over and above any technical expertise in organizing text – an ability to empathize with the author. Along with heroically sustained patience, this was a quality she had to demonstrate in spades with Douglas right from the start. When Douglas was particularly constipated with his writing, her role was the emotionally draining business of providing instant approval and encouragement.

Together they went through peaks and troughs of elation and despair, and inevitably Sue came to care deeply for Douglas, great affection vying with equally great exasperation. 'He was a misfit,' she said, 'a large, left-handed man with an odd perspective who lived in a world that was designed for an altogether more straightforward, right-handed sort of person.' Her connection with him also did no harm to her own career, and his wicked parties provided access to a remarkable network of the élite. It was through Douglas that she met (and later published) Stephen Fry, for instance, a frequent guest at Douglas's table. 'Who is that woman,' Stephen recalls asking Douglas, 'who hangs about the house while we're laughing, to whom you give the occasional piece of paper?'*

The writing itself was not getting any easier. It was around this time that Douglas uttered his remark, cherished in literary circles, that writing was just a matter of sitting in front of a blank piece of paper 'until your forehead bleeds'. He had spent a lot of 1986 editing *The Utterly, Utterly Merry Comic Relief Christmas Book*, to which he had given his time for free, but which proved more demanding than he had expected. It required him to coordinate myriad people and details –

---

* From Stephen Fry's introduction to The 2003 DNA Memorial Lecture.

not a skill that Douglas had manifested to an acute degree as a producer.

He had also been working on *Bureaucracy*, another computer game for Infocom, the company which had sold a gratifying number, mainly in the States, of the first *Hitchhiker's* game. It was inspired by his own move to Upper Street. To his chagrin he had found his credit cards had been invalidated by Barclay's, for they had sent his new cards to his old address despite the fact that he had filled out a change of address card personally and handed it to them, right there in his own branch. Getting the 'system' – an abused word for what is often an inchoate and foolish procedure sanctified only by time – to recognize his new location was a torment that lasted for two years. Douglas was provoked into some excited correspondence. A brief extract from his letter to Miss Wilcox at Barclay's will give a flavour.

[A history of his attempts to inform the bank of his new address plus excruciatingly explicit contact details . . .]

[My Address] is at the top of this letter. It is also at the top of my previous letter to you. I am not trying to hide anything from you. If you write to me at this address I will reply. If you write to me care of my accountant, he will reply, which would be better still. If you write to me at Highbury New Park, the chances are that I won't reply because your letter will probably not reach me, because I don't live there any more. I haven't lived there for two years. I moved. Two years ago. I wrote to you about it, remember?

Dear Miss Wilcox, I am sure you are a very lovely person, and that if I were to meet you I would feel ashamed at having lost my temper with you in this way. I'm sure it's not your fault personally and that if I had to do your job I would hate it. Let me take you away from all this. Come to London. Let me show you where I live, so that you can see it is indeed in Upper Street. I will even take you to Highbury New Park and introduce you to the man who has been living there for the past two years so that you can see for yourself that it isn't me. I could take you out to dinner and slip you little change of address cards across the table. We could even get married and go and live in a villa in Spain, though how would we get anyone in your department to understand that we had moved?

I enclose a copy of my new book which I hope will cheer you up. Happy Christmas. Yours truly

In revenge he was inspired to write *Bureaucracy*, in which the player finds himself unable to get his own money after moving to Paris, whence, via a series of bureaucratic mishaps, he ends up somewhere very much stranger. Having designed the architecture of the game, Douglas became fascinated with learning how to program, when what was needed was simply for him to write all the ramifying text variations. Despite an excellent understanding of computer languages, he lacked the patience for programming; the project started to run late. Infocom staff are credited with helping him finish it (primarily, acccording to the website, the mysterious hacker W.E.B. 'Fred' Morgan), and so is Michael Bywater who was quietly drafted in to help too.

The result of all these commitments was that when Douglas got down to work on *Dirk Gently's Holistic Detective Agency*, it was screamingly late. He'd been thinking about the book on and off for three years, and by the time Sue Freestone started working with him it was already six months past the 'this time we really mean it, absolutely no messing about, this-is-it' deadline. Douglas had written one single sentence. However, Sue reports, it was a brilliant one.

Critical opinion varies about the Dirk Gently novels. I like them a lot, especially the first. Alfred Hickling in the *Guardian* thought that the third, *The Salmon of Doubt*, was shaping up to be the best of the lot when Douglas died. It's certainly complex, very enjoyable and more relaxed than the first two titles. Kate Schechter, first seen in *The Long Dark Tea-time of the Soul*, reappears as a fully rounded female character – unlike Douglas's earlier women characters who tend to be foils for the men to express some impossible romantic and sexual yearning.

Dirk Gently's Holistic Detective Agency is Douglas's authentic voice – darkly funny, full of fresh invention (even though it owed something to his *Dr Who* plot), overly complex, and suffused with anxiety. There isn't the same joke quotient per line as in the *Hitchhiker's* novels, but overall the effect is just as satisfying.

The Electric Monk is a delicious idea; we have labour-saving devices to spare us effort – why not an electric monk who can believe *really stupid* things for us?* The plot is unsynopsizable. It combines jokes about Samuel Taylor Coleridge, Lamarck, quantum mechanics, chaos theory, academia, Schrödinger's Cat, literary magazines, jealousy, death – a whole chocolate box of intellectual goodies – with inadvertently saving the world. Douglas had just read Gleick's book *Chaos* for Heinemann and given it a rare pre-publication quote.[†] Usually he resisted blandishments from publishers to give quotes because he felt it devalued the currency and he was prickly about his acceptability by the literati. But in the case of *Chaos*, he said, 'it was like turning on a light in a dark room'. The ideas of chaos theory underlie much of *Dirk Gently*.[∞]

It is no accident that Samuel Taylor Coleridge is one of the central figures in the story. Like Douglas, Coleridge, one of the greatest narrative poets of all time, took the reader and his Ancient Mariner into the unknown. Coleridge's narrator in that poem is a decent man who makes one mistake. For this, all his fellow mariners die, and he is subjected to an extremity of nightmarish suffering before eventually finding redemption, of a kind. Arthur Dent is in a similar predicament:

---

* When Melvyn Bragg did a *South Bank Show*, the UK's premier TV arts programme, on Douglas, they were so taken with the idea that they arranged for an electric monk on a white horse to climb the steps of Douglas's Islington terrace and walk down the corridor into the house.

† *Chaos* by James Gleick (Heinemann, 1986).

∞ If you are unfamiliar with chaos theory, it is worth reading up on it. It describes how complexity can emerge from the iteration of simple rules (cf. life itself) and how complex systems are exquisitely sensitive both to their initial conditions and to minute perturbations to which they respond in unpredictable ways. In chaos theory outputs are non-linear, and this is satisfyingly like everyday experience. That wobbly table did not half collapse when you put half the pile of books upon it. Our scientific descriptions of events are in some ways an enormous formalism that we impose upon the world which resolutely refuses to behave as it ought. In *Dirk Gently* the tiniest events cascade outwards to mind-boggling consequences.

caught up alone in a bewildering universe – one which sneakily had appeared so safe and familiar – with a whole planetful of people blown to atoms behind him.

Famously Coleridge was also thwarted in the middle of a masterpiece when the Person from Porlock interrupted the composition of 'In Xanadu did Kubla Khan . . .' Douglas, however, was his own man from Porlock. Jane Belson recalls that if he couldn't find a man from Porlock, he'd pull one in from the street.

> It was the desire to get it right. I think his block was more to do with fear than perfectionism. He was frightened he couldn't do it. What he found hard was having these completely off-the-wall ideas which had to be combined with the perfection of the writing. Douglas wasn't confident he could do it, and he did worry dreadfully. I think he went and looked for distractions in order to avoid facing the possibility of failure.

Dirk Gently's Holistic Detective Agency contains within it a brilliant essay about music and mathematics ('Music and Fractal Landscapes' by Richard MacDuff). It's typical of Douglas that he contextualized it within the narrative in a way that gently parodies scholarship, thereby disarming any accusation of pretension before it's been uttered. Nevertheless, that essay is the most beautiful account of the connections not just between music and mathematics, but between mathematics and the universe.

Among mathematicians and physicists the subject of 'MacDuff's' essay is a hot topic. Even for a layman, you'd need a soul like a safety deposit box not to find it fascinating. Is mathematics an organizing principle of the cosmos, or merely a language that helps creatures of our peculiar configuration to isolate aspects of it? A snail does not need to 'know' about the Golden Mean when making its shell any more than a sunflower understands the Fibonacci sequence. The snail and the flower self-organize into those exquisite patterns because of the way atoms interact at the quantum level. But why do atoms behave that way? This is why quantum physics is the science from which all others flow. Is it just coincidence, then, that such phenomena – extending upwards to great spiral galaxies – lend themselves to such elegant mathematical description? Does mathematics define the universe any more than grammar? Maybe both just help us talk about it; much brainpower has been expended and many books written on this subject. It is wonderful to find it so entertainingly touched upon in a popular bestseller. Douglas believed passionately that such apparently arcane ideas were at least as appropriate to so-called commercial fiction as sex and shopping – and a lot more interesting.

This essay within the novel is a reminder of how good Douglas's non-fiction could be. His journalism is beautifully structured, often very funny and always illuminating. Jane remembers that he could do the same in conversation:

> Douglas had this extraordinary capacity to convey information in a most subtle way. He was a natural teacher. His analogies were wonderful. You would get what he was about to tell you about a millisecond before he told you, which made you feel really clever. I've talked to other people who said that was exactly how they felt too. So you felt good talking to him because it made you feel really smart.

Douglas was regularly at Three on the Beaton Scale when writing *Dirk Gently*. It was very uphill, and the complexity of the narrative reflects the discontinuously dripping tap of his inspiration. Sue Freestone spent a lot of time in Upper Street (at this point he had not yet moved into Duncan Terrace) providing sandwiches, encouragement and warmly appreciative feedback. After a particularly pleasing page, he would run downstairs from his office like a child who had done something praiseworthy and give it to Sue, inspecting her with neurotic care to see if she laughed in the right places.

The schedule for the book was so tight that it was almost a conveyor belt with Douglas at one end and the reading public at the other. By writing on his Apple Macintosh Plus and printing the text on a laser printer as camera-ready copy, Douglas cut out several intermediate processes and shaved a couple of weeks off the production time.

Dirk Gently was his first book entirely free of the structural inheritance that comes from converting one medium into another. It even looks different on the page, and resists slipping comfortably into the category straitjacket. Douglas's own quote on the back of the first edition (and still there today) describes his first Dirk Gently thus: 'A THUMPING GOOD DETECTIVE-GHOST-HORROR-WHODUNNIT-TIME TRAVEL-ROMANTIC- MUSICAL-COMEDY-EPIC'.

There is a trajectory to Douglas's books whereby they seemed to get darker and more cynical with every one. Nevertheless, on publication *Dirk Gently* went straight into the charts. He was particularly pleased by the success of the book, a non *Hitchhiker's*, because it seemed like confirmation that he was a real writer and not just a man with a single brand.

The next Gently novel was to follow with what was for Douglas remarkable despatch. *The Long Dark Tea-time of the Soul* was published by Heinemann in the autumn of 1988 and written from the late summer onwards of 1987. It was his first sane publishing schedule for years, though as always the book was delivered under time pressure because of Douglas's longstanding and much postponed promise to go to Australia on a promotion tour.

Meanwhile the improbable hero, Dirk Gently, reappears: plump, bespectacled, addicted to cigs, delinquent about money, randy yet unfulfilled, given to gnomic utterances, exploitative, guilty, not entirely wholesome, irritatingly right and possessed of high-powered but unusually non-linear thought processes. Douglas's friend Michael Bywater shares some of these characteristics and says he is not sure whether to be disgusted or flattered to be thought the model for Gently. Douglas did borrow some of Michael's attributes, but Douglas's creative processes were too horribly complicated for portraiture straight from life; besides, a detective who tries to fathom how the hell the world works was so very useful as a vehicle for his interests. The genesis of the character owes a lot to Chandler and to quantum physics.

Characteristically Douglas challenges the stable world view with jokes. For instance, there's Mr Rational, in the form of a smug, unkind consultant psychologist called Standish (here I standish and can no other . . .?), one of whose patients in his hospital in the Cotswolds has been performing automatic writing. She appears to be taking dictation from the ghosts of Einstein, Planck and Heisenberg. Obviously, such a thing is crazy – except that what she takes down is physics of the highest order, throwing light on the greatest goal of them all, Unified Field Theory, sometimes called a Theory of Everything (or T.O.E.).* Such a theory would be the ultimate triumph of the human spirit. What fun Douglas has in imagining the horror of the scientific mind faced with the paradox of getting such insights from an obviously impossible source.

The Long Dark Tea-time of the Soul is an enjoyable book, though not Douglas's best. It is nicely observed and imbued with such a precise sense of place that one day it might be possible that literary fans will follow Gently's path from Islington to St Pancras Station in the same way that James Joyce buffs walk round Dublin on Bloomsday. In the novel Douglas takes a figure of speech – *'For God's Sake!'* – and rotates it through ninety degrees. What would we do for the sake of the gods? What would they do for themselves? Wouldn't immortality be the most sadistic burden? No wonder Odin (an echo of the master of the universe in *Hitchhiker's*) is so damn tired. For him a nursing home, an infinite supply of clean linen and no responsibilities seem like an appealing arrangement. On the other hand, the alternative to immortality is not such a bundle of laughs, and Dirk discovers it can be disgustingly messy. Gently himself plays a rather passive role in the book, not so much an actor in the drama as a non-participant observer. The novel is full of wit and verbal pyrotechnics, but, stripped of such camouflage, it's bleak.

By this time Douglas and Jane had finally moved into Duncan Terrace. Douglas insisted on the unbelievable stereo and a grand piano, and the rest of the administrative burden of the move fell to Jane. The

---

* The current model of how the universe works has it held together by four binding forces: the strong and weak nuclear forces, electromagnetism and gravity. So far it has been impossible to tie them all together in a coherent account – yet if the Big Bang theory of the universe is correct (and it's beautiful, predictive and compatible with observation) then all the forces must have been at unity before they uncoupled. Unified Field Theory is the Holy Grail of Physics.

mechanics of writing were much the same as before. Sue was on hand for sympathy and feedback. Lisa Glass, the copy editor, also rushed round from time to time to help them chill out. Douglas had a high regard for Lisa whose intelligence saved him from various inconsistencies and solecisms. (He was impressed when she checked, and corrected, some of Dirk's playful sums with his I Ching calculator.) Sometimes Michael Bywater turned up to offer entertainment, stimulation and dazzling conversation.

Once, Sue Freestone recalls, Janet appeared:

Douglas had been angsting at me for days about the increasing length of the grass in his back garden in Islington. At this point I was debating whether to buy a lawn mower on Heinemann expenses and cut it myself to shut him up. His mother, Janet, arrived unannounced bearing a hover mower. A small, determined woman, a quarter-sized spitting image of Douglas, she marched past us without a word out into the garden, unwound the cord, plugged in the mower, marched purposefully up and down until the grass was all cut, unplugged the mower, wrapped the cord round the handle, tucked the whole thing under her arm and marched out again, still without a word. Douglas and I sat looking at one another in stunned silence. He had not said anything to her about his grass worries but somehow she just knew.*

What's more, Janet took the grass clippings all the way back to Dorset.

* * *

As soon as Douglas had finished *The Long Dark Tea-time of the Soul*, he'd promised he would go to Australia for a paperback promotion. So that he felt under unnegotiable obligation, for he had cancelled in the past, Pan had taken the precaution of booking tickets and working out his

---

* This extract by permission of Sue Freestone is from her tribute to Douglas in *Publishing News*.

itinerary in some detail. He had to go, but he was still writing as the car arrived to take him to the airport. He edited while the limo glided across London and he was still fine-tuning the text as he was driven down the M4 to Heathrow.

When he arrived in Perth, Western Australia, twenty hours later, Douglas was still writing. Debbie McInnes, a likeable, energetic woman and one of the best publicists in Australia, remembers picking him up for the first appointment and finding him in his PJs, still making changes. Final corrections had to be faxed to England from the hotel. Debbie is 5'3". Douglas was 6'5". It is a pity there is no picture of them on the streets together.

Douglas had been out there before, in 1983, on promo duty for the Pan edition of *Life, the Universe and Everything*. It had been an enormous success. Brian Davies was the managing director of Pan Australia and Maggie Crystal was in charge of marketing. The company had recently declared independence from Collins and it was determined to do a spectacular job. Maggie remembers Douglas with affection from that first trip:

Our campaign was mainly author-led with plenty of telly. Douglas was a pleasure to promote. He was very clever and rather childlike. He was funny and had absolutely no side to him; the Aussies liked that. His views about British literary snobbery went down very well. He wasn't A-list in literary terms, but he was culty. A cult is when you are enthusiastic about something, but don't realize that millions of others feel the same – and that was certainly true of Douglas's fans. We did TV in all the major cities: Perth, Adelaide, Melbourne, Sydney, Brisbane. Douglas worked very hard. He was easy and could be quite funky and fresh even late at night. We sold a lot of copies. [Brian Davies estimates over 75,000 during that trip.]

For his part, Douglas adored Australia – the climate, the swimming, the space. Everything. He had discovered scuba diving on his first trip to Malibu, but it wasn't until he got to Australia that he realized it could be so indecently pleasurable. Jane says that although he was not one of nature's sportsmen, he was a very good swimmer. He loved diving. Once he'd overcome his natural buoyancy, those large hydrodynamic control surfaces would come into their own. The feeling of weightlessness underwater, and of liberation, the sheer sensual joy of it, are a delight. The colours of the fish, especially on the Great Barrier Reef, are indescribable. The flash of iridescent light as an entire shoal turns as one (how do they do that?) is breathtaking. Douglas found release down there, and spent as long underwater as his schedule and his (always urgent) obligations would allow.

Douglas also liked the Australians themselves a great deal. By and large they were a refreshingly straightforward lot compared to the brittle and competitive ambience shared by many of his Cambridge contemporaries. He was to return to Australia whenever he could. On one occasion – the madness of which must have appealed to his sense of style – he even went to Australia for a day. He'd promised to give a talk at the Adelaide Literary Festival, but he was once again under the gun for late delivery. He flew in and out again in twenty-four hours.

The 1987 trip to Australia coincided with Douglas's need to recoup the truckload of fifties he'd tipped down the Duncan Terrace building site, to say nothing of the money he'd lost to his erring accountant and the taxman. In any event he was planning to do a lot of travelling for his next book. Douglas's relationship with Jane was going through a highly unsettled phase featuring long periods of separation. For all these reasons, but also for tax purposes, Douglas decided to take a year out of the UK.

Starting this period with a promo trip to Australia was ideal. Debbie McInnes looked after him well. She is amusingly no-nonsense about authors, some of whom have been known to throw a 'tanty' (a tantrum) if all is not precisely to their satisfaction. But Douglas, she says, was no problem. It was a massive tour, partly because he had put it off so often. He was popular and in great demand. He seemed genuinely interested in listening to what people were saying and he performed as graciously in tiny radio stations as he did in big telly studios. Debbie recalls:

He could take the piss out of himself very disarmingly. We did sixty-five interviews in five major cities in ten days. The radio stations had to fight over him. Douglas scarcely had a minute to breathe. The schedule was his punishment for being late. He couldn't go to the shops, though he did buy two silver bangles in Perth airport, and he managed to get to a Mac World computer convention. He was passionate about that. He was desperate to go swimming with the dolphins off Palm Beach, but there was no time. He had a huge wetsuit that I ended up storing for him until the next time.

In the evenings he loved food and wine and was good company. He was a very warm person. Once [24 July 1988] we went to dinner with Ben and Sophie Elton [Sophie is an Australian saxophone player] who were in Perth for a tennis match.

We got on very well and the fans loved him. They were absolute devotees. The media loved him too – we all did. When he died, there was a huge piece in the *Sydney Morning Herald*. It was so sad.

Douglas had a great time in Australia, and then the promo tour took him to New Zealand. (Eurocentric Brits might say 'nipped over to New Zealand' but in fact New Zealand is three hours flying time from Sydney.) It is a beautiful country, and Douglas was well looked after by Joan McKenzie, Linda Godley (the publicist) and the whole team at Whitcouls who ran New Zealand's biggest bookselling operation. Jane remembers Douglas calling her from Auckland and describing the Rush Minute – the Kiwi equivalent of the rush hour in more congested cities.

Douglas actually enjoyed promotion tours. Many authors love the initial ego boost, but then settle down to a steady note of plangent whingeing, for a good tour is exhausting and a bad one has huge potential for humiliation. Australia was not the only important market he visited. He went to Germany and the other German-speaking markets of Austria and Switzerland in 1991, 1994, 1995 (when he toured for a week), 1998 and 2000.

But back to tax exile and 1988. Douglas spent much of the rest of that year travelling with zoologist Mark Carwardine and doing the research for what was to become an important and inspirational book (the next chapter is devoted to it). But at the end of 1988 he returned to Australia and rented a large house with its own swimming pool in the millionaires' resort of Palm Beach on the northern beaches of Sydney. Kerry Packer had a place almost next door. At the height of the southern summer it's usually too stifling to do much except drink ice-cold beer and wonder if it's too hot for sex, but over this particular Christmas rain came down like something out of the Old Testament. Even so, it was a lot warmer than London.

Douglas was never much good on his own, so he invited a gang of friends to join him for Christmas. The deal was that they'd have to pay their own fares, but the accommodation would be on him.

Flying into Sydney shortly thereafter were Rick Paxton and Heidi Locher, then Jon Canter, Sarah Mason, an old friend, Ron Cobb, the film designer, Lou Stein, who was in theatrical management, John Lloyd, and finally Annie Watts and Peter Bennett-Jones – who subsequently married each other. (Peter, when he is not nursing Comic Relief, runs a successful management company with more than a fair share of the best comedians in the UK and also an independent TV production company.) It was a collection of the brightest and best – and they were poised to have fun. Only Douglas was a bit low, for he was preoccupied with his emotional predicament and could talk about its complexities – given the slightest encouragement – at interminable length. Indeed he could be uncharacteristically boring. Annie Watts was the best listener.

Peter Bennett-Jones says:

Douglas was looking for people to keep him company really. It was genuine generosity. Of course, he had lots more money than anybody else, but still, if you're not generous you don't do things like that. In fact, you probably do it less in my experience. I also thought he was very generous in his attitude to other people's potential and success.

The weather was just unlucky really, so we went to lots of restaurants and spent a few days in Sydney. He [and John Lloyd] did some work on *The Deeper Meaning of Liff*.

Rick recalls that John Lloyd was in a mercurial mood that Christmas, full of charm, stroppiness and alcohol, and that he had taken on a (thank God, temporary) alternative personality known as Jack Bastard.

Douglas had told everybody they should bring no presents. Absolutely NO PRESSIES was the rule. However, when the guests arrived they found to their embarrassment that he had installed a Christmas tree and furnished everybody with an extravagant gift. By way of thanks they clubbed together and hired a seaplane to take the party for Christmas lunch to the Berowra Waters Inn, at the time only accessible by small boat or seaplane. It is now no more, but in the decadent eighties it was *the* place to go for an indulgent and very expensive lunch. Their Christmas meal was indeed a long, extravagant blow-out; the hope was expressed that they had not taken in so many extra calories that the seaplane would be overburdened. Rick reports that a certain amount of jocular muttering from the other guests was audible as they left. Who are these scruffy pommy bastards who came by bloody seaplane?

Douglas's house guests stayed about two weeks. His next return to Australia would be with Jane, for scuba diving on the Great Barrier Reef, an experience he described as being as near to paradise as he could imagine. Meanwhile, it was time to return to London and Real Life.

Some readers may be wondering by now if the writing continued to become more difficult and whether Douglas ever reached Four on the Beaton Scale. Alas, he did. *Mostly Harmless* (1992) was unmitigated grief. Douglas was convinced that he simply could not do it any more. In 1991 his stepfather, Ron Thrift, a thoroughly decent man respected and loved by all, had died of cancer. It just seemed to happen for no reason. (The book, dedicated to Ron, begins with Zen resignation: 'Anything that happens, happens . . .') Where, if anywhere, was meaning? All his life Douglas was looking for it – and if people die because of nothing, just a predicament of matter, and you are too bright to embrace the spurious comforts of faith, there's little left to fall back on. Creatively, too, Douglas was exhausted by the whole *Hitchhiker's* idea. He'd been doing it for fifteen years despite every effort to stop. In spirit he had long since moved on.

Mostly Harmless is the most solipsistic of all Douglas's books. Without wanting to be too solemn – for the story is full of good jokes – there is the sense throughout the story that Arthur is not sure if anything exists outside himself. Every individual's universe is defined by his or her sense data. Even the seer says so:

'You cannot see what I see because you see what you see. You cannot know what I know because you know what you know. What I see and what I know cannot be added to what you see and what you know because they are not of the same kind. Neither can it replace what you see and what you know, because that would be to replace you yourself.'

'Hang on, can I write this down?' said Arthur, excitedly fumbling in his pocket for a pencil.

Writing this novel was agony. Here and there it reads as if Douglas is faking his own voice (the Sandwich Maker passage, for instance). Sometimes, trying in vain to create something fresh, he lay on the floor in misery. Sue Freestone gave him affection and encouragement. Michael Bywater came round to entertain, chivvy, irritate and stimulate him into writing. Michael says he even wrote some stuff that Douglas rewrote. Both Michael and Sue helped him plot the book, and by way of reward they promised he could destroy everything so utterly that another title would be out of the question. Together they exhorted him to rise from the dead.

Eventually, Michael says, Douglas announced that he just could not do it. 'Don't do it then,' said Michael. 'We're not going to stop being your friends because you didn't finish *Mostly Harmless*, you schmuck.' Jane, at home after a day's combat in the legal arena, took a pragmatic line. Her support and tough mindedness were crucial. The conversation went something like this:

Douglas (prostrate): 'I can't write this book. I just can't do it any more.'

Jane: 'So?'

Douglas: 'I'll be in breach of contract. I'll have to give the money back . . .'

Jane: 'So?'

Douglas: 'But I haven't got the money any more. I'll be bankrupt . . .'

Jane: 'Yes. And so? I can help you do that. It's not the end of the world.'

So Douglas had, as Michael said, 'all the ducks in a row. Everyone he cares about has said: you don't have to do the bloody thing. If you can't do it, you can't do it. You just say: I can't do it and I can't pay back your advance. Your problem.'

Page by excruciating page, Douglas wrote a terrific book. Not surprisingly, it was the darkest of the canon, but before Douglas fell into the pit with his fiction-writing, his life took a surprising and enjoyable turn.

chapter twelve

Last chance to see

'The system of life on this planet is so astoundingly complex that it was a long time before man even realized that it was a system at all.'

Last Chance to See, Douglas Adams, Pan edition p. 192

In 1985 Douglas had received a call from the *Observer* magazine, the colour supplement published every week with the *Observer*, one of Britain's quality Sunday newspapers.

'Do you fancy going to Madagascar?' asked a voice on the other end of the line. 'Umm,' said Douglas, 'Who's that again, please?'

'The *Observer* magazine. You know, the *Observer*. Rather a good Sunday broadsheet. Do you fancy going to Madagascar with a zoologist to look for the aye-aye?'

'Aye-aye what?' said Douglas.

'The aye-aye. A rare, very shy nocturnal lemur. It's got beautiful eyes.'

'Have you got the right person? I'm a humorous science fiction writer . . .'

Later Douglas was to joke that he said 'yes!' before they found out they had the wrong person. But they did have the right person. The World Wildlife Fund and the *Observer* had got together with a scheme to send writers and experts out into the world to find endangered species. The writers would have that freshness of perception that comes from complete ignorance of the subject (but, please God, they could write) and the experts would furnish the background and specialist knowledge. Douglas would be the eyes through which the urban Sunday newspaper-reader would see something wonderful that was quite outside his or her everyday experience. The epitome of Islington Man would voyage – if not to the Heart of Darkness – then to well beyond the restaurant belt.

Douglas didn't hesitate for a femtosecond. He had just returned from a promo visit to the US and was in a state of trance – endless homogenous hotels, airports and freeways had left him anaesthetised. He claimed that concrete floors, complete with giant poisonous spiders, would be a relief. The zoologist who had been paired with Douglas, Mark Carwardine, confirms that his companion liked third-world travelling as a corrective to all that voyaging through American Express-land on expenses. He relished it, said Mark, but for only two weeks:

> He would get more and more scruffy and ravaged looking. He wouldn't shave. His hair would need washing. He'd get terribly tired and look much older. Then we'd get to some nice hotel, he'd have a shower, clean himself up, get some decent sleep and he'd be restored. Ten years younger again. The transformation was almost funny.

Packing for Douglas was a major industrial undertaking. His fertile imagination could scarcely conceive of circumstances in which there was anything he would not need, so he carried astonishing quantities of luggage. Of course pants and socks and all the boring stuff, but in addition a computer was essential, and books,* plus ultra-bright halogen torches charged for seventeen hours from the mains, a medical kit, and his collection of cameras with lenses that ranged from extreme

---

* Douglas took a selection of the works of Charles Dickens to Zaire. The allusion to Waugh's *A Handful of Dust* in which Tony Last is condemned to read Dickens in the jungle forever would not have been lost on him.

close-up to telephotos so long you could pick up the bacteria on someone's nose at half a mile. Burdened with all this kit, Douglas and Jane flew to Paris where they met up with the expedition's affable photographer, Alain le Garsmeur. Together they caught a connection to Antananarivo (pronounced Tananarive) airport in Madagascar.

Mark Carwardine is a delightful person, tall, dark, passionate about his subject. He has the slightly melancholy air of a man who is a committed environmentalist on a planet whose dominant species seems hellbent on its destruction. 'We don't even know what's out there,' he said, 'or what it could do before we wipe it out. Who would have thought that the Madagascar periwinkle, for instance, would provide us with a drug for leukaemia?'

Then only in his late twenties, he was five years younger than Douglas. Mark is a trained zoologist with many books to his credit, and now he presents the excellent BBC Radio Four programme, *Nature*, from the famous Bristol Studios whence the best natural history programming has emanated for decades. From time to time he also takes parties of people out in tiny inflatable boats to see the great whales. A living creature the size of a submarine surfacing smoothly alongside you is such an astonishing experience that the cliché about it being life-changing is literally true. On one such trip recently a nurse and a policewoman decided to retrain as marine biologists.

Mark and Douglas had never met before, but they hit it off. Douglas had a real talent for friendship, and even when he was being egotistical he was so transparent that he was forgivable. Both men were severely put to the test, especially on their travels in 1987/88 when they were away from home on and off for eighteen months, often in stressful circumstances. Their relationship, especially when they were both short of sleep, oscillated between extremes of affection and irritation. In the end affection always won out.

From Antananarivo, via the Hilton, where just some of the luggage was left for safe-keeping, Mark, Alain and Douglas flew by an old propeller plane with rattly windows, like a bus, to Diégo-Saurez. Then they took a battered truck to the coast where they caught a tiny boat to Nosy Mangabé, the last refuge of the aye-aye. Each change of transport had moved them forward in space and backwards in time and technology. The Malagasy boatman who took them to the idyllic, tiny off-shore island was dismayed by Douglas's minor Alp of stuff, and when they arrived he suggested to Douglas that he nip over the side to help get them ashore. The water was so clear and sparkling that the sand looked as if it were only a few feet below the boat, but Douglas disappeared up to his neck to the merriment of (nearly) all.

The aye-aye has always been elusive. Gerald Durrell wrote an amusing account of trying to find one two generations ago, and it hasn't got any easier in the meantime. Douglas and Mark knew where to look, but they were still fortunate. The dizzying instant when Douglas saw one is so beautifully described in *Last Chance to See* that there is little point in recounting it here. It's a moment when a monkey (albeit Douglas was a highly evolved form of monkey) looks at a lemur and the lemur – that 60 million years ago had been top primate – looks back at him with serene incomprehension. Douglas was surprised to find himself utterly captivated. The sense of history on the evolutionary scale was suddenly dizzying. Here he was gazing at a graceful species with its origins in the era when all the continents were together in the huge supercontinent, Gondwana. Isolation had saved it from the monkeys when Madagascar became an island by splitting from Africa and turning into 'a life raft from a different time'. Just possibly the aye-aye might be saved again by a retreat to a much smaller island – this time, as Mark points out, with the help of the monkeys.

What Douglas called 'twig technology' had got him to the refuge. The technology of a tool-using opposable-thumbed animal holding a stick can also eventually build a Boeing 747. The aye-aye deployed twig technology too in the form of a long middle finger resembling a twig that it could use for probing for grubs. There is a telling example of convergent evolution when an unrelated species (the Long-Fingered Possum from Papua New Guinea) has devised a similar strategy to address the same problem. (Douglas was very intrigued by the implications of convergence. What need is there to posit a designer if the operation of random forces, constrained by the reality of the world, produces the same elegant solution, as if there were no choice in the matter?) We monkeys have been more ambitious. Clever primates that we are, we've designed twig mechanisms capable of carrying a few of us to our nearby satellite and for killing each other with an ingenuity unrivalled by less intelligent species.

This first trip to Madagascar was hugely enjoyable for Douglas. Rick Paxton recalls that Douglas was so fired up about it when he returned to St Alban's Place that he went round to their house straight from the airport and talked with wild-eyed energy for hours nonstop, in a state of rapture. Typical writer, though: he returned the following evening after a day of revivifying sleep, showers and pampering and asked, rather plaintively, if Rick and Heidi could remember much of what he had said in his exalted state.

Madagascar also marked a profound expansion of Douglas's view of the world. If you look at the world on the cosmological scale, as he did, you might be forgiven for believing like Descartes that, despite the lacunae in theory, the universe is a huge machine in which humankind is an infinitesimally tiny component. Douglas never found it demeaning to think of himself as a machine of enormous complexity. But life defies the mechanical model; it has – to use the current scientific jargon – emergent properties that are not fully understood. It will obey the laws of physics, but it will never be predictable. A profound tremor in his certainties ran through Douglas when he looked at the aye-aye (and even more so when some years later he gazed into the eyes of a gorilla). He woke up to the variety of life, and for the first time understood his, and mankind's, continuity with the other animals emotionally and not just intellectually. This delicate little creature with its huge eyes and giant finger was a distant cousin. Douglas and it shared some ancestral DNA.*

Douglas plunged into learning more with characteristic enthusiasm. Mark recalls that he was an enviably quick study. Mark only needed to tell Douglas something once for the information to lodge on some burr in his brain. He consumed books at a prodigious rate – and remembered them.

On his first visit to Madagascar, Douglas's awareness of ecology changed up a gear. He wasn't a fierce Green activist in the sense that he would ever dream of zipping up and down in a little rubber boat

---

* We even share an estimated 40% of our genes with a banana.

while Japanese whalers bore down upon him. He gave money to Greenpeace, but he was not an eco-warrior. His amazement was more intellectual. The sheer improbability of life reignited his sense of wonder. That living things as disparate as an aye-aye and a daisy, a rhino and an oyster should have evolved in a comparatively short time is beyond surprising, and the fact an animal has appeared that can dimly understand the process is perhaps the most surprising thing of all. Einstein said that we should seek to explain the universe as simply as possible – but not one bit more simply.

Douglas was incandescent with admiration for what nature and Darwinian processes had achieved, and he understood those processes well enough to realize that there was no great teleological endgame towards which they were striving. In *Mostly Harmless* he observes, 'Anything that, in happening, causes something else to happen, causes something else to happen.'

Everything is contingent. The endless shuffling of the genetic pack and untold billions of biological accidents produced variations. Most were eliminated promptly by a harsh environment or predation; very few were advantageous and conferred some reproductive advantage. Flukishly this blind churning produced a self-aware primate and a breathtaking variety of other flora and fauna. There is no reason why such an unlikely thing should endure. The Earth Mother does not exist save as a comforting metaphor. We do not have to be.

Douglas knew this. He was profoundly influenced by his friend Richard Dawkins and intrigued by the strange detail of what Mark Carwardine had to tell him about various endangered species. His fascination was quite unconventional; it wasn't so much a matter of observing the strange behaviours, bizarre instincts, off-beat mating procedures* and so on that these rare creatures might manifest. What he wanted to imagine was the world as these animals might perceive it. It was for that reason that Douglas was so stricken by the fate of the Yangtze dolphin which assembles its model of its environment through sound. The poor animal has almost certainly

---

* Though, God knows, these can make asking someone out for a Bergman movie, six pints of lager and a Vindaloo look positively rational . . .

vanished from the Earth now and the last remnants of its doomed species were maddened and, as it were, blinded by mankind's marine engines before extinction. Or what, Douglas wondered, does the world 'look' like (we humans are locked into our visual paradigm) if it is mapped mainly by smell? The rhinos with their colossal nasal membranes* (larger than their brains) and terrible eyesight would have seen Douglas like some obsolete computer screen without enough pixels, but they could have smelled him on the wind half a kilometre away. Sight is effectively instantaneous, but smell isn't. Douglas's insight here was to realize that as a result a rhino's view of the world is rich with the sense data of things past – in a way they 'see' in time.

Douglas's determination to master the complexities of zoology was paralleled by his desire to be at least passable in photography. Alain le Garsmeur put up with Douglas standing behind him when he took pictures. Douglas wanted to learn from a professional. Amateurs sometimes delude themselves into thinking photography is all about equipment, but it's not. Douglas favoured motordrive Nikon F3s with those fast, eye-wateringly expensive ED lenses. In the gadget shop in *The Long Dark Tea-time of the Soul*, Dirk describes how he could move from total ignorance of something to total desire for it, and then to actually owning it – all within forty seconds. That was Douglas in a camera shop. But you can have the snazziest equipment on the market and still take pictures of people with telegraph poles sprouting from their heads. Photography is about having an eye, and a good technique for acquiring one is to observe an expert. Douglas's photography improved beyond all measure. This may be why he dedicates the book to Alain, who was good-natured beyond the call. Taking photographs while a Douglas-shaped man-mountain looms over you cannot be easy.

Douglas took a cavalier attitude to money and equipment which on one occasion made Mark terribly angry. They were flying into Beijing; as usual Douglas was pile-driven into the ground by his burden of kit.

---

* Douglas was for a time a contributor to a scientific group concerned with the rhino's preposterously huge nasal membrane.

One of the larger bits was an excellent 400mm Nikkor telephoto lens that Mark coveted but could never have afforded to buy. Later, on location on the Yangtze, Mark noticed it was missing. It was heavy. Douglas had decided to leave it on the plane.

On another occasion in Wunan in China they found themselves in the foyer of a hotel when Douglas just had to write something down before it fell into one of those irrecoverably lost files of mental notes where people over eighteen store their best thoughts. Neither of them had a pen, but there was a shop in the hotel selling rugs and carpets. Douglas asked there if he could borrow a pen. Ungraciously, the shopkeeper refused. 'What is your most expensive rug?' asked Douglas. They showed it to him. 'If I buy it, will you give me your pen?' said Douglas. They would. He did. He was thrilled. Mark was appalled. The rug eventually did arrive back in Islington.

Mark and Douglas had been delighted to find an aye-aye. It was the first official sighting for years, and the only time one had been photographed in the wild. An expedition from *National Geographic Magazine* equipped with helicopters, landrovers and 'a budget you could buy one of the smaller nationalized industries with'* had failed to find one in nine months. Instead a young zoologist and a science fiction writer had located one in the pouring rain on their second night in the jungle. Were the portents good, or what?

For some time Mark had been trying to persuade the BBC to make some programmes – originally planned as six – about endangered species. When he and Douglas found the aye-aye, they were pretty pleased with themselves, and the BBC was pleased with them too. The series was conceived for TV, but as Mark did more research, he found to his dismay that the cost would be prohibitive. Just getting the permit to film on the Yangtze would take nine months and £200,000.

Instead the project was reconfigured as a series for Radio Four. Mark would do the logistics, never Douglas's strongest suit, and provide the expertise. In his head Mark already had the melancholy list of species teetering on the edge of a man-made abyss. Douglas would write the scripts and talk. Add one radio producer, Gaynor Shutte, and there was

---

* This comes from Mark and Douglas's presentation document to the BBC.

a programme in the best traditions of the BBC: funny, wide-ranging, educational, heart in the right place – and, above all, cheap.

The series was commissioned, though the budget was never sufficient for what they had in mind. Fortunately Heinemann came to the rescue by buying the associated book for a hefty advance that Douglas, despite being a bigger name commercially, insisted should be split evenly with Mark as co-author. 'Don't even think about it,' Douglas instructed Ed Victor. Out of the advance Mark and Douglas had to pay for all of their travel and for their own sound engineers. There was usually one per trip: Stephen Faux was a regular, and on several occasions the resourceful Chris Muir, immortalized by Douglas's anecdote about trying to buy condoms in China in order to turn a microphone into a hydrophone. The funds certainly did not cover Douglas flying first class. Despite some refined liberal guilt, he always upgraded, sometimes leaving Mark in scum class at the back of the plane while Douglas was plied with drinks and stewardesses in the front.

Of course, the Douglas deadline factor soon kicked in. They had hoped to go in 1986, but Douglas was under too much pressure. It wasn't until the second half of 1987 that they got on the road, and the bulk of their travels took place in 1988. They could not fly seamlessly from place to place, so had to return to Britain (or, in Douglas's case, often to France) after every sally.

Two minor digressions from this period about Douglas's huge generosity. The first:

The taxman does let tax exiles back into the country for a specified number of days. They have to be careful not to exceed the permitted dose of home for, if it notices, the Revenue will pursue you to the ends of the Earth, or off-planet if necessary. During one of his returns from exile Douglas, following all precedent, had a lavish party in Duncan Terrace. It's one which particularly sticks in my mind because of the suits. He had commissioned some wonderful suits and jackets from a tailor (Topfit Tailors, Kowloon) in Hong Kong while en route to Australia, and he arranged to pick them up on the way back some months later. But in the meantime he went scuba diving and embarked upon a diet of appalling rigour. What's more, the state of his relationship with Jane was making him fraught. Whatever the reasons, when he collected his bespoke clothing from Hong Kong he was two stones (28lbs) lighter than when he had commissioned it.

'I will never put the weight back on,' he lied, 'and if I do, I will get it surgically removed.'

Now back in London Douglas had these superb suits, all raw silk and cashmere. They caressed the body like a naughty liaison, but they were made to measure for a man who was 6'5" and weighed eighteen and a half stone. Fortunately these coordinates also define me. Douglas was a half-inch taller, and I'm a smidgen fatter. In the middle of this party I was made to strip and try on these amazing suits which did indeed fit me extremely well. Sophisticated Islington media folk, emboldened with champagne cocktails, came up to stroke the fabric even as I clambered into these garments. Up till then my tailor was army surplus. Despite being the gaffer of a paperback publisher (Sphere), at that time I only had one suit, and that felt as if it had been made from recycled Shredded Wheat packets. Hmm, I thought, I shall wear a different suit every day for a week and see if my colleagues notice. They did. On day one. My publisher friend Roger, who knew about such things, told me that I'd been given at least three grand's worth of superior suiting (double at London prices).

Second:

Douglas was infuriated with Mark Carwardine because he bought a counterfeit Rolex Oyster watch in Bali for the equivalent of a fiver. It was only partly brand name snobbery on Douglas's part, for he also suffered from a kind of philosophical anxiety about what's real. Mark's knock-off was indistinguishable from the original except for a slight difference in the movement of the second hand. Though exquisitely made, mechanical watches in an age when the second is defined by billions of transitions of a Cesium 133* atom are, of course, obsolete technology. To put a modern quartz movement into a posh case in order to fake obsolete technology that perversely adds value would have appealed to Douglas's sense of the absurd. Anyway, he felt Mark should enjoy the 'real' thing – and bought him a genuine Rolex Oyster for his birthday.

* * *

---

*   9,192,631,770 in case you ever need it.

The *Last Chance to See* expeditions took place in 1988. There is no point in describing them because Douglas himself wrote about them in that book with unmatchable humour and panache. Mark was co-author, and given all he contributed this is eminently just, but *Last Chance to See* is written in the first person and is unmistakably Douglas's voice. It was his favourite book, and if you have not read it yet, please do.

For those unfamiliar with the book, it is a compelling mix of wittily observed travelogue and natural history documentary of the highest intelligence. The story begins with a meeting with an Australian venom specialist, Dr Struan Sutherland, who advises the two adventurers very sincerely not to get bitten. Fortified with this wisdom, Mark and Douglas visit the Komodo dragons (disgusting), the Northern White Rhino, the gorillas of Zaïre (Douglas feels an extraordinary affinity with these primates, our closest relatives), the kakapo in New Zealand (a tragic bird of which more anon), the river dolphins of the Yangtze, and finally the Rodrigues fruitbat on Round Island, Mauritius (strange). Mauritius, the erstwhile home of the Dodo, Douglas considered a significant place in our understanding of life on Earth. 'As Galapagos gave us the idea of evolution, Mauritius gave us the idea of extinction.'* On the way Mark and Douglas encounter some remarkable examples of *homo sapiens*, a number of whom make you feel quite good about mankind. The book is wonderful, full of colour and amusing stories, and all the more powerful for not editorializing too obviously. 'The intention,' Douglas told Michael Leapman in his interview for the *Radio Times*, 'is to be serious, but because I'm a comedy writer the tone will be light.'

There is real anger in *Last Chance* that as a species we could be so careless. For instance, it is so improbable that a rhino could have evolved at all that we allegedly thinking primates should cherish it in astonishment. The rhino is a bad-tempered, nimble, two-ton, armour plated animal with a great nose, crappy eyesight and a complex, multi-chamber biochemical processing plant to digest the otherwise

---

* Transcript of an interview with Michael Leapman used for his article in the *Radio Times*, 17 August 1989. My thanks to Michael Leapman for digging it out of his archives.

indigestible vegetation and turn it into more rhino or heroic quantities of excrement (none of which is wasted). There are now only thirty White Rhino left in the world; that this amazing creature should be shot, not even for its meat, but because of two excrescences of ossified hair on its nose is beyond belief. The wickedness of the slaughter takes on another dimension of stupidity when you realize that the reason is a trade in ceremonial dagger handles as props for Yemeni men to look chunky, or to help credulous orientals reduce fever or get erections (for which rhino horn has no value whatsoever – it's basically hair, guys, for God's sake).

In 1989, the Berlin Wall came down. Large areas of the developed world escaped from a ruthless experiment in large scale social engineering to discover the joys of feral capitalism, and in October and November of that year the radio series of *Last Chance to See* was finally broadcast on Radio Four. It was a success, albeit not another cult on the scale of *Hitchhiker's*, for it worked supremely well on radio. The interpersonal chemistry, the humour, the soundscape, the engagingly snuck-up-upon information (part travelogue and part nature documentary), all wove together with real charm. Douglas had a good radio voice, and he was back to what he enjoyed the most – performing. The admixture of polemical zeal gave the broadcasts an extra bite.

The book, as usual, followed a more vexed path. *Last Chance to See* is truly inspirational, and quite a number of current zoologists and related specialists were attracted to their subjects because of it. Douglas was rightly proud of it. As usual, though, the easy-reading conversational style was hell to produce. In order to write he retreated to a rented villa in Juan les Pins, an enchanting but definitely discovered village near Monaco on the Mediterranean coast of France. Mark came out to join him.

It was a disaster. Between the motion and the act, as Eliot says, falls the shadow. Douglas had sunk into one of his states of listless vacancy and infected Mark with the same condition. Every day they'd get up, have a leisurely coffee, then go for a walk to clear their heads before the serious business. But distractions lay in wait for them. Time stretched. They fell out; they got together again. They'd plan lunch. They'd eat lunch. When their spirits were ebbing, they'd nip into Monte Carlo for some fun. They were suspended, in abeyance, marooned in paradise. Their paralysis had a personal cost for Mark who had a serious girlfriend and was flying back and forth to England most weeks to see her. He's sure that working on the book scuppered that relationship. Somehow over three months passed without the two of them producing very much at all. Sue Freestone visited them to deliver a righteous kick up the collective rectum. Michael Bywater paid a call, and reports that they were in an emotionally charged state. As an emotional man himself, it's doubtful that he would have calmed them down.

In the end, as deadlines whizzed by, they got down to it. Sue Freestone and her Heinemann colleagues told them: 'As soon as there's enough for a respectable book, stop. We cannot wait any longer.' Two expeditions never made it into the final text, not because they lacked interest; Douglas and Mark simply ran out of time. It's a pity, as both concern attractive creatures that need all the help they can get – the Juan Fernandez fur seal of Chile and the Amazonian manatee. I have always thought of Douglas as a manatee, and it would have been interesting to hear his views on these large, gentle marine mammals which live in water so freighted with silt that, like the doomed Yangtze dolphins, their sensorium is largely one of sound. In his long interview with Michael Leapman in the *Radio Times*, Douglas talks about how the threat to the manatee is the threat to the whole rain forest. Its complex ecology is crucially dependent on the free-flowing river systems that even in 1989 were being diverted into hydroelectric schemes that were already silting up.

The book was published in 1990 by Heinemann and by Pan the following year. Douglas's publishers around the world picked it up too. Most of the critics loved it, especially in America (*Atlantic Monthly* said it ranked with the best set pieces of Mark Twain). Only Beth Levene in the *New York Times* was less than ecstatic ('an uneven travelogue') but even she found the heroic efforts to save the animals inspirational. Nothing quite like it had ever been written before. Although it did not explode on the market like one of the *Hitchhikers*, it has steadily reprinted.

Douglas was mortified, and not just for reasons of commercial self-interest, that the book did not immediately sell millions. He cared deeply about the message in it, and was inspired by his experiences to give time and money to Save the Rhino and the Dian Fossey Foundation. Indeed, it was his lecture at the Royal Geographical Society that prompted the UK branch of the Dian Fossey Foundation to write to Douglas. They were thrilled and surprised to receive immediately, by courier, all the cash that he happened to have in the house at the time: quite a few pounds, a number of dollars, some francs and really rather an impressive number (over 2,000) of Deutschmarks left over from a recent tour.

It's worth quoting his account of his first meeting with a gorilla:

> A kind of humming mental paralysis grips you when you first encounter a creature such as this in the wild, and indeed there is no creature such as this. All sorts of wild and vertiginous feelings well up in your brain, that you seem to have no connection with and no name for, perhaps because it is thousands or millions of years since such feelings were last aroused . . .
>
> The feeling I had looking at my first silverback gorilla in the wild was vertiginous. It was as if there was something I was meant to do, some reaction that was expected of me, and I didn't know what it was or how to do it. My modern mind was simply saying, 'Run away!' but all I could do was stand, trembling, and stare. The right moment for something seemed to slip away and fall into an unbridgeable gap between us and the gorilla, and left us gawping helplessly on our side.

Douglas felt deep in his bones that when he looked into the eyes of a gorilla he was seeing a fully conscious creature. Jane Goodall said that Douglas wrote very movingly of the gorillas' lives in the wild and did not ask, like Bentham would have, can they reason? He asked instead: can they suffer?

The charities that are concerned with the welfare of the mountain gorilla and the rhino were delighted to have Douglas as a supporter. Indeed, he became a patron of Save the Rhino International, an energetic organization dedicated to preserving this amazing creature which is in great peril from loss of habitat and, more especially, the depradations of poachers.* Tirelessly he proselytised among his well-heeled mates and his millionaire technology contacts about both causes,† and managed to persuade Bill Gates, no less, to give $10,000 towards saving the silverback gorillas. This was a much greater investment of effort (and of vulnerability) than merely writing a cheque, not that there was anything mere about Douglas's cheques.

In 1995, at the behest of the founders of Save the Rhino International, David Stirling and Johnny Roberts, Douglas was even persuaded to put on a rhino costume and go, accompanied by his sister, Little Jane, for a sponsored climb up Mount Kilimanjaro in Kenya. The rhinoceros has been around for forty million years, and we cannot invent any more of them when they are gone. This is true of all the animals on the CITES list of endangered species. Various kinds of macaws, gibbons, parrots, tortoises, snakes, tigers, rhinos – the list is far too long to be recounted here – will vanish from the world forever. (Inconceivably, there is a trade in stuffed baby tigers.) Douglas was dismayed that the disappearance of the white rhino is a real possibility, and for that he was willing to don the suit. This extraordinary contraption had been on an outing already in New York's marathon. It had been designed by cartoonist Gerald Scarfe∞ for a stageplay about saving the rhinoceros. William Todd-Jones, the Welsh puppeteer and actor, wore it in that production, which is how he also came to be on the sponsored walk. He made friskier progress than Douglas. The insides of the suit reeked of sweat and Dettol; wearing it in the African heat was a torment.

---

* SRI point out that one of the myths is that poachers are impoverished locals, but the reality is that poaching is conducted by ruthless international criminal organizations which are content to see the rhino hunted to extinction if their stockpile of horn thereby increases in value.

† I remember rather ungraciously whinging to Sue as I wrote a cheque that the bloody rhinos never bought any of the books we published . . . I have his letter still, and he even got Polly to make her mark on it thus making it doubly difficult to say no.

∞ Douglas misremembers the artist in his essay in *The Salmon of Doubt* as Ralph Steadman. It is a delightful piece, however, that reminds us how engaging his journalism could be.

Douglas was very game and toiled along for miles and miles, slathered in sunblock so potent that it must have been the pharmaceutical equivalent of tinfoil. But he was too large and pink for the tropics; the rhino suit weighs 30lbs and the heat could reach over 100°F. He did not reach the top. Kilimanjaro, he explained, is the tallest mountain in the world for, although it is 'only' 19,340 feet, it erupts from the ground virtually at sea level whereas Everest starts from the already over-achieving foothills of the Himalayas. He was particularly delighted in the response they got from the children they met on the climb. They shrieked with the kind of happiness, Douglas records, 'that we in the West are almost embarrassed by'.

Douglas's immersion in life in all its variety led him to some serious thinking about its place in the universe. Cosmology is a beautiful subject that concerns itself – *inter alia* – with the origins of the universe and its ultimate fate. Like it or not, these are questions that are also addressed by the religions of the world. Many cosmologists are embarrassed by this overlap, perhaps because they fear they will be tarnished by the touch of woolly religious thinking, or maybe because they are encroaching on areas not susceptible to scientific method. Yet they are the very questions on which they are most often pushed by popular sentiment to express an opinion. We have an appetite for such knowledge.

There is an argument running through the discipline that unavoidably lends itself to the use of that multiply freighted 'God' word; it's called the Anthropic Principle. The argument goes like this: the current state of the universe is the end product of an inconceivably long chain of causal connections. Every link in that chain happened because the conditions were right for it to do so – and not just right, but precisely right – fine-tuned to a degree of scarcely imaginable precision. For instance, if the acceleration of gravity by the tiniest margin were a different value, or ditto the charge on the electron, then our universe could not have evolved to the state we observe. Indeed if any of the fundamental constants* recognized by science were

---

* Actually some of these constants may not be as constant as all that. It's always fun to see the universe pulling a few surprises to keep the theorists on their toes.

changed even infinitesimally, our universe would be very different, or might not exist at all or, if it did, not for long enough to allow for complex evolutionary processes. Similarly if our planet had an orbit just a smidge further from or a little nearer to the sun, it would have been unsuitable for the evolution of life. If there had not been a planetary collision, the odds against being literally astronomical, forming our moon, and stabilizing the Earth's axis of rotation, then it's likely the planet would be sterile. And so on, through any number of benign coincidences. The world has to have the exact properties it has otherwise we would not be around to observe it.

The Anthropic Principle can be expressed in varying ways, but in its strongest version it looks at the cosmos and says: it's too much to expect that these perfect conditions for the emergence of life are a coincidence. Life seems to be the purpose of the universe. There must have been a Designer. Of course, the designer need not be identifiable with any parochially defined deity (no angry old geezers on thunder-clouds yelling 'Thou shalt not'). It could be something more abstract, like initial conditions, or the laws of physics. But however hard you try to finesse it away, there appears to be, according to the argument, an organizing principle at work that favours life, something that gives the universe meaning.

Douglas hated the Anthropic Principle with its comforting notion of putting life, and man, centre stage in the infinity of space. Only Zaphod Beeblebrox, who had laughed in the Total Perspective Vortex, could be that arrogant. Yet a number of extremely smart physicists and astronomers believe something along the lines of the Anthropic Principle, though it has always struck me as a bit like saying that if you win the lottery (i.e. you are the beneficiary of a hugely random process) then you have somehow called the lottery into being by persuading yourself that it has been organized just for you.

He and I would sometimes discuss it, and wonder at its wishfulness. 'Whatever happened to Occam's Razor?' we would sigh, as we stuffed food into our faces. 'The Big Bang stands on its own – any further entity we posit beyond it is unknowably hidden by the event horizon and hardly in a position to take much interest in our affairs. Surely the Anthropic Principle is a confusion between outcome and purpose . . .

Another bottle, do you think?' (We did gossip about trivia too.) A strong urge to believe a proposition does not after all constitute evidence for it. The fact that if the proposition were true it would fulfil needs both obvious and subtle does not make it the case. Consider the proposition that you have a million dollars in the bank.

Once I gave Douglas a copy of *Before the Beginning* by the astronomer, Martin Rees. In that smashing book, Sir Martin suggests that there are sound theoretical reasons for believing that at the time of the Big Bang not just our universe, but an infinity of others, were created. Literally innumerable universes would not have been viable, so the fact that we inhabit one we can observe becomes less surprising. His analogy was that it's like coming across a tailor's shop with a billion suits; finding one that fits perfectly is not so remarkable.

Douglas worried away at this idea. He considered the universe to be more wonderful than any inevitably anthropocentric religious account of it could possibly be. His thought experiment about the Anthropic Principle was one of his favourites, occasionally appearing in print and featuring frequently in his lectures.

What if, he suggested, a puddle on a rock were by some fluke to stir into consciousness? Gosh, it would think, as it looked about itself: how perfectly I conform to this environment. There's not a molecule out of place. This rock suits me precisely. Strewth, it couldn't be a better fit if it were designed for me. Can it be a coincidence? I think not. Somehow I must be the whole purpose of this rock, part of a vast mountain range on an enormous planet I see. What an important puddle I am.

Then as the sun comes out, the puddle starts to evaporate. But even as it shrinks it continues to congratulate itself on fitting into its habitat with uncanny precision. Eventually the puddle, to the very end convinced of its central role in the existence of the universe, disappears without ever waking up to the bigger picture.

Douglas's didacticism was always leavened by great doses of humour. As we've noticed before, in other circumstances he would have been an inspired teacher.

chapter thirteen

The Digital Village

'The best way to predict the future is to invent it.'

Alan Kay

'An assumption is something you don't know you're making.'

Douglas Adams

In 1990, the year Prime Minister Margaret Thatcher resigned (if that's not too passive a word), Pan with Faber & Faber published the delicious *The Deeper Meaning of Liff* by John Lloyd and Douglas Adams. Like their first book, it contained hilarious definitions that would otherwise have been hanging about on street corners getting into trouble. Unlike the first, this one included maps devised by Trevor Bounford, an experienced designer, who underwent some pain when George Sharp, Pan's Art Director, commissioned him. Trevor recalls: 'The brief was to make maps that were deliberately unhelpful, which we managed to achieve despite years of training in producing the opposite.'

Then in 1992, *Mostly Harmless*, the fifth and final novel in the *Hitchhiker's* 'trilogy' was published. The anguish of its creation has already been described. There were spin-offs of various kinds, but this was the last new book that Douglas published in his lifetime.

He had done ironic detachment. He was clean out of cosmic jokes. His hair was going rather thin on top. He was married at last. He even had an office. Now he would discharge his existing contract, give up the painful writing business, and become a futurologist or a games designer/computer consultant. Douglas had moved on.

The world was changing, and at a vertiginous pace. 'Packet switching' so that computers could talk to each other in standardized units of information had been around for decades, and so had the various precursor incarnations of the Internet (like ARPANET), but their use had been largely limited to academics, scientists and the military. Then in 1989 Tim Berners-Lee at CERN devised a universal language (HTML) and the World Wide Web was born. In 1994, the first really powerful browser became available from Netscape. 'Are you on-line yet?' was the question on the lips of every young urban professional, with the United States, Japan and Germany leading the way. The number of users grew exponentially.

Communications technology not only changed how business was done, and hence how whole economies functioned, but it also enabled people who were geographically, economically and culturally remote from each other to be united by shared interests and form communities that had never been possible before in the history of the world. Revolution is an abused word, but the technological changes of the last two decades of the twentieth century were revolutionary.

Ever since he had gazed like a love-struck adolescent at his first Macintosh in the offices of Infocom in Boston in 1983, Douglas had seen much of this coming. The legend is that he bought the first Apple Mac to be sold in the UK – and the second too. Stephen Fry claims he acquired the third. Douglas had gone to Boston to work with the renowned games programmer, Steve Meretzky,* on the first *Hitchhiker's* computer game and had seen the potential with remarkable prescience. Without any encouragement, he would go into lecture mode and – depending on their mindset – either bore or enthral his friends about the coming Cyber Age. He was passionately interested in all aspects

---

* Steve Meretzky was a *Hitchhiker's* fan. He's one of the best games creators in the business, keen on the basics of story-telling and design and not too sidetracked by technology. As well as for Infocom, he has created games for Legend, Blizzard and Boffo. *Planetfall* was huge. *Leather Goddesses of Phobos* should not be missed.

of IT, and especially in the things it could do that the human mind could not.

Computers, for instance, have the ability to crunch through arithmetical calculations with much greater speed and accuracy than the human brain, and in staggering volume. This makes them ideal for sorting mountains of data according to instructions that must be drearily precise. Computers are just irritating machines that have no ability to construe the user's intentions. But unless you take the view that in the end a quantitative change becomes a qualitative one, this capability is not different in kind from that of the human brain. Douglas was much more intrigued by those powers of the new technology that might represent an evolutionary step forward for the species. Famously he defined a computer by what it was not: not a television, not a typewriter, not a calculator, and certainly not a brochure (when linked to a website) – though it could certainly fulfil all those functions.* What it is, he decided, is a modelling device. 'Once we see that,' he wrote in *The Salmon of Doubt*, 'we ought to realize that we can model anything in it. Not just things we are used to doing in the real world, but the things the real world prevents us from doing.'

Douglas wasn't just talking about how a supercomputer could simulate the collision of galaxies, the flow of air over a wing, or the fission of an atom, all of which are for all practical purposes impossible to do in the real world with unaided brainpower. He was fascinated too by the computer's ability to model the emergence of complexity by doing the same thing again and again very quickly. Douglas saw that the old paradigms of how we talk to each other were radically altered by IT. 'One to many' communication abounds (telly, newspapers and so on) but the Internet for the first time makes 'many to many' possible, allowing us to experience distributed intelligence. Even everyday equipment enables us to gain access to the resources of hundreds or thousands of other minds. What if, he wondered, we could carry a device with terabyte storage – just like the Hitchhiker's Guide

---

* Douglas had been expressing and refining these ideas ever since he fell in love with his first Apple, but for an elegant summary, his article in the *Independent on Sunday* (November 1999) collected in *The Salmon of Doubt* is definitive.

in fact – that was constantly updated in real time with information, experience, insights, reviews, jokes even, of a community of fellow owners of a similar device? What's more the device would interact with thousands of other data-storage devices.

Douglas's favourite example of what carrying such a device would mean was that you could be driving along a remote road in Texas, or Surrey for that matter, when the gadget would talk to you. It would 'know' where it was from GPS, and it would also have a detailed profile of your domestic possessions and an intelligent model of your interests. Having recorded what you had done in the past, the device could infer what you wanted in the present. By interrogating some retailer's inventory management system, or perhaps via one of the community of other users, it would alert you to the fact that the missing copy in your otherwise complete collection of rare Beatles' bootlegs happened to be in store in the next unlikely little town.* Such a device would enhance your life not just as some kind of super-enhanced Filofax remembering things for you, but more like a benign Familiar Spirit providing selected information of help and relevance and – perhaps most interesting in a fragmented society in which some find mediated conversation less anxiety-inducing than the real thing – access to company. Another beauty of such a device is that the more people use it, the better it will be.

Mind you, when it came to the nuts and bolts of computing, there were two schools of thought about Douglas's competence: his and the rest. Later, when The Digital Village was up and running, he was to try the patience of some of his very techie colleagues. His intuition about computers was second to none, but he was a compulsive fiddler and easily distracted. His lateral-thinking mind, more like a picture gallery with many branches than a debating chamber, was not fortified against the repetitiveness and shocking literal-mindedness needed for programming. He would make an intuitive leap of the 'Ah-ha, I see what it's doing, the little bastard' variety and then be stymied because there is no substitute for following the manual with an undeviating

---

* I am grateful to Jim Lynn, the technical leader of the H2G2 web project, for his memory of Douglas's dream machine.

and deeply tiresome attention to detail. He liked to play with new software until he understood not just its functionality but its architecture, and confessed to enjoying the new avenues of displacement activity that computers had opened up to authors. The story he often told against himself was that he would happily spend two days programming a macro in order to save himself ten seconds when he opened a document.

From his earliest affair with the computer back in the eighties, Douglas had been tempted by the Apple. He was convinced of the superiority of the Macintosh operating system over that of the sadly ubiquitous PC, and felt that he could doodle on a Mac creatively, even write music, in a way that was impossible, or at least very tricky, on a PC. He was forever trying to wean his friends away from the frustrations of IBM-compatible kit and could bang on about it for a considerable time. The language of computer allegiance is surprisingly theological. Passionate believers in the Apple are always 'evangelical', and people in the IT world have been known just to have the description 'evangelist' on their business cards in the certain expectation of being understood. The undecided – Jim Lynn, The Digital Village's C++ programmer, for instance – call themselves agnostic. Douglas himself had an email exchange about the relative virtues of the Apple versus the PC with the well-regarded computer editor on the *Guardian*, Jack Schofield, which had all the heat of Jesuits arguing heresy.

Douglas relished a good rant, and one of his most entertaining polemical concerned Microsoft Windows. The gist was that Windows is a host of different software services (word-processing, spreadsheet, connectivity and so on) that had all been designed by separate teams and then exported to a foreign country where some real clever-clogs had constructed an overarching bridge onto which all the functions would fit. That's why the final assembly is so complicated, and so many useful options are hidden away in drop-down menus that are not always the obvious ones. But, he said, Apple had not started that way. Their departure point had been what the user *actually wanted to do with the equipment*. Once Douglas met Bill Gates at a Paul Allen party (two of the billionaire founders of Microsoft and the IT revolution) and said to him: 'You can't run the world.' But they can – the software world at least.*

Douglas's family were on the receiving end of his passion for Apple Macs, as part of his ever-present generosity. One Christmas they had gathered in Duncan Terrace – Little Jane, James, Sue, and Janet – for one of those blow-outs that leave you anchored to your seat for the rest of the day. But Douglas had a surprise for them. Each one was handed the end of a colour-coded string that they had to follow around the house, up the stairs, round corners, mischievously back again, until they came to the present at the end of it. And there, for each of them, was a brand new Apple iMac.

Ever since its first famous superbowl ad in 1984 (directed by Ridley Scott), Apple had always positioned itself as the computer for those who dared to be different. The idea was that by all means you could run your budget on a PC, but you should write your symphony on a Mac. In the nineties, as part of this continuing campaign, Kanwal Sharma, Apple's inspired marketing man, had devised and managed a 'great minds' scheme whereby about one hundred high profile celebrities (Apple dislikes the word celebrity and prefers 'visionaries') let their names be published as Apple users. Douglas was delighted to join.

What the 'macophiles' in this scheme had in common was that they were leaders in their fields who worked creatively with their computers and found that they were liberated by them rather than (as is often the case with PCs) driven to rage and intemperate effing and blinding. The celebrities did not get paid, but they did get some of the latest equipment and software. From time to time they were brought together at Apple's expense for extraordinary conferences where they could talk about anything to each other, and indulge in what the management books call 'out of the box' thinking. In return they were expected to sit down occasionally and talk with the Apple team. The generic title for the scheme was the Apple Masters. Apple got input from some of the brightest people around and reinforced their role as the creative

---

* Perhaps the open source software like Linux will still prevail . . . but don't hold your breath.

person's computer company. The celebrities were flattered to be on a list of the charismatically brainy and interesting, and they saved a lot of money on equipment and got to go to some stimulating meetings. Douglas adored being an Apple Master. There is no doubt, however, that he preferred their kit and would have used it regardless.

The Apple Masters were a wonderfully eclectic collection of people. Mountaineers (Sir Chris Bonnington) could rub shoulders with actors like James Woods or Jennifer Jason Leigh, Richard Dawkins could chat with Richard Dreyfus, Peter Cochrane (the futurologist employed by BT) could swap ideas with Nobel Prize-winners Murray Gell-Mann or Donald Glaser (the physicist who invented the bubble chamber). Douglas was thrilled – where else could he encounter Harrison Ford or Muhammad Ali? It's hard to imagine other circumstances in which a British comic SF writer would meet Sinbad, the African American stand-up comedian, and discover they had a rapport.

Douglas thought highly of Kanwal Sharma and they struck up a friendship. In Kanwal's opinion, Douglas was one of the most creative people he had ever come across, able to juggle around many multi-disciplinary subjects with enthusiasm and knowledge. He'd toy with ideas, said Kanwal, in a way that was quite childlike: 'What would happen if I did this?' Kanwal recalls that Douglas had extraordinary presentational skills, and was brilliant with the Silicon Valley crowd. He remembers him on spectacular form in 1998 giving an address at a conference in San Jose about convergent technologies and the next generation of PDAs. Stop thinking in terms of tweaking existing gadgets, urged Douglas. Think instead of your P.E.T. – your Personal Electronic Thing – and what you would like it to do for you. Why would you want to use an ancient keyboard design to talk to it? Why not just talk? The audience of software engineers and technologists was delighted.

Though their relationship was largely telephonic, Douglas and Kanwal were close. Douglas's phone bill – especially when he should have been chipping away at the word face of his current book – must have been considerable, for he had a circle of pals whom he would call frequently, sometimes every day, especially when he was in California for that last frustrating pass at the *Hitchhiker's* movie. The phone was how he maintained his many friendships. If he and Douglas were both feeling low, Kanwal recalls, they would cheer themselves up by competing over just how miserable they were. Once Douglas called Kanwal in Hong Kong. After they compared notes about angst and jet lag, Douglas asked Kanwal how he had enjoyed life in seat 3A. Through his contacts, Douglas had wangled Kanwal an upgrade and continued to do so whenever he could.

Kanwal cited the Joni Mitchell song 'You never realise what you've got until it's gone' in connection with Douglas's death. 'I was as upset as at the death of my own father,' he said.

Douglas's role in Silicon Valley and the whole IT revolution is more subtle and important than it may at first appear. His sales in the USA were always huge, especially among high school kids and college students, and with a readership almost certainly more male than female.* Some of those teenagers grew up to be the technologists and engineers of the IT revolution. Certainly Douglas commanded enormous respect among the techies. When he was with The Digital Village, Robbie Stamp, a decent family man who can talk to an Olympic standard, recalls the awe that Douglas could evoke:

Douglas was a big star. There was part of him that took pleasure in it, but would get embarrassed if you told him. I remember going to meetings at Microsoft and being with junior programmers who were simply overwhelmed, especially if they hadn't been expecting to see him. In one set of meetings, with a woman called Linda Stone who works at Microsoft, we were wandering around the offices in Seattle and went into one. There was this guy who was so excited he literally could not speak.

---

* I have no proper demographic figures here, just a feeling . SF used to be more of a male market, but that has changed over the years. Fantasy has a readership that is better balanced between the sexes. Douglas had very many female readers, but he also had a particular gift for speaking to slightly alienated men for whom Douglas's sense of the cosmically absurd was sympathetic. The fan correspondence and the postings to the website after Douglas's death were preponderantly from blokes.

When it came to inventing gadgets, Douglas burst through the barriers of the conventional by positing the fantastic. Why add a cosine key to a calculator when you could be developing an interactive, constantly updated talking encyclopaedia with attitude? It is not too far-fetched to say that a generation of clever American techies grew up with their imaginations fired by the guide itself in *The Hitchhiker's Guide to the Galaxy*. The Palm Pilot and PDA (Personal Digital Assistant) might never have been developed without the seed planted by Douglas a decade and a half before they first came onto the market.

In fact the *New York Times** quotes Bob Stein as crediting Apple with unintentionally creating the first electronic book in 1991 (Sony's Discman had failed, possibly because the screen was too small). Apple, with their new generation of snazzy portables, seemed to be the business, 'complete with animation, drawings and hypertext links'. The early titles were, of course, the *Hitchhiker's* trilogy plus Michael Crichton's *Jurassic Park* and Martin Gardner's *Annotated Alice in Wonderland*. Years later Douglas was peeved when Stephen King was the first major author to publish a novel on-line. 'I should have done that,' he told me.† But, despite some brilliant technology and all the benefits of search engines, the book market has by and large remained stubbornly wedded to blocks of laminated wood-pulp.

When the idea of joining a new media/technology company reached Douglas, it was not a bolt from the blue. The ground had been long prepared for him to be receptive to such a suggestion. Robbie Stamp, Managing Director of The Digital Village, was working as a producer for Central Television in 1991. He takes up the story:

> The way it happened was this chap, Paul Springer, who was a
> would-be film producer, had managed to get a meeting with
> Douglas. He was hoping Douglas would help him to write a
> feature film of an idea he had. So he and I went to see Douglas in
> his house in Islington with those great big, huge sofas in that

---

* Article by John Markoff, the *New York Times*, Sunday 29 December 1991.

† Stephen King's brilliant novella *Riding the Bullet* was e-published by Philtrum Press and Simon & Schuster in March 2000.

upper room in Duncan Terrace. He was charming, and played
Bach to us because there was a point he wanted to make about
music and mathematics. I just thought: 'What a fascinating man,'
and we stayed in touch.

We had lunch periodically, and I think that one of the projects
he was looking to do was a big series about evolution. He'd been
looking for a producer to work with, and that was another reason
why we were talking because with my TV producer's hat on,
maybe I could have been that person . . . He would have been a
superb live storyteller, and a really good presenter because he had
that fantastic capacity to find the image, the metaphor, *the* way of
describing something even if it's quite complex. He had a number
of TV ideas though, frankly, in the end he got fed up with having
to go through the 'pitch'. He felt that he had established himself
by then, and that TV producers could approach him with projects.

At that stage I was going to be leaving Central [TV] for a
variety of reasons, and I'd decided it was time to set up a
company. I'd been looking at cable opportunities at Central and I
had an idea for a company called Cable City. I'd been examining
the economics and had felt that they did not work unless you
could do two or three low-cost channels from the same base
technically – satellite sharing and so on – so you had the
opportunity of building cable channels and of using the material
you were creating to distribute through other media.

So I was talking about this idea to Douglas, and he said 'How
much would it cost to invest in this company?' And I plucked a
figure out of the air and said '£25,000', and he said, 'Well, I'm in.'
And that was that, really. That was how The Digital Village [TDV]
started.

Of course, there were hurdles to overcome. It took some years before
the company was funded and running, or jogging a bit. Douglas still
had a book to write (destined to be published nearly ten years later as
The Salmon of Doubt) and his publishers around the world were getting
cheesed off with being kept waiting.

In fact, he took a bruising blow to his morale when his long-term publisher, Sue Freestone (whom he had followed from Heinemann to Cape) suggested that his non-delivery was hanging over them like some terrible illness that neither wanted to mention, and that it would be a lot easier for their friendship if it were not. Through a rococo process of corporate assimilation that characterized publishing in the eighties and nineties, she was then in the huge Random House complex. It happened that Random also owned the assets of Heinemann, following their acquisition of the Reed Trade Publishing Group. Simon Master, who had been at Pan when Douglas began his career there as a writer, was also at Random as Group Deputy Chairman. The contractual complexities are too boring to recount, but what happened essentially was that Random decided to get out from under its obligation to publish Douglas's next book by selling its interest to Pan, its co-venture partner and Douglas's faithful paperback house. This was prompted by Random's decision to say no to the *Starship Titanic* novelization; evidently at a senior level (for Sue would not have been able to initiate this on her own) their commitment to their wayward author was wavering. In fairness, Douglas was already over half a decade past his deadline.

Random was not exposed by having a huge amount of money out on signature. On the other hand, they did have a substantial liability if and when Douglas delivered his next novel, as they would be obliged to pay him a large delivery advance. In the circumstances it seemed to make sense to consolidate all his work with one publisher, Pan, and its hardcover imprint, Macmillan. Douglas, insecure as ever, felt that Random's decision was hardly a vote of confidence in him. They clearly did not believe that he would deliver or, if he did, that it would be a worthwhile commercial bet to hang on.

The argument that followed was exacerbated by the fact that Heinemann had the rights to an attractive hardcover omnibus of the *Hitchhiker's* novels which was still selling over ten thousand copies a year. OK, said Ed Victor, if the rationale for this assignment of the whole contract to Pan is to publish Douglas under one roof, please could we have the hardcover omnibus rights back too? Ian Chapman at Pan then offered £50,000 to buy the rights in the omnibus from Random. In fairness the loss to Random would have been the entire margin on the sales so £50,000, though a decent offer, did not represent the profit on those sales for much more than a year. Publishers hate giving up copyrights for these are all they possess, and there is a certain intangible loss of credibility in the trade when the booksellers notice the change of publisher. Simon Master said no. Ed and Simon argued. Battle lines ebbed and flowed. Douglas himself wrote a plaintive letter (unusual in itself, for he was not a frequent correspondent) to the formidable Gail Rebuck, the boss of Random UK, asking for the omnibus to be released. The answer was still no. Random House was within its rights, of course, but this decision was exceedingly hard-nosed.

Part of Random's icy calculation to reassign their contract may have been based on the market's notorious amnesia. Although Douglas's body of work was more than respectable, it's damaging if there are too many years between each book. The momentum is lost. Commercially he was still big, but not quite as hot as he had been. Besides, Douglas no longer had the genre to himself. Terry Pratchett's humorous Discworld novels were deservedly selling by the truckload.* What's more, they were being written at exactly the right rate of one per year.

It was important that Douglas not stall completely, and, after the agony of *Mostly Harmless*, it looked very much as if he might. Ed Victor was so concerned that he had rented Douglas the top floor of his office in Bedford Square in the vain hope that having a place to write would make the whole process seem more like a routine, just a job where you did your stuff without too much anguish. There Ed and his sympathetic colleagues, particularly Maggie Phillips and Sophie Hicks (now joint Managing Directors), could keep a kindly, well-focused eye upon him.

For a while Douglas kept quiet about his interest in The Digital Village, but then Ed was approached by Weidenfeld & Nicolson to see if Douglas would create – or at least present – a series of non-fiction science CD-ROMs. Publishers at the time were twitchy about the new

---

* In case anybody thinks that Terry Pratchett spotted Douglas's market and wrote for it, I must point out that Terry's comic SF just preceded Douglas's though it took longer before Terry broke through, as they say. *Strata*, for example, a pre-Discworld novel, is a little gem featuring time travellers who deliberately place cola bottles in ancient sediments in order to bewilder archaeologists of the future.

media and anxious lest their book sales evaporate while they were still struggling to understand the new ways of distributing what everybody learned to call content (a hateful word that seemed to homogenize everything). Publishers owned a lot of 'content' and hoped that the CD-ROM would offer a supplementary market for it. There is now a market that exploits the huge storage capacity of the CD-ROM. However, for most general applications, it turned out that there was already a well-established technology that got the vote of the general trade – a portable, cheap, searchable, user-friendly, large-capacity information module requiring no power by hours of daylight, and with an indefinite storage life. It was called a book.

Douglas had to come clean about his interest in TDV, and a meeting was arranged with him, Robbie, Ed Victor and Douglas's lawyer, Leon Morgan, in Bedford Square. Ed was not thrilled, and confessed to Robbie later that his intention had been to squash the idea. But he was won over and became a supporter with a place on the board. Besides, he could see that Douglas was not in the writing vein and that this new venture gave him an interest and stimulating company.

With Douglas as the resident genius and brand name, and Apple likely to come in as strategic partners (which they did in 1996), plus some serious TV experience and general management *nous* from Robbie, TDV looked a good bet. At this time investment in Internet-related companies in the UK was still gathering momentum. It was a couple of years before stories were appearing in the press that a company worth sixpence on Thursday had floated on the market on Saturday, thereby making two speccy sixteen-year-olds and a venture capitalist obscene wads of money. Nevertheless, feverish rumblings had started. Retrospect lends a spurious clarity to one's view, but in the mid-nineties the atmosphere was heady. The possibilities of the new technology, and the uneasy sensation that the ground was shifting beneath one's feet, were enormously exciting. The feeling that the technological tide might go out leaving a few dying species of commercial dinosaur dehydrating on the beach added to the urgent sense that this was a technology that had to be embraced.

Robbie began to pull all the strands together. Douglas, Robbie, and Robbie's former boss at Central, Richard Creasey, were the three original partners. Robbie recalls:

We took our first offices on top of Ed's in Bedford Square, and wrote a business plan and found other partners. Then Ian Charles Stewart joined us as the business brains [a smart ex-Pearson's venture capitalist]. He had a lot more fund-raising experience than I had. Richard Harris joined us on the technical side because I knew we had need of technical expertise. And we had Ed on board, and Mary Glanville [a lively, clever TV executive] joined us to help with the TV deal-making and so on . . .

So that's how we got going. There was a huge amount of excitement. We raised seed capital relatively easily from [venture capitalist] Alex Catto to whom we had been introduced by John Lloyd. Alex came in at an early stage, buying 10% of the company for £400,000. I think it was 19 December 1995 when we closed that deal – and what a wonderful feeling it was. I really felt that we had a shot at building something very special.

With the initial investment and with the expert help of Ian Stewart, Robbie finalized a professional business plan complete with spread-sheets that looked set to march confidently into the future. Those nasty figures in brackets were soon to be replaced by positives. Now it's too easy to say that some of the assumptions were founded on false premises. Nobody at the time knew how quickly the fundamentals were changing. The best advice about on-line advertising revenue, for instance, predicted some remarkable growth, and it was by no means clear then that the access providers, the ISPs, would hog so much of that income. New technologies like nano-billing were also coming on stream that would make it possible to receive tiny amounts of money from multitudes of people in such a way that the cost of collection was low enough for the exercise to be worthwhile. The problem with nano-billing was that the availability of the means did not create the market; people tend to go straight to the source if they are buying on-line rather than paying a fee, however minuscule, to be linked to it. All this, however, is post-hoc wisdom. At the time the potential looked exhilarating.

TDV's original executive team looked something like this: Robbie Stamp, Chief Executive; Douglas Adams, Chief Fantasist; Ian Charles

Stewart, Director, Dollars and Sense; Richard Creasey, Creative Director; Mary Glanville, Director, International Television and Marketing; Richard Harris, Chief Technology Officer; and Ed Victor and the Hon. Alex Catto, Non-Executive Directors. In addition, Robbie had lined up a very high-powered board of technology advisors, each of whom was a key figure in his field. For communications there was Bob Lucky of Bellcore Research Labs; Alan Kay, whom many regard as the father of the personal computer, was their advisor for computer science; Kai Krause, head of MetaTools, the ground-breaking graphics software company, was on the board for technology and design; and David Nagel, the President of AT&T Labs, was there for research. In the IT world, these men were royalty. With KPMG as auditors, and media-establishment Olswang as the company lawyers, all the credentials were in place for a sensible round of fund-raising with the hard-eyed men in stripy shirts and spotted ties in London, and the even tougher men with hard eyes and open shirts in California.

But first, what would the company actually do? The goal, to quote from the business plan, was 'the creation of a global on-line consumer transaction business which will exist on the World Wide Web and its successors. It will sell interactive entertainment and information experiences to a worldwide audience.' There is a misconception that the company would be mainly a vehicle for Douglas's talents, but, although his presence was essential, TDV was always planned to be much broader than that. It was one of the new generation of multi-media organizations being made possible by new technology.

There were to be three planks on which TDV would rest.

Firstly, *The Hitchhiker's Guide* (H2G2) – a guide to the Earth in this case, not the galaxy – would be created as a next-generation Internet service, a huge, living miscellany of useful information and opinion offering its users much more than a directory or a search engine. It wouldn't be a semi-detached source of cool information or a portal out to the World Wide Web; the idea was that it would become something innovative and altogether warmer by providing society and fostering a sense of personal belonging. 'Community' is an overused word, but H2G2, with its legions of passionate fans, stood a good chance of becoming one of the first 'virtual' communities with a truly cross-cultural and international nature. One way it would achieve that was by getting the members to participate in the evolution of H2G2 by writing much of the guide themselves, with some editorial shaping in-house. For instance, instead of getting on-line to read a stodgy review of your local Italian restaurant from some established reference work, you could find the real info from no-nonsense H2G2 users. ('Saw a mouse on the stairs . . . full of braying advertising men with pony tails . . . watch for the heart-stopping cleavage of the waitress . . . better off at the great sushi bar two doors down.' You know.) H2G2 would be rich in editorial content and informed by Douglas's own voice. It was always conceived as the Earth edition of the *Hitchhiker's Guide* – free to members and supported by sponsorship and advertising.

Secondly, there was *Starship Titanic*, a massive CD-ROM game of staggering visual panache and narrative complexity for which Robbie had closed a co-production venture with Peter Yunich at Simon & Schuster Interactive in New York. S&S would put up the money which was originally budgeted at over $2 million. This sum was immediately negotiated downwards, a typical corporate reflex that caused TDV problems from the outset. TDV would create and manage the project and have a 50% share of revenues. A linked website would provide further extension of the brand.

Finally, TDV planned to develop a second multiple-media brand, Avatar, and later Avatar Forest, which would appear first as a low-cost, long-running one-hour television series for Disney/ABC. In turn, they hoped, it would generate a 3-D virtual world based on the series. All the joint ventures would be 100% funded by the outside partners with their deep pockets and distribution muscle, and this would lessen TDV's financial risk in the early years of the business.

With first-round money in place, TDV was able to expand and soon moved out of Bedford Square into a whitewashed, former industrial space in Camden Street in Camden Town. The offices were attractive, but on a main thoroughfare with one-way traffic droning down it all day and night like a reminder of mortality. On the other hand Camden Town is lively, with one of the city's best street markets, and endowed with that essential for any area housing Douglas and colleagues – a surfeit of restaurants.

Funding in the UK was always tight. The wall of money heading like a tsunami towards all things dotcomish did not really pick up speed until the late nineties. In the UK in 1996 such ventures still looked speculative and hard to quantify, and it's also always tricky striking a balance between how much equity to sell and how much to keep back so that the founders of the company still feel it's theirs. Robbie also wanted the staff to have an opportunity of participating in the success of the company. To his credit, he admits that with their ambitions for TDV and their uncertainty about how to value it, they made a strategic error:

> In the early spring of 1996 we had made an absolutely egregious mistake. It was a very, very slow death in many ways and it gave us a wound from which we never completely recovered. The scar tissue healed up, but it was fragile and was ripped open easily when the going got tough. And that mistake was when we were offered £3 million from Apax Partners for 30% of the company [valuing TDV at £10 million], we turned it down. It was a lower valuation than we'd expected because we'd set the threshold at something like £15 million. There were some ratchets put in for Alex [Catto] so that he would have the chance to buy more shares to equalize him up.
>
> Frankly we were barking not to take that money from Apax. It was because we had an over-inflated sense of the value of the company. We were driven by some West Coast dream stories. But we weren't there – we were in Camden, in London, in 1996 and the Internet was not a great big thing yet in Europe. There were still a lot of people for whom you'd have to spell the word 'Internet', let alone talk about what the financial models might be. And Apax was a blue-chip investment company.

Though the lack of development capital was to torture Robbie and the executive team throughout the life of the company, they did have some seed money and funds from their co-venture partners. Robbie, Richard Harris and Richard Creasey soon recruited a team of bright youngsters, many of whom were *Hitchhiker's* fans. Kate Salmon joined as Douglas's

P.A. (When Kate moved on, Sophie Astin, a graduate in French from Leicester University, replaced her and soon became indispensable.) Tim Browse, a brilliant programmer, and Adam Shaikh, a terrific games designer, were recruited. Some were so young that like 'Yoz' (Yoram) Grahame, a web technologist, they'd been introduced to *Hitchhiker's* by their mums and dads.

It was a terrific company that at its height employed about thirty people either on the staff or on contracts. The atmosphere was both frantic and relaxed. Robbie was a humane boss who believed in a horizontal rather than a vertical management structure, and he was very approachable. They nearly all worked dementedly hard. The usual amount of intra-company flirting took place (probably more than the usual amount), and the prevailing spirit meant that you did not stop in mid-task if it happened to be going-home time. As a result, people got terribly tired, and if they really needed to recharge their batteries it was possible to take what were known as 'duvet days' lying at home, groaning. Of course there were interpersonal tensions and wrangles, but it was a happy and well-motivated company.

Richard Harris, the Chief Technology Officer, a bouncy beardy generalist, had a degree in zoology from Aberdeen as well as a deep knowledge of IT. His background was in biological computation and his range of interests – *inter alia*, quantum physics, population modelling, motorbikes, the red-throated bee eater, gorillas, beer – was almost as catholic as Douglas's. The two of them got on well, though they tended to compete over their high-tech toys – a dangerous game to play with Douglas.

London at the time, Richard believes, was the most creative city in the world (not excluding Palo Alto/San Francisco) for software design. The engineers and designers they recruited were 'really brilliant, talented and obstreperous'. Douglas loved the atmosphere and the stimulation of the office. One of his colleagues said the affection and support he got at the office was 'worth a hundred of his showbiz pals'.

Initially, with Avatar to one side, the company was structured into two teams, the larger one working on *Starship Titanic* and the other on the H2G2 website. (The latter 'very unladdish', Yoz reports. 'Extremely witty, great fun, but they hardly drank at all, and never talked about girls or made rude jokes . . .') A certain amount of competition for resources ebbed and flowed between the two, and there was the traditional joshing between the techies and the so-called creatives. Courtesy of Apple (the partnership was announced at MILIA in Cannes in 1996), TDV enjoyed some state-of-the-art equipment, though Yoz recalls a certain amount of obsolete stuff also got dumped on them. Technically the all-Apple environment did give the programmers a headache. What Apple had available at the time was not ideal for game programming.

But it soon became clear that the revenue from H2G2 was some way off in the future. There was no shortage of potential users, but to persuade advertisers to part with their money you have to demonstrate that you have a regular audience, and that takes time to establish. Sponsorship is also notoriously tricky, a stately, slow dance of inching forwards and shuffling backwards again. Your contact at Megacorp says: 'That's interesting. Write me a proposal and I will take it to next month's marketing meeting.' A month goes by. Then she says, 'This is so new – more research needs to be done before we commit to this.' The following month the key decision-maker is in Japan, and the one after that is the end of Megacorp's financial year so they've spent the budget. Another month passes and now 'we're reconsidering our Internet strategy so this little sponsorship deal is on hold. The tail cannot wag the dog . . .'

Another problem with H2G2 lay with the users writing the material. Robbie and the team knew that the members would not somehow create an innovative reference source collectively without a great deal of effort at the centre; he always strove to get the balance between public writing and in-house editorial right – and looking at the guide now with its rich variety and volume of entries the mix is very appealing. In retrospect the directors may have underestimated the work needed in-house, though their innocence in that respect reflects well on H2G2's determination not to talk down to their audience. Some of the entries were wonderful, but many were not – and all of them reflected the many personalities, voices, styles and viewpoints of the writers. In aggregate the result just did not cohere into a usable resource.

And all the while Robbie and the other directors were acutely aware of how quickly they were spending money – something known in the jargon by the apt expression 'the burn rate'. They threw themselves onto venture capitalists and well-heeled technology companies like Zero Mostel in *The Producers* launching himself on Little Old Lady Land. Intel came close but insisted on a local partner, and the UK market proved very steely indeed for a start-up multi-media company. Poor Robbie had to keep everybody motivated and fix a confident smile on his face until it ached, while in the privacy of his brain he worried about their finances.

Raising money had its lighter moments. Richard recalls what fun they had in California in 1997. Douglas, Ian Stewart, Richard and Robbie had flown out there to make a series of presentations. Douglas was essential, Robbie recalls. The esteem with which he was regarded 'on the Coast' enabled their small but smart British company, as he said, to punch above its weight.

The local car hire company had a special offer, so for an increment of only $6 per day they tooled about in a large, red, convertible Ford Mustang with Douglas's head sticking over the top like some mad tank commander's. It was stressful, but an adventure. On that trip, Ian Stewart recalls, they made a pitch to Vulcan North-West, Paul Allen's investment company. Paul Allen and Douglas had met several times and seemed to have a good rapport. Douglas was naïvely hurt that despite this good relationship with Paul, the investment decision had been pushed down the line to the analysts. They declined. The locals, despite the Grateful Dead T-shirts, flip-flops and 'hey dude' laid-back manner, have a cool grasp of the basics when it comes to business. Douglas complained, 'We only wanted a mere $1–1.5 million. It's pocket money for Paul.' In fairness, Douglas understood that Paul's investment company had to make their own judgements.

The TDV team met all the Microsoft billionaire aristocrats while they were touting for investment. Charles Simonyi entertained them in his mansion that had the size and content of an art gallery. He even showed them his bedroom with its vast picture window overlooking one of Seattle's many lakes and a revolving bed enabling him to track the sun. It must have been difficult for the visiting Brits not to grin. But Simonyi did not invest in TDV either.

Jim Lynn, the technical leader of H2G2, thinks that the technology was ten years behind what Douglas's imagination wanted it to do both on the game and for H2G2. He and his fellow programmers, all *Hitchhiker's* fans, worked heroically to try to realize Douglas's dreams. Douglas was particularly close to software engineers Tim Browse and Sean Solle who worked well beyond the call of duty to make the H2G2 vision come true.

'He was always so disappointed when we said "no",' said Jim, 'and didn't always understand why some of the simplest things were the hardest to deliver.' Douglas wasn't very good at saying 'well done' even though – as resident star and genius adored by the troops – this was something they wanted very much to hear. The TDV programmers worked wonders, but they were not a huge team in some billion dollar research park in Palo Alto. There was just a handful of them in Camden Town; their Chief Fantasist's expectations were not always realistic.

Organizational life was something for which Douglas did not have the subtlest reflexes. He could be unreceptive to creative ideas from others – as if creativity was exclusively his job – and it was apparent almost immediately that the role of benign Godfather to other people's projects (a role that all had hoped he might fulfil) was just not one that suited him, even if there were sufficient time. Douglas was out of practice in large meetings – after all it had been nearly twenty years since the BBC – and he would sometimes address his remarks just to one person in a way that could make colleagues sensitive to these nuances cringe inwardly. On the other hand, he often showed great warmth and kindness and never deliberately hurt anybody's feelings; indeed he would be mortified when he realized that he had been a clodhopper. Douglas making amends was almost more embarrassing than the original slight. Despite the surface sophistication, in unfamiliar contexts the shy and gawky schoolboy could rise from his past.

The H2G2 site was very advanced technically for it was one integrated whole rather than lots of linked components, and was written in the computer language C++, which is unusual for a website. But despite its sophistication, Douglas's dream for TDV was that it could develop some kind of artificial intelligence that would pass the famous Turing Test. That is still a long way off.* Instead he had to settle for something that looked like it, and thereby he came up with one of his engaging analogies.

'Think of it this way,' he told the team:

> It's a magic trick. When a magician saws his shapely assistant in half on the stage, we see her feet wiggling at one end of the box and her head, clearly too far from her feet, at the other end. We know she hasn't actually been sawn in half, but the illusion is bloody good. We don't want to know how the trick is done. That's the kind of illusion of artificial intelligence I want with *Starship Titanic*.†

Not being embarrassed by a surfeit of cash put all the more pressure on the timely production of *Starship Titanic*. Unfortunately this game, inspired by a joke in *Life, the Universe and Everything*,∞ was hugely ambitious in scope, and almost beyond their resources to produce in the relatively short development time available to them, especially as the S&S money did not come through quickly. After a false start (Douglas's fault, as he later admitted) over the buying in of some specialized software, the engineers wrote their own bespoke tools. Starting in the summer of 1996, delivering a giant game by September 1997 was always going to require a Himalayan effort.

The game itself is a remarkable achievement. From the outset Douglas had wanted a game with wit and humour that was also

---

* What's more, it will be immensely difficult. Wittgenstein pointed out that the meaning of words cannot be analysed atomically because what he called the performative context in which they are uttered is essential for understanding. There is more to intelligence than logical reasoning: you have to want to interact with the world and be aware of yourself as an actor in it. So far, only organic creatures have feeling and appetite and self-consciousness. There is no reason in principle why consciousness cannot be created from some configuration of matter, but evolution has billions of years' lead on our efforts.

† My thanks to Yoz Grahame for this story.

∞ The one about the interstellar liner that undergoes SMEF – Spontaneous Massive Existence Failure.

beautiful to watch. He had admired the graphics in *Myst* and loved the intriguing world it created, but he found it characterless and lifeless.* *Starship Titanic* would be richly inhabited by characters, in this case robots, many of whom were obstructive in ways too baroque to be described.

Visually it was stunning. Douglas had been attracted to the work of the artist and designer team Oscar Chichoni and Isabel Molina, an Italian/Argentinian partnership of extraordinary talent. They were hired on a short-term contract and ended up working flat out for eighteen months. The look they created was that of an elegant but slightly sinister French ocean liner of the 1930s. The colours are unusual. Every surface is highly polished and elegantly decorated in an art deco style that is somehow suffused with an off-beat eroticism. The robots (the bots) with their smooth yet expressive faces and their sudden unfoldings, like mechanised bats, are both funny and disturbing. In fact there is something both comic and nightmarish about the whole enterprise. Isabel found Douglas very appreciative of the artwork, and receptive to suggestions that emerged from it to the extent of sometimes writing them into the script. The only problem with graphics so detailed and finished was the sheer amount of information they contained. Sometimes, Isabel says, the polygon count had to be trimmed because otherwise the screen would just take too long to refresh itself.† As it is, *Starship Titanic* is a colossal game requiring no less than three CDs to run. Quite possibly it is the most elegant computer game ever produced.

Some of those CDs' capacity was taken up with a plot which rested on narrative foundations as big as a castle. Making something as complex as a computer game is a team effort, so it may be unfair to list some individuals and not them all. However, the software engineers – Tim Browse, Sean Solle, Rik Heywood, and Mike Kenny – did an exceptional job delivering far more than seemed possible. Adam Shaikh

---

* Interview in *Computer Game* magazine, November 1997.

† The polygon count represents the number of visual elements in the image. The higher the number, the greater the resolution. I am grateful to Isabel Molina for her assistance with this part of the story.

worked heroically on the architecture of the game. Douglas could not really program, though he admired those who could, and sometimes he drove the techies mad trying. Robbie said 'he wanted to be the Michelangelo who chips away the stone to reveal the statue'. TDV employed experts to do that. Wix, Douglas's old friend, wrote some evocative music; Terry Jones was typecast as the parrot; John Cleese made a cameo appearance as the mystery voice of the bomb.

The story of *Starship Titanic* itself is deceptively simple and characteristic of Douglas's view of the human condition: you're on your own, the world doesn't quite make sense and it operates according to rules that you haven't yet worked out. The player has to negotiate an upgrade to a higher class of cabin while the desk bot politely but intractably closes off every rational route to that goal. Simultaneously a stroppy talking bomb is counting down to detonation, and the player has regularly to defuse it since the bomb has a perverse habit of rearming itself. The ship is deserted apart from a demented parrot and a weird collection of nicely observed bots, some of whom will drone on about their war wounds at heartbreaking length. The key to success in the game is talking to the bots – and this takes discretion and subtlety, for first-class minds have invested ingenuity in making the job horribly tricky.

There is a gigantic language engine built into the game. If you are so minded, you can talk to it for fourteen hours without it repeating itself. There are over three thousand sentences and phrases available to the bots, and they have a surprising range of cultural references at their disposal. It is an intellectual achievement of the highest order, one that required an endlessly inventive anticipation of player input and the subtle teasing of the audience along the route that the authors prepared for them. The language engine was very advanced – probably more so than the market required – but the culture of the company strove for excellence. Parsing natural language into recognizable components so as to generate an appropriate response from a library of possible replies is immensely complicated and it raises some interesting philosophical questions about meaning and the role of grammar in thought. An American baby and a Chinese baby are born with indistinguishable brains, and both set about learning their local languages thanks in part (according to Chomsky and others) to innate pattern generation and recognition talents built in by millions of years of evolution. A computer, on the other hand, is many orders of magnitude simpler than a baby's brain, and its operating system (without which it is just an inert assemblage of components) may be all of ten years old. This is not the place to explore these notions, but one example of almost identical sentences with radically different syntax will suffice to illustrate the problem: 'Time flies like an arrow' and 'Fruit flies like an apple.'*

Douglas created the game concept and the basic architecture, and he and Neil Richards and Douglas's old friend, Michael Bywater, wrote nearly all the character dialogue. Neil Richards also managed the text, and Douglas and Michael are credited with the game outline.

Not surprisingly such a groundbreaking game took longer to produce than they had planned, a grim outcome because the revenue from the game was effectively their only source of income. If they ran out of money before the game was on the market, they'd be bust. If they got more money from S&S Interactive, they would delay the receipt of their own income from the game – possibly for years. What's more they would miss the Christmas 1997 market, and run the risk that the launch would be stillborn. It's often impossible to rekindle excitement if something is announced, then delayed. Cash flow can kill a business even at its moment of triumph because it takes time to collect debts from the market whereas expenditure always increases before the launch of a new product.

In the end, after several missed dates, Robbie, who can be very persuasive, pleaded with S&S Interactive for more time and money – not an easy thing to do, for S&S prides itself on being tough. Gilles Dana, the Publisher of S&S Interactive who had taken over from Peter Yunich, flew over from New York to assess whether to pull the plug or extend some help. It was a frightening time.

Gilles Dana happens to be a strictly orthodox Jew, and the TDV management was not quite sure what to feed him. There were a couple

---

* These witty examples are from Steven Pinker's *The Language Instinct* (Penguin Books, 1995).

of Jews on the staff who were consulted. Yoz remembers Douglas listening intently and without the slightest hint of satire while Yoz explained some of the unusual culinary regulations:

> I laid everything on the table, and before Gilles arrived I lined up all the TDV directors and everybody who was going to be having lunch and carefully explained to them, 'Look, this goes in here. If you've eaten that, you don't eat this with that . . .' Enough for them to get the idea. Douglas was there. This was my first proper interaction with one of my all-time heroes, who happens to be the most famous, staunchest atheist in the world, and I have to explain to him how to keep kosher . . . It was deeply frightening. Douglas was very tactful, and asked a lot of questions. He knew how not to tread on people. Mind you, when Douglas was back in his office and, as he thought, I was safely out of earshot, he had this conversation with Alison [a colleague]. He was hitting his forehead with a cry of, 'This is the twentieth century, for God's sake.' And Alison said: 'It's *religion*, Douglas, it's century-independent.'

As it turned out, Gilles brought his own food. He was, says Robbie, tough but totally straight, and he extended both their deadline and their funding, though on rigorous terms. Games are not like books which enjoy a market stable enough for there to be confidence that the 'product' would still sell even if a year late. There was no leeway at all for further delay.

Emma Westecott was appointed as producer of the game, and she did an astonishingly good job in motivating the team and making up time. Nearly all the company's efforts were now directed to getting *Starship Titanic* finished while a small team maintained the H2G2 site – though it was not commercialised. The website venture taking second place compounded Robbie's difficulties in raising money, for his multimedia company was now engaged on only one product. There was a running joke in TDV that H2G2 was operating on the *South Park* 'Three Phase' business model. Apparently in *South Park* (the anarchic cartoon series) the underpant gnomes abduct the infant heroes and take them back to a huge, cavernous lair in the middle of which is a gigantic pile of underpants. There's a flip chart behind the pile, and on the chart it says, 'Phase One – collect underpants. Phase Two – [a giant question mark]. Phase Three – profit.' The underpants business model, one can't help thinking, basically sums up much of the strategy behind the dotcom explosion. Despite this gallows humour, everybody I have spoken to who worked on H2G2 was proud to have contributed to it regardless of whether it made a profit or not.

The pressure became overwhelming. The technicians frequently worked overnight and their room soon held mountains of print-out, tottering towers of discarded pizza boxes and changes of clothes. Robbie used to bring in food parcels for them when they were working on Sundays.

Under this crushing pressure, another of Douglas's intense friendships became a casualty. Never employ your friends, they say, if you want to keep them.

Michael Bywater had known Douglas since Cambridge. Michael is a phenomenon. Once, Peter Bennett-Jones reports, after Michael had been consistently late for Footlights rehearsals, at which he played the piano, he had been threatened with the scrotal shears if he were late again. But at next rehearsal he turned up two hours after the appointed time looking wild-eyed and dishevelled. 'Don't ask,' he said. 'I've just crashed a plane.' Michael does indeed have a private pilot's licence (you will recall that he once flew a house party down to Douglas's place in Provence). He plays the piano beautifully. He knows a great deal of stuff across an unusual range of subject matters. Once, at one of their smart dinners, Douglas and Jane, fatigued by Michael's incontinent trickle of esoterica, especially of the medical variety, placed him next to Annie Coren, the wife of Alan, the humorist and writer. Annie is a highly respected consultant anaesthetist at a major London teaching hospital. After dinner she and Jane compared notes: 'Michael,' Annie reported to Jane, 'has a bluff that cannot be called . . .'

Michael Bywater is the most intellectually competitive person anybody is ever likely to meet. He is ferociously bright, and not inhibited from letting others appreciate the fact. He does not wear his erudition lightly. In an age when the uneasy journalism of self-revelation is popular, it was nevertheless surprising when Michael told his readers in the *Independent on Sunday* about an incident in his childhood. His parents, believing on medical grounds that he would be a singleton, adopted a baby girl. Michael adored her, but for whatever reason she did not bond well with his mother, and after a short time she was returned with great regret to the agency. All his life, Michael confessed, he had been at some emotional level convinced that if you did not pass muster *you could be sent back.* Human beings are so complex that the idea of a single motivational key to their behaviour is obviously crass – or best reserved for movies as with *Citizen Kane's* Rosebud motif. Nevertheless, there is something driven about Michael's need to impress. For God's sake, *relax*, one wants to say: every sentence need not be a winner.

Intellectually Douglas and Michael were very much on the same wavelength. Both stood proudly on the bridge between arts and science. Given the interconnectedness of all things, in a more sensible world such mischievous distinctions would not need bridge-builders at all. Michael can talk about Heine and Heisenberg with equal facility. Some of his younger colleagues at TDV loved going for a beer with him. Though there was one lion and the rest were Christians, he could put on a coruscating performance. Other colleagues thought differently. Richard Harris and Michael, for instance, had personalities that grated upon each other. There were even occasions when Michael used his column in the paper to write about the company in easily penetrated disguise, something his co-workers considered bad form. Once, when one of Michael's articles was published at a sensitive time for TDV, Robbie was almost inclined to reach for his lawyers.

If most of us talk like bottles of pale ale, Michael talks like champagne, and he had fizzed at Douglas before when he had been under the cosh over several novels – especially *Mostly Harmless*. The two of them had been close for years: Douglas helped Michael out financially when he was struggling, and had stood by him, often proselytising about his talents. Douglas had nagged me, for instance, to commission Michael's novel that was eventually bought by Sue Freestone and (as of February 2003) is yet to be published. In return Douglas got a lot of attention, a great deal of charm, editorial feedback and effervescent conversation. When Douglas and Michael were on song, gales of laughter would emerge from Douglas's office in TDV.

Such intimacy made their falling out all the more bitter. The immediate *casus belli* was the novel of *Starship Titanic* that Pan wanted to issue to coincide with the launch of the computer game. Douglas had flirted with the idea of writing it himself, but eventually became determined not to do so. As he explained, he just didn't have the time to work on the game and a book simultaneously – a reasonable position given his rate of production.

At first the great SF author, Robert Sheckley, was commissioned to write the *Starship Titanic* novel. Robert Sheckley is a wonderful American writer who has lived for many years in Europe, mainly the UK and Ibiza. His witty, surreal imagination always seemed best deployed on the short story, a form at which he is a master, though his shortish novels are objects of delight. *Mindswap* and *Dimension of Miracles*, written in the 1960s, are both masterpieces, and full of tropes and alarming reality displacements that years later could be described as Adamsy. But Robert Sheckley, a gentle, funny man, frequently hard up, and then in his late sixties, had not been very productive for some time. He and Douglas had something in common inasmuch as Sheckley once endured a ten-year writing block (though he was having an inordinate amount of fun on Ibiza). Douglas had read his work, and I know they met many years before *Starship Titanic* because on 31 August 1984 Douglas, Robert, Jane Belson, my friend Nick Austin (another publisher), my sister, Anna, and Sue Webb (spouse and diary writer) had dinner at our place in Hackney, north-east London.

Unfortunately, the novel that Robert delivered was not suitable. It's difficult to say why. Robert may not have been on form, or his voice may have been so unlike Douglas's own – or so different to the *Starship Titanic* source material – that it just would not do. It wasn't until the autumn that they finally decided that the novelization was completely unusable, and this left Douglas and Robbie under time pressure on the delivery of the novel as well as the game. There was also money riding on it – a commodity of which they had a distinctly finite supply – for this piece of intellectual property resided in the company and not with Douglas. Pan, believing that the game would be issued in December

1997, wanted the book at the same time. Douglas never saw why two such different media had to coincide, but Pan was insistent. Besides, for books as with games, the Christmas market is vital. Robbie describes *Starship Titanic* at this time as a black hole sucking in all their money and resources. The famous advice in the *Hitchhiker's Guide*, DON'T PANIC, seemed to be mocking them. Robbie, to his credit, never did panic, but he endured many a restless night with runaway brain.

Michael had the answer. He would write the novel. Pan would publish at blinding speed, and Michael would hole up somewhere with his Apple, vast quantities of chocolate, cigs and black coffee, and emerge three weeks later – trembling, bearded, hallucinating, eyes the colour of Spam – with the novel in his hands. After all, he knew the dialogue and the architecture of the story as well as anyone. Pan agreed, and so did Peter Guzzardi, the American publisher. There was no formal offer, but Robbie's email log confirms that everybody expected Michael would be writing the book. He was thrilled. Not only would he be paid to do it (for this was a task over and above his contract with TDV) but also he would gain a credential – a novel, albeit with an odd genesis, with his name on it. (The packaging was going to say 'Douglas Adams's *Starship Titanic*' at the top and the author's name at the bottom.) Perhaps like John Lloyd, Michael also felt a need to show the world that he too could hack it creatively up there with Douglas.

In the event, Douglas changed his mind. Jane recalls that he came home after an exhausting day at TDV and told her about the problem over the timing of the novel. He was vaguely thinking of giving the book to Michael. 'Well, if I were you, I'd vaguely unthink it,' said Jane, with her characteristic grasp of the practical. 'You've only got a few weeks, and will not have any options left when they're gone. Michael has never finished a book on time.'

Douglas pondered, and then phoned his friend, Terry Jones, and asked him to do it instead. Terry, innocent of the history, agreed and managed to write a more than competent, good-natured novel in only three weeks. It does not catch fire on the page like one of Douglas's, but it does the job. Pan published it just before Christmas 1997 when the shelves of the book trade are so swollen with stock that it is almost impossible to shoe-horn in another title. It sold about 80,000 copies – not bad at all, though nothing like the sales of a Douglas Adams novel.

Michael went spare. To say he was upset would be like describing the US navy as a bit miffed about Pearl Harbor. He felt betrayed. He believed that he had been made to look foolish in front of publishers in the UK and the States. For a man like Michael, who bears his intelligence like a banner before him, this was humiliating. Fluency can be dangerous. Never a man to curb his linguistic skills, his articulate screech of outrage was so over the top that his relationship with TDV was almost irreparable, though Richard Creasey, exercising his prodigious skills of persuasion and diplomacy, lured him back into the fold for the short term. The schism is a pity, for Michael had a point, and he and Douglas had a huge capacity for amusing each other intellectually. Douglas wrote Michael a carefully considered letter, but the response was terse. There was even talk of lawyers. Both parties were hurt. Even now there is a deep and complex ambivalence in Michael on the subject of Douglas.

Eventually *Starship Titanic* was completed, but, despite the superhuman efforts of Emma and the team, it did not make the US Christmas market. It was finally released for the PC market in April 1998 – 'a horrible year' Robbie remembers with a shudder – and the multi-language and Apple versions came out a year later. Apple Master Douglas took a lot of flack on-line for the delay in releasing the Apple version, but he was unfailingly polite about explaining the economic realities despite receiving 'some of the rudest emails ever written'.

Everybody admired the graphics, but the sheer scale and density of the game and the tortuous ingenuity of the tactical traps make playing it a big investment of time, and in the end it gets frustrating. The team had become just too immersed in it, a world unto itself. Perhaps TDV was overly confident about the power of the brand to pull in buyers. *Starship Titanic* was also at the cerebral end of the computer game spectrum, whereas the mass market was to be found at the other end, home of Garth Gonad-Crusher shoot-'em-up violent graphics. S&S Interactive worked very hard to promote the game, though there was one occasion, Ed Victor reported, when Douglas was dismayed to find one of his college lecture audiences (the key market) had not heard of it at all. However, the game did win an industry award, the Codie, for the best Adventure/Role-Playing game.

Unfortunately the sales were insufficient to change the company's fortunes. After the release of *Starship Titanic*, there was not enough operating capital to fund TDV until another game or new revenue earner could be developed. All the more innovative sources of income were just not there yet in sufficient volume, and at that time investors were becoming more interested in the potential for on-line commerce than in computer game companies. They had realized that the games market was as volatile as the music charts. A hit could make a fortune, but there was a high incidence of expensive dogs. When Thomas Hoegh of Arts Alliance, an enlightened Norwegian/American venture capital company with a strongly innovative arts bias, expressed interest in *Starship Titanic*, it made perfect sense for them to take over the games division and for TDV to be relaunched as H2G2, concentrating solely on building the Earth Edition of the guide. In September 1998, Thomas Hoegh and Robbie closed the deal for *Starship Titanic* and all its associated intellectual property to be transferred to Arts Alliance. It seemed like a good new home. Douglas said:

> What a wonderful change. So many investors in the UK have
> almost no idea what the Internet even is. Thomas Hoegh
> understands it intensely and knows that the old rules no longer
> apply, that the medium will belong to those who can think the
> most radically and creatively. I couldn't be more pleased to have
> him on board.

The balance of the company moved to smaller offices – though, if anything, even more fashionable – in Maiden Lane, in London's Covent Garden, where the Earth Edition of the guide was relaunched. All through 1999 they experimented with various business models – banner ads, tie-ins with mobile phone companies, new forms of sponsorship and so on – and lived on their wits in the meantime. After one false start, the site began to grow. As it expanded, the importance of peer review and the rigorous sifting of the entries grew correspondingly, and Mark Moxon was appointed as the full-time editor. Eventually a workable structure emerged for a truly original and useful website service. Alas, the company was still chronically short of cash and Robbie started preparing for a private placement using Bear Stearns, the international trading and brokerage company, which put a potential value on H2G2 of over $20 million.

By now Douglas himself was largely absent, either in California working on the movie, or on the lecture circuit. But he visited as often as he could both in the flesh and on-line. It says a lot for the soundness of their friendship that Douglas and Robbie never seriously fell out. Even when Douglas had moved to Santa Barbara, he remained in close touch with Robbie. Douglas's self-imposed exile in California must have been a boon for Pacific Bell.

'Douglas was always there for the company,' Robbie recalls. 'Even when the consequences were painful I could always rely on his support.'

All through 1999 H2G2 lived frugally, while slowly establishing the on-line business and preparing the business for a private sale. Due diligence had been done on the accounts. All the cupboard doors had been opened. They were, as Robbie says, 'all dressed up with nowhere to go'.

Then, at the beginning of April 2000 (the 'tech wreck' as it was known), the world of finance jolted awake like some sleepwalker on the edge of a roof whom nobody had wanted to wake up in case of an accident. The day of reckoning had arrived. Technology and dotcom stocks fell through the floor, and Bear Stearns told Robbie that there was no point in taking the company out to the market. They were, as Robbie said, 'now holed below the water line'.

Robbie and his fellow directors paid themselves nothing for as long as they could manage. Jim Lynn said he didn't care if H2G2 made money because developing it was 'just so wonderful'. Their remaining money melted away like butter on a hot rock, and negotiations began with the BBC, always possessive about what it considered to be one of its brands, to buy the company. This deal was finally executed in January 2001 and Robbie stayed on for a while to oversee the transition. Some of the staff were made redundant, but many were re-employed by the BBC.

TDV/H2G2 consumed about six years of Douglas's life; apart from writing it was the longest he had devoted to any venture in his adult life. It was a brave experiment, years ahead of its time, with some bold and imaginative thinking from Douglas and his colleagues. Some very smart people worked desperately hard to create something fresh and extraordinary, and one day it might be seen as a prototype of a new kind of on-line company – one in which the customers and their relationship with the organization are in a sense the enterprise itself.

Meanwhile, H2G2, rehoused in the BBC, the world's most famous media brand, and free from immediate financial pressures, is starting to bloom. At the time of writing H2G2 has about 5,000 articles available and over 60,000 entries, and it is growing steadily. The community now has more than 200,000 registered users. Internet communities can be savage, forever 'flaming' and slagging off each other. But the H2G2 membership has not had that problem for it seems to attract decent, above averagely bright and imaginative people.

In Douglas's honour the operating system running H2G2 has been named DNA by the BBC. It has found the right home.

Finally Douglas's vision for a real on-line Guide is coming true.

chapter fourteen

Turtles all the way down

> There is one peculiar model of the universe that has turtles all
> the way down, but we have gods all the way up. It really isn't a
> very good answer, but a bottom-up solution, on the other hand,
> which rests on the incredibly powerful tautology of anything that
> happens, happens, clearly gives you a very simple and powerful
> answer that needs no other explanation whatsoever.
>
> Douglas Adams, speech at the Digital Biota II Conference

We inhabit a world in which we tend to put labels on each other and expect that we will then march through life wearing them like permanent sandwich boards. Douglas's category was Comic SF writer with philosophical bent, and that's true as far as it goes. But he was also an important thinker. He wasn't a scientist; he was a well-read and supremely intelligent generalist whose unearthly imagination was much in demand.

Don Epstein, an energetic and sophisticated New Yorker, is the president of GTN, the Greater Talent Network, one of the leading lecture agencies in the United States. If you want to hear President Clinton's talk about geopolitics after your corporate dinner, it can be arranged; Don is the man to contact.

America is a big market. Perhaps in the middle of a vast landmass, where you could be more than fifteen hundred miles from the sea in all directions, you have a hunger to hear about the world at large. The college-educated public in the States is also huge, and many American corporations are global in their scope. America is a culture with a passion for the new. Fashionable ideas, in self-help or business for example, sweep over the land where they are consumed voraciously – and sometimes discarded the next season.* The lecture circuit reflects that volatility. Maybe the local TV is just too arse-numbingly boring. Whatever the manifold reasons, lecturing on a catholic variety of subjects is a well-established business in the USA, rather giving the lie to snotty European slanders about American parochialism. Colleges, companies, chambers of commerce, clubs and societies will pay good money to hear talks from articulate people if they have fame, opinions, charisma or an interesting idea to flog.

Don had read *The Hitchhiker's Guide to the Galaxy* and enjoyed it, and he and his colleagues kept their sensitive professional antennae attuned to the strange appetites of the public. He knew that Douglas enjoyed a popular profile with the student audience rather like that of the saintly Kurt Vonnegut. Don had first been contacted by Ed Victor in 1989, but it wasn't until 1992 that he and Douglas met when Douglas was in New York and they had dinner together. Don and Douglas soon struck up a business arrangement. Eventually their mutual affection meant that Douglas became a friend as well as a client.

Douglas, Don says, had a tremendous following in the colleges and universities. His was quite an intellectual market, not hugely main-stream, but 'very keen, well informed and receptive. Quite bohemian too'. Douglas, back to his first love of performance, made incredible speeches – witty, stimulating, occasionally a little over people's heads, but that did not matter. It is better to emerge from an after dinner speech with the IQ challenged than to endure the speaker, the booze and the caterer's bleached chicken in a conspiracy of torpor.

'Douglas was quite easy and low-maintenance,' Don reports, 'always a pleasure to manage and always about responding to emails quickly.' One cannot help thinking, as admin was not Douglas's strongest suit, that he must have been poised waiting for offers to lecture. Not only did he love doing it, but it was a guilt-free flight from his keyboard.

---

* In publishing the self-improvement market is colossal in the USA and much smaller proportionately in the UK. Do Americans still hope to be perfectible? Are Brits just too embarrassed and constipated?

There is more to the lecture circuit than just turning up, giving a speech and promptly doing a runner. Often there's a reception, or dinner, a little drinks party to meet the faculty, questions after the talk, and a trip to the bar to discuss evolution, sex and football with the students . . . in short, a whole host of informal obligations that the speaker can skimp on or discharge with grace. Douglas was always 'on' as actors say. He liked meeting new people and was charming to everybody, from the driver who picked him up from the airport to the receptionist who wanted him to autograph a book for her son. He loved it; he was performing to an audience which had paid to hear him specifically, and he was earning his keep. When he had an auditorium laughing, and hanging on his every word, it was a high.

In the early nineties Douglas's lectures were mainly in colleges and universities, but from 1996 the technology market took off. Every programmer in Silicon Valley knew the name of Douglas Adams, and the desire to get him to talk to corporate America often came from the rank and file, the infantry in the IT wars, rather than the top. But he was such an amusing and interesting speaker that his fame spread, and meeting-planners in high-tech companies were soon competing to book him. His fees grew correspondingly, and eventually GTN could charge up to $20,000, plus expenses, per lecture to the big players in the IT world. (Prime Ministers and Presidents – the undeserving famous – are paid at a much higher rate, but Douglas's income from this source was substantial and helped sustain him through the decade.)

Don tells a story of Douglas's celebrity in the techie world. In 2000 Douglas was speaking at Sun Microsystems in San Francisco when Don had to get hold of him urgently. Unfortunately it was 10 p.m. in California and Sun's main switchboard was closed. Douglas was somewhere in San Francisco, a city not lacking in restaurants, his most likely location. The only number available was Sun's technical support line which at that time was connected to a team in Kuala Lumpur, the burgeoning capital of Malaysia.

'I'm trying to track down Douglas Adams somewhere in San Francisco,' Don explained. 'He's been talking to you guys, and I really need to get hold of him.'

'If you're talking about *the* Douglas Adams,' said the helpful tech support person in Kuala Lumpur, 'I'll find him for you.' Mobilizing some underground network of techies and fans, he did – in less than thirty minutes.

The range of institutions that wanted Douglas was quite broad. Universities, from small colleges to Stanford and M.I.T., remained faithful fans. Once he gave a talk to *Architecture and Interiors* magazine. Telecoms, science-based and software companies were all fascinated to hear him speak about the future of technology.

His approach was interesting for it was not led – as is often the case – by where the developments in hardware seemed to be heading. Douglas pretty much took it for granted that Moore's Law, about the doubling of capacity in the speed and memory of computers every eighteen months, would continue to run until some fundamental quantum-scale limit was reached, and he was sure that human ingenuity would still find a way of increasing efficiency. Instead his approach was intuitive. Smart technology will not necessarily be useful just because it has been developed. It is social rather than technical innovation that will bring about change. You have to understand, Douglas argued, where we've been in order to see where we might be going, because the past gives us some idea about what we actually want this stuff to do. We have to think beyond tweaking our existing gadgets and instead imagine self-organizing systems, akin to life itself, that could do almost anything we want of them. The question is: do we know what we want? It is the human spirit – infinitely adaptable yet resolutely the same – and not the hardware that is the key.

As an outstanding generalist, Douglas also spoke at scientific conferences on a non-commercial basis. He did not see that creativity in science was of a different order or nature to artistic creativity. There is always that eureka moment when you've thought of the perfect image or realized that the world works in a particular way. Douglas knew a lot of scientists, and understood that scientific method does not consist of collecting an ocean of data to see if some pattern emerges. To devise the experiment for collecting the data in the first place, you need a theory about what you might find. Art and science both involve intuition and a feel for the subject. Experimental method is to test your intuition against observation. It is only then that scientific procedure kicks in to ensure that the relevant variables have been isolated, the result can be replicated and – *pace* Popper – if necessary tested for falsifiability.

For instance, Douglas was a fan of Steve Grand, the brilliant programmer who devised the artificial life computer game, *Creatures*. In his astonishing book, *Creation*,* Steve Grand urges the readers to try and liberate their imaginations by not seeing the world in the discrete categories given to us by language and our sensory apparatus (a chicken and egg conjunction best not contemplated here). Instead he suggests we try to perceive the continuity between things as if they were not separate objects at all but part of a continuous surface. Steve Grand cites Douglas as possessing 'a tremendous feel for such concepts'† and Douglas in turn gave him an enthusiastic quote for his book: 'A giant leap forward into a new and unknown world . . . awe-inspiring.'

So Douglas was flattered when he was asked to moderate a high-powered conference of neo-Darwinists (The Digital Planet, 1998) in Germany. He was also thrilled to be asked to chair the debate at the second Digital Biota conference that took place at Magdalene College,∞ Cambridge, on 10–13 September 1998. The first had been held in Banff in Canada the year before, and had raised so many questions that the organizers soon realized the conferences represent a life-long commitment.

At Digital Biota II Steve Grand gave the opening address, followed by Professor Richard Dawkins. Cybernetic specialists, evangelists of A-life (artificial life), cutting-edge programmers, professors of cognitive science, innovative technologists (including TDV's own Richard Harris), computer science academics – there was a remarkable concentration of brain-power drawn from the computing and natural

---

* Weidenfeld & Nicolson, 2000.

† *Creation*, op.cit. p. 32.

∞ Such are the mysterious shibboleths of English that the organizers felt obliged to tip off their foreign visitors that the college is pronounced 'maudlin'.

sciences. Their aim was nothing if not ambitious. They would consider how best to go about fusing biology with machine to create the first 'radically new kind of life on this planet in nearly four billion years'.*

In the process they would speculate about new, partly organic adaptable technologies of the future and try to design some kind of roadmap showing how to get there. The thinking involved is not easy, but it is exhilarating. Somehow you have to step outside yourself as a living entity and consider yourself as a system. It's akin to pulling yourself up by your bootstraps, and it requires knowledge of many disciplines and a flexible mind.

Far from being outgunned by the specialists, Douglas was in his element. Life is something you know when you see it, but it's fearsomely tricky to define. It seems too complicated to be the result of the mechanical process whereby sexual recombination, mutation and the elimination of duff variations by their relative lack of reproductive success could have produced things as beautiful and as disparate as orchids and whales. However, computer modelling shows us how astonishing complexity can arise from a feedback loop and the iteration of simple rules. Indeed, computer programs that emulate aspects of evolution by introducing variation and passing the most successful algorithms on to the next generation are now very powerful tools in their own right, and – were it not incipiently anthropomorphic – we would have to call them creative.[†] These simulations are particularly illuminating, said Douglas, because there are not many ways available to us of analysing the property of being alive. If you take a cat apart to see how it works, he pointed out, you very quickly have a non-working cat.

'What survives, survives' is the most fertile tautology in evolution. Douglas saw that it was not just our physical form that has been shaped by evolution. It's difficult to see things other than the way we do 'because we are evolved beings who evolved in a particular landscape with a particular set of skills and views of the world that have enabled us to survive and thrive rather successfully'. Trying to think outside

---

* From the Overview on the conference website, paragraph four.

† See, *inter alia*, 'Evolving Inventions' by Koza, Keane and Streeter, *Scientific American*, February 2003.

that bone-deep evolutionary conditioning, encoded in our very cells, requires an exceptional imagination. Douglas's speech in Cambridge was remarkable, and as a tribute to him it has been posted on the Internet at www.biota.org/people/douglasadams. Do read it. It's a bit migraine-inducing, but truly an effort of genius.

In the eighteenth century Douglas might have been a great scientist along the lines of the 'natural philosopher' interested in everything. The esteem of the men and women who were doing science for real meant a great deal to him. Once he was attending a lecture at the famous NASA Ames Research Center in Moffett Field in the heart of Silicon Valley when the speaker was told that Douglas was in the audience. The proceedings were stopped, and an auditorium full of scientists gave Douglas a spontaneous round of applause. He was embarrassed but ecstatic. This was recognition from an audience that he rated infinitely more highly than he did the British literary critics turning up their noses at SF. His relationship with NASA Ames was so close that they have subtitled their monthly scholarly journal on astrobiology *Life, the Universe and Everything*, with an explicit thank you to Douglas for his permission to do so. (As if he would refuse – he must have been delighted beyond measure.)

Douglas continued to give lectures right up until his untimely death. Don Epstein was talking to him the day before he died about updating his potted bio for a commencement speech at the University of Santa Barbara. In many ways lecturing was his perfect job. It combines performance art, a chance to show off his high intelligence, his gift for the explanatory analogy, lots of stimulation, decent pay, and, almost certainly, restaurants and travel.

Of course, not even Douglas could come up with new lectures on every occasion though he could speculate interestingly if given a specific topic (for instance, in September 2000 he was invited to San Jose to talk about the Future of Systems). His lectures were akin to his anecdotes, and Sophie Astin, his assistant at TDV, was a little shocked to discover how cleverly he could appear to be thinking on his feet, umming and ahhing with the effort of original thought right under the audience's nose – while in fact repeating himself perfectly. Douglas always was a bit of a thespian.

Douglas could slip into lecture mode easily, and just occasionally his mates would crave the small change of human transactions rather than an intellectually demanding brain dump. 'Enough already,' one would gasp, even though it was good stuff that would command a fee when done professionally.* Douglas's didacticism was, however, deployed brilliantly on the circuit. Although he had many variations and could wander into new topics during Q & A sessions, his basic repertoire comprised four lectures with interesting sub-routines depending on the audience. He had grasped the first rule of public speaking – one that comes even before 'look up, don't gabble, try not to read wads of text' and so on. Know who your audience is. Three of his lectures circled around the theme of the future of technology, though one of these – specifically for the college crowd – was a humorous examination of the technology in *The Hitchhiker's Guide to the Galaxy*. The fourth, probably the one least in demand, says Don, was an inspired talk based on *Last Chance to See*. It was both wise and funny.†

Do you remember the kakapo whose fate is described in that book? It's the large parrot from New Zealand that has forgotten how to fly. New Zealand is in some ways a huge evolutionary experiment, for it never formed part of a larger land mass, but consisted of what Douglas called gunk emerging from the sea. As a result creatures that could fly there enjoyed an early advantage. The ecology is spectacular. New Zealand was bird heaven. There were no predators.

Flying is expensive (here Douglas was wont to make a joke about whatever aviation cartels had brought him to that location), expensive,

---

* The last time we met he bought me lunch at Fredericks, in Islington, and we argued about evolutionary psychology. Beware of a key that seems to open all doors, was my line. Not all our character traits stem from the deep past. Don't be so self-deceiving about our capacity for reason, was his (though I do him an injustice synopsizing so drastically). Note, he said, how restaurants fill up from the sides, an ancient reflex. He laughed when I said that may be true, but in this case the maitre d' showed us to the best table.

† My thanks to Christoph Reisner for his time and his kindness in getting me a CD of Douglas lecturing. I am sorry that reasons of space prevent me from using more of this excellent material from Germany.

that is, in terms of energy. A bird needs a lot of food to sustain flight, and the more food ingested, the heavier the bird becomes, and the more difficult it is to fly. Flight, of course, is also a survival mechanism, but it is one not needed when there is nothing to escape from. Eventually the kakapo evolved to flightlessness. Sometimes, Douglas reminded us, it forgets and topples from a tree with the grace of a six or seven pound bag of flour. But there is a problem with being in such a protected environment: you could breed beyond the ability of the environment to sustain your population, which would then crash catastrophically. For a truly harmonious existence in such a paradise, a really slow rate of reproduction is advantageous.

The kakapo has one of the slowest and oddest. The male attracts the female by hollowing out a concavity, a resonance chamber, on a promontory over a valley and then making a bass sound so low that it is almost felt rather than heard. Bass sound travels for miles, but it is non-directional, which is why some stereo systems have a separate woofer that can be hidden anywhere in the room. The female kakapo can therefore hear the male at an enormous distance, but, even assuming she's in a receptive mood, she has no idea where he is. We've all had relationships like that, Douglas asserted. If, by happy chance, they find each other, the female may lay one large egg every two years.

This reproductive strategy worked well for the kakapo until, with the aid of their twig technology, the monkeys arrived by boat, bringing with them animals that had evolved in altogether more competitive circumstances. Cats, stoats, possums, and, worst of the lot, the ship's ineradicable stowaway, *rattus rattus.* These alien species tore through the kakapos in a welter of blood. The birds simply didn't know the form when confronted with a predator, not that they could have done much even if they did. By the time the monkeys woke up to the problem, kakapo numbers had fallen from possibly as many as millions to forty-five. Rather like the aye-aye, they barely hang on to life on a small island off an island.

The more stressed the kakapo became, the more it relied on the old strategy that had worked so well in the past – i.e. it bred even more slowly – and the more endangered it became. Now, said Douglas, look at us monkeys. We evolved in circumstances when our most successful strategy for dealing with the environment was to regard it as ours for the taking. There were so few of us that for all practical purposes we could treat the planet as infinite.

Consider the kakapo and how its evolutionary strategy now serves it in changed circumstances. Do you think, he would ask ingenuously, that this stupid bird may have something to teach mankind?

It was an intellectual coup – Douglas at his very best.

* * *

In the *New Scientist* magazine, 9 November 2002, there's a letter from an Alain Williams on the rather esoteric subject of Grigori Volovik's attempt to infer the structure of the early universe from the distribution of helium isotopes. Mr Williams says that this scientist found out what readers of *The Hitchhiker's Guide to the Galaxy* already knew, *viz* that you could learn a lot about the universe from small bits of it – though in Douglas's case he suggested fairy cake rather than helium.

It's a tiny example of how Douglas's ideas have permeated into world. Richard Dawkins posits the idea of 'memes' – ideas, notions, cultural artefacts, fashionable connections, turns of phrase even, that have one thing in common: they replicate like viruses. Considered from this viewpoint, Douglas has left a huge and benign footprint on the world.

Recent references to Douglas and his ideas – spotted on a quite unsystematic basis – include a website, 'the homepage of God', where God's son is not Jesus but Zaphod Beeblebrox (*Sunday Times*, 14 July 2002). Or *Astronomy Now* magazine quoting his words about being at the unfashionable end of the galaxy (February 2002). Life, the universe and everything, for instance – those words in that order, have become ubiquitous as a jokey way of positing some all-embracing answer. Examples are too numerous to quote, but one recent sighting was an editorial in *The Times* about anti-matter. Indeed the words are now so deeply embedded in our consciousness that variations of them can be uttered, and printed, in the confidence that the allusion to the original will be recognized with a smile. 'Earth, the Universe and Everything' was a recent headline to the Review section of the *Guardian*'s G2 supplement (23 November 2002). Even the *Sun*, one of Britain's more frivolous tabloids, ran a recent story about models and their rapacious divorce settlements under the headline 'Strife, the Universe and Everything.' Another *Sun* headline along the same lines was 'Wife, the Universe and Everything'.

A clever piece of translation software is named Babel, not as an Old Testament reference to the tower and the fragmentation of language, but in honour of Douglas's Babel fish. Neal Stephenson, in his brilliant SF novel *Snow Crash*, alludes to the Babel fish argument in *Hitchhiker's* when he talks about how, if the Bible were provably true, there would be no room for faith. Stephen Fry's book *Making History* and Rob Grant's *Colony* also show signs of the Adams influence. The computer that finally beat humanity's strongest chess player, the awesome Kasparov, ran a program called – guess what? – Deep Thought, a reference to the computer in *Hitchhiker's* that took seven million years to ponder the question. Douglas even has an asteroid named after him.

Listing all the manifold ways Douglas left his mark on the world would take several volumes. If you want to try an experiment, put 'Douglas Adams' into the Google search engine. In February 2003 this produces 941,000 references.

Over the years Douglas's books have sold over 17 million copies. He has given us lots of excellent jokes, many expressions that entered the general currency of the language, and a great deal of pleasure – not all of it innocent. He was serious and funny – *seriously funny*. If Dawkins's memes really are viral, then the most infectious and enduring of Douglas's legacies is his sideways view of the place we ape descendants occupy in the world and the absurdly trivial place that our world has in the cosmos. It's what has become known as a paradigm shift, a pattern-altering template-busting change in the shape not just of a philosophical argument, but of a whole way of seeing. The pity of it is that we will never know what more he may have achieved. Very sneakily, while we were laughing at the jokes, he gave us back a sense of wonder.

It's why Douglas Adams was so important. There he was, apparently living in Islington or California, but often inhabiting another planet, and looking back at ours with a mixture of amazement, grief, not infrequent anger and overwhelming humour. 'It's just so improbable,' you can imagine him saying. 'How did the human condition ever get to be so bloody silly?'

*   *   *

Douglas Adams, one of the most creative thinkers of his time, the man who put his imagination through the Total Perspective Vortex on our behalf, was born on 11 March 1952.

Douglas's publishers worldwide

Britain:	Pan, Heinemann and Macmillan were his principal publishers. Arthur Barker published some early sub-licensed library editions of *The Hitchhiker's Guide to the Galaxy*, *The Restaurant at the End of the Universe*, and *Life, the Universe and Everything* (now collectors' items)
Bulgaria:	Hemus Publishers, also Yakov Publishers, Sofia
Croatia:	Zdenko Vlainic
Czechoslovakia:	Hynek Publishers, Prague
Denmark:	Aschebourg Dansk Forlag
Estonia:	Olion Publishers, Tallinn
Finland:	WSOY, Helsinki
France:	Editions Denoël, Paris
Germany:	Rogner & Bernhard and mareBuch Verlag, both Hamburg
Greece:	Vita Brevis, then Editions Stachi, Athens
Holland:	De Fontein, Baarn

Hungary:	Tamás Földes, Budapest
Israel:	Keter Publishing, Jerusalem
Italy:	Mondadori, Milan
Japan:	Shincho-Sha, Tokyo
Norway:	Familienvennen, Oslo
Poland:	ZYSK I S-KA, Poznan
Russia:	AST, Moscow
Slovenia:	Tehniska Zaozba and Zalozba Tuma, both Ljubljana
Spain:	Editorial Anagram, Barcelona
Sweden:	Bonniers, Stockholm
United States:	Harmony Books/Crown published everything except as follows: Easton Press (autographed, leather-bound edition of *Hitchhiker's*); Simon & Schuster (the Dirk Gently novels); and Byron Preiss Visual Publications (for trading cards and the three-volume graphic novel version of *Hitchhiker's*)

Also published/distributed in China, Korea and Turkey

Chronology of the

major works

1978 First radio series of *The Hitchhiker's Guide to the Galaxy* starts 8 March. Christmas special in December.

1979 First stage production in May by The Science Fiction Theatre of Liverpool.
The Hitchhiker's Guide to the Galaxy published by Pan in October
Double LP or double cassette recording available from November by mail order.

1980 Second radio series broadcast from 21 January.
Records and cassettes sold through shops from May.
Theatr Clywd production in January/February (much liked).
Rainbow Theatre Production in July (massacred). Hundreds of amateur and professional productions follow.
The Restaurant at the End of the Universe published by Pan in October.

1981 The television series broadcast on the BBC from 5 January.
Theme music single released from Original Records.
Two Marvin singles from Polydor.

Abridged Talking Books *Hitchhiker's* from Listen For Pleasure read brilliantly by Stephen Moore.

1982 *Life, the Universe and Everything* published by Pan, and by Arthur Baker in hardcover, in August.

1983 *The Meaning of Liff*, with John Lloyd, published by Pan in association with Faber & Faber.

1984 Infocom releases the computer game of *Hitchhiker's* – a big hit, especially in the US.
So Long, and Thanks for All the Fish published by Pan in November. Pan's first hardcover.

1986 'Young Zaphod Plays it Safe' for *The Utterly, Utterly Merry Comic Relief Christmas Book*.

1987 *Dirk Gently's Holistic Detective Agency* published by Heinemann in June.
Bureaucracy computer game from Infocom in August.

1988 *The Long, Dark Tea-time of the Soul*, the second Dirk Gently adventure, published by Heinemann in October. Coincides with the Pan paperback of the first Gently novel.

1989 Pan edition of *The Long Dark Tea-time of the Soul*.

1990 *Last Chance to See* published by Heinemann.
The Deeper Meaning of Liff, with John Lloyd, published in hardcover by Faber & Faber.

1991 Pan edition of *Last Chance to See*.

1992 *Mostly Harmless* published by Heinemann.
Pan edition of *The Deeper Meaning of Liff*.

1993 Pan edition of *Mostly Harmless*.

1994 Unabridged (6-hour)Talking Books version of all the *Hitchhiker's* novels issued by Isis. Douglas reads them himself with great panache.

1997 *Douglas Adams's Starship Titanic* by Terry Jones based on the TDV computer game published by Pan in December.

1998 *Starship Titanic* CD-ROM game released in April in the US.

2002 Posthumous publication of *The Salmon of Doubt* by Macmillan in March.

2003 Pan edition of *The Salmon of Doubt* in January.

Full credits for the
radio series

Cast:

The Book . . . . .Peter Jones
Arthur Dent . . . . .Simon Jones
Ford Prefect . . . . .Geoffrey McGivern
Frogstar Prison Relation Officer . . . . .David Tate
Gargra Varr . . . . .Valentine Dyall
The Ventilation System . . . . .Geoffrey McGivern
The Nutrimat Machine . . . . .Leueen Willoughby
Zaphod Beeblebrox the Fourth . . . . .Richard Goolden
Bird One . . . . .Ronald Baddiley
Bird Two and The Footwarrior . . . . .John Baddeley
The Wise Old Bird . . . . .John Le Mesurier
Lintilla (and her Clones) . . . . .Rula Lenska
The Film Commentator and The Computeach .David Tate
The Pupil . . . . .Stephen Moore
Hig Hurtenflurst . . . . .Mark Smith
Varntvar the Priest . . . . .Geoffrey McGivern
The Allitnils . . . . .David Tate
Poodoo . . . . .Ken Campbell
Airline Stewardess . . . . .Rula Lenska
Autopilot and Zarniwhoop . . . . .Jonathan Pryce
The Man in the Shack . . . . .Stephen Moore

Prosser & Prostetnic Vogon . . . . .Bill Wallis
Lady Cynthia Fitzmelton . . . . .Jo Kendall
Barman . . . . .David Gooderson
Eddie the Computer and Vogon . . . . .David Tate
Deep Thought . . . . .Geoffrey McGivern
Majithise and Cheerleader . . . . .Jo Nathan Adams
Computer Programmer and Bang Bang . . . . .Ray Hassett
Second Programmer . . . . .Jeremy Browne
Vroonfondel and Shooty . . . . .Jim Broadbent
Frankie Mouse . . . . .Peter Hawkins
Benjy Mouse . . . . .David Tate
Garkbit the waiter and Zarquon . . . . .Anthony Sharp
Max Quordlepleen . . . . .Roy Hudd
B-Ark No. 2, Haggunenon Commander and Hairdresser . . . . .Aubrey Woods
B-Ark No.1 and Management Consultant . . . . .Jonathan Cecil
Captain and the Caveman . . . . .David Jason
Marketing Girl . . . . .Beth Porter
Gag Halfrunt . . . . .Stephen Moore
Arcturan no. 1 . . . . .Bill Paterson
Arcturan Captain, Radio Voice, Receptionist and Lift . . . . .David Tate
Frogstar Robot and Air Traffic Controller . . . . .Geoffrey McGivern
Roosta . . . . .Alan Ford
Zaphod Beeblebrox . . . . .Mark Wing-Davey
Trillian . . . . .Susan Sheridan
Slartibartfast . . . . .Richard Vernon
Marvin the Paranoid Android . . . . .Stephen Moore

Production:
David Hatch . . . . Head of Department
Simon Brett . . . . .Producer (Episode One)
Geoffrey Perkins . . . . .Producer
Paddy Kingsland . . . . .BBC Radiophonic Workshop
Dick Mills . . . . .BBC Radiophonic Workshop
Harry Parker . . . . .BBC Radiophonic Workshop
Alick Hale-Munro . . . . .Chief Sound Engineer
Anne Ling . . . . .Production Secretary

Technical Team:
Paul Hawdon
Lisa Brown
Colin Duff
Eric Young
Martha Knight
Max Alcock
John Whitehall

Douglas's favourite Beatles' tracks in order of preference

25 May 1999 – St John's Gardens W11

Douglas Adams's Top 20 Beatles' Songs
 1 Hey Jude
 2 A Day In The Life
 3 Drive My Car
 4 Don't Let Me Down
 5 I Will
 6 If I Fell
 7 Hello Goodbye
 8 Rain
 9 Martha My Dear
10 Strawberry Fields
11 We Can Work It Out
12 This Boy
13 Ticket to Ride
14 Can't Buy Me Love
15 All You Need Is Love
16 I'm Fixing A Hole
17 And Your Bird Can Sing
18 She's A Woman
19 You Can't Do That
20 Here, There & Everywhere

Douglas Adams's Top 10 Beatles' Solo Projects

1 Maybe I'm Amazed
2 I Found Out
3 Dear Boy
4 Woman
5 Little Willow
6 Happy Xmas (War Is Over)
7 Baby's Request
8 Jealous Guy
9 No More Lonely Nights
10 Imagine

Index